THE CENSORSHIP

OF THE

CHURCH OF ROME

AND ITS INFLUENCE UPON THE PRODUCTION

AND DISTRIBUTION OF LITERATURE

*A study of the history of the prohibitory and expurgatory
indexes, together with some consideration of the effects
of Protestant censorship and of censorship by the state*

By

George Haven Putnam

Volume II

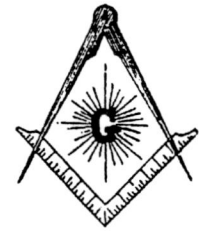

CONTENTS

PAGE

I.—THEOLOGICAL CONTROVERSIES IN FRANCE, GERMANY, ENGLAND, AND THE NETHERLANDS, 1600–1750 . 1
   1. The Protestant Theologians of France, 1654–1700.
   2. Theological Contests in the Netherlands, 1654–1690.
   3. The Protestant Theologians of Holland in the 17th Century
   4 The Protestant Theologians of England, 1676–1732.
   5. The Protestant Theologians of Germany, 1600–1750.

II.—THE TREATMENT OF THE SCRIPTURES UNDER CENSORSHIP 11
   1 Germany
   2. France
   3. The Netherlands
   4 Spain
   5. England
   6 Scriptures in the Vernacular

III —THE MONASTIC ORDERS AND CENSORSHIP . . 31
   1. Writings on the Monastic Orders, 1600–1800
   2. The Jesuits, 1650–1800
   3 The Dominicans, 1510–1600
   4 The Casuists, 1600–1610
   5. The Seculars and the Regulars, 1600–1700

IV —ROMAN INDEXES, 1758–1900 49
   Index of Benedict XIV, 1758
   Issues of the Roman Index, 1763–1900

V.—METHODS OF PROHIBITION AND THE CONTINUATION OF CLASS I 69
   1 Papal Prohibitions in the 17th and 18th Centuries

Contents

PAGE

V.—METHODS OF PROHIBITION, etc.—*Continued*

    2. Prohibitions by Bishops

    3. Publication of the Book Prohibitions

    4. The Continuation of Class I

    5. Catalogues of Books Approved

VI.—ISSUES BETWEEN CHURCH AND STATE   .   .   90

    1. Venice and the Papacy, 1606–1696

    2. Spain and the Papacy, 1559–1770

    3. Controversies concerning the Gallican Church, 1600–1758

    4. Ecclesiastical-Political Contests, 1700–1750

    5. England and the Papacy, 1600–1853

    6. The Gallicans and Liberal Catholics, 1845–1870

VII.—EXAMPLES OF CONDEMNED LITERATURE .   .   121

    1. Writings concerning the Papacy and the Inquisition

    2. Writings concerning the Churches of the East

    3. Patristic Writings and Pagan Classics

    4. Jewish Literature

    5. Historical Writings of the 17th Century

    6. Protestant Jurists of the 17th Century

    7. Writings of Italian Protestants

    8. Philosophy, Natural Science, and Medicine

    9. Books on Magic and Astrology

    10. Cyclopedias, Text-books, Facetiae

    11 Secret Societies

    12. Manuals for Exorcising

    13. Fraudulent Indulgences

    14. Works on the Saints

    15. Forms of Prayer

    16. Mariology

    17 Revelations by Nuns

    18. The Chinese and Malabar Usages

    19. Fraudulent Literature.

    20. Quietism

    21. Fénelon

    22. The Doctrine of Probability

    23. Usury

    24. Philosophy and Literature, 1750–1800

    25. Philosophy and Natural Science, 1800–1880

Contents

PAGE

VII.—EXAMPLES OF CONDEMNED LITERATURE—*Continued*

26. The Synod of Pistoja, 1786
27. The Festival of the Heart of Jesus, 1697–1765
28. French, German, and English Catholic Theologians, 1758–1800
29. The French Revolution, 1790–1806
30. The French Concordats of 1801, 1801–1822
31. Protestant Theologians, 1750–1884
32. The Eastern Church, 1810–1873
33. The Theologians of Pavia, 1774–1790
34. French, English, and Dutch Literature 1817–1880
35. German Catholic Writings, 1814–1870
36. La Mennais, 1830–1846
37. The Roman Revolution of 1848, 1848–1852
38. Traditionalism and Ontology, 1833–1880
39. *Attritio* and the *Peccatum Philosophicum*, 1667–1690
40. Communism and Socialism, 1825–1860
41. Magnetism and Spiritualism, 1840–1874
42. French Authors, 1835–1884
43. Italian Authors, 1840–1876
44. American Writings, 1822–1876
45. Periodicals, 1832–1900
46. The Roman Question, 1859–1870
47. The Council of the Vatican, 1867–1876
48. Example of a License.

VIII.—THE CENSORSHIP OF THE STATE AND CENSORSHIP BY PROTESTANTS 205

(I) General
(II) Catholic States
  1. Catholic Germany
  2. France
  3. Spain and Portugal
(III) Protestant States
  1. Switzerland
  2. Protestant Germany
  3. Holland
  4. Scandinavia
  5. England
(IV) Summary

Contents

PAGE

IX.—THE BOOK-PRODUCTION OF EUROPE AS AFFECTED BY
    CENSORSHIP, 1450–1800   270
        1. General
        2. The Universities
        3. Italy
        4. Spain
        5. France
        6. Germany
        7. The Netherlands
        8. England
        9. The *Index Generalis* of Thomas James, Ox-
           ford, 1627

X.—THE CENSORSHIP OF THE STAGE   .   .   .   376

XI.—THE LITERARY POLICY OF THE MODERN CHURCH   .   379
        1. The Indexes of Leo XIII, 1881–1900
        2. Index Revision and Reform, 1868–1880
        3. "Romanus" and the *Tablet*, 1897
        4. The Present Methods of Roman Censorship

XII.—THE AUTHORITY AND THE RESULTS OF THE CENSORSHIP
    OF THE CHURCH   446
    Schedule of Indexes issued under the authority
        of the Church or compiled by ecclesiastics and
        published under authority of the State, 1526–
        1900   480

INDEX   483

CENSORSHIP

CENSORSHIP

CHAPTER 1

THEOLOGICAL CONTROVERSIES IN FRANCE, GERMANY, ENGLAND, AND THE NETHERLANDS, 1600-1750

1. The Protestant Theologians of France.... ..... .1654–1700.
2. Theological Contests in the Netherlands.. ....1654–1690.
3. The Protestant Theologians of Holland in the 17th Century
4. The Protestant Theologians of England... ....1676–1732.
5. The Protestant Theologians of Germany.. ...... .1600–1750.

1. The Protestant Theologians of France, 1654-1700.—The Protestant theological literature of France and of French Switzerland is more fully represented in the Index than are the corresponding groups of Holland and Germany; but in the case of the French authors also the selection is rather haphazard, the names of important authors being omitted, while of others only single books, and of these the least characteristic, have been included. Certain works also which escaped condemnation at the time of the first publication secure attention from the censors only a number of years later. Such Protestant writers in the first half of the 17th century as Chamier, Picter, Capel, and Bochart were overlooked altogether.

Jacques Abbadie (1654–1727) comes into the Index

in connection with his *Traité de la Vérité de la Religion Chrétienne*. The edition prohibited was that of 1688, the entry finding place in the list of 1703. Remond's treatise, *L'Antichrist Romain opposé à l'Antichrist Juif, du Bellarmin,* secured naturally fairly prompt attention, being condemned in 1609, the year after its appearance.

La Bastide's monograph, *Exposition de la Doctrine de l'Église Catholique sur les Matières de Controverse,* was prohibited in 1693, twenty years after its publication. This is the only one of the series of replies to the treatise of Bossuet which secured condemnation.

Isaac la Peyrère published in Holland, in 1655, a treatise entitled *Praeadamitae s. Exercitatio super V. 12–14, cap. 5. epistolae ad Romanos item Systema theologicum ex Praeadamitarum Hypothesi.* The book was censured by the Bishop of Namur, and copies were publicly burned in Paris. In 1656, Peyrère was imprisoned in the Spanish Netherlands, but, on his application, was sent to Rome for trial. In advance of his trial, he became Catholic and retracted the utterances in his book. Later, he wrote a second treatise in confutation of the first. Notwithstanding the emphasis given to the earlier book, it is not included in the Index lists.

2. Theological Contests in the Netherlands, 1654-1690.—The issues that arose in the Netherlands during the second half of the 17th century between the Jesuits and the Franciscans on the one side, and the theologians of the University of Louvain and the leaders of the other orders and of the clergy on the other, had to do not only with the doctrine of Grace but also with questions of theological morality and pastoral theology (the administration, for instance, of confession and communion), and, after 1682, were also concerned with some of the contentions that had been brought up by the Gallican Church. As a result of a long series of controversies that arose concerning these issues, a very considerable number of the works of theological writers of the Low Countries came into the Index. It was the practice of the leaders on either side to make application to Rome to have condemned the works brought into print by their adversaries. The authorities in Rome appear to have condemned with a fair measure of impartiality the controversial writings on both sides. In 1677, the University of Louvain sent to Rome, with the approval of the Spanish King (Charles II), four professors who were charged with the duty of securing the condemnation of a series of propositions described as adverse to sound morality, and at the same time to defend against the assaults of the Jesuits the true doctrine of Grace. In response to this application, Innocent XI, in March, 1679, caused to be condemned by a decree of the Inquisition sixty-five propositions. The decree followed the lines of that issued in 1665 for forty-five propositions then defined as unorthodox. In regard to the doctrine of Grace, the Holy See decided that the teaching presented in the censures promulgated in 1558 by the faculties of Louvain and Douay, was sound and was to be upheld. As was the case with the decrees in 1665 and 1666, the particular works from which the condemned propositions had been cited were not specified. A number of monographs in which the question was brought up as to the authors who were responsible for these condemned propositions, and particularly as to whether these authors were or were not Jesuits, were themselves condemned. After the publication

of the decree of 1679, the Inquisition gave attention
to the investigation of certain propositions which had
been denounced by the opponents of the Louvain
divines as contained in the writings of these, and as
also contained in certain other works classed as Jansenist. In 1690, was published by Alexander VIII
a decree which had been framed under the instructions
of Innocent XI, condemning as unorthodox thirty-one
propositions which had been found in this group of
writings. The propositions condemned had to do in
part with what may be called the moralities and in part
with the doctrine of Grace. The proposition bearing
in this series the number twenty-nine, took the ground
that the claim for the superiority of the pope over the
general council of the Church, and for the infallibility
of the pope in the decision of questions of dogma, was
a claim for which there was no foundation (*Futilis et
toties convulsa assertio*). Certain monographs written
to criticise and oppose this decree were promptly
prohibited. The action taken during these years gives
evidence of the development of the policy of the
Church in the matter of defining or of approving or
condemning doctrinal assertions, or propositions having
to do with theology or morality, apart from the condemnation by title of any works in which such propositions may have been contained. A condemnation
of this kind freely interpreted constitutes, of course,
a condemnation not only of all books which had
been brought into print up to that time containing
such propositions or doctrines, but (without the
necessity of specific prohibition by title) a condemnation which may serve as a prohibition of all books
coming into print at a later date containing similar
doctrines. On the other hand, the fact that the

propositions as specified were often found open to different interpretations (as in the case of the famous five propositions of Jansen), and the further fact that it was not always easy to determine whether the statements or expressions in certain works brought into question were actually identical with propositions, classed as heretical, had the result of bringing into print after every such condemnation of propositions, a group of writings undertaking either to analyse the propositions themselves or to confirm or to deny the application of the condemnation to works with which they had been connected. The necessity for analysing, and in large part for condemning, the writings of this class, involved probably in the end a larger amount of detailed labour for the Index authorities than would have been required if, in place of condemning general propositions, the original condemnation had been connected with specific writings. The thirty-one propositions condemned in the decree of Alexander VIII of 1690 were described as *temerariae, scandalosae, male sonantes, injuriosae, haeresi proximae, . . . schismaticae et haereticae*, etc. Certain of the propositions were taken from the writings of Lupus, Huygens, Havermans, Gabrielis; *La Fréquente Communion* of Arnauld, and the *Monita* of Widenfeld. Arnauld speaks of this as *un décret pitoyable*,[1] and Gerberon says: *Cette censure ambiguë est le scandale de la Cour Romaine, la honte du Saint Office et la confusion du Pontificat d'Alexandre VIII*.[2]

3. The Protestant Theologians of Holland in the 17th Century.—The compilers of the Index selected from the Dutch writings of this period only such books as

[1] III, 350. [2] *Procès*, ii, 10.

were issued in Latin or as were printed later in French versions. It appears that the Dutch language constituted a sufficient barrier to secure a practical protection against the condemnation of the Church. It is noteworthy to remember, however, that this condemnation would in any case not have been likely to influence those readers who took their literature in the Dutch form, and it is quite probable that the majority of these Dutch readers never even knew that their authors had the distinction of being prohibited. Even in the case of those authors whose books did appear in the world language of Latin, the selections of the Index compilers were made at haphazard and omitted a number of the most noteworthy names. Arminius, Voetius, Gomarus, Coccejus, and a number of other leaders of thought in Holland are not found in the Index. The Congregation did succeed in getting into their lists the names of a number of obscure authors whose books had been printed originally in Latin, but who were forgotten excepting in connection with this record. The treatise by Grotius, *De Jure Belli et Pacis*, and a few of the writings of Heinsius, Fossius, and Horne were prohibited.

4. The Protestant Theologians of England, 1676–1732.—Up to the time of Benedict XIV, none of the English theological writings which had been printed in the vernacular received attention at the hands of the compilers of the Indexes. Certain works were condemned which had been originally issued in Latin or of which French translations had been printed. The English writers begin to receive attention after 1676, although even in these later Indexes the selections, as in the case of the writers of Germany and Holland, are curiously incidental and have apparently been made with no consistent principle. The list for the 17th century includes among the more noteworthy titles the following: *Reformatio Ecclesiae Anglicanae quibus gradibus inchoata et perfecta sit*, London, 1603; the writings of Bishop Hall († 1656); the works of the scientist Robert Boyle, founder of the Boyle lectures (1627–91); the Polyglot Bible of Walton, the *Synopsis Criticorum* of Reginald Pole; the *Cantabrigensis tributa* of Thomas James; the *Gravissimae Quaestiones de Christ. Ecclesiarum,* of James Usher, Archbishop of Armagh; certain works of Isaac Casaubon (1559–1614) (Casaubon was by birth a Swiss, but in connection with his long residence and the place of publication of the greater portion of his books, he came to be classed with English scholars); the latest work of Casaubon to be condemned, the title of which has been continued in modern Indexes, is the *Corona Regia,* a panegyric of James I; the *Regii sanguinis clamor ad coelum adversus parricidas Anglicanos* (This was first printed in The Hague in 1652, and later in London in 1655. It constituted an answer to Milton's essay *Pro populo Anglicano defensio.* The author was later identified as Pierre du Moulin, a canon in Canterbury); *The History of the Reformation of England* of Burnet (1643–1715) and the same author's *History of his Own Times* (These two books are described in the Index in the French editions. Burnet's other writings escaped condemnation); Robert Baillie († 1662), *Operis historici et chronologici a creatione mundi ad Constantinum magnum,* printed in Amsterdam in 1668; Pearson's *Exposition of the Creed;* the sermons of Bishop Sherlock (in the French version) and those of Archbishop Tillotson; a treatise on *Christian Perfection* by Lucas; Bartley's *Apology for the True*

Christian (printed in the French version in 1702, prohibited in 1712); Andrew Marvelle's († 1678) *An Account of the Growth of Popery and Absolute Government in England* (1675–76). (This was prohibited in its French edition; the Parliament had, shortly after its first prohibition, offered a reward of £50 for the identification of the author.) Williams, Bishop of Chester, finds place in the Index in connection with his treatise on the *Discovery of a New World*, in which the author undertakes to prove that the moon is inhabited. This had been first printed in 1638; the condemnation in 1703 had to do with the French edition printed in Rouen in 1655. Selden's *De jure naturali et gentium*, together with a number of his later treatises which had appeared between the years 1640 and 1679, were prohibited in 1714. Prideaux's *The Old and the New Testament connected in the History of the Jews and Neighbouring Nations*, printed in 1716, was prohibited in the French edition in 1732.

5. **The Protestant Theologians of Germany, 1600–1750.**— The cancellation of Class I of the Index may be considered as constituting one of the more distinctive modifications of the activity or assertions of authority on the part of the Congregation of the Index. Through the 16th century, the view had obtained that in this class should be brought together practically all of the heretical authors who had ventured to treat of religious matters. After the Index of 1596, however, the attempt had been abandoned to specify in full the names of all of the works which on the ground of their heretical character came under the proscription of Rule II. After that time, it was considered sufficient to place under a general condemnation all

works on religious subjects which came from writers outside of the Church. To this general principle, however, certain noteworthy exceptions were made. There continued to be a separate prohibition, by title, of books which had, on one ground or another, been brought to the attention of the Congregation. The decrees of 1686–1700, 1703–1709, included, in addition to certain lists of Protestant theological writings, a series of the works of jurists of which the treatise by Grotius above cited is a good example. The works so selected were for the most part concerned with questions as to the sources of authority, whether of Church or of State.

One peculiarity of the condemnation of this particular group of books is the fact that their pernicious character came to the attention of the Congregation or of the examiners in many cases only a number of years after the publication of the books themselves, and, as has been pointed out, there are commemorated in this manner, as deserving of attention, not a few books which had gone out of print and had been practically forgotten in the communities in which they had been published. Of the works on exegesis and in Church history published in Germany during the 17th century and the first half of the 18th, a number of the most important never found their way into the Index. The titles selected covered in the majority of cases comparatively insignificant books. There is, for instance, a long list of the controversial German writings directed against Bellarmin, Becanus, and Grester, which escaped attention altogether in Italy. Among the better known names which did come under condemnation during this period are those of Joh. L. Mosheim, for his *Ecclesiastical History* and his treatise on the *Institutions of Christianity*, and Swedenborg for the *Opera philosophica et mineralia*, published in Dresden in 1734 and prohibited in 1737. In the Index of Benedict, the *Opera philosophica* is omitted and in its place is given the *Principia rerum naturalium*. The other treatises of this voluminous author escaped condemnation. The prohibition of Mosheim's Church History was not sufficiently conclusive to prevent the book from being read in Italy. In 1769, an Italian translation by Roselli was published in Naples in ten volumes. This particular edition was never listed in the Indexes.

CHAPTER II

THE TREATMENT OF THE SCRIPTURES UNDER CENSORSHIP

1. Germany.	4. Spain.
2. France.	5. England.
3. Netherlands.	6. Scriptures in the Vernacular.

1. Germany.—The cordial co-operation extended by the Church to the work of the printers continued until the Humanists, more than a generation before the protest of Luther, began to assail the authority of the Church and the infallibility of the pope. The ecclesiastics now took the ground that errors and heresies arose through a wrongful understanding of the Scriptures, and from the beginning of the 16th century, took measures to discourage, and finally to prohibit, the circulation of the Scriptures.

In 1479, was printed in Cologne a fine edition of the Scriptures in Latin which bears record of the approval of the University of Cologne. The term is *admissum et approbatum ab alma Universitate Coloniensi.* This appears to be the earliest instance of the exercise of censorship by a university in connection with a printed book. Cologne had extended early hospitality to the printing art and it was there that Colard Mansion, the associate of Caxton, secured his training. It was only through the oppressive censorship of the faculty of theology in the University that during the succeeding century the business of book production became seriously burdened and the city lost its relative importance as a publishing centre.

The first Hebrew Bible printed in Europe was issued in Soncino, in 1461, from the press of Abraham Colonto. In 1462, Fust brought to Paris from Mayence a supply of his folio Bible, copies of which he was able to sell for fifty crowns. The usual price for manuscripts of this compass had heretofore been four to five hundred crowns. The first Bible printed in the vernacular was issued, in 1466, in Strasbourg by Heinrick Eggestein.

Among the earlier printers of Zurich (in which the work of printing began in 1504) was Christ Froschauer, who is known chiefly through his association with Zwingli. Froschauer, who devoted himself earnestly to the cause of the Calvinists, had a religious as well as a business interest in securing a wide circulation for the works of Zwingli and his associates, and together with these he printed editions of the Bible not only in German but in French, Italian, Flemish, and English. Froschauer's editions were the first Bibles printed on the Continent in the English tongue. For these Bibles, which were distributed at what to-day would be called popular prices, very considerable sales were secured and the presses of Froschauer were thus made an important adjunct to the work of the Reformation.

Anthoni Koberger of Nuremberg, at that time one of the greatest publishers of Europe, brought into print, in 1481, an edition in eight volumes folio, of the Bible of Cardinal Hugo. This work had been produced about 1240, the editor having been made a cardinal by Innocent IV. It was used for two centuries (of course in manuscript form) as one of the theological text-books of the Sorbonne. The text of the Scriptures as revised by Hugo, together with his notes, were utilised by Luther and by a number of the later editors and translators of the Scriptures. Koberger's publishing catalogue included in all no less than fifteen impressions of this *Biblia Latina*. In the year 1483, the year in which Luther was born, Koberger published his German Bible. The text was translated from the Latin of the Vulgate and was illustrated with wood-cuts. It is not clear who was responsible for the version or what was the German idiom utilised for it, but it was a form that never took any permanent place in the literature of the country. Luther, referring to this Nuremberg Bible, declares that "no one could speak German of this outlandish kind." The catalogue of Koberger constituted a very good representation of the foundations of scholarly Catholicism. The Catholic teachers who rested their contention for the supremacy of the Roman Church upon the Scriptures as interpreted for fourteen centuries by the scholars of the Church, depended for the material of their teachings upon such folios as those produced by Koberger. Weighty as were these folios, and assured as appeared to be the foundations upon which had been raised the great structure of ecclesiasticism, their instruction and their authority were undermined, at least for a large portion of the community, by the influence of the widely circulated pamphlets and sheets, the *Flugschriften*, which brought to the people the teachings of the reformers. A series of Latin Bibles were printed by Froben of Basel between 1500 and 1528. His undertakings, like those of Koberger, were addressed almost exclusively to scholars. He added later a series of works of the Fathers and an edition of the New Testament in Greek edited by Erasmus. The Testament included, printed in parallel columns, an improved Latin version. This was the first edition of the Greek text and it was utilised by Luther in the preparation of his German version. The text as shaped by Erasmus was based in part upon the previous issue of Laurentius Valla, to whom must be given the honour of having been the first scholar to attempt a revision of the Scripture text by a comparison of authorities.

Notwithstanding the approval given to the book by the pope, its publication brought out many and bitter criticisms. Accusations were heard of heresy and Arianism. Erasmus had departed from the version of the Vulgate and in his Latin text had substituted pure Latin for the monastic barbarisms; he had even, it was said, charged the Apostles with writing bad Greek. He had had the temerity to correct a number of texts in such a way as materially to alter their meaning, and in the first Epistle of John had ventured to omit altogether the testimony of the " Three Witnesses." This unfortunate verse, after being accepted by the Protestants on the strength of its retention by Luther and of the later and more scholarly authority of the editors of the King James version, was finally condemned, as an interpolation, by the revisers under Victoria, who were thus in a position, after an interval of three and a half centuries, to bear testimony to the scholarship and the editorial boldness of Erasmus. That Erasmus did possess the courage of his convictions was evidenced by the character of the notes throughout the volume; for instance, in commenting upon the famous text, Matt. xvi, 18, "Upon this rock will I build my church," he takes occasion to deny altogether the primacy of Peter and to express his surprise that words undoubtedly meant to apply to all Christians should have been interpreted as applying exclusively to the Roman pontiff; and this is said, it should be remembered, in a volume dedicated to the Pope.[1] The paraphrase of the New Testament, printed by Erasmus in Basel in 1524 was reprinted in an English version in London, and the work was so highly appreciated in England that a copy was ordered to be placed in every parish church beside the Bible.

It was the influence of Erasmus (who was at the time in good favour with the Pope, Leo X) that secured for Froben, in 1514, a papal privilege for a term of five years for the works of St. Jerome.

2. **France.**—Up to the close of the 12th century, the Church appears to have issued no regulations in regard to the use of the Bible in the vernacular or to the reading of the Bible in any form by laymen. In the 13th century, several of the synods in France prohibited the use of French versions of the Bible, and forbade the laity from reading theological writings or the Scriptures in any form (excepting the Psalms).[2] These regulations failed, however, to secure any uniform or enduring obedience.

In 1522, Robert Estienne of Paris, working as the assistant of his stepfather Colines, undertook the preparation of an edition in Latin of the New Testament. The text followed, in the main, the version of the Vulgate, but the youthful editor found occasion for certain corrections. The textual changes ventured upon at once called forth criticism from the divines of the Sorbonne, and Robert found himself classed

[1] Drummond, i, 412. [2] Reusch, i, 43.

with the group of heretical persons. It appears from his correspondence that he held himself ready to justify on critical grounds the corrections that he had ventured to make in the text of the Vulgate. The divines, while continuing their invectives, took pains to avoid any direct controversy on the points at issue.[1] In 1540, Robert was brought into special jeopardy through an impression of the Decalogue executed in large characters and printed in the form of a hanging map for placing on the walls of schoolrooms. Such an undertaking seems to our present understanding innocent enough, whether considered from a Romanist or a Protestant point of view, but in this publication of the Ten Commandments, the divines discovered little less mischief than in the heresies of Luther. The censors caused to be put into print a counter-impression of the Decalogue in which the first two commandments were combined into one, with the omission of the prohibition of making and worshipping images, while the tenth commandment was divided into two in order to make up the complete number. During the same year, various proceedings were taken against Estienne on the part of the Sorbonne, and on more than one occasion he was compelled to leave his home and to betake himself for safety to the King's court. The fact that a publisher, in order to protect himself against the violence of officials who were (at least nominally) the King's censors, should take refuge at court, throws a curious light on both the strength and the weakness of the Crown. With all the authority of the kingdom at his command, Francis was evidently unable to control the operations of the ecclesiastical censors who, in their dogmatic and unruly zeal, did

[1] Greswell, i, 191.

what was in their power to throw the influence of the university against the literary development of France and Europe.　On the other hand, the doctors of the Sorbonne, although backed by the authority of Rome, were not strong enough, at least for a number of years, to put a stop to the publication in Catholic Paris of works stigmatised by them as dangerously heretical.

Fénelon takes the ground in regard to the use of the Scriptures, that originally the Church permitted such reading without restrictions; that with increasing degeneracy, restraint was found to be necessary; that the necessity became increasingly manifest when the Vaudois, the Albigenses, and the later heretics, Wyclif, Luther, Calvin, and their associates, utilised the Scriptures as the basis of attacks upon the true Faith and the authority of the Church; Fénelon's conclusion is: *Enfin, il ne faut donner l'écriture qu' à ceux qui, ne la reçevant que des mains de l'Église, ne veulent y chercher que le sens de l'Église même.*

In 1686, an edition of the New Testament in French was printed at Bordeaux.　The edition is described in a tract by Bishop Kidder, printed in London in 1690, entitled *Reflections on a French Testament.*　This tract was reprinted in 1827 by Doctor H. Cotton in connection with a Memoir of Bishop Kidder.　The Bordeaux Testament is described as rare; but five copies are recorded as having been in existence in Great Britain in 1827.　The immediate occasion of the production of this special version of the Testament was the revocation, in 1685, of the Edict of Nantes. Strenuous efforts were made after the revocation, by the Church, and by the State acting in co-operation with the Church, for the recall to the fold of the various groups of Protestants who still remained in the kingdom. The publication, under the authority of the State, of the volume in question has been referred by Catholic writers (including among others Mr. Butler in his *Book of the Roman Catholic Church* [1]) as a contradiction to the charge that the Church was averse to the dissemination of the Scriptures. Mr. Butler reminds his readers, on the authority of Bausset in his *Life of Bossuet* that, under the orders of Louis XIV, no less than fifty thousand copies of the French translation of the New Testament were, "at the recommendation of Bossuet, distributed among the converted Protestants." Bausset refers to this version as being the work of Père Amelotte, and says that with the Testament were distributed copies of a translated missal. Mendham points out that among the several peculiarities specified by Kidder in the Bordeaux version, the more noteworthy have to do with references of a special character to the Mass, to Purgatory, and to the Roman Faith, which have been made to find place in the text of the Testament. Among the examples cited are the following:

Acts xiii, 2, given in the King James version "As they ministered to the Lord," is given in the French version *Comme ils offraient au Seigneur leurs sacrifices de la Messe*, or "They rendered unto the Lord the sacrifice of the Mass."

1 Cor. ii, 15, where the Apostle writes they shall be saved as "by fire," this version has *par le feu de Purgatoire*, "by the fire of Purgatory."

1 Tim. iv, 1, "In the latter times," says St. Paul, "some shall depart from the faith," is rendered *de la Foy Romaine*, "from the Roman faith."

These instances will serve as examples of the char-

[1] Mendham, 183.

acter of the accusations brought by Kidder, Cotton, and Mendham,[1] against the trustworthiness and good faith of the Catholic censors who undertook to present to the Protestants who were to be recalled to the true Faith the doctrine of the Scriptures. It would certainly appear as if the zeal of these editors had outrun their standard of accurate scholarship.

3. The Netherlands.— In 1559, Plantin printed a French edition of the New Testament and found sale within the year for nearly twenty-five hundred copies. In 1568, Plantin completed the publication of the most important of his undertakings, *La Bible Royale*, or *Bible Polyglotte*, which was produced under the editorship of the great scholar Arias Montanus. This was the most scholarly edition of the Scriptures that had thus far been put into print. A polyglot Bible had been planned by Aldus but he had not lived to complete it. In 1517, the Cardinal Ximenes had had printed at Alcala a polyglot edition of the Old Testament, and in 1547, an edition of the Pentateuch, prepared under the supervision of certain Jewish editors, was printed in Constantinople in Hebrew, Latin, Greek, and Syrian. Plantin secured for his Bible from King Philip II a subvention (or at least the promise of a subvention) of twenty-one thousand florins, which amount was to be repaid to the King in copies of the book. The editor Montanus had himself been appointed by the King, and he selected as his associates members of the theological faculty of the University of Louvain. The enterprise received also the co-operation and support of Cardinal Granvelle.

One of the most important, and also one of the

[1] Mendham, 146.

most difficult, parts of the undertaking was the securing of the various privileges required to authorise the sale of the work, and to protect it from infringement in the several countries in which a demand for it was expected. A general privilege was first obtained from the governor of the Netherlands acting in behalf of the King, and this secular authorisation was supplemented by a certificate of orthodoxy issued by the theological faculty of Louvain, which was naturally prepared to approve of its own work. The Pope, Pius V, or his advisers, took the ground, however, that any general circulation of the Scriptures might prove dangerous, and in spite of the approval given to the work by Louvain, he refused to sanction its publication. This refusal blocked the undertaking for some years and brought upon the publisher Plantin serious financial difficulties. The history of this work presents a convenient example of the special difficulties attending the publishing enterprises of the time. The examiners or censors, whether political or ecclesiastical, were prepared to make their examinations and to arrive at decisions only when the book in question was already in printed form. It was necessary, therefore, that the outlays for the editing, the typesetting, and the printing should be incurred before the publisher could ascertain whether or not the publication could be permitted. It was quite possible also that the plan of the publication might be approved by one authority, while the work, when completed, might fail to secure the sanction required on the part of some other or succeeding authority. With Plantin's Bible, the history took a different course. Pope Gregory XIII, who succeeded Pius V, was finally persuaded to give his approval to the work and, in

1572 (that is to say four years after the book was in readiness), he issued a privilege for it which gave to the publisher exclusive control for the term of twenty years, and which brought upon any reprinter excommunication and a fine of two thousand livres. The editor, Montanus, after finishing his editorial labours and supervising the printing of the final sheets of the Bible, was obliged to devote some years to travelling from court to court and to a long sojourn in Rome, before he could secure the privileges required for its sale. Even after the work had secured the approval of Gregory, it was vigorously attacked by a group of the stricter Romanists, led by Leon de Castro, professor of Salamanca. De Castro took the ground that the Vulgate had been accepted by the Church as the authoritative text, and that all attempts to go back to the original Hebrew, Greek, or Syriac must, therefore, be sacrilegious. As early as 1520, Noël Beda, Dean of the Sorbonne, had taken similar ground in connection with the editions of the Bible printed by Henry Estienne. Beda contended that the study of Greek and Hebrew would bring religion into peril, as it would tend to undermine the authority of the Vulgate. When Montanus, after completing his work in Antwerp, returned to Spain, he was accused of being a partisan of the Jews and an enemy to the Church, and was threatened with a trial for heresy. He was able, however, through his own scholarship and with the backing of the Pope, to hold his own against his accusers, and no formal trial ever took place.

4. **Spain.**—The earliest censorship in Spain was undertaken in Aragon and was directed against vernacular versions of the Scriptures. In 1234, the

Cortes of Tarragona adopted a decree of King Jayme I forbidding the possession by any one of any portion of the Old or New Testament in Romance.[1] The Church in the 13th century, as later, was satisfied with the Latin Vulgate. It authorised no translation into modern tongues and preferred that popular instruction should come from learned priests who could explain obscurities in orthodox fashion. The sects of the Cathari and the Waldenses, whose growth was for a time a real danger to the establishment, were ardent students of Scripture and found in it a potent instrument of propagandism. The Cathari, who rejected nearly the whole of the Old Testament, had translations of the New. The Waldenses had versions of the whole Bible.[2] In Castile, literature remained until the 15th century without interference on the part of either Church or State. The first instance of general censorship of which I find record in Spain was exercised on the library of the Marquis of Villena, after his death in 1434. The marquis had dabbled in occult arts and had won the reputation of a magician. At the command of Juan II, his books were examined by Lope de Barrientos, who by a royal order publicly burned such as were deemed objectionable.

In 1479, Pedro de Osma, a professor of Salamanca, was condemned by the Council of Alcala for certain heresies. The professor was required to make public recantation holding a lighted candle, and the book in which his errors were set forth was burned by the secular authorities. In 1316, the inquisitor, Juan de Llotger, on the report of an assembly of experts,

---

[1] *Constitutt. Apostt.*, Lib. 1, c. vii.
[2] Lea, *Religious History of Spain*, 17.

assembled at Tarragona, condemned the works on spiritual Franciscanism by Arnaldo de Villanneva. The sentence in which the tracts were condemned formed the model of a long series of similar prohibitions. Towards the close of the 14th century, Nicholas Eymerich, who won fame as a strenuous inquisitor, secured the condemnation of a long series of books including some twenty works by Raymond Lully and several of Ramon de Tarraga.[1] In Castile, during the latter part of the 13th century, the censorship of the Scriptures was evidently relaxed. In 1267, Alfonso X caused a Castilian translation to be made of the Bible, a copy of which, in five folio volumes, is preserved in the Escorial.[2] In 1430, Rabbi Moyses aben Ragel completed the work of translating the Old Testament which had been undertaken in 1422, under the instructions of the Master of Calatrava. He secured for his task the aid of certain Franciscans and Dominicans who supplied the Catholic glosses. An illuminated manuscript of this version still exists in the collection of Condé, Duke de Olivares.[3] During the 14th and 15th centuries, a number of versions of different portions of the Scriptures were executed in Catalan. One of these was prepared by the Carthusian, Bonifacio Ferrer. Of this, an edition was printed in 1478 at Valencia, which edition had been revised by the Jesuit, Jayme Borell. This volume was issued on the eve of a general proscription of the Scriptures in the vernacular.

Excepting for the instance of censorship in Aragon, there appears to have been up to the close of the 15th century, no obstacle to the printing or the distribution in Spain of versions of the Scriptures in the

[1] Lea, 19.   [2] *Ibid.*, 19.   [3] *Ibid.*, 19.

vernacular. Carranza, Archbishop of Toledo, writing in 1557, says that before Lutheran heresies emerged from hell he knew of no prohibition of the Bible in the vulgar tongue. [1]

Cardinal Ximenes at first took strong ground against the circulation of all versions of the Scriptures, and even stopped the work that had been begun by the Archbishop of Granada, in translating into Arabic the Scripture text used at the matins and in the mass. In 1519, however, the Cardinal had printed at Alcala a polyglot edition of the Old Testament, known in bibliographies as the Ximenes Bible. In this edition, the text of the Vulgate was placed in a column between the text in Greek and that in Hebrew. Mendham quotes the Cardinal as saying that the arrangement recalled the crucifixion where Christ was placed between two thieves.[2]

In 1533, Maria Cazalla, when on trial before the Inquisition, speaks of its being customary for Catholic women to read portions of the Scriptures in Castilian, and Carranza in his *Comentarios* complains of the "number of female expounders of Scripture who abounded everywhere," as an evil to be suppressed.[3] Alfonso de Castro takes the ground that from the misinterpretation of the Scriptures spring all heresies; as the keenest intellect and widest learning are required for their interpretation, they must be sedulously kept from the people; reverence for the Scriptures would be destroyed if they were allowed to become common.[4] The Spanish Index of 1551 includes among books prohibited, Bibles translated into Spanish or other vulgar tongue. In this year, Valdes issued an

[1] Lea. 45.   [2] 134.   [3] *Comentarios, Prologo al Lector.*
[4] *Haereses*, Lib. I, c. xiii.

edict directed particularly against the importation of heretical Bibles. In 1554, Valdes issued a special expurgatory Index in which were examined fifty-four editions of the Scriptures and lists of the objectionable passages were given. The owners of these Bibles were required to present them to the inquisitors within sixty days in order that the objectionable passages might be obliterated. In 1554, was printed at Salamanca the edition of the Bible of Vatable which had been thoroughly expurgated, but this expurgated edition was prohibited in the Index of 1559. A further expurgation was undertaken and the second revised edition appeared in 1584. Even this contained additional expurgations inserted with the pen. In 1613, and 1632, the much revised book endured two further series of expurgations. Its circulation appears thereafter to have been permitted without further interference. The Bible edited by Montanus and printed in Antwerp by Plantin, was denounced by de Castro and others as full of heresies, but the charges do not appear to have been adequately supported. The Index of 1583 contains in its general rules a sweeping prohibition of vernacular Bibles and of all portions thereof. An Edict of Denunciations, published annually after 1580, classes among works absolutely prohibited, the writings of the Lutherans, the Alcoran, and Bibles in the vernacular. It appears to have been the conclusion of the Spanish censors that the effect of the Bible on the popular mind was on the whole more to be dreaded than that of the Koran.[1]

The Spanish writer Villanueva has endeavoured to show by extracts from religious authors whose writings were issued between 1550 and 1620, that there was

Lea, 54.

a large body of educated opinion which favoured the study of the Scriptures. He finds such utterances from Carmelites, Franciscans, Benedictines, and even Dominicans. Lea points out, however, that, with the first quarter of the 17th century, the authorities of Villanueva come to an end. The generation which had witnessed the prohibition of the Scriptures had died out and the Scriptures themselves were forgotten in the intellectual gymnastics of casuistry. The work of the Inquisition had been accomplished among both priests and people.[1] Villanueva, himself a *calificador* (councillor) of the Inquisition, writing in 1791, says that the people are now practically ignorant of the existence of the Scriptures and those who have knowledge of such existence regard the Scriptures with horror and detestation.[2]

In the fifth of the series of the rules in the Index of 1790, the Inquisitor announces that the Church authorities have become sensible of the benefits to be secured from the perusal of the Scriptures and that they are prepared to repeat the declaration given in the Index of Benedict and to permit, under similar restrictions, the reading of the Bible in the vernacular. This Index repeats the condemnation first published in the preceding Index of 1747, and withdrawn under the protest of Pope Benedict, of the *History of Pelagianism* by Cardinal Noris.

The Protestants had little success in getting into Spain their great weapon of attack, a vernacular Bible, little I mean compared with their success in Italy. The Spanish Bible upon which they chiefly relied is the one of 1602 which was prepared by

[1] MS. of David Fergusson, cited by Lea, 87.
[2] Villanueva, 29.

Cypriano de Valera, but which, in fact, is a second edition, much improved, of that of Cassiodoro de Reyna, printed in 1559, which in its turn used for the Old Testament the Jewish Bible in Spanish, printed at Ferrara in 1553. De Reyna was a native of Seville and had been educated at the university there. Becoming a heretic, he escaped from Spain about 1557 and went first to London and then to Basel, where, with the aid of the Senate, he published his Bible in 1559.

In 1836-37, the Cortes made an attempt to reconcile the liberty of the press with the repression of certain abuses. It was at this time that George Borrow undertook to test the censorship conditions in Spain, by printing and circulating the New Testament. Lea points out[1] that he utilised for his work a version prepared from the Vulgate by Father Scio and that he was, therefore, presenting Scriptures which were entirely orthodox. Borrow succeeded in having an edition of his New Testament printed in Madrid and in opening a shop for its sale. With a change of ministry, the sale was blocked and Borrow was for a few weeks placed in prison. Later, his supplies of books were seized and cancelled.[2] The later issues of the Bible Society for circulation in Spain are reprints of the translation by de Valera. The constitution of 1876 gives to all Spaniards the right to express freely in speech or in print their ideas and opinions without subjection to a preliminary censorship. Article XI concedes liberty of thought and belief.[3]

[1] Equizabal, 162, cited by Lea, 179.
[2] *Bible in Spain*, c. xix.   [3] Lea, 128.

In an encyclical letter of Leo XII, written to Spain in 1824, occur the following passages:

"A certain sect not unknown certainly to you, usurping to itself undeservedly the name of Philosophy, has raked from the ashes disorderly crowds of almost every error. This sect, exhibiting the meek appearance of piety and liberality, professes Latitudinarianism or Indifferentism. . . . You are aware, venerable Brothers, that a certain society, commonly called the Bible Society, strolls with effrontery throughout the world; which society, contemning the traditions of the Holy Fathers and contrary to the well-known decree of the Council of Trent, labours with all its might and by every means, to translate—or rather to pervert—the Holy Bible into the vulgar languages of every nation; from which proceeding it is greatly to be feared that what is ascertained to have happened as to some passages may occur with regard to others; to wit that, by a perverse interpretation, the Gospel of Christ be turned into a human Gospel, or, which is still worse, into the Gospel of the Devil (Hier. Cap.l, *Ep. ad. Gal.*). To avert this plague, our predecessors published many ordinances. . . . We also, venerable Brothers, in conformity with our Apostolic duty, exhort you to turn away your flock, by all means, from these poisonous pastures. Reprove, beseech, be instant in season and out of season, in all patience and doctrine, that the faithful entrusted to you (adhering strictly to the rules of our Congregation of the Index) be persuaded that if the Sacred Scriptures be everywhere indiscriminately public, more evil than advantage will arise thence, on account of the rashness of men. . . . Behold then the tendency of this Society, which, to attain its ends. leaves nothing untried. Not only does it print its translations, but wandering through the towns and cities, it delights in distributing these among the crowd. Nay, to allure the minds of the simple, at one it sells them, at another with an insidious liberality it bestows them. Again, therefore, we exhort you that your courage fail not. The power of temporal princes, will, we trust in the Lord, come to your assistance, whose interest, as reason and experience show, is concerned when the authority of the Church is questioned "[1]

5. **England.** The Synod of Canterbury, held at Oxford in 1408, forbids the translation into English under individual authority (*auctoritate sua*) of any portion of the Scriptures. It further forbids, under penalty of the greater excommunication, the reading or the possession (except with the approval of the bishop or provincial council) of any versions of the Scriptures which had been issued since the time of Wyclif, or which might thereafter be issued.[2] This prohibition appears not to have been very thoroughly enforced. Sir Thomas More speaks of seeing old versions of the Bible in the hands of the laity, without criticism from the bishops.[3] It is the case, however, that, between 1408 and 1525, the date of Tyndale's Bible, no English version of the Scriptures was printed.

The first Bible published in England was Tyndale's English version of the New Testament. This was, however, printed not in England but in Cologne at the press of Quentell. Tyndale was by birth a Welshman. After studying in Oxford and in Cambridge, he sojourned in Antwerp and in that city he completed, in the year 1525, with the assistance of John Fryth and Joseph Royes, his translation of the New Testament. The supplies of the book when forwarded to London, came into immediate demand, but as soon as

[1] Printed in a volume of *Pastoral Instructions* issued by Richard Coyne in Dublin, 1824, cited by Mendham, 353.

[2] Wilkins, iii. 317.

[3] Blunt, *Reformation of the Ch. of Eng.*, i, 505.

the ecclesiastical authorities had an opportunity of examining the text, the book was put under ban and all copies that could be found were seized and destroyed. At the instance of Catholic ecclesiastics in England, Tyndale was. in 1536, arrested at Antwerp, under the authority of the Emperor Charles V and after being imprisoned for eighteen months, was burned. In 1535, a complete English Bible, comprising Tyndale's version of the New Testament and the Pentateuch and a translation, prepared by Coverdale and others, of the remaining books of the Old Testament, was printed somewhere on the Continent. probably at Zurich by Trochsover.

Fortunately for the freedom of the English press and for the spread of religious belief through the instruction of the Scriptures, it happened that shortly after the completion of the Coverdale Bible, Henry VIII wanted to marry Anne Boleyn. With the close of the supremacy of the papal power in England, and with the addition of Great Britain to the list of the countries accepting the principles of the Reformation, the printing and the distribution of the English versions of the Scriptures became practicable. It would not be correct to say that from this date the printing-press of England was free, but it was the case that it became free for the production of the Protestant Scriptures and of other Protestant literature, while it was also the case that the censorship put in force by the English ecclesiastics, or by the authority of the State, never proved as severe or as serious an obstacle to publishing as had been the case with the ecclesiastical censorship of the Catholics.

The first English Bible printed in England was the translation of John Hollybushe, which was issued in 1538 by John Nicholson, in Southwark. The great Cranmer Bible was printed between 1539 and 1541, the funds for its publication being supplied by Cranmer and Cromwell. The magnificent illustrations are ascribed to Holbein.

When the Scriptures were no longer interdicted in England, the printers themselves began at once to supply reasons why certain of their editions should be suppressed. In the year 1631, in a Bible and Prayer Book printed in London by R. Barker, the word "not" was omitted in the seventh commandment. This discovery led to a further examination of the edition and it was stated by Laud that no less than one thousand mistakes were found in this and in another edition issued by the same printers. The impressions of both books were destroyed and the printers were condemned by the High Commission to be fined two thousand pounds, a condemnation which naturally ruined their business.

6. The Reading of the Scriptures in the Vernacular.—The various Protestant versions of the Scriptures were prohibited in so far as they came to the knowledge of the Inquisition or the Congregation. The same course was taken with a number of translations into the language of the people, which were the work of good Catholics. In 1668, the New Testament of Mons was condemned by a brief of Clement IX; and in addition to the New Testament text with the commentaries of Quesnel, were prohibited French versions that had been prepared by Sinori and by Hure and a Dutch translation by Schurius. A number of editions for popular use escaped prohibition and some of these secured a very wide circulation; but in Italy, in Spain, and in Portugal, a general regulation was kept in force prohibiting any reading of the Scriptures in the language of the people. In the last decade of the 17th century, the question of the use of the Scriptures by the unlearned brought about some active controversies. The Jansenists maintained from the outset that the fourth of the Ten Rules of the Index of Trent was not to be accepted as binding. This question brought into the Index a number of controversial writings of the time, and in the Bull *Unigenitus* were condemned a series of specific propositions, a condemnation which carried with it the prohibition of any works in which could be identified the doctrines contained in the propositions.

In the Index of Benedict XIV, Rule IV, cited from the Trent Index, is printed, with an addition based upon a decree issued by the Congregation of the Index in June, 1757:

Permission can be given for the use of versions of the Scriptures or of portions of the Scriptures printed in the language of the people, when these versions have been prepared by devout and learned Catholics or have been issued with commentaries or annotations selected from the writings of the Fathers of the Church, and when said editions have been specifically approved by the Holy See. For the reading of all editions not carrying such specific approval, permission must be secured in each individual case.

This modification of Rule IV was, however, itself

revoked under Gregory XVI through a *Monitum* issued by the Congregation of the Index in January, 1836, which *Monitum* has, since 1841, been printed in the successive issues of the Index.

"It has come to the knowledge of the authorities of the Congregation that, in certain places, editions of the Scriptures, printed in the language of the people, have been brought into circulation without reference to the restrictions and regulations imposed by the Church. The Congregation recalls therefore to believers that, according to the decree of 1757, only such versions of the Scriptures can be permitted which have secured the specific approval of the Holy See. For all other editions of the Scriptures the provisions of Rule IV must be enforced."

In 1699, a provincial synod of Naples had declared that editions of the Scriptures in the vernacular were not to be possessed or read, even with the authorisation of the bishops, because an Apostolic mandate had taken from the bishops the authority to grant such permission. The editions of the Scriptures prepared by the Catholic divines for the use of the faithful appear for the great part to have been made up with carefully selected citations, the selections being restricted to the portions which were not doctrinal. Care was taken also to omit certain of the stories and historical episodes in the Old Testament which were considered to be not edifying or wholesome in their teaching. Hilgers contends that under the present policy of the Church, each Catholic is, as far as the Church is concerned, at liberty to utilise in his home reading the text of the entire Bible. The spiritual protectors of the faithful emphasise, however, the importance of securing for each division of the Scriptures the interpretation of the Church and the guidance of those who are made responsible for the shaping of sound doctrine.

CHAPTER III

THE MONASTIC ORDERS AND CENSORSHIP, 1600–1800

1.   The Monastic Orders...... .... 1600–1800.
2.   The Jesuits. 1650–1800.
3   The Dominicans. . . . . .1510–1600.
4.   The Casuists. . . . . .1600–1610.
5.   The Seculars and the Regulars. . . . . .1600–1700.

1. **Writings on the Monastic Orders.**—The Index contains the titles of a long series of writings having to do with the Orders of the Church. Certain of these are controversial in character, raising contentions against the whole system of the Orders or against the work or the character of particular Orders. The larger portion of the number are, however, the work of members of the Orders who have undertaken, in an exaggerated and improper manner, to maintain unfounded claims for their own Orders or to point out the defects of their rivals, or which are devoted to petty differences and strifes that have arisen between the Orders. The *Decreta Gen.*, ii, 12, contain a prohibition, dated 1568, of the printing or of the distribution in written form of any works that have not secured the approval of the Index Congregation, which have to do with the controversy concerning the actual succession of the Sons of St. Francis, or concerning the detail of the true form of the hood worn by the saint. The *Decreta Gen.*, iii, 8, print the prohibition, issued in 1663, of all reproductions of the inscriptions on the

pictures of St. Francis and St. Antonio of Padua, which inscriptions may undertake to specify the form of the garments worn by the saints or in which any reference may be made to the true and legitimate succession from these saints.

The Index also contains the series of works having to do with the long contests between the Franciscans and the Dominicans, the Augustine hermits and the Augustine choristers, the Augustine choristers and the Benedictines, the Benedictines and the Hieronymites (followers of St. Jerome), the Mercedarians and the Trinitarians. The list also includes certain writings presenting the traditions or records of the Carmelites. In 1698, Innocent XII issued a general prohibition in regard to the printing or the distribution of the whole group of writings concerning the controversies of the Orders.[1]

The long contest carried on between the Carmelites and the Jesuits brought about the condemnation in Spain, in 1695, of the *Acta Sanctorum* of the Bollandists, printed in fourteen volumes. This prohibition was recalled in 1715. In Rome only one volume was prohibited and this on another ground. In 1755, was prohibited a work issued under the title of *Ordres Monastiques; Histoires extraites de tous les auteurs qui ont conservé à la postérité ce qu'il y a de plus curieux dans chaque ordre.* The work, printed in 1751 in seven volumes, bears the imprint of Berlin but was supposed as a matter of fact to have been issued in Paris. It was ascribed to the Abbé Musson. The *Pragmatische Geschichte der vornehmsten Mönchsorden*, printed in Leipsic in 1774, in ten volumes, was based upon the *Histoires* of Musson.

[1] Reusch, ii, 260 ff.

2. The Jesuits, 1650–1800.—Books written by, and books concerning, the Jesuits make a considerable group among the dogmatic and controversial works in the Index. In 1659, Alexander VII issues a decree condemning a treatise which had been issued anonymously, in Paris, under the title, *Apologie pour les Casuistes contre les calomnies des Jansénistes.* In 1689, Innocent XI condemns forty-five propositions, cited from Jesuit works; and in 1690, he issues a decree against the Jesuit doctrine of philosophical sin. Of the books written against the doctrines and the practices of the Order, the most important are those by Mariana, Scotti, Pasquelin, and other ex-Jesuits, by the Capucin, Valerianus Magni, by Arnauld (the elder), Pasquier, and Scioppius. The great mass of Protestant writings against the Order are hardly represented. Scotti, whose catalogue name is Julius Clemens Scotus, had become a Jesuit in 1616. In 1664, he abandoned the Order and later secured a chair in Padua as professor of philosophy and of ecclesiastical law. The treatise which was condemned in 1651, was issued under the title of *De potestate pontificia in societatem Jesu . . . ad Innocentium X, etc.* Scioppius comes into the Index in connection with a volume entitled *Infamia Famiani,* prohibited in 1687. The following treatises which were also his work but which were published anonymously, were condemned in 1682: *Actio perduellis in Jesuitas S. Rom. Imperii juratos hostes, Anatomia Soc. Jesu seu probatio spiritus Jesuitarum* A third book in the list was also attributed to Scioppius, *Mysteria Patrum Jesuitarum.* In 1725, was forbidden a treatise bearing the rather vague title *Cura Salutis, sive de statu vitae mature ac prudenter deliberandi methodus.* It had been published in Vienna in 1712, and had been utilised as a proselyting tract in behalf of the Jesuit Order. In 1646, was forbidden in Spain a volume by the Jesuit Solier, printed in Poictiers, under the title of *Trois très excellentes prédications prononcées au jour et fête de la béatification du glorieux patriarche le bien-heureux Ignace.* The volume had been denounced before the Sorbonne by the Spanish Dominican Gallardo as scandalous, blasphemous, and heretical. As an example of the blasphemy, Gallardo cites a sentence in which the author claims that Ignatius had, with a piece of paper bearing his written name, worked more miracles than Moses and as many as the Apostles In 1752, was placed upon the Index a volume by Marcus Fridl, presenting a record of the miraculous life of Mary Ward, founder of the English Society of the *Jesuitissae.* With this, were condemned another biography of Mary Ward by Unterberg, printed in Tübingen in 1735, and an account of the Order by Khamms. The Order had been founded in England early in the 17th century on the model of the Order of the Jesuits. The counsellor of Mary Ward's *Jesuitissae* was the Jesuit Roger Lee. The Order never secured an authorisation or confirmation from the Pope, but houses of it were established in Belgium, Germany, and Italy. In 1636, the principal and her chief assistants were arrested and brought to Rome where, after a trial, their Order was formally condemned and they were then released. New houses were, however, shortly after instituted in England and one in Munich, and, in 1703, the rules of the Order were approved and confirmed by Clement XI at the instance of the Elector of Bavaria.

Twenty years after the condemnation of the teachings of Michael Bajus, arose in Spain the controversy between the Jesuits and the Dominicans concerning the doctrine of Grace. The leading representative of the latter was Domingo Bañez of Salamanca (†1604) and of the Jesuits, Luis Molina, professor at Evera (†1600). The issues were referred to Rome more immediately in connection with the treatise by Molina, *Concordia liberi arbitrii cum gratiae donis*, which had been denounced by the Dominicans, and, between 1602 and 1606, a series of disputations were carried on under the direction of Clement VIII and of Paul V at the sessions of the Congregation *de Auxiliis*. In December, 1611, a decree of Paul V prohibits the printing thereafter, without the specific authorisation of the Inquisition, of any writing having to do with the contest. This decree was confirmed by Urban VIII in 1625 and 1641, and again by Alexander VII in 1657. The latter added a prohibition for the printing, without the approval of the Inquisition, of any writings which were concerned with the *materia auxiliorum divinorum ex professo*, or which brought this subject-matter into print in connection with commentaries on the writings of Thomas Aquinas. This general prohibition is entered in Alexander's Index under the term *libri* and, since the time of Benedict, finds place in the *Decreta Gen.*, ii, 1. Under the terms of the *Decreta*, all writings under this heading, printed since 1657 without a specific approval, are to be held as condemned. The Index contains, however, but three specific titles and these of comparatively insignificant monographs. Reusch points out that the bitter controversial treatises of the Dominican, Hyacinth Serry, and of the Jesuit, Livinus de Meyer, failed to be recorded in the Index.[1]

Among the Jesuits whose writings secured special attention on the part of the Index authorities were J. B. Poza (†1660) and Théophile Raynaud (†1663).

[1] Reusch, ii, 294.

Poza, who was a native of Bilboa, printed in 1626 at Alcala, under the title of *Elucidarium Deiparae*, a treatise that is described as one of the very worst among the many books concerning the Virgin. This volume was prohibited by the Congregation of the Index in 1628, and as a result of Poza's bitter protests against the action of the Congregation, a prohibition was issued in 1632 covering all of his writings. In Poza's contentions against the judgment of the Roman authorities, he had the support of the Spanish Inquisition, which refused to confirm both the individual and the general Roman prohibition. Raynaud, born in 1583 near Nizza, became a Jesuit in 1602. He was a scholar and an active writer. He first came into conflict with the Congregation in connection with a bitter satire against the Dominican theories of the doctrine of Grace. Shortly thereafter, was condemned a monograph of his written to oppose the view that those who died of pestilence were to be held as martyrs. In 1659, was prohibited a monograph of Raynaud on the ecclesiastical system of censorship. Thereupon he published, under a pseudonym, a satire treating of the control exercised by the Dominicans over the Inquisition, which was promptly placed on the Index.

Clement X, who is classed as favouring the Jesuits, found occasion to condemn a number of treatises written in defence of Berruyer's *Historia Populi Dei*. This work was prohibited in Spain, 1759 (see also p. 42). Under Benedict XIV and during the first years of Clement XIII, were placed upon the Index a long series of publications written in opposition to the Jesuits.

Among the works antagonistic to the Jesuits which were prohibited during the decade after 1750 may be mentioned the following: Quesnel, *Histoire des*

Religieux de la Compagnie de Jésus, Utrecht, 1741;
*Procès contre les Jesuites, pour servir de suite aux causes
Célèbres*, Brest, 1750; Mesnier (†1761), *Problême
Historique, qui des Jésuites ou de Luther ou de Calvin ont
le plus nui à l'Église Chrétienne*, Utrecht, 1758; de
Silva, *Histoire de l'Admirable Don Inigo de Guipuscoa,
Chevalier de la Vierge*, The Hague, 1738.

The author of the *History of the Jesuits* (published in
London in 1816, and ascribed to John Poynder) writes:
"The doctrine of probability, our ignorance of the law
of nature, and the necessity of actual reflection upon
the quality of an action in order to its becoming sinful,
are the foundations upon which the moral corruption
of the Jesuits is built."[1]

In 1610, the treatise of Mariana, already referred
to, was burned in Paris under the command of the
Parliament. The condemnation was on **The Jesuits**
the ground of the doctrine maintained by **in France,**
Mariana that, under certain conditions, there **1610-1625**
rested with the people the right to slay a tyrant.
During the succeeding fifteen years, a number of the
works by leading Jesuit writers, such as Bellarmin,
Suarez, Santarelli, etc., were prohibited by the Parliament or by the Sorbonne or by both. The ground for
the condemnation of this group of books was the assertion of the right of the pope to depose princes and
generally to control the authority of the State. In
1613, Paul V directed the Index Congregation to
prohibit with a *d.c.* a treatise by Becanus, in order, as
was stated, to prevent the total condemnation of this
treatise by the authorities in Paris. Curiously enough,
however, the volume by Becanus is not included in
the Index of Paul or in any later lists. The decree itself

[1] Mendham, 184

appears to have been cancelled. In 1612, was placed in the Index a treatise entitled *Anti-Coton* which had been written to oppose the writings of the Jesuit Coton. The latter had undertaken, after the condemnation of the work of Mariana, a fresh defence of the doctrines of his Order. In 1603, Clement VIII ordered the condemnation of a treatise by the Italian Carerius, a writer who had undertaken to oppose the teaching of Bellarmin in regard to the authority of the pope in matters of State. The same Pope caused to be removed from the Index the treatise of Bellarmin which had been condemned under Sixtus V.

In 1665, was published in Lyons a collected edition of Raynaud's works comprising no less than nineteen folio volumes. This set does not include the prohibited writings; but, in 1669, the Jesuits issued, with a false imprint, a twentieth volume bearing the title *Apopompaeus* (scape-goat, *see* Levit. xvi., 10). In this volume are presented the several prohibited writings together with certain others. The book was duly prohibited in 1672.

In 1739, the Congregation prohibits the *Opera Electa* and *Opera Varia* of the learned Jesuit Hardouin (1646–1729), and, in 1742, his Commentary on the New Testament. The *Opera Electa* had been published as far back as 1709, and had been promptly condemned by the authorities of the Jesuit Order. The *Opera Varia* appeared after the death of the author; for these also the Jesuit rulers disavowed responsibility. The works of Hardouin do not appear in the Spanish Index. In 1734, the Congregation prohibited a *History of the People of God* which was the work of Berruyer (1681–1758), a pupil of Hardouin. The first part of this history had been issued in 1728 with the approval of the French rulers of the Order, but under the decision of the general of the Order, it was recalled for revision. The second part, published in 1753, was disavowed by the Jesuit rulers as having been issued without their permission, and Berruyer was obliged, under the condemnatory decision of the Archbishop of Paris, given in 1754, and of the Parliament, given in 1756, to make recantation of certain of the statements contained in the volume and to promise to cancel the original issue and to correct the text. The third division of the history was issued in 1757, and this secured condemnation through a brief of Clement XIII.

After the middle of the 16th century, the most important influence working against the freedom of the press and the undertakings of the publishers was that of the Jesuits. Members of the Order secured positions as councillors with the imperial Government in Vienna, with the Elector of Bavaria, and in other Catholic States, and promptly brought their influence to bear to strengthen the censorship regulations. The publication of books lessened or became active almost in direct proportion to the extent of the Jesuit influence in one State or another.

Under the reign of Clement XIII (1758–1769), there came into print a long series of controversial writings directed against the Order of the Jesuits, but of these only a small number of titles were placed upon the Clementine Indexes. In a brief issued in September, 1762, the Pope says that he has caused to be condemned as invalid the edicts and orders issued by the Parliament of Paris against the Jesuits; but these orders do not find place in Index lists. Under Clement XIV (1769–1774), no single one of the writings against the Jesuits was prohibited. Under

Pius VI (1775-1799), was prohibited but a single and comparatively unimportant monograph of the long series of memorials written by Jesuits concerning the suppression of their Order.

3. **The Dominicans.**—As stated in an earlier chapter, the work of the Congregation of the Index had, from the outset, been left very largely under the direction of the Dominicans. After the beginning of the 16th century, the Dominicans came into practical control of the censorship operations in Germany, excepting only in Vienna where the influence of the Jesuits prevailed. In 1510, under the direction of these Dominican censors, a strenuous attempt was made to suppress altogether the literature of the Jews. The influence of the censors was directed not merely against instruction in Hebrew in the university centres, but against the printing, for the use of the Jews themselves, of editions of the Jewish Scriptures, the Jewish commentaries, or of any works by Jewish writers. The fight led by Reuchlin in behalf of Hebrew literature was really a fight for the freedom of the press. Reuchlin, with the all-valuable aid of Erasmus, had in view more particularly the interests of scholarship, but the principles asserted by him and in the end successfully maintained, were those upon which depended the intellectual freedom of the people, of the more common folk as well as scholars. The fight of Reuchlin against the Dominicans led by Pfefferkorn was a hundred and thirty years in advance of the publication of Milton's *Areopagitica*, but the arguments shaped by Reuchlin and by Erasmus were substantially identical with those presented so eloquently by Milton. In 1512, Reuchlin's treatise entitled *Augenspiegel* was prohibited by the emperor and this prohibition was confirmed in 1520

by the pope (Leo X). In 1515, *Epistolae obscurorum virorum*, a work which exerted an important influence in the Protestant contest, secured the honour of prohibition both from the emperor and from the pope.

4. **The Casuists.**—In 1602, under the direction of Clement VIII, the Inquisition formally condemned the opinion that under any circumstances confession could be made other than in person, that is to say by letter or by messenger, and that a confession other than in person could secure absolution. The publication of this conclusion appears to constitute the first example of a decision by the Roman Inquisition securing general distribution and enforcement. As a result of this decree, were placed upon the Index treatises by the Jesuits Henriquez and Sa (books which contained, to be sure, other opinions that called forth disapproval) and a work by Vivaldus. The latter came under the *d.c.* class. Certain writings of F. Suarez, one of the most noted theologians of the Jesuits, were thoroughly discussed and, according to report, escaped the Index only by a close vote. During the following ten years, a considerable series of writings by Jesuits found their way into the Index, in part, however, with the *d.c.* addition. Among names to be noted are those of St. Bauny and Fra. Amico, who rank with the more important of the advocates of the Jesuit morality, and with these a number of treatises by the Theatins, Vidal, Verricelli, and Pasqualigo. Suarez had defended strongly the contention that there was authority for accepting confession from one absent and for giving to the same absolution. He based his argument in part upon an interpretation of Thomas Aquinas. A series of investigations were held in Spain concerning these teachings of Suarez and it was ordered by the

Inquisition (which was under the control of the Dominicans) that he should be suspended from his functions and that the distribution of the books should be stopped until they had been amended. In 1604, Suarez came to Rome and presented, first before Clement VIII and later before Paul V, the defence of his opinions. The Inquisition of Rome decided that the opinions of Suarez were unsound and ordered him to have his treatise corrected. The book escaped therefore being entered in the Index. The treatise by Sa was condemned not merely on account of its teachings concerning the confession but on other grounds. The title reads *Aphorisma conf. hactenus impressa*, etc. An expurgated edition, approved by Brasichelli, was printed in Rome in 1608. The condemnation of the original work was never confirmed in the Spanish Indexes.

5. Contests between the " Seculars " and the " Regulars," 1600–1700.—With the beginning of the 17th century, fierce contests arose concerning the relation of the regular Orders to the bishops. The authorities of the Orders claimed that they held their responsibilities directly from the pope and that the work of their Orders was to be carried on free from the interference of the bishops. A number of the bishops, on the other hand, took the ground that they were themselves the territorial representatives of the central authority of the Church in their own dioceses and that, without direct authorisation from the bishop, no member of an Order could be permitted to exercise in the diocese clerical functions. Dr. Richard Smith, who, under the title of Bishop of Chalcedon, had been appointed Apostolic Vicar for England, took active part in a controversy with certain Jesuit writers in maintaining

the authority of the bishops. As a result of the antagon-
isms raised by his writings, he was obliged, in 1628, to
leave England, and until his death in 1655, he remained
in France. Among the French writers who took part in
the controversy were François Hallier and Jean du
Vergier de Hauranne, later abbé of Saint-Cyran. In
1633, the Index Congregation condemned all the
controversial writings that had come into print concerning the issues between the Bishop of Chalcedon
and the English Regulars. To this condemnation was
added the specification that the Congregation had not
undertaken to express any decision in regard to the
issues involved. The continuance of the controversy
was, however, considered undesirable and a general prohibition, under the penalty of the excommunication *latae sententiae*, was made of any further writing
in regard to the matter. This prohibition did not
succeed, however, in preventing the publication of a
number of further treatises on the subject, and was
itself placed in the Index, and, since Benedict XIV,
remains in the *Decreta Gen.*, ii, 4. In 1642, a special
prohibition with a *d.c.* was issued for the volume by the
Jesuit Cellot. In 1659, the Inquisition formally condemned the writings of a number of the French representatives of the Regulars, including certain treatises of
Bishop Arnauld of Angers. At the same time, were
condemned the replies to these writings. Shortly
afterwards, were placed on the Index a treatise by
Chassaing written in behalf of the Regulars and one by
de Launoy maintaining the claims of the Seculars.
In 1664, the Sorbonne censured a monograph that
had been printed under the name of Jacques Vernant,
in which large claims were made not only for the
privileges of the Regulars but also for the general

authority of the Papacy; in 1665, this censorship of the Sorbonne was itself separately condemned in a brief issued by Alexander VII.   In 1693, was prohibited a treatise by the magistrate Karg, dedicated to the Bishop of Bamberg and Wurzburg, which took ground against the privileges of the Orders.

CHAPTER IV

ROMAN INDEXES, 1758–1899

1.   Index of Benedict XIV.............................1758.
2.   Issues of the Roman Index ....1763–1899.

1. Index of Benedict XIV, 1758.—In 1758, an Index was compiled under the direction of Benedict XIV which is of importance as marking a new departure in the censorship policy of the Church. The accompanying papal brief, which bears date December 23, 1757, states that the Indexes heretofore issued are in various respects incorrect, and that the present work has been prepared in order to place at the service of the faithful trustworthy lists of the books prohibited. In a Bull, issued as far back as July, 1753, the Index Congregation had been charged with the duty of the compilation, and five years had been devoted to the task. The Index was printed at once in two editions, one containing pp. xxxix–268, and the other pp. xxxvi–304. The title-page reads:

Index Librorum prohibitorum SSmi D.N. Benedicti XIV, Pontificis Maximi, jussu Recognitus atque editus. Romae 1758, ex typographia reverendae Camerae Apostolicae. cum summi Pontificis privilegio.

Both editions contain a copper plate vignette. The papal brief is followed by an introduction by Thomas Augustus Ricchini, Secretary of the Congregation; the

Tridentine Rules with the commentaries of Clement VIII and Alexander VII, together with a new note on Rule IV (on the reading of the Scriptures); the Instruction of Clement; the Bull of 1753, and a summary (peculiar to this Index) entitled: *Decreta de libris prohibitis nec in Indice expressis*. Such summaries are in later Indexes entitled *Decreta Generalia*. In the preface to the *Decreta*, it is explained that as, on account of the increasing mass of printed books, it is no longer possible to present all the titles in the lists, it has seemed best to classify these into certain general divisions or categories, and to shape general regulations based upon the subjects treated or on the general character of the literature, which shall serve as guides to the faithful, who with this aid need have no difficulty in determining for a book not specifically catalogued, whether or not it belongs to one of the prohibited classes. In the editor's introduction, Ricchini says: "In the arrangement of the lists, the family names rather than the forenames of the writers have been followed as far as practicable. In the previous Indexes, the forenames were utilised for the main entry, with occasional cross-references to the family name. We have accepted as family names names that have been adopted by the writers. Theses and disputations stand under the names not of the students but of the instructors. Anonymous works are alphabeted under their titles." Against the entries of books which were condemned in the Tridentine Index, is noted *Ind. Trid.*, and for those condemned under Clement, *Append. Ind. Trid.* For the prohibitions after 1696, the year is specified, and occasionally the Bull itself. In the cases in which the entry includes the place and date of publication, the prohibition applies not to the work as a whole, but only to the particular edition cited ; but in the absence of such specification, the condemnation applies to the work in all its issues. The addition of the term *donec corrigatur* or *donec expurgetur* indicates that the responsibility for the corrections rests with the Index Congregation. Reusch points out that the lists in this Index, while presenting corrections of many of the errors contained in the Tridentine and Clementine, are themselves by no means either correct or complete. A number of the names of the Clementine lists have been omitted simply through the oversight of the transcribers.

The *Decreta Generalia* have the sub-heading: "Prohibited books which have been written or published by heretics or which have to do with heresies or with creeds of unbelievers." This part of the work contains the following subdivisions:

1. The prayers and offices of the heretics.

2. *Apologia* in which their errors are defended or favoured.

3. Editions of the Scriptures edited or printed by heretics, or containing notes, *scholia*, or commentaries prepared by unbelieving writers.

4. Any portions of the Scriptures put into verse by heretics.

5. Heretical editions of calendars, martyrologies, and necrologies.

6. Poems, narrations, addresses, pictures, or compositions of any kind in which heretical beliefs are commended.

7. Catechisms, A.B.C. primers, commentaries on the Apostles' Creed or the Ten Commandments, instructions in doctrine.

8. Colloquies, conferences, disputations, synodical

proceedings concerning the creeds, edited or printed by heretics.

9. Articles of Faith, confessions, or creeds of heretics.

10. Dictionaries, vocabularies, glossaries. and thesauri compiled or printed by heretics (as examples are specified the works of the class bearing the names of the Stephani, Scapula, and Hoffman); these books may, however, be permitted when they have been purged of heretical passages or of entries that could be utilised against the Catholic faith.

11. Works presenting or defending the creeds of any of the Mohammedan sects.

Certain of the above specifications of classes are entered in the alphabeted lists under the headings: *Apologia, Catechesis, Colloquium, Confessio, Disputatio*, etc. The titles of individual works belonging to such classes, titles which had found place in many preceding Indexes, are then omitted. In some instances a specific work is entered as an example or type of the class to be prohibited, as *Apologia Confessionis Augustinae*, with the *addendum, et caeterae omnes haereticorum apologiae; vide Decreta.*

Under the heading of "Prohibited Books on Special Subjects," are classed together works condemned under certain prohibitions of the last half of the 16th century and the first half of the 17th; for instance, works on duelling, and letters or pamphlets in which the so-called laws and rules of duelling are presented. Forbidden also are *Pasquilles* (broadsides or tractates), printed or written, which make citations from the Scriptures, or which in any fashion "approach too near" to God or to the saints, or to the sacraments or other holy things of the Church.

In certain letters addressed to the Inquisitor-General of Spain, Benedict XIV names a number of writers whose works had, on the ground of special consideration for the authors, been spared from the insertion in the Index, although they had fully deserved such measure of condemnation. Among the books so specified are those of the Pope's friend, Ludovico Antonio Muratori (1672–1750). When this letter of the Pope with reference to Muratori was made public, the latter wrote to the Pope for some specification of the grounds for the condemnation of his writings. The Pope replied that he had had in view in this reference, not the theological writings of his friend, but the treatise on the civil jurisdiction of the Pope in the papal States. A number of the writings of Muratori came into sharp criticism and were the subject of controversy, but although these were thoroughly investigated and formally denounced in Rome, no one of them finds place in the Index.

In the list of authors is retained the name of Poza for his complete works, in continued antagonism to the approval of these works by the framers of the Spanish Indexes. Another noteworthy entry is that of the *Bibliothèque Janséniste, ou Catalogue Alphabétique des Livres Jansénistes, Quesnellistes, Baganistes ou Suspects de ces Erreurs* (Decr., September 20, 1749). This is the work that supplies the material for the anti-Jansenist appendix in the latest Spanish Index. Its condemnation here constitutes a fresh instance of the antagonism which continued in regard to literature and in regard to certain points of doctrine as presented in literature, between the Church of Rome and the Church of Spain.

Raynaud, whose work had been prohibited in the

preceding Index, had added his protest to that of Poza
at the injustice of being condemned unheard. In his
Genitus Columbae, is printed as a parody on the methods
of the censors, a critique on the Apostles' Creed in every
article of which is discovered some latent and insidious heresy. The work was itself, naturally enough,
promptly condemned.[1]

This Index of Benedict represents the beginning of
what may be called the modern policy of the Catholic
Church in regard to the censorship of literary production and the control or supervision of the reading of
the faithful. By the middle of the 18th century, the
Church authorities were finally prepared to admit the
impracticability, with any such commissions or examining bodies as could be maintained, of making an
individual examination of each work produced from
the printing-press. Such a conclusion might with
better wisdom have been arrived at a century earlier.
The most direct evidence of the futility of the attempts
on the part of the Congregation of the Index, of the
Roman Inquisition, and of the local inquisitors to
inform themselves intelligently concerning the nature,
the orthodoxy, and the probable influence for good or
for bad of the increasing mass of books brought into
print from year to year, is presented by the Indexes
themselves. The work of the compilation of these
successive Indexes was placed in the hands of scholarly
men, and, in the large majority of cases, of men whose
integrity of purpose and devotion to the higher interests
of the Church need not be brought into question. These
devout and scholarly compilers were, however, willing
to put into print, under the authority of an infallible
Church, instructions for the reading of believers which

[1] Cited by Mendham, 243.

the most faithful of Catholics must have found difficulty in obeying with any consistency.

The Index lists are marvels of bibliographical inaccuracy. The names of the authors, frequently misspelled, are entered almost at random. at times under their surnames or locality-names, sometimes in the vernacular, sometimes in the Latin forms. This method, or lack of method, necessarily resulted in duplicate entries, while the copyists, instructed to transfer for printer's copy for a later Index the titles from an earlier, succeeded not infrequently (possibly in the desire to avoid duplications) in omitting altogether writers and books of unquestioned heresy. More serious, however, than these bibliographical blunders, the responsibility for which rested in part at least with copyists or with compositors, were the errors which were undoubtedly due to editorial ignorance. It was increasingly impossible for the compilers to secure personal knowledge of the contents of more than a very small proportion of the books which were to be passed upon and classed as either safe or pernicious. Descriptions or impressions of current publications such as are available to-day through reviews were. prior at least to the middle of the 18th century, non-existent. The judgment arrived at concerning an unfamiliar book depended in part on the name of the author. and in part on that of the printer or the place of publication. Certain printing offices and certain publishing centres came to be associated in the minds of the Roman censors with heretical opinions. The general policy seems to have been that it was safer to condemn a few books not assuredly either pernicious or heretical, than to run the risk of omitting from the lists any single work which might constitute an influence against the authority of the Church.

The selections were also largely influenced by the doctrinal issues and by the party prejudices that arose between the great Orders of the Church. The direction of the censorship work in Rome, both of the Inquisition and of the Congregation, has, since their institution, remained in the hands of the Dominicans. The natural result was a strong bias of opinion and of action against the writings of the Jesuits and of the Franciscans. When, as occasionally happened, the two latter Orders secured representation on the boards of examiners, opportunity was taken to pay off literary scores against the Dominican writers. Of these three great bodies in the Church, the Jesuits included by far the larger proportion of scholarly workers and were responsible for the larger mass of dogmatic and theological literature. It is the books of the Jesuits, therefore, that furnish the largest number of titles to the lists of prohibited doctrinal works by Catholic writers.

Up to the time of Benedict, the authorities who had directed the work of the compilers had thought it necessary to give consideration to the literature produced by Protestant writers, as far as they could secure knowledge concerning the character of the books, or could secure at least information as to their existence. Such knowledge and information were at best but imperfect and fragmentary. The selections from Protestant writers that appear in the Indexes of Pius IV, Paul IV, and Clement VIII impress one as curiously haphazard. It is difficult to understand under what instructions the work of the compilers was done. The names of the larger heretics of the Reformation period, such as Luther, Calvin, Zwingli, Oecolampadius, find place in the greater number of the Indexes, although even with these larger names there are occasional curious omissions.   In no one of these earlier Indexes, however, in which the attempt was made to present a complete list of the doctrinal writings of these leaders of the Reformation, have the compilers been successful in making a list that was either complete or correct.   It is possibly on the ground of some consciousness of probable omissions that, after having inserted in the alphabeted lists the titles (more or less correctly worded) of certain books, it was thought safer to make a second entry by the name of the author, followed by the term "*Opera omnia.*"   With the second and third groups (considered in the order of their relative importance) of the Protestant doctrinal writers, the selection both of the writers themselves and of their books becomes much more incidental or accidental. In certain instances, the most important controversial production of such an author is left uncondemned, while for some comparatively insignificant tract space is made in the catalogue.

While the selections from writers other than Catholic are devoted in the main to doctrinal and controversial literature, and were probably made up as the result of a general instruction to place on the list of prohibitions all works inimical to the true Faith, the Indexes include also a curious sprinkling of titles of what may be called miscellaneous literature, that is, of books having nothing to do with matters of doctrine, theology, or religion.

The attempt to have some consideration given in the Indexes to the literature of the whole of Europe, caused the compilers to depend for their titles upon catalogues which, in many cases, they could not have had an opportunity of verifying.   The Italian editors transcribed for these Roman Indexes titles of books which appeared from year to year in the announcement-lists of the Frankfort Book-Fair. Their opinions or guesses as to the pernicious character of a book so announced could be based only upon the name of the author, if this happened to be a well-known name, or upon the imprint and general character of the publisher whose name indicated of course the place of production. It was the case, however, with the publishing catalogues of Frankfort in the 16th and 17th centuries, as with similar catalogues in later centuries, that a certain proportion of the books announced never came into print at all Either no sufficient subscriptions were secured, or there was a change in the plans of the publisher, or the author did not secure the necessary resources to ensure the undertaking, or the author died before the completion of his work. As a result, distinction and commemoration were secured in the Index for a number of books which never came into existence.

In the Index of Benedict, while no specific statement to such effect is made, the compilers had evidently been instructed to concentrate their censorship labours upon books which, bearing the names of Catholic writers, and printed, for the most part, within Catholic territory, were likely to have influence with readers among the faithful. The authorities of the Church had finally recognised, after a series of experiments continuing during two centuries, that it was not practicable for a group of Italian priests, working in Rome, to keep themselves adequately informed concerning the productions of the printing-press throughout the civilised world. It was not only a physical impossibility to secure knowledge of the contents of these books, printed no longer in one universal language of literature and scholarship but in all the languages of civilisation; it was even impracticable to obtain and to utilise for Index purposes any fairly complete bibliographies of their titles. From the time of Benedict to the present day, the censorship of the Church has therefore restricted its efforts in the main to the supervision of Catholic literature. It is necessary, however, to use the term "in the main" because the Index of Benedict and the succeeding Indexes, including even the two promulgated by Leo XIII, include, in connection with the long lists of doctrinal works by Catholic writers, a curious sprinkling of books written by Protestants for Protestant communities, the majority of which books have no concern whatsoever with doctrinal matter. It it very difficult to arrive at any understanding of the policy on which these selections, comprising a few dozen volumes out of many thousands, have been arrived at. It does not seem to have been based on the relative importance, as hundreds of productions which secured a world-wide reputation, and the influence of which has been decidedly adverse to the contentions of the Church, have received no attention, while volumes of lesser significance have been found worthy of condemnation.

The lists of the Catholic books have also, under the system pursued by the editors of Benedict and their successors, been largely reduced. The method pursued by the Benedictine compilers of condemning *in toto* certain classes of literature and all books relating to certain specified subjects, saves the editors from the necessity of presenting long lists of titles. In no other manner, in fact, could the conclusions of the censors of the 18th and 19th centuries in regard to the current productions of the printing-press have been brought within reasonable compass. The Index of Benedict marks the beginning of the modern policy of the Church in the matter of censorship.

Hilgers lays stress on the wise toleration of Benedict, as expressed in these regulations of 1758, in insisting that in all cases of doubt, and particularly when the book under examination was a work of a Catholic of repute, the advantage of the doubt should be given to the author; that the author should, if within reach, be given an opportunity, before the decision concerning his book was reached, of being heard before the examiners; that the examination of any book the subject of which might not be one for general understanding should be committed to "consultors" or "qualificators," one or more of whom must have expert knowledge of the subject-matter; that the judgment should be based upon, not the view of any one Order or group or school, but upon the whole policy of the Christian Church and with reference purely to the welfare and instruction of believers. Hilgers also commends the wise liberality of Benedict in regard to works of science. He adds: "So valuable for the influence of the people is the example of men of science, that it is not too much to say that even in the work of scientific investigation, it is their duty, irrespective of the regulations of the Church, to secure a dispensation for the reading of prohibited books or doubtful books." [1]

The Constitution of Benedict, issued under the title *Sollicita ac provida*, was considered to be so wisely framed that Leo XIII, while repealing all the earlier regulations, found it desirable to confirm and to republish this in the Index of 1900.

2. Issues of the Roman Index, 1763–1899.—The Index of 1758 constitutes the foundation of all later

[1] Hilgers, 138.

issues of the Roman Index. A series of appendices were compiled at irregular intervals (from five to ten years) in such form that they could be bound in with the Benedictine Index. At longer intervals (from twenty-five to fifty years), the lists were consolidated into one alphabet and the Index, so printed, constituted a legitimate new edition. The responsibility for the compilation of these additional lists rested with the successive secretaries of the Congregation of the Index. The introduction, written by the secretary to each new appendix, follows pretty closely the wording of that of Ricchini, printed in 1758.

Appendices issued in 1763, 1770, and 1779 were printed in the printing-office of the Holy See. A number of the better printed editions which, according to the title-page, were the work of this office, were, as Reusch points out, actually printed in places other than Rome. Certain of these have been identified with the typography of offices in Parma, Venice, and Florence. The Index issued in 1786 was continued with five appendices; and, in 1806, was reprinted with the six lists in one alphabet. The first Roman Index of the 19th century was issued in 1819, with an introduction from Alex. Aug. Bardani. The second Index of the century was published under Gregory XVI in 1835, and the third under the same Pope in 1841. Both issues contained prefaces by Thomas Ant. Degola. These three Indexes were reprinted in a number of impressions, and the practice had now obtained of recording correctly the place of issue. Italian issues, printed with the papal privilege, were published at Monza, Monreale (in Sicily), and Naples; and an edition printed in Mechlin also carries a papal privilege. Editions for which no such privilege was secured appeared in Paris and in Brussels   Under Pius IX, were published two editions of the Index, one in 1865 and the second in 1877.   Under Leo XIII, were also published two, one in 1881 and the second in 1900 (the preface bears date 1899).   This latter is at the present date (January, 1907) the latest issue in the papal series.   It is described in detail in Chapter XI.   These two Indexes contain each an introduction by the same editor, Hieronymus Pius Saccheri.   The second Index of Leo represents a higher standard of bookmaking than had been reached by any previous Index either papal or Spanish.   The lists are remarkably free from bibliographical or typographical errors and the printed page is not only readable but artistic.   The previous issues of the 19th century, and those of the 18th and 17th, present but very little advance in the matter of consistent and uniform bibliography or in freedom from misprints.   According to the routine obtaining after the accession of Benedict, all the more important of the changes which took shape in the successive Indexes were decided upon in sessions of the Congregation at which the Pope himself presided.   Such was the case, for instance, with the elimination of the general prohibition of the Copernican writings, with the cancellation of the series of entries connected with the issues between Paul V and Venice, and with the recall of the prohibition of the writings of Cardinal Noailles.

What may be called the editorial division (that is to say, the introduction and official entries) in the Index of Benedict is repeated without change in all the later Indexes through the 19th century.   In the Index of 1835, are added to this division two papers.   The first is a *mandatum* of Leo XII, issued under a decree of the Congregation of March 26, 1825, which reads in substance as follows:

"His Holiness has ordered that all patriarchs, archbishops, bishops, and other ecclesiastical dignitaries shall carefully bear in mind their responsibilities under the Rules as promulgated by the Council of Trent, together with the additions to the same which were published by Clement VIII, Alexander VIII, and Benedict XIV. It is evidently impossible to bring into the Index the titles of all publications appearing from year to year which are pernicious in character or dangerous in doctrine. It is no longer practicable to apply the authority of the Church through prohibitions of specific books or cautions as to these, to prevent the faithful from being injured by such pernicious literature. The Church authorities must therefore issue general instructions based upon the Index Rules, by means of which instructions, the faith of believers can be protected against heresy and demoralisation."

The second is a *monitum* of the Congregation of the Index, dated March 4, 1828. The Congregation enjoins upon all patriarchs. archbishops, bishops, confessors, and local inquisitors the importance of making thorough application of the provision of the second of the Tridentine Rules: "Works by heretics which have to do with religious or theological subjects are prohibited without reservation." The *monitum* makes reference also to the instruction of Clement VIII: "All works which are prohibited by the Holy See in the original text are also forbidden in all translations of the same."

In the Index of 1841, was included a *monitum* concerning translations into the vernacular of the Scriptures. In the Index of 1877, was included a statement concerning the modification of the penalties that had been prescribed under the Bull of 1869, and also a declaration concerning books on the doctrine of the Immaculate Conception.

In May, 1844, Gregory XVI had included in an encyclical a *monitum* cautioning all believers to guard themselves not only against the reading of all books prohibited by title, but against the use or the influence of any literature belonging to the classes which are condemned and prohibited under the general instructions of the Index. This *monitum* of Gregory's was, however, not itself reprinted in any of the succeeding Indexes.

The *Decreta Generalia* have received no additions since the time of Benedict. A number of general prohibitions have, however, been issued which are analogous in their character and authority to the *Decreta*. These are printed in the text of the Index proper and, in certain cases, under headings where they would hardly be looked for. Some of them are entered under *libri (omnes incredulorum)*; the prohibition of books on spiritualism is entered under the term "matter." Some of these general prohibitions, such as that of the writings of the Carbonari, escaped being repeated in any of the Indexes.

A formula which finds place in the Index first under Benedict reads: *Auctor laudabiliter se subjecit et opus suum reprobavit.*

When a work has been condemned by the Inquisition or by the Congregation on the ground of heretical propositions, the determination of such propositions is based upon certain general principles laid down by the Inquisition. The author has the alternative of cancelling the book altogether or of agreeing to reprint it with the elimination of the propositions condemned as heretical.

In later years, it has been the practice of the Congregation in the case of authors to whom, on one ground or another, it is thought desirable to extend consideration, to give to such authors, in advance of the publication of any condemnation, the opportunity of making the eliminations or corrections required. If the author promptly assents to such a course, his work is not included in any of the official lists of condemnation. Catholics who learn first through the publication of the official reports that their writings have come into condemnation and who thereupon make submission and promise of correction, are recorded in a supplementary decree of the Congregation. Such decree makes announcement of the fact of the submission and gives approval to the text as corrected, of the work in question. The form of announcement is as follows: *Auctor laudabiliter se subjecit et opus reprobavit* In the case of works which have been prohibited with a *d.c.* the formula reads: *Auctor laudabiliter se subjecit et reprobanda reprobavit* or *et opus amendavit.* There are various examples of the use of this formula between the years 1873 and 1881.

In a decree of Pius IX, issued in June, 1848, the censorship concerning material of a religious or doctrinal character, printed either in books or periodicals, was restricted to the territory of the States of the Church. A decree of the inquisitor-general, issued in September, 1851, states :

"It is become known to us that either on the ground of malice, of wilful disobedience, or of ignorance, certain persons fail to give information to the Holy See concerning the undertakings of heretics and the spread of Protestant contentions, or concerning the publication of attacks or satires against the Pope or against ecclesiastical Orders, or as to the distribution of writings in which the Holy Scriptures have been misused or misquoted, or the distribution of works printed without the official permit, or the reading, printing or possession of such works. It is hereby ordered that all such delinquents shall incur the penalty of excommunication *latae sententiae*. This edict is to be placed in every sacristy. It is further ordered that all printers, booksellers, collectors of customs, janitors, landlords, and shopkeepers of any kind shall place copies of this edict in their premises in such manner that it shall be read by all."

In an instruction given in July, 1878, by the cardinal vicar of Rome, which has to do particularly with the regulation of divine service, of the sermons, and of the schools of heretics, "whose operations are carried on under the very eyes of the Teacher of Infallible Youth," is printed the announcement:

"The typesetters who, in order to prevent themselves from losing their work, put into type the writings of heretics, come into grievous sin. This is essentially the case with those who lend themselves to the production of works maintaining or defending heretical doctrines for which works the Pope has ordered the larger excommunication."

1806. Rome. Index Prohibitorius. This Index, issued under Pius VII, is a reprint of the Index of 1786 with continuations of the lists up to the year of its publication.

1819. Rome. Index Prohibitorius. Index Librorum Prohibitorum, Sanctissimi Domini Nostri Pii Septimi Pontificis Maximi jussu editus. The only article in this volume which is distinctive is the "Address to the Catholic Reader" by the editor, Alex. Angelicus Bardani, of the Order of St. Dominic and Secretary of the Congregation of the Index. This address refers, with congratulation, to the pious interest of the faithful which had exhausted the edition of the Index of 1786 (making, curiously enough, no reference to the intervening Index of 1806). The volume was reprinted in 1822 with two appendices and two decrees. The closing portion of the second decree is devoted to a denunciation of five works in English relating to papal controversies in North America, as follows:

"An Address to the Congregation of St. Mary's Church, Philadelphia."

"Continuation of an Address," etc.

"The Opinion of the Right Reverend John Rico on the Address."

"Address of the Committee."

"Address of the Right Reverend Bishop of Pennsylvania," etc.

A further edition of this Index with some revisions was printed in Paris in 1825—*Le Catalogue des Ouvrages mis à l'Index, contenant les noms de tous les Livres condamnés par la Cour de Rome, depuis l'invention de l'Imprimerie jusqu' à 1825, avec les dates des Décrets de leur condamnation.* The lists are preceded by an *Avis de l'Éditeur* in which an account is given of the Congregation of the Index at Rome with reference to the work of Catalani. It proceeds to say that the works comprehended in this Index are those which had been prohibited by Pius VI and Pius VII, together with all which are known to have been since censured *sous l'heureux gouvernment de l'Église Universelle par N.T.S. Père le Pape Léon XII.* It is not clear what authority this general Index may have been held to possess in France as, under various preceding utterances, the Gallican Church had taken the position that the Indexes of Rome were not to have authority in France unless re-issued with the specific approval of the rulers of the French Church.

This Index contains a condemnation of the "Defence of the Ancient Faith," by the Rev. Peter Gandolphy, published in 1816, a work which had secured the approbation of the master of the sacred palace and of Damiani, master of theology. The appendix includes also Lady Morgan's volume on Italy, and a special decree in regard to the New Testament.

A reprint of the Index of 1819 was issued in Brussels in 1828.

1835. Rome. Gregory XVI. Prohibitorius.

1841. Rome. Gregory XVI. Prohibitorius. Reprints of these two Indexes were issued (with papal privileges) in Mechlin, Monza, Monreale, and Naples.

1855. Rome. Pius IX. Prohibitorius.

1871. Rome. Pius IX. Reissue, with an appendix, of the Index of 1841.

1877. Rome. Pius IX. Prohibitorius. Each of these Indexes contains an introduction by Hieronymus Pius Saccheri. The lists of titles in both present a number of errors, bibliographical and typographical, and are in fact much less correct than those of Benedict.

1881. Rome. Leo XIII. Index Prohibitorius, reprinted with appendix in 1884.

1896. Rome. Leo XIII. Index Prohibitorius. A reprint of the Index of 1884, with appendix carrying the titles to 1895.

1899–1900. Rome. Leo XIII. Index Prohibitorius: for specification of contents, see Chapter XI.

CHAPTER V

METHODS OF PROHIBITION AND THE CONTINUATION OF CLASS I

1. Papal Prohibitions in the 17th and 18th Centuries.
2. Prohibitions by Bishops.
3. Publication of the Book Prohibitions.
4. The Continuation of Class I.
5. Catalogues of Books Approved.

1. Papal Prohibitions in the 17th and 18th Centuries.
—As in previous periods, there are in the 17th century numerous examples of papal prohibitions, through constitutions, bulls, or briefs, of individual books which were held to be sufficiently important to call for such special action. In 1602, Clement VIII condemns the works of Carolus Molinaeus; in 1642, Urban VIII condemns the writings of Jansen together with a number of treatises by the followers of Jansen; in 1661, Alexander VII condemns a French version of the missal. The formula generally utilised for these individual prohibitions was as follows:

"We condemn this work after mature consideration, on our personal judgment (*motu proprio*) and with assured knowledge (of its pernicious character), on the Apostolic authority (vested in us); and we prohibit to all persons, whatever may be their rank or position, the printing, reading, or possession of the same. The penalty for disobedience shall be the *excommunicatio latae sententiae*. We direct that the existing copies of said work be delivered to the bishop or to the inquisitor of the diocese, by whom such copies shall be promptly burned. This order shall be placed on the doors of the Basilica of the Church of the Apostles and on the doors of the Apostolic Chancellery, and on the gateway of the Campus Florae, and when so published, shall be held to have been delivered in person to each individual affected by it."

In the case of a Bull, the wording of the first paragraph was:

"Through this Constitution, which shall remain in force for ever, and under the authority of the blessed Apostles Peter and Paul, and of ourselves."

After the time of Alexander VII, 1665, the condemnation is made to follow the decisions arrived at by theological examiners appointed for the purpose, or by the cardinals of the Inquisition. The greater number of the prohibitions continued, however, to emanate from the Congregation of the Index, while for a few, the responsibility rested with the Inquisition.

In 1753, Benedict XIV in the Bull *Sollicita* (printed later in connection with the Index of 1758) gives consideration to the regulation of the proceedings of the two bodies. The substance of Benedict's ruling is as follows:

In the case of a book which is denounced by the Inquisition as deserving of condemnation, and the prohibition of which has not been confirmed by the Index Congregation, the following measures shall be taken. The book shall be examined by a commission appointed for the purpose, and the written report of these examiners shall be submitted (with the book itself) to the cardinals. The conclusion of the cardinals shall be referred to the pope, who will give the final judgment in the matter. In the case of a book by a Catholic author, the condemnation shall not be permitted to rest on the decision of one examiner. His adverse report must secure the confirmation of a second censor appointed by the Congregation. If the judgments of the two differ, the matter must be passed upon by the cardinals. The Congregation of the Index is always to include several cardinals. The *Magister* of the papal palace is a member *ex officio*. The secretary shall be a Dominican selected by the pope. The Congregation has the assistance of a number of counsellors selected from the clergy and from the Orders and from the judicial class (*Relatores*). The sessions of the Congregation are not regular, as are those of the Inquisition, but are called in response to the report of the secretary that there is business requiring action. This leaves to the secretary a large discretion in the initiating of action and in the selection of matters to be passed upon. In the case of a book by a Catholic author of good repute (*integrae famae*) in which pernicious material is found, the prohibition shall, if practicable, be made not general, but conditional, under the heading of *donec corrigatur* or *donec expurgetur*. The decree shall not be made public at once, but opportunity shall be given to the author or to some representative of the author to make the required corrections. If the author shall agree to withdraw from sale the original edition, replacing this with the corrected text, no public prohibition need be made. If the original edition has come into general circulation, the condemnation shall be so worded as to apply only to such uncorrected text. The loss incurred through such cancellation and reprinting appears to have fallen upon the publisher unless the edition were the property of the author, or the publishing agreement made the author responsible for losses incurred on the ground of heresies. In reply to the complaint that books had from time to time been prohibited without an opportunity being given to the author to defend his production against the charge of heresy, the Bull takes the ground that the purpose of the action of the Church is not to pronounce judgment on authors, but to protect the faithful against injury through heretical doctrine. Any detriment caused to the repute of the author is an incidental result which cannot be avoided. In any case, the judgment on the character of the production is to be arrived at with due deliberation and full knowledge.

The Pope expresses his intention to be present at sessions of the Congregation when matters of first importance are to be considered. Decisions concerning the works of unquestioned heretics, in regard to books containing direct attacks on the doctrines of the Church, can, however, be disposed of without his counsel and under the Rules of the Index of Trent. The members of the Congregation bind themselves to secrecy as to its proceedings. The secretary is, however, at liberty to give information to the author or the publisher of the book condemned.

"The counsellors and examiners of the Congregation are cautioned to proceed with their work with due conservatism. They are by no means to assume that a work submitted is certainly to be condemned but are to assure themselves by diligent investigation whether it may not be possible to declare it fitting for circulation, either in its original form or with certain omissions or emendations. Care is to be taken to place each book in the hands of examiners having expert and scholarly knowledge of the subject-matter. The examiners must free themselves from prejudices of race, native school of thought, or ecclesiastical order. They must keep before them that the essential purpose of their work is the defence of the faith, and the preservation of the doctrines of the Church as set forth by the decrees of the general councils, the constitutions of the popes, and by the teachings of the Fathers and of their learned successors, and the maintenance of the authority of the Church universal. The examiners must bear in mind that it is not possible to judge fairly of the character of a book without reading the entire text, and that the statements in the different divisions of the work must be carefully collated one with another. It is frequently the case that a sentence taken apart from its context may give a wrong impression of the author's meaning, or that a sentence which taken alone may seem of doubtful purport, will have the thought made clear by comparison with other portions of the text. (Conservative counsel which was by no means always followed by the censors.) In the case of the work of a Catholic author whose orthodoxy is of good repute, it is proper, if a sentence or statement may be open to more than one interpretation, to give to it the most favourable (*i.e.* the most orthodox). There are books which, while quite sound and orthodox in their purpose and teachings, contain references to pernicious writings, or extracts from such writings. The knowledge of the heresies thus referred to may do injury to the faith of innocent readers. Such books call, therefore, for very careful consideration, and if the quoted material is sufficient in amount and in character to exert a pernicious influence, the work must be expurgated or placed upon the Index. Authors are cautioned against the wrongdoing of abusing each other whatever may be the difference of opinion, or of using harsh and condemnatory language against other writers whose works have not been condemned by the Church. These instructions and counsels are to be accepted as carrying the full Apostolic authority and as binding upon the Congregations, the examiners, and all others concerned."

Certain of the other Congregations, such as those on confession, on the rites of the Church, and on propaganda, assumed the right to prohibit books having to do with their particular subjects, but their prohibitions had to be confirmed by, and promulgated through, the Congregation of the Index.

The *Magister* of the palace had authority to issue in his own name prohibitions which were valid for the city of Rome. The individual edicts published by him in the name of the pope were of course general in their effect. From the time of Clement XI, 1700–1721, the prohibitions of individual works through bulls and briefs became much more frequent. After Benedict XIV, 1756, such prohibitions are to be found in allocations and in encyclicals. In 1664, Alexander VII ordered that the injunctions and penalties of Pius IV, as specified in the Index of Trent, should remain in force, but that all the other constitutions and decrees in regard to books, excepting only the *Bulla Coenae*, be revoked.

In the introduction to the Index of 1758, Benedict XIV presents certain principles as controlling, from that time, the work of the censors. Books by heretics are to receive consideration only in the instances in which they treat of the Catholic faith, or teach heresies. The task of examining and supervising the entire literature of the world was at last recognised as one beyond the powers of the Church authorities.

In 1869, a Bull of Pius IX restricts the penalty of the excommunication *latae sententiae* to the reading, possession. etc., of books written by heretics, only when these not only contain heresies, but make a formal defence of the same, or when they have been specifically prohibited by title.

In the case of a writer who had already been condemned for uttering heretical opinions, his later books were likely to be placed on the Index irrespective of the character of their contents. In 1615, for instance, the opinions of Copernicus were condemned by the Inquisition, and, a year later, his astronomical treatises were duly prohibited.

The condemnation of a book by the Inquisition

carried as a rule more weight than a prohibition by the Congregation. On the other hand, the Inquisition found difficulty in keeping up with its work.

In 1711, the Jesuit Daubenton writes to Fénelon: "The Inquisition has such a mass of business on its hands, and has available for its consideration so few men who are capable and who are ready to give attention to it, that a period of years may be required to secure the condemnation of a book, particularly if it is of considerable compass." The control of the Inquisition, as of the Congregation, rested with the Dominicans. The commissary of the former and the secretary of the latter, always Dominicans, retained in their hands the continuity and the general direction of the business of their respective bodies.

In 1633, Lucas Holstenius (a "consultor" appointed by Alexander XII) writes from Rome to Peiresc:

"We have here a few learned men who would be glad to be of service to scholarly literature if there were any possibility of securing for their views any recognition. . . . But the opinions of scholars have no weight with these ignorant censors . . . One of the cardinals who thinks of himself as an intelligent man and who has a large control of the business, says openly that he is in favour of condemning and burning practically all works of a humanistic character (*qui de literis humanioribus et de liberali eruditione agunt*) and of leaving in existence only the theological treatises, and the writings of a few jurists. . . . You will have heard of the recent condemnation of the scholarly works of Scaliger, Heinsius, Rivius, and Godenius. . . . My indignation grows and I find myself unwilling to attend any more sittings of the Congregation. . . . I speak thus, for your ear only, as here, it is perilous to make any complaint or opposition to such proceedings."[1]

[1] Epp., ed. Boissonade, 1817, 252.

In 1686, the learned Benedictine Mabillon, being in Rome, was asked by the Congregation to give a report on the writings of Vossius, and later he was appointed a "consultor."

In the compilation of the Roman Indexes of the 16th century, the announcement catalogues of the Frankfort Fair were largely utilised. As before pointed out, one result of this practice was to bring into the Index lists the titles of not a few books of but trifling importance (which otherwise would have been entirely lost sight of), of others which contained no doctrinal material and in fact nothing pernicious or objectionable, and of still others which, while announced as in preparation or in plan, never came into print at all. After 1600, the Fair catalogues appear to have been but little used, but information concerning published books was secured from the *Acta Eruditorum*, the *Journal des Savants*, and similar periodicals. Bourgeois is authority for the statement that after 1650, it was the routine, with both Inquisition and Congregation, to take up for consideration only such books as had been specifically denounced.

In 1690, Cardinal Ciampini proposed the establishment of a seminar or commission of ten or twelve scholars, selected from different countries, who should be charged with the task of examining the books issued from the different publishing centres and of making reports upon which could be based the selections of the Congregation of the Index. He proposed to bequeath to such a seminar his library and a capital sufficient to secure for each member an annual payment of one hundred scudi. The foundation never, however, came into existence. At the time of Benedict XIV, Cardinal Querini submitted a plea for the better organisation of the Congregation and offered an endowment to be utilised for the printing of the censorship opinions, but the offer appears not to have been taken advantage of. In 1622, Gregory XV instituted the *Congregatio de Propaganda Fide*, and to this body was confided the task of examining, and when necessary of prohibiting, books in oriental and other "exotic" tongues. In 1674, Clement X issued a brief prohibiting the printing, "even by Jesuits or other Orders," of any works relating to the missions except with the authority of the Congregation. The penalty was cancellation of the edition and excommunication of those responsible for its production.

After 1610, the edicts of the *Magister* prohibiting individual books are infrequent. In 1690, we have an example of such an edict in the case of a treatise on the Immaculate Conception by the Jesuit Saliceti, which was printed in Rome with the censored passages duly cancelled in the text. It continued, however, to be the practice for each *Magister*, in taking office, to issue a general edict setting forth the regulations controlling the production of books. One of the most important of these required the comparison page by page, by examiners appointed by the censor, of the text of the book as printed with that of the manuscript which had been approved (and possibly corrected). Until this comparison had been made, no copies of the edition could be offered for sale.

Certain general prohibitions are included in the Clementine Index. In the earlier years of the 17th century, further similar prohibitions or decrees are published. In 1621, for instance, is printed the series of decisions of the Congregation of the Council of Trent. The Pope had prohibited the publication of any unauthorised translations of the decrees of Trent, but the above work, carrying with it no authorisation, does not find place in the Index lists. In 1601, appears a prohibition of all litanies with the exception of the Laurentian and that bearing the name of All Saints. In 1603, appears a general prohibition of all writings concerning the Mohammedan religion. In 1633, a decree of the *Magister S. Palatii* prohibits all *Elogia Haereticorum*. With this prohibition, is included a condemnation of all pictures or medals in honour of heretics. This general prohibition was interpreted to bring into condemnation a long series of important bibliographical works in which had been printed, either with approval or without condemnation, the names of heretical writers. In April, 1621, an announcement was made, on the part of the Congregation of the Council of Trent, protesting against the publication, nominally under the authority of the council, of so-called collections of the declarations of the council, and pointing out that such publications had been specifically condemned under the Bull of Pius IV. With the authority of Gregory XV, all such collections or reports of the decisions and conclusions of the council, issued without specific authority of the council, which had thus far been printed or which should later come into print, were condemned and prohibited. Among the works included under this condemnation, were a number which had been prepared by orthodox Catholic theologians and canonists, such as Prosper Farinaccius, Vincenzio de Marzilla, etc.

In the course of the 17th century, the Congregation of Rites condemned a series of prayers and litanies. Reusch states that "up to the present day" (he is writing in 1884) only one such litany, that described as "In the name of Jesus" had secured approbation. The general decree of 1601 prohibiting litanies has never been recalled; and under this decree stand condemned and prohibited all books of service which contain other than the two, or at this time, the three brief litanies. This decree, would, according to Reusch, prohibit nine tenths of the service books in use in the Catholic Church.

The prohibition issued by Alexander in decree number IV with the title: *Instructionum et rituum sectae Mahumetanae libri omnes*, seems to have had for its immediate text a work entitled: *Liber de Russorum, Moscovitarum, et Tartarorum religione*, which was printed at Spires. In the Index of Benedict, the title was for the first time given complete with the name of the author, Lasitzki, Jo., *de Russorum rel. sacrificiis, nuptiarum et funerum ritu e diversis scriptoribus.* Under the general prohibition of bibliographical works in which any terms of approval are connected with the names of heretical writers, is included (in 1687) the following English work: Crowaei Guil, *Elenchus scriptorum in s. scripturam tam graecorum quam latinorum*, London, 1672. A work of similar character, compiled by Thomas Pope Blount, under the title *Censura celebrium auctorum*, printed in London in 1690, escaped the attention of the compilers.

2. **Book Prohibitions by the Bishops.**—During the 17th and 18th centuries, were published no lists of books condemned under the authority of the bishops which compare in importance or in influence with the Indexes issued during the 17th century from Louvain and from Paris. During the 17th century, however, there are a number of instances of individual books condemned by the divines of the

Sorbonne. of Louvain, and of other theological faculties. One Index of some comprehensiveness was issued by the Archbishop of Paris, but the work was undertaken at the instance of the Parliament. Two Indexes were issued by the Archbishops of Prague, and the decree of Precipiano, Archbishop of Utrecht. has already been referred to. As late as the last half of the 18th century, the bishops have utilised the form of pastoral letters and pastoral instructions for the condemnation of individual books and, occasionally, of lists of books. A pastoral letter, for instance, of the Vicar-General of Augsburg, issued in 1758, presents a list of fifty-five works which are condemned on the ground of their association with the "new sects and new teachings of mystics and fanatics." In 1752, similar lists were connected with a decree of the Bishop of Turenne and a pastoral instruction of the Bishop of Luçon.

Clement XIII (1758–1769) condemned, in briefs issued in January and in September. 1759, the treatise by Helvetius, *De l'Esprit*, and the encyclopaedia compiled by the same author, both of which had been published anonymously. For the encyclopaedia, the specification was added that it belonged to the class of books permission for the reading of which could be given only by the pope himself. In a brief addressed in November, 1765, to the Archbishop of Rheims, Clement praises the assembly of the clergy for the condemnation of pernicious writings, and in an encyclical issued in November, 1766, he reminds the bishops of their responsibility for the repression of irreligious works, and reminds them further that they are to secure in this work the aid of the State authorities.

In an encyclical issued in 1769, Clement XIV repeats

to the bishops the injunction of his predecessor in regard to the essential importance of maintaining the fight for the stamping out of wicked books. In the decade succeeding 1758, the Inquisition and the Congregation of the Index condemn and prohibit the works of Voltaire, Rousseau, La Mettrie, d'Holbach, Marmontel, Raynal, and others. The list includes also a treatise by Helvetius, in addition to his work *De l'Esprit*, and single monographs of Diderot and d'Alembert in addition to their contributions to the Encyclopaedia.

In 1864, the Congregation of the Index issues, under the authority of Pius IX, a circular letter to the bishops authorising and instructing them to carry out the prohibitions of the Congregation. Reference is made to the Edict of Leo XII, of 1825, and emphasis is laid on the importance of checking the irreligious influence of the newspapers.

3. Publication of the Book Prohibitions.—During the earlier years of the 17th century, the lists of the books condemned by the Congregation or the Inquisition were published by the *Magister*. After 1613, the lists passed upon by the Congregation were prepared for the press by the secretary, printed in the papal printing-office, and distributed through the local inquisitors and the nuncios. This was the course taken, for instance, with the condemnation, in 1616, of the books of Copernicus, and in 1633, with the writings of Galileo. Later, the practice obtained of printing the special lists on the annual lists in the *format* of the latest edition of the Index, so that they could be bound in with this. After 1624, the secretaries of the Congregation brought into print a number of collections of the various decrees.

In the reprint, in 1667, of the Index issued by Alexander VII in 1664, are included no less than ninety-two of the separate decrees. Of the later decrees there is no official or complete collection. According to the contention of the Curia, the publication of a decree in Rome rendered it binding on Catholics throughout the world, but this view was by no means generally accepted. In Spain as in France, it was held that the papal bulls and decrees were in force only after they had been formally confirmed and published under national authority, but in Spain this authority was delegated to the Inquisition. Francis I refused altogether to recognise the decrees of the Congregation or of the Roman Inquisition. In Venice, Naples, and Belgium, these decrees became authoritative only when confirmed by the State authorities. The circulation outside of Italy of copies of the Roman Indexes was very trifling, and (with the exception of that of Trent) the reprinting of these occurred but seldom. If the work of the papal printing-office is to be judged by the Roman Indexes and decrees of the 16th and 17th centuries, the standard was by no means high. The bibliographical lists abound in errors, the responsibility for which must be divided between the compilers and the type-setters. In not a few instances, the names and titles have been so seriously twisted that it is often not easy to identify the work condemned. The Index of Benedict XIV was the first of the Roman series in which any serious attempt appears to have been made to secure any measure of bibliographical accuracy.

An *Abrégé du Recueil des Actes du Clergé*, first issued in 1762, divides the bulls and briefs of the popes into two classes: those which have been confirmed and accepted in France, and those which have been rejected and which are, therefore, not binding on the French Church.[1] The chronicler explains that it is the general rule to accept the Roman rescripts which may prove useful for Church or for State, even although it is often necessary to repudiate certain formulas and expressions contained in them. In certain cases, however, the formulas are so repugnant that they cause the rejection of the Bull itself, as for instance when the king is threatened with excommunication or deposition. The French authorities, ecclesiastical as well as political, refused from the outset to accept the Roman formula that publication of a decree in Rome made it binding throughout the realms of the Church, and they refused also to accept the authority of any general penalty of excommunication which might be made to include the head of the State.[2]

The Advocate-General Omer Talon, in an address delivered in 1647 before the Parliament of Paris, says: "We are prepared to recognise and to accept the authority of the pope but neither the authority nor the jurisdiction of the Congregation or of the Curia." The Chancellor d'Aguesseau writes in 1710: "It is well understood that the Roman Index carries no authority in France where, while the primacy of the pope is accepted, the authority of the Congregation of cardinals is not in force."[3]

Bossuet writes in regard to such a papal brief:[4] "We hold that these constitutions are not binding in a French diocese until (and unless) they have been published by the bishop." Fénelon says: "We are not

[1] 2d edtn., Paris, 1764, 186.
[2] Reusch, ii, 20.
[3] *Oeuvres*, xiii, 409.
[4] *Oeuvres*, 37, 75.

willing through the acceptance of a papal brief to acknowledge the authority (for France) of either the Index or Inquisition."

As before stated, within the dominions of Spain, the Spanish Indexes alone were accepted as authoritative, and the Spanish authorities very frequently refused to condemn books that had been prohibited by the editors of Rome.   In other of the States classed as Catholic, the authority of the Roman censorship was in like manner contested.   In 1759, Charles Alexander, Stadtholder of Lorraine, prohibited the printing or sale of certain theological treatises by Dens, on the ground that these asserted the authority of the *Bulla Coenae*, and of the Roman censorship and the immunity of the bishops, and that this constituted an assault on the authority of the emperor and on the general policy of the Netherlands.

4.   **The Continuation of Class I, 1603–1876.**—The list of heretical authors of the first class, all of whose works (past and future) were condemned, were,

Later Heresiarchs.

in the first group of Roman Indexes, printed without change or additions. The authorities do not appear to have considered the later heretical writers to be entitled to the dignity of being classed as heresiarchs.   In the Decree of 1603, the name of Frac. Guicciardini and that of Peter Frider are added by the Roman editors to Class I; but these constitute the only additions for the series of years given.   On the other hand, new Spanish Indexes of this class receive from decade to decade continued additions.

Among the authors, all of whose writings were prohibited in Indexes printed prior to Alexander VII (1664), may be noted Hugo Broughton (of Oxford),

Thomas White (of London), Ludwig de Dieu, Gregorius Richter, Giordano Bruno, Claudius Salmasius, J. B. Poza. Between 1664 and 1756, the list includes among the more noteworthy names, the German writers J. H. Buddaeus, Georg. Calixtus, J. H. Heidigger ; the Hollanders Jo. Clericus, Simon Episcopius, Jac. Laurentius, and Lambert Velthuysen; the Frenchmen J. Daillé, Ch. Drelincourt, Jean d'Espagne; the Englishmen G. Bull (Bishop of St. Davids), W. Cave, J. Lightfoot, Henricus Morus, J. Prideaux, and Thomas Hobbes.

To these may be added the names of Molinos van Espen and Colbert, Bishop of Montpellier. It is difficult, in an examination of the complete lists, to arrive at any principle or basis on which the compilers made their selections. Of forty-one Protestant writers whose names were placed on the Index during one sitting of the Index Congregation in May, 1757, sixteen were Germans, ten, Hollanders, eleven, Frenchmen, and four, Englishmen. At the same session, were prohibited the entire series of the theological writings of Hugo Grotius. Between 1757 and 1821, there is no instance in the Roman Indexes of the use in connection with the name of an author of the term *Opera omnia*, although as a fact in a number of cases every book produced by some particular author was included under its own title. Between the years 1821 and 1827, the authors whose complete works were thus specifically condemned by title include G. Mordai, David Hume, and Colin de Plancy. In 1852, were added, among other names, those of V. Giorberti, Proudhon, and Sue. In 1862, the prohibition included Dumas father and son, Georges Sand, Murger, Stendhal, Balzac, Champfleury, Feydeau, and Soulié. In 1876, three names are to be noted, Vera, Spavente, and Ferrari. The works of John Locke called for special attention in two of the Indexes of the first half of the 18th century. The reading or possession of these books is forbidden under penalty of excommunication, *sub anathemate*.

In 1610, was prohibited the treatise that had been published in the previous year by Hugo Grotius, *Mare liberum S. de jure quod Batavis competit ad Indicana commercia*. The entry was alphabeted under *H*. The title has been preserved in the later Indexes of the 19th century under the proper heading, Grotius. The purpose of the treatise was to contest, on the ground of natural right and of the *Jus gentium*, the monopoly, which had secured the support of Alexander VI, of the Spaniards and Portuguese over certain lines of sea trade. The Pope had taken the ground that his authority was sufficient to institute trade monopolies either by land or by sea. If the Pope were in a position to grant ownership of territories and of peoples, the smaller matter of the connecting trade might naturally be assumed as the conclusion. Grotius, however, asserts that no authority vested in the Pope had given to the Spaniards the control of the Indies (of the West) and that such control as had come to the Spaniards had been secured through force of arms and not through the papal diploma.

5. **Catalogues of Books Approved.**—There is ground for surprise that while in the four and a half centuries since the publication of the first papal Index, the Church has promulgated such a long series of lists of books condemned and prohibited, the authorities have not been interested in giving a larger measure of attention to the selection of books which could safely be recommended for the reading of the faithful, and

which to some extent at least might be suggested as taking the place of the literature that was to be cancelled as pernicious. I can find record of but four or five lists, issued under the authority of the Church, of books recommended for the reading of the faithful, and no one of these recommendation catalogues was prepared in Rome or was published under direct authority from Rome. The first Index in the Church series, that published in Louvain in 1546, contains a short list of books recommended. This list is referred to in the description of the Index itself (see Volume I); a similar recommendation list, including in part the same titles, is connected with the second Louvain Index of 1550. In 1549, a provincial synod was held in Cologne under the direction of the Archbishop Adolf of Schauenburg. A decree was issued by this synod addressed to "the simple and unlearned priests who might not be qualified to distinguish the sound from the unsound doctrine, and who had therefore from time to time been misled by books that were placed in the market with misleading titles." These pastors and their followers were particularly charged against any books, whatsoever might be their titles, which contain writings of Luther, Calvin, Melanchthon, Oecolampadius, or of their followers. The decree of the synod was connected with a brief list of the heretical authors whose works were particularly to be guarded against, and the statement was made that this would be followed by a general and comprehensive catalogue or Index. No such general Index was, however, prepared. In 1550, however, the diocesan synod issued a list of books recommended for the use of the instructors and teachers in the Church schools.

The third recommendation list of which I find record

was issued in Munich in 1566, under an edict of Albert V. This is a comprehensive catalogue of books which have secured privilege for publication throughout the duchy, and which, having been selected under the direct supervision of the Church authorities, can be safely recommended for the use of students and readers.

The heads of convents and Church libraries are cautioned to cleanse their collections from the books which have been condemned under the previous prohibitory Index, and to replace these books with the works now recommended by the authority of the Church. In the second issue of this recommendation catalogue are presented, curiously enough, the titles of certain works which had been prohibited in the Index of Trent. Examples of these are the writings of Bohemus, J. P., of Geiler Kaisersperg, Conrad Klingius, Jo. Ferus, F. Guicciardinus.[1] Between the years 1606 and 1619, there came into annual publication in Mayence, as a result apparently of the recommendation of Peter Canisius, the energetic head of the Jesuits in Germany, a catalogue, prepared more particularly for the use of booksellers in Catholic countries, of books recommended for the reading of the faithful. This annual catalogue bore the following titles: *Index novus librorum imprimis Catholicorum, theologorum, aliorumque celebrium auctorum quarumcunque facultatum et linguarum, causas religionis tamen non tractantium . . . pro italia ceterisque nationibus confectus.* On the back of the title-page of the issue for 1606, is presented a preface bearing the signature Valentinus Leuchtius. *S. Sedis Apost. librorum revisor, imp. Rodolphi II*, etc. In this preface, the reviser undertakes to lay down the principle for the elimination of

[1] Reusch, i, 467.

pernicious literature and for the selection of books of wholesome doctrine and sound influence.

The above series describes the few fragmentary efforts made in any formal fashion by the Church authorities during the centuries of censorship to guide with any positive advice the reading of the faithful. The dependence for counsel in regard to the books to be read seems to have been left to the individual action of the confessors or other ecclesiastical advisers.

CHAPTER VI

ISSUES BETWEEN CHURCH AND STATE

1559-1870

1. Venice and the Papacy.... .... 1606-1696.
2. Spain and the Papacy........................... 1559-1770.
3. Controversies concerning the Gallican Church..... 1600-1758.
4. Ecclesiastical-Political Contests.. .... 1700-1750.
5. England and the Papacy........ .... 1606-1853.
6. The Gallicans and the Liberal Catholics. ....1845-1870.

1. Venice and the Papacy, 1606-1696.—The contest that arose between Paul V and the Venetian Republic caused to the Pope a larger measure of trouble than had arisen in connection with the controversy *De Auxiliis*. The Venetian Senate, in laws enacted in 1603 and 1605, had brought under its direct control the building of new churches, monasteries, and hospitals; it had prohibited the transfer, either by sale or by gift, of real estate to any ecclesiastical bodies, and it had brought for trial before the civil court two ecclesiastics who were charged with common crimes. In December, 1605, Paul writes a brief to the Doge and a second brief to the Senate in which he declares these laws to be annulled and demands the delivery to the papal nuncio of the two clerical delinquents. The Venetians refused obedience to the demand in the briefs; thereupon the Pope transmits to the ecclesi-

90

astical bodies of Venice in April, 1606, a *monitorium* in which he places under excommunication the Doge and the members of the Senate unless, within twenty-four days after the publication of this *monitorium*, the demand of the brief be complied with. The Doge, Leonardo Donato, prohibits the publication of the papal decree. The Jesuits, the Capucins, and the Theatins, the only bodies who were affected by the interdict placed upon the territory of the Republic, were expelled. The Pope now threatened the Venetians with war, but in the course of a few months, through the intervention of the French Ambassador and of Cardinal Joyeuse, the two priests were delivered to the French Ambassador, with the declaration that the Republic reserved for itself the right to punish ecclesiastics for civil offences. The laws in regard to such procedure were not recalled, but the Senate agreed to have the same administered with due reserve. The Senate also recalled its manifesto against censorship. The Cardinal, in the name of the Pope, thereupon recalled the several decrees issued against the Republic. The Venetians refused, however, to take back the order expelling the Jesuits, and it was not until fifty years later, in 1657, that the latter again found place for themselves within the Republic

In 1606, were included in the Index a number of controversial treatises which had been written for the defence of the contentions of the Republic or which concerned themselves with the interdict issued by the Inquisition. During the time of Alexander VII, was placed upon the Index a general prohibition of the record of the interdict issued by Paul V against the Venetian Republic. This entry was cancelled by Benedict XIV. During this contest, were placed upon the Index certain treatises by Suarez and by Sanchez, both leaders among the Jesuits, on the ground that editions of their works, printed by Venetian printers, had omitted passages which sustained the authority of the Holy See. The printers had been able to secure from the Senate a privilege for the printing of these volumes only on condition of the elimination of these passages. The most famous of the representatives of Venice in this contest was Paolo Sarpi (1552–1626). Sarpi was, in 1626, ordered by the Inquisition to report to Rome, but he refused obedience and made a formal protest against the order. Sarpi's *History of the Council of Trent* was prohibited promptly after its publication in 1619, and later, several other writings of his found their way also into the Index lists. There is, however, no condemnation under the name of Sarpi of his *Opera omnia*. In 1656, was published the official *History of the Council of Trent*, compiled by Pallavicini. The Index contains the titles of a number of writings which were written in criticism of this history.

In the *Discorso* concerning the Inquisition in Venice (printed in 1639), Sarpi (in a reference to certain decrees issued in 1609 and 1610 by Yotella, master of the palace) complains of the attempt on the part of the papacy to undermine and violate the Concordat made in the year 1596, between the Republic and the pope, which among other obligations stipulated that no other Index than that of Clement VIII should be enforced or allowed. In contravention of this stipulation, new decrees were year after year being imposed, "chiefly through confessors, which were to be enforced in all cities, territories, and places of whatever kingdom or nation, and which were to have authority even without publication."

In the latter part of 1607, Sarpi was set upon by three assassins (two of whom were monks) and was very nearly killed. He was in fact stabbed in fifteen places. The attempt was (not unnaturally) charged to the papal representatives in Venice and did not a little to embitter the contest between the city and the pope.[1]

Sir Henry Wotton, writing from Venice to the Earl of Salisbury in September, 1607, says of Sarpi:

"Now to say yet a little more of this man upon whom and his seedes there lyeth so great a work, he seemeth as in countenance as in spirit liker to Philip Melanchthon than to Luther, and peradventure a fitter instrument to overthrow the falsehood by degrees than by a sodayne, which accordeth with a frequent saying of his own: That in these operations *non bisogna far salti*. He is by birth a Venetian, and well-skilled in the humour of his own country. For learning, I think I may justly call him the most deep and general scholar of the world, and above other parts of knowledge he seemeth to have looked very far into the subtelties of the Canonists, which part of skill gave him introduction into the Senate. His power of speech consisteth rather in the soundness of reason than in any other natural habilitie. He is much frequented and much intelligenced of all things that passe, and lastly, his life is the most irreprehensible and exemplar that hath ever been known."—Public Record Office, State Papers, Venice, Misc. 12, f. 805.

In November 1607 the Earl writes to Wotton:

"SIR HENRY WOTTON,—His Majesty hath well approved your care and industry, and he hath commanded me to return you thanks for it, being much pleased in the constant and magnanimous proceedings of that State upon all occasions offered, and particularly in the carriadge of the

[1] Robertson, 118.

matter concerning il Padre Paolo, of whose escape from so foule an assassinate his Majesty is right glad, as he expressed himself to the Venetian Ambassador here at his last audience, to whom he did also make known his particular good declination towards il Padre Paolo, for his learning, modesty and zeale in the defence of so good a cause as is the sovereign power of an estate which hath dependence of none but of God against the usurpations of the Pope of Rome, who being not only contented to have intruded himself into the sole power and authoritie for matters belonging to religion, doth seek also cunningly to wynd himself, by little and little into the civil government and lift himself up above all the Monarchs of the Earth, as the examples in that State and elsewhere to make manifest; for which also his Breve against the oath of obedience here may serve for an instance, whereof I do send you a copy here enclosed, together with another Breve, which for better explication of the former hath since been published at Rome, to prevent all exceptions that might be conceived against it, both which you may impart to the partie you wrote of, for his better satisfaction and encouragement in the course he hath begun, to which His Majesty wishes all good success, for the propagation of God's glory."

In 1892, a Monument to Sarpi was erected in Venice with funds secured by public subscription. This monument commemorates not only the life and work of a high-minded, far-seeing patriot, but the successful issue of the long contest waged by Venice against Rome in behalf of the freedom of the press.

2. **Spain and the Papacy, 1559-1770.**—From the beginning of the policy of censorship down to the date of the issue of the latest Index, the Papacy maintained its claims as the sole authority to make definitions of faith or of morals and to the exclusive control of the supervision of literature. The record shows, however,

that outside of certain divisions of Italy, the papal decrees in the matter of censorship secured scant obedience. Spain, which continued through the centuries to be the most orthodox of States, proved the least willing to recognise, in the matter of censorship, the authority of Rome. Montanus is authority for the statement that the issue in 1559, of the first Roman Index of Paul IV excited the indignation of scholars throughout the world, and that in Spain the Index was not permitted to be published. Valdés, the Inquisitor-General, announced that a catalogue of books had been issued in Rome and further lists in Louvain and in Portugal, and that the Inquisition would itself prepare an Index or catalogue based upon these. This first Spanish Index was, however, framed with little respect for the papal decisions, and this policy was followed in the whole succeeding series. Books prohibited in Rome were permitted in Spain, and certain books were condemned in Spain which had secured the approval of the papal authorities. After the Index of Trent (published in 1564) had given evidence of a more liberal policy on the part of the Roman Church, the Spanish authorities declined to accept the modifications. Valdés, the Inquisitor-General, actually suspended the publication of the decree of Pius IV and remonstrated with Philip II for permitting currency to these lax papal regulations. The decree in question had permitted the reading of Bibles in the vernacular and also works written by heretics which had to do with matters outside of the domain of theology and religion. The Spanish authorities thereafter asserted the right of issuing Indexes under their own name and authority.[1] Condemnation of a book in

[1] Llorente, i, 492. Ticknor, ii, 96.

Rome carried no weight in Spain unless such condemnation was itself confirmed by the Inquisition. When a book had been examined by the Inquisition, it was forbidden to make any appeal in the matter to Rome.

In 1599, Juan de Mariana published in Valladolid a Latin treatise on the *Institution of Royalty* and dedicated it to Philip III. The work was liberal in its general political tone and even intimated that there are cases in which it may be lawful to put a monarch to death; but it sustained with great acuteness the power of the Church and it tended to the establishment of a theocracy. The work was regularly approved by the censors of the press and is said to have been favoured by the policy of the Government which, in the time of Philip II, had sent assassins to cut off Elizabeth of England and the Prince of Orange. In France, where Henry III had been thus put to death a few years before, and where Henry IV suffered a similar fate a few years afterward, the book excited a great sensation. Indeed, the sixth chapter of the first volume directly mentions, and by implication countenances, the murder of the former of these monarchs and was claimed, although without foundation, to have been among the causes that stimulated Ravaillac to the assassination of the latter. . . . Among the papers found after the death of Mariana was one on the errors in the government of the Society of Jesuits. It would appear that, notwithstanding the strong support of the authority of the Church, the learned author had incurred the enmity of the great Order which directed the Inquisition.

The Congregation of the Index was instituted by Pius V in 1571. Gregory XIII, in 1572, issued letters stating that the operations of the Congregation were in no way to interfere with the powers and jurisdiction of the Holy Office in Spain. This utterance was in line with that made by Paul III in 1544, in which the Pope declared, in reference to the Roman Inquisition that had been instituted in 1542, that this was not to come into conflict in any way with the powers and the jurisdiction of the Inquisition in Spain. A similar statement was made in 1587 by Sixtus V, and in 1595, Clement VIII specifically committed to the inquisitor in Spain cognizance in the matter of prohibiting books. There were, however, notwithstanding this series of papal briefs, occasional protests from Rome concerning the independent action of the Spanish Inquisition. Catalani, writing in 1680, pronounces it "ridiculous to suppose that any one could confer on the Spanish Inquisition the power to rescind the judgments of Rome." [1] A letter written by the secretary of the Congregation of the Index to the Bishop of Malaga, takes the ground that the decrees of the Congregation were binding on all Christians, and that the bishops were under obligations, in virtue of their episcopal authority, to punish those who transgressed their decrees. Lea is of the opinion, however, that few Spanish bishops would have ventured to put themselves in opposition to the Inquisition. [1] This conflict of authority produced a series of issues in regard to certain authors, among whom the most noteworthy were Poza, Sa, and Moya. There is not space here to give the details of these issues. It may simply be said that, in the larger number of instances, the Spanish Inquisition succeeded in maintaining, at least for Spain, its own authority.

The contentions for the independent control of the national Church were maintained with no less vigour

[1] Lea, 102.

in Spain than in France although a somewhat different
ground was taken by the Spanish writers. Whatever
success may have been secured in the claim of the
Kings of Spain to control the affairs of the Spanish
Church, this control never took the secular character
which characterised much of the action of the administration of France on ecclesiastical matters. The
throne of Spain was so directly and so completely
under the influence of the Spanish Inquisition that
the direction of the affairs of the Spanish Church,
while often entirely independent of Rome, was, with
hardly an exception, kept within complete ecclesiastical
control. Under Urban VIII, were placed in the
Index certain Spanish writers who had been prominent
in maintaining the authority of the Crown in the control
of the Spanish Church. The writers of this group
came to be known as Regalists. The most noteworthy
among them were Cevallos and Salgado. The condemnation of these authors was, however, by no means
accepted in Spain and was vigorously protested against
by Philip III and by Philip IV. Later, there came into
the Roman Index a long series of treatises by Spanish,
Portuguese, Neapolitan, and Sicilian Regalists who were
maintaining the views originally presented by Cevallos
and Salgado. In 1610, a treatise by Cardinal Baronius,
in which strong ground was taken for the authority of
the pope to control Church appointments and Church
property in Sicily, was, under an edict of Philip III,
prohibited for Sicily and also for Spain, and the printing
or circulation of copies was forbidden under heavy
penalty.

The Spanish kings had in practice usually been able
to maintain the *regalias* or rights which they held to be
inherent in the Crown, but there were still questions

left to be debated by publicists and canon lawyers.
The advocates of the royal prerogative were known as
Regalists and came naturally into antagonism with
the authority of Rome and with the contentions of the
Ultramontanists.   The issue was complicated by the
determination of the Inquisition to maintain at any
cost the supremacy of its jurisdiction over that of all
secular tribunals.[1]   The Inquisition was able to utilise
its powers of censorship to sustain its aggressions upon
the other departments of government.   In the Index
of Clement VIII, published in 1596, the instructions
that had been reprinted in the successive Indexes
ordered the expurgation of all propositions which were
antagonistic to ecclesiastical liberty, immunity, and
jurisdiction.   In 1606, the Jesuit Henriquez, in his
treatise entitled *De Clavibus Romani Pontificis*, defended the right of appeal from the ecclesiastical courts
to the Royal Council (of Spain).   By order of the
papal nuncio, the edition was cancelled so successfully
that only three or four copies survived.   In 1618, in a
treatise by Cevallos, a similar contention was maintained on behalf of the authority of the State.   In
1624, this work was prohibited by a separate decree,
notwithstanding the application made by the King
(Philip III) through his ambassador at Rome, to
prevent the condemnation of a book that maintained
the rights inherent in the sovereign.   The censorship
authorities of Spain declined to ratify the papal
decree.   In a case such as this, the Inquisition and
the Crown had interests in common.   If the Crown
had failed to vindicate its independence, the Inquisition would have been reduced to subjection to
the Roman Congregations.[2]   When the Inquisition

[1] Lea, 125.   [2] *Ibid.* 130.

failed in its duties in regard to the examination of books before publication, the State assumed for itself the direct exercise of the functions of condemnation and suppression. In 1694, a treatise attributed to Barambio was issued under the title of *Casos reservados a su Santidad*, in which the royal prerogative was impugned. The book was never placed upon the Index, but it was formally condemned under royal decree, and the edition was ordered cancelled. In 1760, King Carlos III issued regulations prescribing the rules respecting papal briefs, and prescribing further the system under which the censorship functions of the Inquisition were to be kept under subordination to the State. The decree was recalled in 1763, but was reissued in 1768 with an appeal to the spirit of the *Constitution* of Benedict XIV, issued in 1753, under which *Constitution* the proceedings of the Roman Congregations had been reformed. No edict concerning censorship was thereafter to be published until it had been submitted to and approved by the King. The Inquisition was thus placed under wholesome restrictions, but, although it could not openly resist the royal prerogative, in practice it continued to condemn books in secret without giving a hearing to the authors, and to a great extent rendered the submission to the King a mere formality after the publication of the edict of prohibition. It is Lea's conclusion that, as a result of the long series of contests, the State gradually succeeded in asserting for its own protection the power of sovereignty, and did not hesitate to exercise the function which had at first been relegated exclusively to the Inquisition.

In 1751, an issue arose between Spain and Rome over the Catechism of Mesengui. In this case the

Spanish and Roman censors were in accord. The contest represented an attempt on the part of King Carlos III to free the throne from the domination of the Inquisition. The catechism in question was contained in six volumes entitled *Exposition de la Doctrine Chrétienne*. It was published in 1744 and was placed on the Index in 1757. It proved particularly obnoxious to the Jesuits and, at the instance of their general, Ricci, it was again condemned under a formal Bull. The main ground for the antagonism to the book was its utterances in regard to the claim of the popes to supremacy over sovereigns. Its condemnation was virtually a challenge to all the monarchs of Europe. King Carlos forbade the publication of the Bull in Spain; the inquisitor-general, in defiance of the royal authority, caused the Bull to be distributed throughout the churches and convents of Spain.[1] A royal edict of 1762 ordered that no Bull or papal letter issued from Rome should be published without having been first presented to the King by the nuncio and having been approved. This edict was withdrawn in 1763 under pressure brought to bear upon the King by his confessor, but it was reissued in 1768. With the close of the reign of Carlos, the royal edict fell, however, into abeyance, and the Inquisition again secured for itself full control of the matter of censorship.

3. Controversies concerning the Gallican Church, 1600-1758.—While there was an increasing tendency on the part, not only of the civil authorities in Paris but also on that of the divines of the Sorbonne, to bring into condemnation the works of the more extreme of the Ultramontane writers, this policy had as one result the directing of the attention of the authorities

[1] Lea, 136.

in Rome to the series of treatises by French jurists
and theologians in which was contested the claim of the
pope to authority in civil matters, and in which was
upheld the claim to independent authority on the
part of the Gallic Church and the right of the king to
control the appointments in the Church.   The French
writers gave special attention to the responsibilities
of the French bishops in regard to the control of the
Church property of their dioceses, responsibilities which,
according to the French view, were to be discharged
not to Rome but to the State authorities.   Among the
writers of this Gallican school of thought whose names
came into the Index during the 17th century may be
noted the jurists, Simon Vigor, Louis Servin, and Pithon
Du Puy; the theologians Edmond Richer, Véron, de
Marca, Gerbais, and Boileau.   The treatise of the latter had been written under the instructions of Richelieu.
These censorships of the Holy See secured as a series
no recognition in France.   The condemnation of
the treatise of Rabardeau was, however, confirmed
by an assembly of the French clergy.   In one way
or another, the authority of the Holy See made itself felt in France.   Richer, for instance, even before
the formal prohibition in Rome of his writings, was,
at the instance of the authorities in Rome, dis-
possessed by the French Government from his post as
syndic of the Sorbonne.   De Marca, who in 1642 had
been nominated as bishop, was refused confirmation
by the Holy See on the ground of the condemnation of
his treatise *De concordia sacerdotii et imperii*, and it
was only in 1647, when after long negotiations he had
made retractation of the doctrine presented in this
thesis, that he was given authority to take charge of
his diocese.   In the Spanish Index, are entered a few

only of the titles of these French defenders of the authority of the State which had been condemned in Rome.

In May, 1663, the divines of the Sorbonne, on the ground of the development of extreme Ultramontane views, published the following declara- **Declaration of** tion: I. It is the contention of this fac- **the Sorbonne,** ulty that the pope possesses no authority **1663** whatsoever concerning matters belonging to the State or affecting the control on the part of the most Christian King over matters of State. This faculty has, in fact, always opposed the contentions of those who hold for even an indirect authority on the part of the Church in State matters. II. It is the doctrine of this faculty that the Christian King recognises in matters of State no higher authority than God himself. III. It is the doctrine of this faculty that the subjects of the king can, under no pretext or suggestion, be freed from their obligation of loyalty and obedience to the monarch. IV. The faculty can approve no propositions or theories which are opposed to the complete freedom of the Gallican Church or to the full authority for this kingdom of the canon law of France. The faculty denies that the pope has the authority to issue instructions that are contrary to the authority of these canons. This faculty holds that the authority of the pope does not take precedence of that of a general council of the Church. V. This faculty holds that without the collaboration of the Church as expressed in a general council, the pope does not possess infallibility. This declaration was the view which was later confirmed, first by the Parliament of Paris, and later by the King (Louis XIV). The King at the same time prohibited the printing or distribution of any writings

maintaining contrary doctrine. In 1664 and 1665, the
Sorbonne published a censure of certain Ultramontane
propositions which had been found in books by de
Vernant and Guimenius. These censures were themselves condemned in very sharp terms in a Bull issued
in 1665 by Alexander VII. The Parliament of Paris
promptly prohibits the publication of the Bull and
confirms the censures of the Sorbonne. Diplomatic
negotiations followed but did not succeed in bringing
any satisfactory conclusion for the issue. In 1671,
was published the *Exposition de la Doctrine de l'Église
Catholique*, by Bossuet, a treatise which, while it
by no means supported the contentions of the Holy
See, found in Rome a favourable reception and
secured the individual commendation of Innocent
XI.

In 1673, Louis XIV made claim for a material
extension of the rights of the Crown over the appoint-

The Rights of the Crown in Ecclesiastical Matters ments in the French dioceses and for the
control of the property of the French
Church. This declaration of the King
brought about a sharp conflict with Innocent XI, which continued until 1682. In that
year, a statement of principles arrived at by the
Gallican Church and presented in four articles
brought the earlier issue to a close. As a result of this
first contest, one or two French publications came into
the Index. Among these was a treatise by the Jesuit
Rapin (published anonymously), prohibited in 1680.
As late as 1710, was prohibited, by a brief of Clement
XI, a volume by Andoul on the matter of the Regalia
rights. This papal brief the Parliament of Paris refused to confirm and, in 1712, the Inquisition therefore
condemned the declaration that had been issued by

the Parliament. A similar course of condemnations had taken shape in 1680, in which year a previous letter or enactment of the Parliament had been in like manner condemned by the Inquisition of Rome. In 1682, the assembly of the French clergy presented a conclusion in support of the contention of the Crown in regard to the Regalia rights, which conclusion was expressed in the following declaration:

I. To the pope has been given by God no authority over civil matters of State. In these matters, kings and princes are subject to no ecclesiastical authority. and they cannot either directly or indirectly be brought under the control of the Church, nor can their subjects be freed through any ecclesiastical intervention from the loyalty and obedience due from them to their civil rulers.

II. The pope possesses full control in spiritual affairs, as specified in the conclusions arrived at during the fourth and fifth sessions of the Council of Constance. The Church of France takes the ground that these conclusions arrived at in the council did not apply only to the time of the schism but remained of binding authority.

III. The Apostolic authority is always to be exercised subject to the restrictions of the canon law; and as far as France is concerned, the laws of the monarchy and the old customs and regulations of the French Church are not to be interfered with.

IV. It is the case that in matters of faith, the decision of the pope retains a controlling influence and his decrees are rightly to be issued to all the churches of the world. The papal judgment is, however, not to be held as infallible, final, or not open to modification unless and until it has secured the assent of the Church universal, such assent as is expressed through the conclusions of the general council.

This declaration was, in March, 1682, confirmed under the edict of Louis XIV, duly registered by the Parliament of Paris. The declaration brought out not a little antagonism and criticism in Rome but was not at once condemned. In 1691, however, a brief of Alexander VIII declared that the conclusions of this convention of 1682, and the edicts in which the same were represented, were to be considered as null and void. Through the prohibition of various writings in which the opinions of this declaration were defended, the papal view in regard to the same was also made clearly evident. In 1684, was prohibited, under a special brief of Innocent XI, a treatise from Natalis, in 1685, one from Neimburg, in 1688, one from Dupin. During the same period, the Index Congregation condemned writings to the same purpose by Choiseul, Borjon, Fleury, Févret, Arnauld, and others. The defence of the French position made by Bossuet was also under consideration for condemnation but was never formally prohibited.

The following statement from the historian Dejob, while referring to issues that were under discussion at the Council of Trent, is equally applicable to opinion in France on ecclesiastical organisation in the succeeding century:

"Frenchmen of the sixteenth century found as a rule no attraction in puritanism, in mysticism, or in epicureanism. They approved of the conclusions of the Council of Trent in maintaining against the Protestants the invocation of the Saints, the use (as symbols) of images, the feeling for the ceremonials of religious observance. Feeling assured that all homage was actually and finally addressed to God, they approved the action of the Council in maintaining for the government Church a monarchical hierarchy, always provided that the national clergy should lose none of its privileges, and that the prerogatives of the King should not be assailed. Finally, they realised that Catholicism had the advantage of being in accord with the feeling of the people and with justice and common sense, in defending against the partisans of predestination the belief in the freedom of the will and in justification by works; for, while concerning themselves little with equality under the law, they held stoutly to equality before God. It may, in fact, be said that their theory of relations of man before God could be summed up in the three famous words that were adopted by their descendants in expressing a political ideal: liberty, equality, fraternity. . . .

"They believed further that while it was not the duty of believers to abandon the joys of this world, their salvation in the world to come could be assured only through self-denial and penitence. In accepting the aims and the ideals of the Counter-reformation, France was, therefore, called upon for no sacrifice of convictions or of practice."[1]

In 1684, 1685, and 1687, Innocent XI prohibited in special briefs the Church history of Alexander; in 1685, an historical treatise by Neimburg; **The Gallican** in 1687, the same author's biography of **Church** Gregory I, and in 1689 a group of other **Historians** of his writings. Between 1662 and 1693, a series of treatises by de Launoy on Church history and Church law were prohibited. In 1688, a brief of Innocent XI prohibits the treatise on Church law of Dupin, and in 1693, the Inquisition prohibits the *Bibliothèque* of the same author. Later, the remainder of his works came into the Index. In 1707, the writings of Tillemont were denounced, but were saved from prohibition

[1] Dejob, 342

through a protest on the part of certain Roman scholars. The Church history of Fleury escaped the Index and of his works on Church law, only the *Catéchisme Historique* was prohibited and with a *d.c.* The learned Mabillon came under consideration with the Index authorities more than once. In 1703, a treatise of Mabillon, which had to do with the misuse and misinterpretation of certain relics taken from the Roman catacombs, was sharply criticised but escaped formal prohibition with the instruction that Mabillon must produce an improved edition. His *Traité des Études Monastiques* was prohibited in the Italian edition. The Church history of the French Jesuit Avrigny, covering the period of 1600–1718, was prohibited on the ground of its Gallican views. Through a special brief was condemned, in 1740, the translation by Le Courayer of Sarpi's *History of the Council of Trent*. Benedict XIV decided to recall the prohibition of the Church history of Alexander, but at the same time placed on the Index a series of treatises of Roncaglia the conclusions in which were practically identical with those of Alexander.

Among the works condemned by the State may be cited:

Bellarmin, *Tractatus de potestate summi Pontificis in temporalibus*, Rome, 1610, condemned under a decree of the Parliament of Paris in November, 1610, on the following ground: *Contenant une fausse et détestable proposition, tendante à l' éversion des puissances souveraines ordonnées et établies de Dieu, soulévement des sujets contre leurs princes, soustraction de leur obéissance, induction d'attenter à leurs personnes et états, troubler le repos et la tranquillité publique.*

Casaubon, Isaac, *De libertate ecclesiastica.* This book was condemned by Henry IV, who undertook to have collected and destroyed all the copies that had been brought into print.

Charron, Pierre, *Traité sur la sagesse*, Bordeaux, 1661. The first edition was condemned by the Sorbonne until it should have been expurgated. The later revised editions secured approval.

In 1729, Benedict XIII wrote a monograph which was to be read before the Church universal on the commemoration of the feast of Gregory VII, and in this paper he gave particular emphasis to the statement that Gregory had deposed the Emperor Henry IV. This papal utterance brought out protests on the part of a number of the parliaments and bishops of France. In four briefs, Benedict condemned and ordered cancelled pastoral letters of three bishops which contained animadversions on his monograph, and he included at the same time in a general condemnation all resolutions, decrees, or protests which had emanated from civil authorities concerning the same matter. The *Officium* containing the objectionable statement which Benedict had ordered to be read on the feast-day, was itself prohibited throughout the Austrian dominions.

Works Connected with the Gallican Church

Under Benedict XIV, were prohibited a series of writings which undertook to defend certain measures attempted in 1749 by the Government of France for the taxation of the clergy. The *Decr. Generalia*, ii. 9. contain a general prohibition of all works which bring into question the immunity (from taxation) of the property of the Church. Shortly after the death of Benedict XIV, a group of six monographs came into the Index which had to do with the question whether a converted Jew, by name Barach Levi, was to be permitted to take to himself another wife during the lifetime of the original wife, who had decided to remain in the Jewish faith. The same question had arisen a little earlier in France and had been decided in the affirmative by Benedict XIV. The authority for the contention that the convert was free so to act rests upon 1 Corinthians vii. 15.

4. Ecclesiastical-Political Contests, 1700–1750.—Clement XI (1700–1721) plays an important part in the history of the Index. He is the author of the Bull *Unigenitus*, of the Bull *Vineam Domini Sabaoth*, and of the Bull concerning Chinese usages, and he was responsible for the schism of Utrecht. He issued a longer series of briefs than are to be credited to any other pope for the prohibition of particular works, and to these are to be added a great number of decrees published under his orders by the Inquisition and by the Congregation of the Index, which carried general prohibitions of whole classes of publications. Clement found himself involved, during the twenty years of his rule, in serious contests and complications with the several States of Europe, contests which had as one result the swelling of the Index lists with a great number of controversial writings. Under the Index policy of this period, were condemned not only works which took ground antagonistic to the claims of the pope, or in defence of the claims of civil authority, but a great series of civil enactments, State decrees, and court decisions, with the purport of which the Holy See found reason for dissatisfaction. Public documents and official records of this general character could of course be formally condemned, and could in form be prohibited; but it was not practicable, under any authority possessed by the pope, to do anything to prevent such enactments, court decisions, etc., from becoming known and from remaining in force in the territories in which they applied. The so-called prohibition on the part of the pope may be considered as simply the expression of a pious opinion, and differs therefore in its purpose and in its application from the prohibitions previously attempted by means of the Index. Among the decisions of magistrates which came into the Index during this period, were a long series taken from the Neapolitan courts, decisions which indicated strained relations between the Government of Sicily and the Holy See.

The most important book of the time having to do with these Sicilian complications was the *Political History of the Kingdom of Naples*, by Pietro Giannone. This was published just after the death of Clement and was promptly prohibited under the general policy that had been in force. By the time of Benedict XIV, the complications between the Holy See and the Governments of the Catholic States had been pretty well straightened out and the Index of Benedict contains therefore the titles of but very few political works. Through a special decree of the Congregation of January, 1729, was prohibited a history written by Count Franc. Maria Ottieri, and published in Rome in 1728, of the *War of the Spanish Succession*, 1696–1725. The book was condemned on the ground that it contained expressions injurious, if not libellous, concerning certain princes and political leaders. There seems in this case to have been no objection on theological or ecclesiastical grounds. The decree states that the condemnation had received the personal approval of Benedict XIII. Under the instructions of Benedict XIV, however, the title was taken out of the Index.

In 1746, Benedict XIV ordered the prohibition of
a treatise by Garrido, general of the Spanish Congregation of the Benedictines, which had been printed
in Madrid in 1745 under the title: *Concordia prelatorum:
Tractatus duplex de unione ecclesiarum et beneficiorum,*
etc. This work was also condemned by the Spanish
Inquisition, which was as heretofore under the control
of the Dominicans.

It is the contention of those upholding the reasonableness of the claims of the Church that there need be no
conflict of authority between the powers spiritual and
the powers temporal, that the allegiance and obedience
should be entire towards the sovereign in matters
temporal and entire towards the pope in matters
spiritual. In the application of this apparently
simple principle, it was inevitable that there should
arise differences of interpretation. From the ecclesiastical point of view, it was claimed that all ecclesiastical
property was to be classed with the matters spiritual;
to the same class belonged of necessity ecclesiastical
persons, thus securing for such persons immunities,
both personal and real; while from these two claims
arises the jurisdiction of the Church in matters both
civil and criminal. In marriage, for instance, the
sacrament is the essential thing, from which arises the
inference that marriage is to be regulated by ecclesiastical law. Finally, every human act may be the subject
of sin, and on this ground the Church has received
divine precepts and has instituted ecclesiastical laws
for the regulation of all actions.

It is evident that, if these assumptions be accepted,
there are very few human activities the regulation of
which belongs outside of the authority of the Church.
This is in substance the view presented by an Austrian

Romanist previously quoted, who was writing on behalf of the liberties of the Austrian Church.[1]

The Rev. Joseph Berington, writing in 1760, uses,
in describing the ecclesiastical polity, the following
language:

"The mode of government which Rome maintains in
this kingdom (England) and from which in no kingdom
it ever departed but when driven by hard necessity, draws
very near to that feudal system of polity, to which the
nations of Europe were once subject. It contained one
sovereign as suzerain monarch in whose hands was lodged
the *supremum dominium*, and this he apportioned out
to a descending series of vassals who, all holding of him
in capite, returned him service for the benefits they received
in honours, jurisdiction on lands; and to this service they
were bound by gratitude, which was strengthened by an
oath of fealty. The application of the system to the sovereign power of the pontiff and to a chain of descending
vassalage in archbishops, bishops, and the inferior orders
in the ministry, is direct and inevitable."[2]

Catalani, writing in 1738, contends that the oath of
allegiance to the pope expresses not only a profession
of canonical obedience, but an oath of fealty not
unlike that which vassals took to their direct lords.[3]
He cites as an example, the first oath of the kind, that
taken by the Patriarch of Aquileia to Gregory VII,
in 1079.

Mendham concludes, after reference to other authorities, that allegiance and obedience are divided in the
most unfavourable sense and degree (particularly in

[1] Dal Pozzo, *Catholicism in Austria*, 182.
[2] *The Decline and Fall of the Roman Catholic Religion in England*,
London, 1760, 275.
[3] *Commentary on the Roman Pontificate*, i, 178.

the case of heretical rulers) when the soul and conscience are to be given to a foreign (so-called) spiritual sovereign, while the actual temporal ruler can claim only what remains of his subject.[1]

A long series of works came into print during the last half of the 18th century having to do with the issues that had arisen between the Papacy, under Clement XIII and Pius VI and the Governments of Venice and of Naples. With a few exceptions, doubtless accidental, these works were duly prohibited, either by the Inquisition or the Congregation. The similar contests between Clement XIII and the Duke of Parma did not bring into the Index any fresh titles. A series of Spanish works written against the claims and contentions of the Holy See, printed during the same period, also escaped the attention of the editors of the Roman Indexes. The Indexes of this period contain the titles of a number of treatises on Church and State issued by the French author, Richet, and also of a series of monographs on the reform of the religious orders and on the policy to be pursued by the State with its non-Catholic citizens. The list also includes a monograph on the authority of the pope, published in Amsterdam in connection with the controversy concerning the Church at Utrecht.

In 1764, were prohibited under a separate decree of the Congregation, a treatise by Bishop Frevorius, published in 1763, together with a series of less important works, all of which were concerned with the issues that had arisen between the Holy See and certain of the German bishoprics. In 1784, the Congregation prohibits the Introduction to Ecclesiastical Law written by Eybel; and in the following year was condemned,

[1] Mendham, 217.

by a brief of Pius VI, the treatise by the same author on Confession. In 1786, the monograph by Eybel, issued under the title of *Was ist der Papst?*, was also prohibited in a separate brief. The editors of the Index evidently found it impracticable, however, to make place for the long series of similar publications by the controversial writers of Germany which came into print during the same period. The two or three titles selected cover some of the least important of the series. The selection was apparently made without any adequate knowledge of the material to be considered.

5. England and the Papacy.—On the 25th of February, 1570, Sixtus V issues his Bull against Queen Elizabeth, a copy of which Bull was, on May 15th, nailed on the door of the palace of the Bishop of London. The Pope describes Elizabeth as "a bastard and usurper," the "persecutor of God's saints." He declares that it would be "an act of virtue to be repaid with plenary indulgence and forgiveness of all sins, to lay violent hands upon Elizabeth and to deliver her into the hands of her enemies." He declares Philip of Spain to be the rightful King of England and the Defender of the Faith. In the same year, Cardinal Allen, an Englishman, printed in Antwerp a pamphlet entitled *An Admonition to the Nobility and People of England and Ireland*, in which, says Motley, Queen Elizabeth is "accused of every crime and vice that can pollute humanity." These charges are set forth with "foul details unfit for the public eye in these more decent days."

An important question in the relations between the Papacy and England that called for attention under Paul V, was the issue that arose with James I of

England after the discovery of the Gunpowder Plot. An order had been issued by King James in July. 1606, **The English Oath of Allegiance 1606-1853** for a fresh oath of allegiance to be taken by English Catholics. The Pope forbade the Catholics to take this oath because it included the statement that the claim of the Pope to have the right to depose kings and princes and to absolve their subjects from allegiance was godless, infamous, and heretical. The several statements brought into print on behalf of King James in defence of the wording of the oath, were themselves condemned by the Inquisition. The treatises of the English Catholics, William and John Barclay and Thomas Preston ("Roger Widdrington"), in reply to the defence by Bellarmin of the papal contentions, were promptly placed upon the Index in connection with a long series of later monographs on the same subject. The oath of allegiance was, under Urban VIII in 1626. and later under Innocent X and Alexander VII, again declared to be invalid. Towards the end of the 18th century, an oath of allegiance substantially identical was, however, approved by six theological faculties in England and by the Apostolic vicar in England and this decision was accepted without protest by Rome. In the oath of allegiance (which is not to be confused with the oath of supremacy, the latter not being required from his Catholic subjects) James required the Catholics to acknowledge that he was the rightful King of England, that the pope had no authority to dispossess him or to incite a foreign prince to war against him or to pardon his subjects for disobedience to British law. They were further called upon to swear that, irrespective of any papal decrees of deposition or any threat of excommunication, they would remain loyal to the King, and further they were to declare as godless and as damnable the theory that the pope could release any subject from obedience to his rightful sovereign. Finally, they were called upon to declare the belief that neither the pope nor any other authority could release them from this oath. In 1608, James wrote a defence of the oath, which was printed in a Latin version prepared by Henry Savile. In 1609, this treatise was prohibited by Paul V under the penalty of *excommunicatio latae*, etc. A further prohibition was issued by the Inquisition some months later. A treatise by William Barclay, a Scotch Catholic, printed in 1609 (after the death of the author), presents the arguments against the authority, either direct or indirect, of the pope in secular matters. This was duly condemned in Rome in 1610 and in Paris in 1612. It formed the text for the famous treatise by Bellarmin, *Tractatus de potestate summi Pont. in rebus temporalibus.* The treatise written by the Benedictine, Thomas Preston, under the nom-de-plume of Roger Widdrington, *Apologia Card. Bellarmini pro jure principium adv. suas ipsius rationes pro auctoritate papali*, etc., printed in London in 1611, was prohibited in Rome in 1613 in a general decree. In 1614, the Index of the Congregation issued a special decree prohibiting this work together with a second treatise of the same author. Later, were placed on the Index a further group of essays by Widdrington. Sarpi published in April, 1614, an analysis of the two earlier books of Widdrington, giving high praise to the scholarly authority of the author's conclusions. These had an immediate bearing upon the contention of the Venetian Republic to control, without interference from the pope, its own civil affairs. In 1680, sixty divines of the Sorbonne rendered a judgment to the effect that the Catholics in England could with a safe conscience swear loyalty to King James and accept the oath of allegiance. A monograph making record of this judgment, printed in London, in 1681, under the title of *English Loyalty Vindicated by the Divines*, or a *Declaration of Three-score Persons of the Sorbonne for the Oath of Allegiance*, was, in 1682, prohibited by the Inquisition. A monograph that secured a wide circulation, being printed in fact thirty-five times in fifteen years, under the title of *An Abuse Misrepresented and Represented*, escaped formal condemnation, although it took strong ground in behalf of the English contention. In 1760, the theological faculties of Paris, Louvain, Douay, Valladolid, Salamanca, and Alcala united in a declaration to the effect that the pope possessed in England no authority over civil affairs and had no power to release the subjects of the English king from the oath of allegiance, and that no Catholic was under obligation to accept instructions from the authorities of the Church that would interfere with this allegiance. In 1853, Professors Russell, Patrick Murray, and others of the Catholic College of Maynooth declared, in connection with a Parliamentary investigation, that, according to their own opinion and to the purport of their teachings to their students, the pope possessed neither direct nor indirect authority in the United Kingdom in secular matters. They stated further that the contrary doctrine was now considered as practically obsolete.

6. **The Gallicans and Liberal Catholics, 1845-1870.** —The contest of the Congregation of the Index against theological Gallicanism began in 1851 under Pius IX. Certain books of instruction utilised in the seminaries

of France were, for the purpose of maintaining them in use against the criticisms of the Ultramontane press, revised with the elimination of material that could be classed as Gallican. Among the works belonging to this period which were condemned on the ground of their Gallican or Liberal Catholic views may be noted the following:

Dupin, André M. J. J., *Manuel du Droit Publique-ecclésiastique Français*, printed in 1844, prohibited 1845. This manual presents in eighty-three articles the "Liberties" of the Gallican Church, the declaration of the clergy made in 1682 on the limits of ecclesiastical power, and the text of the Concordat.

Bailly, Louis, Canon of Dijon, *Theologia Dogmatica et Moralis, ad usum Seminariorum*, completed in eight volumes in 1789, reprinted with the revision by Receveur in 1842, prohibited in 1852 with a *d.c.*

Lequeux, J. F. M., *Manuale Compendium Juris Canonici ad usum Seminariorum*, printed in 1839, prohibited in 1851. The work had been denounced by five of the French bishops. A decree of the Congregation issued in 1852 states that the author had "submitted himself."

Guettée, l'Abbé, *L'Histoire de l'Église de France*, volumes i to vii, printed in Paris, 1847, condemned in 1852. The work had secured the specific approval of no less than forty-two of the French bishops.

Thions, C., *Adresse au Pape Pie IX sur la Nécessité d'une Réforme Religieuse*, printed in 1848, prohibited in 1852.

Montalembert, *Les Intérêts Catholiques au XIXme Siècle*, published in 1852, received very sharp criticisms from the Ultramontane journals and from a number of the bishops, but escaped the Index. In fact no work of this author was formally condemned in Rome.

A number of the dioceses of France had, on the authority of a Bull of Pius V, issued in 1568, retained their individual mass books and breviaries. In 1848, Pius IX issues a Bull recalling the permission given three centuries earlier by his predecessor and directing the use in all the dioceses of the Roman liturgy. One or two of the long series of writings which the Bull brought out were placed upon the Index. From 1852 on, there came into print a number of controversial writings concerning the use in the schools of the heathen classics. No one of these was placed upon the Index, but Pius IX, in an encyclical issued in March, 1853, emphasises the importance of a very careful selection of the heathen texts to be so utilised and the necessity, in the case of certain authors, of providing expurgated texts.

Bellarmin, in his treatise *De Summo Pontifice*, condemned pure monarchy in the name of a limited monarchy. By the former he appears to have understood a government (hardly to be conceived as practicable) in which the king would have ruled entirely by himself, while under the second he was describing a restricting body made up of delegates who, having been drawn from the ranks of the people, were invested by the prince with an absolute authority and were made responsible to him alone. He denied for the pope the right to exercise a direct control over the states of the world, but claimed for the Papacy the privilege of interfering at will.

CHAPTER VII

EXAMPLES OF CONDEMNED LITERATURE

1. Writings of the 17th Century concerning the Papacy and the Inquisition.   2. Writings concerning the Churches of the East.   3. Patristic Writings and Pagan Classics.   4. Jewish Literature.   5. Historical Writings of the 17th Century.   6. Protestant Jurists of the 17th Century.   7. Writings of Italian Protestants.   8. Writings in Philosophy, Natural Science, and Medicine.   9. Books on Magic and Astrology.   10. Cyclopaedias, Text-Books, Facetiae, etc.   11. Secret Societies.   12. Manuals for Exorcising.   13. Fraudulent Indulgences.   14. Works on the Saints.   15. Forms of Prayer.   16. Mariology.   17. Revelations by Nuns.   18. The Chinese and Malabar Usages.   19. Fraudulent Literature.   20. Quietism.   21. Fénelon.   22. The Doctrine of Probability.   23 Usury.   24. Philosophy and Literature, 1750–1800.   25. Philosophy and Science, 1800–1880.   26. The Synod of Pistoja, 1786.   27. The Festival of the Heart of Jesus, 1697–1765.   28. French, German, and English Catholic Theologians, 1758–1800.   29. The French Revolution, 1790–1806.   30. The French Concordat of 1801, 1801–1822.   31. Protestant Theologians, 1750–1884.   32. The Eastern Church, 1810–1873.   33. The Theologians of Pavia, 1774–1790.   34. French, English, and Dutch Literature, 1817–1880.   35. German Catholic Writings, 1814–1870.   36. La Mennais, 1830–1846.   37. The Roman Revolution of 1848, 1848–1852.   38. Traditionalism and Ontology, 1833–1880.   39. *Attritio* and the *Peccatum Philosophicum*, 1667–1690.   40. Communism and Socialism 1825–1860.   41. Magnetism and Spiritualism, 1840–1874.   42. French Authors, 1835–1884.   43. Italian Authors, 1840–1876.   44. American Writings, 1822–1876.   45. Periodicals, 1832–1900.   46. The Roman Question, 1859–1870.   47. The Council of the Vatican, 1867–1876.   48. Example of a License.

1. Writings concerning the Papacy and the Inquisition, 1600–1757.—The Index contains but few of the polemic writings of this period against the Papacy.   A few however of the historical works on the Papacy, both by Protestants and Catholics, were prohibited. The lists include a treatise of the Jesuit Riccioli on the infallibility of the pope, but this is entered with a *d.c.* The lists include also a group of writings on the Inquisition, on the Index itself, on the finance system of the papal chancellery, etc. Among these are some monographs by Gregorio Leti (1630–1701), whose entire works secured condemnation in 1686. Reusch points out that the history of the Papacy by Archibald Bower, which was first published in 1748 in seven volumes, and of which a number of editions appeared later, was overlooked by the Index compilers. Bower was born in Scotland, but, becoming a Jesuit, had held a professor's chair in Italy in Fermo and in Macerata. In 1726, he left Italy and became a member of the Church of England. His treatise was of a character that might naturally have met criticism on the part of the Congregation. The *History of the Inquisition* by Limborch, printed in Brussels, in 1693, was promptly prohibited in 1694. In the same list, are included the titles of a number of less important treatises on the Inquisition.

2. **Writings concerning the Churches of the East.**—The Index lists of the 17th and 18th centuries contain but few of the works of the Greek theologians. Among the authors of this group are to be noted the names Lukaris, Nektarius, Philippus Cyprius, Catum Syrittus, and Sylvester Syropoli. Robert Creighton, professor in Cambridge, later Bishop of Bath, had printed in The Hague in 1660 the *Vera Historia* of Syropoli, a record of the relations between the Greek and the Latin Church, which includes an account of the Council of Florence. This was prohibited in 1682.

3. Patristic Writings and Pagan Classics.—During the 17th century, a number of editions of the writings of the Fathers are placed on the Index on the ground of the notes and commentaries of the heretical editors. It was the case in the 17th as in the 16th century that the editors who had interested themselves in producing the editions of these works of the Fathers were in large part men whose orthodoxy had come into question. There were, in fact, but very few editions of the Fathers of the Church the editorial work in which had been in the hands of orthodox or conservative believers. Among the editions so prohibited, were the works of Cyprian with the notes of the Frenchman Maran, and the Letters of Chrysostom in the edition printed in Basel. Prohibited also was a work by Erigena in a German edition and the history of the Council of Constance by von Hardt. In the list of classics are to be found Italian editions of the works of Caesar, Ovid, Anacreon, and Lucretius.

4. Jewish Literature.—In 1703, prohibitions were issued covering a series of rabbinical writings, selected, as Reusch points out, with hardly any apparent policy or plan from a great mass of literature of the same kind. The compilers had utilised in making up their titles the *bibliotheca rabbinica* of Bartolocci and Imbonati, which had been published between the years 1675–1694. In 1755–1766, was printed a supplementary Index with additional titles of the same character. A further list, printed separately, covered certain rabbinical writings which had been printed in Latin and in Spanish versions. In 1776, was prohibited a treatise by the Italian monk Vincenti. which was strongly anti-Semitic, and a little later a response to this treatise also secured condemnation.

5. Historical Writings of the 17th Century.—The list of historical writings prohibited during the 17th century is very considerable but, as has been indicated for the lists of other groups of literature, is by no means comprehensive nor does it give evidence of any consistent scholarly selection. The prohibitions are by no means confined to works by Protestants. A number of Catholic historians succeeded in getting into their texts phrases or statements that aroused opposition. In the Index of Alexander VII, are given in the class of history only works in Latin; the later Indexes include a series of French and Italian titles and two English works, but nothing from the German writers. Reusch points out that during the 17th and 18th centuries there were produced in Italy no works deserving of preservation having to do with general history. A translation of the *History of the World* by Dupin and an Italian version of a condensed history published in London were both prohibited. The larger number of the titles comprise monographs on the various issues that arose in Italy and throughout Europe between the ecclesiastical and the civil authorities. Among the historical names to be noted is that of de Thou, whose History of his Own Times was prohibited in 1609. In 1610, in connection with certain applications made to the authorities, the prohibition was modified to an instruction for an expurgation of the work, but no expurgated edition ever came into print. The work continued in circulation not only in France and other European States but in Venice. The *Histoire du Gouvernement de Venise*, by Houssaye, was prohibited in 1667. The miscellaneous works of Francis Osborne, published in 1673, secured the honour of a prohibition in the list of Benedict in 1757. Johnson is quoted as saying of Osborne: "A conceited fellow; were a man to write so now, the boys would throw stones at him." The Italian historian, Pietro della Valle, on returning in 1626 from a series of journeys, had a favourable reception from Urban VIII, and his account of Persia, printed in Venice in 1628. was issued with a license and with a special privilege. It was, however, in 1629, prohibited with the specification *cum auctor at suum tantum agnoscat librum qui Romae impressus est.* As a fact, however, no edition of this work was ever printed in Rome.

6. **Protestant Jurists.**—During the first decade of the 17th century, the Index includes the names of a group of Protestant jurists, chiefly Germans and Hollanders. The titles specified cover, in the main, books which had no material importance and which never even reached the honour of a second printing. The subjects include not only books having to do with canon law or ecclesiastical relations but works of purely political importance. In the Spanish lists, the compilers have taken the pains to add after the number of the book the term *d.c.*, and for a few works they themselves presented the expurgations required. In editions of the pandects and in the treatises having to do with the pandects, the prohibitions cover a number of books on such subjects as *de summa trinitate de fide Catholica* and *de haereticis et paganis.* The Spanish Indexes include also certain treatises on usury (the authorities taking the Church ground that interest was indefensible) and two essays having to do with the requirement of the permission of parents for marrying. A number of books which in the Roman Index are prohibited altogether, are presented by the Spanish compilers with the term *d.c.* The noteworthy treatise of Puffendorf,

De statu Germaniæ Imperii, first published in 1667, did not come to the attention of the Index compilers as a pernicious work until 1754. Other works by the same author which secured condemnation are the French edition of his introduction to the history of the great States, published in 1687 and prohibited in 1693; the *De jure naturae et gentium*, published in 1672 and prohibited in 1714; the *Introductio ad historiam Europaeam*, published in 1704, prohibited in 1737; the *De officio hominis et civis*, published in 1743, prohibited in 1752.

7. **Italian Protestant Writings.**—During the 17th and 18th centuries, Protestant writings printed in Italian were published chiefly in Switzerland. The only author of this group whose work came into any general circulation was Pincenino, a preacher in Soglio. Four of his controversial treatises were prohibited by the Inquisition between the years 1704-1714, and the publication of these brought out a number of replies from Catholic theologians. The name of Vicenzo Paravicino came into the Index in connection with a number of translations of French Protestant writings, and also with editions of the Scriptures printed in the vernacular. Edwin Sandys, a son of the Archbishop of York (who is himself listed in Class I), printed, without his name, in 1605, and with his name in 1629, a treatise entitled *A View of the State of Religion in the Western Part of the World, wherein the Roman Religion and the pregnant Policies of the Church of Rome to support the same are notably displayed, with other memorable Discoveries and Commemorations.* The French and German translations of the book, printed in Geneva in 1625 and 1626, were both condemned.

In 1621, was prohibited a history, printed in 1620, by Luglio (or Paravicino) of the persecution and massacre by the Papists of the Protestants of Valtellina. This has to do with one division of the long series of persecutions of the Waldenses.

8. Philosophical Writings, Natural Science, and Medicine, 1660-1750.—In 1663, the Congregation of the Index prohibits with a *d.c.* the chief writings of Descartes (1596-1650); and in 1722 prohibits with no restriction his *Meditationes*. This second prohibition was issued some eighty years after the publication of the work. Reusch [1] explains that the prohibition of 1663 was intended to cover only specific divisions or propositions contained in these writings, but no specification was made by the Congregation as to the passages charged with heresy nor was any expurgated edition ever brought into print. The commentators on Descartes point out that in any case it would not have been practicable, without practically destroying the entire statement of his system, to modify or correct the statements that had evoked criticism. The chief objection raised by the Roman critics was the view taken by Descartes of the philosophy of Aristotle. It seems probable that in the case of this particular work the use of the term *d.c.* did not indicate any expectation that the work would be issued in an expurgated edition, but was intended simply to express the condemnation in somewhat milder form. The works of Nicholas Malebranche (1638-1715) were, with hardly an exception (although not under the term *Opera omnia*), prohibited; but the philosophical writings of Gassendi, Mersenne, and Maignan, writings expressing the same general school of thought, escaped the Index. In 1772, the writings of the Neapolitan Grimaldi, in reply to the treatise issued in 1694 by the Jesuit de Benedictis,

[1] II, 598.

opposing the views of Descartes, were prohibited with a special condemnation. In 1679, nine years after its publication, was prohibited the treatise by Spinoza entitled *Tractatus theologico-politicus.* This remains on the later Indexes, but as an anonymous work. In the same year were prohibited the *Opera postuma* of Spinoza which had been printed in Amsterdam, in 1667. The works of Protestant philosophical writers are but sparsely represented in the Index and were probably but little known to the examiners of the Roman Congregation. The names of Leibnitz and Christian Wolff, for instance, do not appear in the Index lists. The Spanish authorities declined to place in their Indexes the works of Descartes, of Malebranche, or of Spinoza.

Under the heading of Philosophy, the Indexes of the 17th century contain the names of Montaigne, Charron, Ramus, Bacon, Hobbes, Fludd, and Herbert of Cherbury. In 1709, Hobbes secured the distinction of condemnation in the Roman list for his complete works, of which in the earlier lists only single books had been prohibited. His writings escaped the attention, however, of the Spanish compilers. Julius Caesar Vanini, who was in 1619 burned in Toulouse as a propagator of atheism, and whose name stands in the Spanish Index in Class I, with the specification *Impiissimus atheus,* finds place in the Spanish Index of 1623 only in connection with one work and that with the restriction *d.c.* In the Index of Benedict XIV, the title was repeated but the *d.c.* was cancelled.

In the Index of Alexander VII, the natural scientists are, with the noteworthy exception of Galileo, represented only by a few alchemists and a group of physicians. Among the names here to be noted is that of Lionardo di Capua, on the ground of certain sharp criticisms by him of the accepted scholastic philosophy.

The name of the mystic Jacob Boehme is not included in any Roman Index but finds place in Class I of the Spanish lists.

The prohibition in 1676 of the essays of Montaigne is connected with the specification "in whatever language they may be printed." The essays of Bacon that received attention from the Roman compilers are the *De dignitate et augmentis scientiarum* and the *De sapientia veterum*. Sotomayor has entered Franc. Baconus and Franc. Verulam in his first class as two distinct authors. The Spanish Index of 1707 condemns of Bacon *Opera omnia*. The full name, Baron Verulam, appears first correctly in the Spanish Index of 1790. Of the many writings of Robert Fludd (†1637) only one, *Utriusque Cosmi*, etc., appears in the Index. The first work of Thomas Hobbes to receive attention was the *Leviathan*, prohibited in 1703, about forty years after its publication. In 1709, however, thirty years after the author's death, the prohibition was made to include the *Opera omnia*.

9. Books on Magic and Astrology.—The lists of the 17th century include the titles of a number of works on magic and astrology, books which apart from this record would long since have been entirely forgotten. The *Steganographie* of the Abbé Trithenius was included among the books so prohibited, evidently under the impression that it had to do with magic. In April, 1631, Pope Urban VIII issued a Bull against the astrologists, that is to say against those who undertook to produce calculations concerning the future of Christendom or of the Roman Curia or in regard to the life of the pope. In 1732, the Inquisition issued a prohibition of the reading of any books having to do with fortune telling, the interpretation of dreams, or the art of numbers. The books referred to under the latter designation were those that undertook to prophesy the successful numbers for lotteries.

10. **Poems, Facetiae, Text-books, Periodicals, and Cyclopaedias.**—A number of works of no intrinsic importance, belonging under the class of *facetiae* and text-books, were condemned during the 17th century on the ground of certain references, characterised as disrespectful, concerning Church matters. Certain text-books also found their way into the list because they were reproducing the texts of classic authors who were classed by the ecclesiastics as obscene or immoral. The action of the authorities in regard to literature of this kind was curiously varied and it does not seem to be possible to find for it any consistent policy or principle. The German satirical literature of this period appears to have escaped attention on the part of the examiners. The only German book of this character prohibited during the latter part of the 17th century was the *Visiones de don Quevedo, die Wunderliche Satyrische und Warhafftige Geschichte Philanders v. Sittewald,* by Moscherosch, printed in 1645 and prohibited in 1662. The next German work of this special character to find place on the Index was Heine's *Reisebilder,* published a century and a half later. The prohibition of cyclopaedias on the ground of objection to certain entries or references, proved of special inconvenience to Catholic students and instructors. The greater publishing activity of the Protestant communities and the keener scholarship of heretical editors had caused the production of works of reference of this kind

to be much more considerable and important in the territories outside of those controlled by the Church. It not infrequently happened that the condemnation of a work of this class left the scholars of the Church without the use of any equivalent work. As late even as Benedict XIV. the Congregation found occasion to add to the list of prohibited cyclopaedias.

The English titles of the first half of the 18th century include the *Tale of a Tub* by Swift. *Pamela* by Richardson, and *Robinson Crusoe* by Defoe. The latter came to the attention of the indexers through a French edition printed in 1750 and prohibited in 1756. The French names of the same period include the *Contes et Nouvelles* of La Fontaine; the *Vie de Jacqueline, Comtesse de Hainaut*, of Mlle. de La Roche-Guilhem, printed in 1702 and prohibited in 1727; *Lettres Historiques et Galantes de deux Dames de Condition*, by Mme. Dunoyer, printed in 1704 in seven volumes, prohibited in 1725 and again by Benedict in 1758; *Les Emportements Amoureux de la Religieuse Étrangère*, printed anonymously in 1707, prohibited in Rome 1727, and in Spain in 1790. Molière escapes condemnation in Rome as well as in Spain. The *Don Quixote*, of Cervantes was marked by Sotomayor for correction but only in the case of a single sentence. The Lisbon Index of 1624 finds occasion for the cancellation in the same work of a number of paragraphs.

11. Secret Societies. — Clement XII and Benedict XIV condemned, in Bulls issued in April, 1738, and March, 1751, the associations of *Libri Muratori*, or freemasons. The members of these societies were rendered liable to the excommunication *latae sententiae*, and bishops and inquisitors were instructed to take measures against them as heretics. In September,

1821, Pius VII issued a similar Bull against the *Carbonari*. A Bull issued in March, 1825, by Leo XII repeats the text of the three Bulls above specified and confirms their instructions. In the Bull of Pius VII, is prohibited the possession or the reading of all catechisms of the *Carbonari*, of the minutes of their meetings, of their statutes and statements of purposes, and of all works written in their defence. whether these be in print or in manuscript. Through some oversight, this important general prohibition did not find its way into the Index. It is also the case that but very few titles of works on freemasonry are included in the Index lists after Clement XII. The Church seems to have relied, for the suppression of this literature, on its general prohibitions. In May, 1829, Pius VIII issued an encyclical condemning the teachings of the freemasons and of kindred secret societies. Pius IX takes similar ground in an encyclical of November, 1846, and in the allocution of September. 1865. In April, 1884, Leo XIII devotes an encyclical to the injurious teachings of the sect "*masonum.*" With this encyclical, is connected an instruction of the Inquisition under which the faithful are forbidden to have any dealings with such societies. In January, 1870, the Inquisition declared, in response (apparently) to some formal application for instructions, that the Irish and American Fenians had placed themselves under the general condemnation.[1]

In 1739, after the publication of the Bull of Clement XII, the Inquisition prohibited the *Relation apologétique et historique de la société des Francs-Maçons,* by J. G. D., F. D., Dublin, 1738. In the same year, Crudeli was imprisoned by the Inquisition on the

[1] *Acta SS.*, i, 290, v, 369.

charge that he was a freemason, that he had ridiculed or scoffed at the Madonna of Saint Cresci, and that he had read prohibited books. He was sentenced to confinement for one year with the penance of praying from day to day the seven Penitential Psalms.

In 1789, the necromancer, Cagliostro, was imprisoned under the orders of the Inquisition. In April, 1791, the Inquisition issued a judgment arrived at in a session at which the pope presided, declaring that Cagliostro had fallen under the penalties adjudged by canon law, and also by municipal law, against heretics, heresiarchs, astrologers, magicians, and freemasons. The pope decided, as a special grace, to restrict the punishment to a life-long imprisonment, under the condition however that he should abjure his heresies. Cagliostro died in prison in 1795. His collection of books and instruments was publicly burned. The destruction included a manuscript in which the Inquisition was declared to have made the Christian religion superstitious, godless, and degrading. A work of Cagliostro's, apparently also left only in the form of manuscript, bearing the title *Maçonnerie Egyptienne*, was in April, 1791, placed in the Index. The Spanish Index of 1789 prohibits the *Mémoires Authentiques de Cagliostro* by Beam, published in Hamburg, in 1786.

In 1836, the Congregation prohibits various histories and treatises on freemasonry published during the preceding three years in Paris and in Brussels. In 1820, was prohibited a treatise published in Madrid giving an account of the persecution of the freemasons under Clement XII and Benedict XIV. In 1846, was prohibited by the Inquisition a history of freemasonry published anonymously in Madrid.

In 1880, the Congregation prohibited a treatise by

Falcioni, *Coup d'oeil sur le Christianisme, par un Franc-Maçon, Disciple de la Philosophie Positive.* Falcioni had been secretary of the Pontifical chapel. His book had been published in Paris in 1879.

12. Manuals for Exorcising.—In 1604, was issued an edition of the Roman ritual containing a brief of Paul V, in which brief, bishops, abbots, and pastors are instructed to secure the exclusive use of this particular ritual. There continued in use, nevertheless, a number of rituals varying to some extent from the text of this official Roman ritual. There were also in use a number of companion volumes which contained collections of blessings, forms of oaths, etc. In a decree of March, 1709, five exorcising manuals were prohibited which had been in print for more than a century with proper ecclesiastical approval and privilege. After the prohibition had been issued, it appeared that a certain Daniel Francus had printed a collection of so-called scandalous passages taken from these books, and had then pointed out that there was no prohibition in any of the Indexes of these passages or of the collections containing them, nor any instruction in any of the Indexes for the expurgation of the books containing these passages. Francus stated further that the worst of the five books, that bearing the name of Hieronymus Mengus, had been printed in Frankfort, in 1708, for the express purpose of bringing the Catholics to ridicule. During the following decade, a number of similar books of exorcising ritual were prohibited and a decree of December, 1725, makes a general prohibition of all rituals printed after the Reformation without the specific authorisation and approval of the Congregation of Rites. This prohibition includes a condemnation of all forms of exorcising and even of benedictions which had not secured such approval. The bishops are instructed to say that no such forms are permitted. As late as 1832, the Congregation of Rites was asked to take into consideration a collection of forms of absolution, benedictions, forms of exorcising, etc., bearing the name Bern. Sannig, which had been first printed in 1733 and had been in general use for a century. The Sannig collection was declared to be prohibited under the general regulation above specified. The work finds, however, no place in any of the Indexes either under the name of Sannig or under its own title. In the middle of the 18th century, were prohibited certain books for exorcising which had been in use among the faithful for a long series of years and which contained such formulas as the following: *Hel, Heloym, Heloa, Eheye, Totramaton, Adonay, Saday, Sabaoth, Sota, Emanuel, Alpha et Omega, Primus et Novissimus, Principimus et Finis, Hagios, Ischyros, Ho Theos, Athanatos, Agla, Ichona, Homousion, Ya, Messias, Esereheye,* etc. Before each term of ejaculation was to be made the sign of the cross. Capellis, in some treatise or manual for the use of exorcisms, explains that in order to ascertain whether or not the suspected person is certainly under possession, this series of names should be written out on a strip of consecrated paper and the paper should be placed somewhere on the person of the patient without his knowledge. If the patient becomes restless after the placing of the paper, it is evidence that he is possessed. Capellis maintains stoutly that a test of this kind is not to be considered as superstitious. Mengus[1] gives a series of similar formulas with the same specification that before each utterance should be made the sign of

[1] *Flag.*, 86.

the cross. Mengus also gives the instruction for the burning of a picture or representation of the demon through whom the patient is supposed to have become possessed. Upon the picture is to be written one of the several series of magic names. In the fire in which the picture is to be placed should be cast, after the imposition of a blessing, portions of sulphur, galbanus, assafoetida, aristolochia. hypericon, and ruta. Mengus gives further a list of formulas for the blessing of oil which is to be bestowed upon the possessed person, both inwardly and outwardly; one of these formulas is ascribed to St. Cyprian. In regard to this particular group of publications, which, as stated, were in very extended use among the faithful, a use that in many cases at least was approved by their spiritual advisers, the censorship of the Church may be considered as having come into action rather late and with not too much effectiveness. In 1752, Benedict XIV publishes a new edition of the official Roman ritual. This contains but few new forms of benedictions. In 1874, the Benedictine ritual was reprinted in Rome with a supplement containing forms of benedictions for railroads, telegraphs, springs, foundries, and brickyards. and also for the production of beer, cheese, butter, medicine, for the care of cattle, of horses, of birds, and of bees; in this appendix are also presented special forms of prayer against mice, grasshoppers. and other destructive creatures.

13. **Fraudulent Indulgences.**—After 1603, prohibition was made, first by the Inquisition and the Congregation of the Index, and later by the Congregation of Indulgences. of a number of books, monographs, and sheets in which indulgences are recorded which either had never been granted or which had been garbled

from their original text. Many of the false indulgences owe their existence to the general superstition and stupidity of the people, and it is to be noted that it has been necessary, from the beginning of the 17th century until the present day, to continue to make disavowal of certain of the most fabulous and absurd of the series. Cardinal Baronius writes January 20, 1601, to Antonio Talpa[1] : "Last evening I had occasion to apply to the Pope for a general indulgence. I found to my surprise that the Pope had decided thereafter to give no general indulgences for a single person or for a specific place. I praised him for this conclusion; for it is the case that many wrong uses have crept into the general use of indulgences. I have had occasion more than once to call the attention of the Congregations to these abuses and in so doing have had the support of many of the more thoughtful of my associates."

In the *Decreta Generalia* of Benedict XIV, there are four specifications concerning indulgences. In the Index of Benedict are forbidden, under the term *compendio*, four Italian indulgence records, and under the term *indulgentiae*, eleven similar publications. Under the term *sommario*, the entries include twelve Italian works, and under the term *ablass*, one German issue. Indulgence publications are also recorded under such terms as: *diario, dovizie, folium, giornali, notizia*, and *orazioni*. The entries are also sometimes made under the names of the publishers or editors, as, for instance, in the names of Dumensis and Lorenzo. It is the conclusion of Reusch, however, that but a very small proportion of the literature of this class finds place in the Index. In the *Decreta Generalia* (iii)

---

[1] *Epp.*, ed. Albericius, 3, 125.

are recorded for instance all indulgences which had
been issued before the decree of Clement VIII of
1598, *de forma indulgentiarum pro corona, grana seu
calculi, cruces, et imagines sacrae;* all indulgences which
had been issued before the Bulls of Clement VIII
in December, 1604, and of Paul V, May, 1605, and
November, 1610, to orders, brotherhoods, etc.   As late
as 1856, a decree of the Congregation of Indulgences
was communicated to the bishops in which attention
is called to a long series of fraudulent indulgence
announcements which had been issued in comparatively recent years in Italy, for the most part in
Florence and which are ordered to be condemned.
Of the false indulgences so specified, is one credited to
Pius V in which, in consideration of a certain prayer,
the beneficiary was to have as many indulgences as
would be equal " to the stars in the Heaven, the grains
of sand in the sea, and the blades of grass in the fields ";
another specification is that of nine prayers in consideration of which Gregory (it is not clear which of the
Gregories) and his successors, extend indulgences during
a period of eighty thousand and a hundred and forty-
nine years for each Friday, and for Good Friday eight
additional indulgences; on a picture somewhere in
Poland is printed a prayer ascribed to the Madonna,
spoken as she held in her arms the body of Christ.
It is stated that to the believer uttering this prayer,
Innocent XII had promised that he should be able
to save fifteen souls from the eternal fire or to convert
fifteen sinners whose names he was to specify.

14. Works on the Saints and Pictures of the Saints.
—Under the decrees of Urban VIII of 1625 and of
1634, it was forbidden to publish or to distribute writings concerning the lives and the miracles of persons

classed as holy until such writings had secured the specific authorisation of the Congregation or of the Inquisition. It was also forbidden to select for honour or worship as saints any persons not announced as such by the authority of the Church; and, finally, it was forbidden to place upon pictures of any persons not officially saints the insignia of saintliness (*cum laureolis aut radiis sive splendoribus*). In the *Decreta Gen.*, iii, 1, production of such unauthorised pictures is forbidden. In the Index stand also, in addition to the prohibitions of writings concerning unauthorised or unofficial saints, works on the saints duly recognised as such, unless and until such works have been, page by page, examined and approved. Such a prohibition became necessary in connection with the increasing mass of absurdly superstitious legends and stories which (in spite of the watchfulness of authorities) continued to get into print and to secure a wide circulation. The lives of Joseph and of Anna proved to be a tempting subject for the writers of these stories.

The decrees of Urban VIII were in the beginning carried out with full thoroughness. Janus Nicius Erythraeus, writing in 1642,[1] says that he had had in plan the publication of a life of Ancina of Saltuzzo, but that the permission to print had been withheld because in his narrative he had found occasion to record wonderful or miraculous things done by persons who had not been canonised. He had proposed to re-shape his biography, omitting the separate passages concerning persons other than the bishop himself, but giving some fuller measure of consideration to the virtues of Ancina; but even then had not been able to secure the authority to print. He complains bitterly

[1] *Epp. ad. Tyrrh.*, 70.

that writers are permitted to bring into print stories of shameful deeds and words of wicked men but that the devout authors who desire to record for the elevation of the faithful the virtues of pious men are discouraged. In 1648, the Congregation of Rites instructed the Archbishop of Naples to confiscate a book presenting the life and the miracles of Ursula Benincasa (†1618), the founder of the Order of the Theatins. The author of the book, Maria Maggio, a Theatin, was ordered to be brought to trial. Ursula is described on the title-page as *beata* and as she had not been canonised, this was apparently the main difficulty with the volume. In the decree of 1625, it is stated that the prohibition of the use of the term "saint" or "blessed" in connection with uncanonised persons is not in itself to be considered as any reflection on the piety or orthodoxy of such persons. It is also not to be considered as bringing into question persons who on the ground of the general consensus of the faithful or from time immemorial, in the writings of the Church Fathers and of the earlier writers, or through the personal knowledge extending over a series of years on the part of the local bishops, have been deservedly honoured. This reservation was not unnaturally the cause of a series of controversies in regard to the standing in the Church of holy persons who had secured what may be called a local repute for saintliness but whose claims were not sufficiently assured to have obtained universal recognition.

15. Forms of Prayer.—In 1626, Urban VIII confirmed the earlier prohibition of all breviaries or mass-books printed without the approval of the Congregation of Rites. The same prohibition was made to apply to unauthorised editions of the offices, of the litanies, or of the saints. The Index includes in addition to these general prohibitions the titles of a series of prayers mainly superstitious in their character. In the *Decreta Gen.*, iv, 8, are prohibited all rosaries other than those which have been specifically authorised by the Curia

16. Mariology.—In the *Decreta Gen.*, ii, 4, are prohibited (in 1617) all works in which the contention is maintained that Mary had partaken of any earthly sin. It is the conclusion of the Church that those who maintain that Mary had any part in such sin are heretics and godless ones (*impii*). This prohibition stands in the Index of Alexander VII under the term *libri*. It is cited from a Bull of this Pope issued in 1661. In 1617, Paul V caused the Inquisition to prohibit the presentation in sermons, lectures, or theses of any suggestion concerning the possible sinfulness of Mary. Paul takes pains to add, however, that his prohibition is not to be considered as undertaking itself to present a final conclusion on the question. It is the case that the several Indexes include the titles of a long series of books in which the doctrine of the Immaculate Conception is defended. The ground for the prohibition of books presenting this doctrine has been the tendency to misapprehensions and misstatements in the form of presentation. It appears that the Dominicans, who have controlled the policy of the Inquisition and largely that also of the Congregation of the Index, have had the chief responsibility for the condemnation of all doctrinal treatises which did not present precisely according to the Dominican theories the doctrine of the Immaculate Conception. A number of other works on Mariology are forbidden on the ground of exaggerations of statement, of bad taste in expression, and of confusion in the analyses of doctrinal issues.   Among the worst of these is a treatise of Maria of Agreda and one by J. B. Poza.   There are also in the Index a group of writings condemned on the ground of their exaggeration of the worship of Mary.

In 1439, the Council of Basel decreed that the doctrine of the Immaculate Conception must be held by all orthodox Catholics.   The divines of the Sorbonne, in 1497, issued an order referring to the above decree and instructing that each candidate for the doctorate must be prepared to maintain this doctrine.   The decree of the council was naturally not confirmed in Rome, but in 1483, a Bull of Sixtus IV condemned the contention that the doctrine of the Immaculate Conception is heretical and that the observance of the festival instituted under this name is in itself sinful. At the same time, however, he prohibits the declaring of the contrary doctrine as in itself heretical.   In 1661, a Bull of Alexander VII says, while confirming the approval given by his predecessors to the doctrine, that it is not to be permitted to charge with heresy or with mortal sin those who have not accepted this doctrine, as the Church universal and the Holy Chair are not yet prepared to decide all the difficulties involved.   In 1708, Clement XI declares that the festival of the Immaculate Conception is to be universally observed, but in the same year he orders to be confiscated and prohibited a reprint of the Bull in which this festival was first instituted.   Gregory VII was the first Pope who permitted the term Immaculate Conception to find place in the Book of the Mass and to have included in the Laurentian Litany the words *Regina sine labe originali concepta*.   In 1854, the doctrine of the Immaculate Conception is confirmed by Pius IX as a dogma of the Church.   Through some oversight, the *Decretum Gen.*, ii, 2, continued, however, to find place in the Index that was published in 1854. In December, 1854, is printed in connection with the publication of the *Decreta* a declaration in substance as follows: "As the dogma of Immaculate Conception has now been authoritatively defined, works which treat of the same and which have in previous years been placed in the Index, are now to be eliminated from the Index, unless it may be that certain of these works are entitled to condemnation on grounds other than their conclusions in regard to this doctrine." It appears therefore that no prohibition now rests upon books, whether placed on the earlier Indexes or not, which make defence of the doctrine.

The first important book written in defence of the doctrine of the Immaculate Conception which was formally condemned, was the work of the Italian Capucin, J. O. Maria Zamora, *De eminentissimae Deiparae V. M. perfectione*, published in Venice in 1629 and placed on the Index in 1636. The list of prohibitions of the works of this group during the succeeding half-century is very considerable. I will note here but one additional title, *Quatres Sonnets à l'honneur de la très-pure et très-immaculée conception de la Vierge Marie*, by le Père Anne Joachim de Jésus-Marie.

In 1667, there came into controversy questions in regard to the bodily ascension of Mary into heaven. These controversies brought into the Index a number of treatises written on either side of the issue. Benedict XIV (in the decree *De Festis*, ii, 8, 18) says that the bodily assumption of Mary may be held as a pious and probable belief which it would be rash to contest; it is not, however, to be accepted formally as a dogma of the Church. The passages from the Scriptures which are cited to sustain the belief can be otherwise interpreted.   The text of the announcement proceeds: *Nec est ejusmodi traditio, quae satis sit ad evehendam hanc sententiam ad gradum articulorum fidei.*   Reusch is of opinion that the tendency during the 19th century has been to develop this pious belief into a dogma. Dom. Arnaldi, in a treatise entitled *Super transitu B. M.*, printed in Genoa in 1879, undertook to prove that Mary had never suffered death.[1]   Several monographs, written in honour of the Madonna of Loreto, found their way into the Index on the ground not of the substance of their teachings but of the extravagance of their language.   In 1654, a work by Vincenzo Caraffa (later general of the Jesuits) was prohibited (with a *d.c.*) which had been published under a pseudonym in Naples and later reprinted in Rome under the title *Camino del cielo overo prattiche spirituali, del P. Luigi Sidereo.*   The book was brought into the Index under the instructions of the general of the Dominicans on the ground that it maintained the theory of the Immaculate Conception.   An examination of the text showed that this was not the case, whereupon the following new grounds for condemnation were presented: first, the author claims that the Virgin during her sojourn in the temple had been fed by the angels with heavenly nectar;   second, the author says that the grace of Mary from the first moment of her life was greater than that of any created being;   the author states with approval the opinion of Bernardino of Siena that Mary is to be worshipped as a goddess.

Scheeben points out [2] that, during these later years,

---

[1] Scheeben, *Dogm.*, iii, 281.   [2] *Ibid.* iii, 516

the teaching of the Church holds that the power of the grace of Mary, at least after the birth of Christ, must be held as being greater not only than the heavenly grace given to the highest of mankind but even than that possessed by the highest among the angels. In 1700, was prohibited, twenty-seven years after its publication, a volume by Zepherin de Somèire, a French Franciscan, printed in Narbonne under the title of *La dévotion à la mère de Dieu dans le très-saint Sacrement de l'autel, fondé sur les unions qui sont entre son fils et elle en ce divin mystère.* The list of books on Mariology condemned in the Indexes is, as stated, very considerable, but the larger number of the more important works treating upon different phases of the worship of Mary escaped attention.

In 1854, under the authority of Pius IX. the belief in the Immaculate Conception of Mary was elevated into a dogma. A number of treatises written against the new dogma were placed on the Index and the authors, in so far as they were ecclesiastics, were excommunicated. The list of these includes Thomas Braun of Germany, J. J. Laborde of France, Braulio Morgaez of Spain, and Grignani of Italy. A pastoral brief on the subject, signed by the three bishops of the Church of Utrecht, was prohibited by the Inquisition. A German treatise by H. Oswald, professor at Paderborn, was condemned on the ground of extravagance of utterance in defence of the dogma.

17. Revelations by Nuns.—For a long series of visions and of so-called revelations the imagination of the nuns is responsible. Many of these revelations from the convents have called for the attention of the Roman censors, but the writer whose productions received the largest measure of consideration was

Maria of Agreda (†1665). Her monograph on the mystical nature of God, first printed in 1670, was condemned by the Inquisition in 1681. The prohibition was, however, suspended by Innocent XI at the instance of the court of Spain. Up to the close of the century, there continued to be conflicting utterances and instructions in regard to the book. The judgment of the Inquisition was neither formally published nor recalled, and there was therefore continued question as to whether or not the book of Agreda belonged to the list of prohibited works. The title never found place in the Index, while a number of editions of the volume were actually issued with the privilege and approval of the Church authorities. Towards the end of the 17th century, there came into the Index titles of a number of writings of a similar character by another Spanish nun, Hippolyta Rocaberti, and the Index of Benedict contains a prohibition of another thesis of the same general character by the nun Clarissa, which had been printed in Munich.

18. Controversies concerning the Chinese and Malabar Usages.—Under Clement XI, was decided, adversely to the contentions of the Jesuits, through a decree of the Inquisition in 1710 and a Bull of 1715, an issue that had continued during a series of years between the missionaries of the Jesuits and those of the rival Orders, concerning the propriety of permitting the Chinese converts to retain certain special usages. The Inquisition prohibited the publication, unless with the special authorisation of the pope, of all writings which were concerned with these Chinese usages or with the controversies that had arisen concerning them. This prohibition was entered by Benedict XIV in the *Decreta Gen.*, iv, 6, and, in 1722, the division of the great history of the Jesuits by Juvencius, which treated of this matter, was condemned separately. This action aroused fresh controversies and, in 1742, Benedict found occasion for a further Bull devoted to them. In 1744, another Bull was issued, in which decision was given in an analogous issue that had arisen with the Malabars; and, in 1745, Benedict caused the Inquisition to prohibit, on the ground of some antagonistic opinions expressed in it in regard to this decision, a comprehensive history by the Capucin Norbert. The two controversies continued during a long term of years and produced a mass of controversial publications, but few separate titles of these writings came into the Index; the See appears to have considered the general prohibitions above specified sufficient to meet the requirements.

19. Fraudulent Literature.—In the *Decreta Gen.*, ii, 10, are prohibited all books, pamphlets, criticisms, and commentaries, whether written or printed, which had to do with certain lead tablets (*Laminae plumbeae*) which had been dug up in Granada and which bore ancient Arabic characters; with these were condemned certain manuscripts which had been unearthed in the foundations of an old tower in Granada. The condemnation covers also works not devoted to this subject-matter but in which references are made to said tablets or writings, until and unless such references have been eliminated. The fragments of tablets and of manuscripts, which, according to their text, had been inscribed in the time of the Apostles, were discovered between the years 1588 and 1597; but it was not until 1682 that they were officially pronounced by the authorities in Rome to be fraudulent. The false monographs of Flavius Lucius Dexter which belonged to the same group of manufactured documents, were never forbidden either in Rome or in Spain. Of the long series of treatises written concerning the letter said to have been addressed by the Madonna to the residents of Messina, two only have come into the Index.

In the *Decreta Gen.*, ii, 8, are forbidden all books, codexes, and sheets, whether printed or written, which had to do with the visions and utterances, the alleged saintliness, etc., of the Anchorite Johannes Cala; later, were also forbidden all pictures or representations presenting Cala as a saint. This prohibition has to do with an alleged discovery made in 1660, by one of the ecclesiastics in Naples, of Johannes Cala as a saint of the 12th century. Cala secured saintly honour for a term of twenty years but his saintliness was finally discredited in 1680.

20. Works on Quietism.—In 1680, the Jesuit Segneri brought to the consideration of the Index authorities two ascetic writings of the Spaniard Molinos, on the ground that they were maintaining, under the doctrinal name of Quietism, a fraudulent holiness. In 1685, the Inquisition of Rome initiated proceedings against Molinos on the ground both of his life and of his instruction. He was condemned to imprisonment for life, and, under a special Bull of Innocent XI confirming a decree of the Inquisition, his doctrine was condemned, and all of his writings, whether printed or written, were prohibited. Shortly thereafter, the Inquisition prohibited also the ascetic writings of the friend of Molinos, the Cardinal Petrucci, together with certain French writings presenting similar doctrine. Among the latter were works by Mallavel, Boudon, Lacombe and Madame Guyon. Towards the close of the 17th century, the Inquisition found occasion to condemn a long series of ascetic writings including a number which had been published many years back, but which had apparently only at that time been brought to the attention of the examiners. Some of these books had been printed in Rome and had been distributed for many years without check. In this group may be mentioned the works of Falconi, Canfeld, Bernières-Louvigny, etc. As early as 1675, the Inquisition had prohibited the *Opera omnia* of the Italian writer Lambardi, who is described as in his doctrinal views a predecessor of Molinos.

21. Fénelon.—In 1697, Fénelon, who had with Bossuet interested himself some years earlier in the protection of Madame Guyon, published his volume on the Saints and the Inner Life. The doctrines therein presented on contemplation as distinguished from meditation, and in regard to the pure and unselfish love of God, which. as he contended, caused to be put to one side selfishness and the demand for individual salvation, were sharply criticised by Bossuet and other of his fellow bishops. The volume was by Fénelon himself forwarded to Rome for a decision as to its orthodoxy. Louis XIV demanded from Innocent XII, in July, 1697, the condemnation of the book. It was placed for examination in the hands of the censorship committee of the Inquisition. The reports of the representatives who had been sent to Rome in regard to the business, represented that the votes of the Inquisitors would have decided in favour of Fénelon's treatise if it had not been for the requirement of Louis XIV. In a brief of March, 1699, the book was prohibited under the penalty of excommunication, and twenty-three propositions cited from it were specifically censured.   In this brief, pains had been taken to avoid the use of any expressions which would be likely to cause annoyance in France and in fact no reference was made in it to the Inquisition.   The brief was confirmed by the French Church and was formally published, and Fénelon submitted himself to the judgment. The earlier prohibition of the writings of Lacombe and Madame Guyon (the opinions in which were substantially at one with those presented by Fénelon) appears hardly to have become known in France, where it certainly never was acted upon.   Fénelon's correspondence from Rome states that the influence of the Jesuits there had been exercised in his favour.   The Jesuits were, at the moment, in connection with some conditions in China, in opposition to the Pope and were willing on this ground to support the contentions even of a Jansenist.   Chanterac, who was Fénelon's representative in Rome, suggested to the bishop that ground could be found for denouncing before the Inquisition the writings of his opponent Bossuet, but Fénelon appears to have been unwilling to have any such matter brought into question in connection with the pending issue.   The brief of the Pope was published in France under the direct authority of the King by means of letters patent.   The Maxims of Fénelon (in which had been found the larger number of the propositions condemned) were never placed in the Spanish Index. An edition of the *Télémaque* which had been printed in London was, however, under an edict of 1771, expurgated before being authorised for circulation in Spain.

22. Contest concerning the Doctrine of Probability.— During the rule of Benedict XIV, a sharp controversy arose between the Dominicans and the Jesuits in regard to the doctrine of Probability, the immediate cause being the publication of a treatise on morality by the Jesuit Benzi, which is described as "shameless." The leading representative of the Dominicans was Concina (1687–1756), and of the Jesuits, Faure (1702–1779). Benedict XIV brought into his Index certain of the monographs by both authors, but the principal treatise of Concina, sharply condemned by the Jesuits, was not prohibited. Benedict took occasion, however, to instruct Concina to publish, over his signature, a comprehensive explanation of his treatise. Clement XIII prohibited the sermons of the German Jesuit, Neumayr, and, at the same time, a biography of Concina. Concina's teachings against the doctrine of Probability were continued and developed by his associate Patuzzi (1700–1769). Patuzzi was replied to by Liguori (1696–1787), founder, in 1732, of the Congregation of the Redemptorists. Benedict XIV appears to have given his official acceptance to the doctrine of Probability as expounded by Liguori, the later edition of his treatise having been issued with a specific approval from the Pope. This approval secured, later, confirmation on the part of the Church as a whole, as, in 1839, Concina secured canonisation, and, in 1871, his name was included in the list of doctors of the Church, being, through this act, associated with St. Athanasius, St. Augustine, St. Bernard, St. Thomas, and other pillars of the Church. After the giving of this honour, the Jesuits, under the lead of Ballerini, took the ground that certain of the conclusions of Liguori had been too rigorous and that the doctrine termed by him *Regni probabilismus* must in order to be maintained, be interpreted in the sense of "ordinary probability." The

Jesuits came in this contention into controversy with the Redemptorists, who insisted upon the distinctive importance of the differentiation expressed by their founder. The treatise of Ballerini was however reprinted in Rome with a special privilege from the master of the palace.

23. The Controversy concerning Usury, 1600–1800. —In a long series of decrees from popes and from councils, the Church has announced its conclusion that the taking of interest, even although the rate should not be extortionate, comes under the head of the sin of usury. This contention was maintained constantly throughout the 17th and 18th centuries, and the several classes of trade in which the taking of interest was a necessary factor, were condemned as not to be permitted by the Church. As a result of this policy, a number of legal treatises which undertook the defence of interest that was not exaggerated into extortion, were prohibited. There were also placed upon the Index certain other monographs in which the question had been treated from a purely academic standpoint. Under Benedict XIV, the controversy came to the front in connection with the publication of monographs by Broedersen, an ecclesiastic of Utrecht, and by the Marquis Sipio Maffei, in which ground was taken against the theories of the Church. Benedict XIV published, in 1745, an encyclical in which he confirms as the present utterance of the Church the old contention. The two treatises which had formed the text for the utterance of the Pope were, however, not prohibited. In fact that by Maffei was, in 1746, reprinted in Rome contemporaneously with a monograph by the Dominican Concina, in which Maffei's conclusions were stigmatised as heretical.

It is the conclusion of Reusch that the earlier Church view, while in theory confirmed by Benedict, had practically been abandoned. The controversy continued throughout the 19th century, and several of the later popes have taken the ground that the practice of taking interest that was not extortionate could be permitted until the question had received a final decision from the Holy See. During this latter period, only one work on the subject was placed on the Index, a monograph by Laborde, who was a sharp opponent of the earlier Church theory. No final conclusion of the issue has, however, ever been reached by the Church. It has probably been withheld because it would be difficult to frame a conclusion that would not either directly or indirectly constitute a reflection on the good judgment and wisdom of the earlier papal utterances.

In July, 1745, Benedict XIV instituted a special Congregation comprising four cardinals and clever theologians to give consideration to the subject of usury. The theologians included two Jesuits, one Dominican (Concina), and one Observant. The Pope himself presided over the sessions. The conclusions arrived at were published on the first of August in the form of three propositions. These were utilised by Benedict as the basis of the encyclical to the Italian bishops issued in November, 1745.

1. All return for the use of money given in the form of interest is to be classed as usury and characterised as unlawful.

2. One may not say that it is unlawful only to receive extortionate interest or to take interest from the poor.

3. It may be permitted for the lender to receive

some return or compensation for his service from some person other than the borrower or person benefited; but it may not be permitted to make provision that such second person or guarantor should always be at hand.

In 1746, the year following the publication of the encyclical, Maffei had published a second edition of his treatise, which bears the imprint of the master of the palace. In a letter printed in this edition, Maffei writes that he had not as yet learned what had been the precise subject of condemnation in the encyclical. He was, however, of the opinion that he had been able in his treatise to anticipate the doctrine of the encyclical.

In the same year, Concina brought into print three essays in which he makes sharp criticism of the heresies of Broedersen and Maffei. These essays are dedicated to the pope. Muratori, writing in February, 1747, says: "A curious history is this! The Holy Father accepts dedication on the one hand from Concina and on the other from Maffei and yet neither the one nor the other is to be classed as unsound or heretical."

After 1820, there arose also in France an active controversy on the question of interest. The earlier orthodox opinion adverse to the use of interest was maintained by Abbé Pages in his treatise *Dissertation sur le prêt à intérêt*, published in 1821. The contrary view was maintained by La Luzerne, Bishop of Langres, in his *Dissertations sur le Prêt de Commerce*, published in 1823 in five volumes, and by the Abbé Baronnat in *Le Prétendu Mystère de l'Usure Dévoilé*, published in 1822. In the course of the following half-century, the question was repeatedly brought from France and from Italy to the attention of the Inquisition. In 1873, the Congregation of Propaganda printed together the decisions that had been issued by the Inquisition on this subject between 1780 and 1872. The conclusion presented in 1873 is in substance as follows: Those who, under the authority of the law of the land, may take interest at a moderate rate (up to five per cent.), whether laymen or ecclesiastics, are not to be called to account in the confessional or otherwise for so doing until it has seemed wise to the Holy See to present a final conclusion in the matter. They must, however, hold themselves prepared at any time to accept and to abide by the final instruction of the Church.

24. Philosophical Writings, between 1750 and 1800, Condemned as Irreligious.—In the Spanish Index, are prohibited all the writings of Voltaire and Rousseau. The Roman Index of 1824 includes the name of David Hume.

In February, 1778, Pius VI issues a general prohibition as follows: *Libri omnes incredulorum, sive anonymi sive contra, in quibus contra religionem agitur.* This prohibition, instead of being included in the *Decreta Generalia*, where similar decrees had heretofore been printed, is placed under the term *libri*. Connected with the decree, is the specification that the permission to read books of this class can be granted only by the pope himself. It is probable that this general prohibition did not prove particularly effective, as it was hardly possible for the average reader to be able at once to identify a work as irreligious in tendency or to have knowledge by name of all of the writers who were to be classed as unbelievers. The difficulty was naturally greater in the case of anonymous works.

In the Spanish Indexes of 1747 and 1790, the editors have indicated by a mark the books the reading of which is prohibited even to those who have secured permission for the use of works included in the general Index lists.

There was published in Paris an encyclopaedia under the title *L'Encyclopédie ou Dictionnaire raisonnée des Sciences, des Arts, et des Métiers, par la Société des Gens de Lettres*. It bore the names, as editors, of Diderot and d'Alembert. In 1759, at the time of the prohibition, seven volumes only had been published. The first two volumes, printed in 1751, had been condemned in 1752, under an order of the Council of the King; but two years later, the king issued a privilege for the continuation of the work. The papal brief states that the volumes first issued had been condemned and that the later issues, described as a revised edition, had been carefully examined by the Inquisition and again condemned on the ground that the teachings and propositions contained in them were false and pernicious and tended to the destruction of morality; and further that these teachings promoted godlessness and the undermining of religion. In 1759, the royal privilege under which the publication was being continued, was withdrawn. The editors and printers succeeded, however, in carrying on the work without coming into open conflict with the authorities, and by 1772, twenty-eight volumes had come into print.

In April, 1757, a decree of Louis XV prohibits, under penalty of death, the production and distribution of any writings against religion. There does not appear, however, to be on record any instance of the carrying out of this penalty.

The papal brief issued in 1759 in regard to the treatise of Helvétius, *De l' Esprit*, describes the book as " antagonistic to the Christian religion and to natural moral-ity, and as maintaining the pernicious and damnable views of the Materialists and of the Epicureans," and further, "as maintaining many godless and heretical propositions."

In 1762, a prohibition of the Inquisition contains the title of *La petite Encyclopédie ou Dictionnaire des Philosophes, oeuvre posthume d'un de ces Messieurs.* The entry is followed by the remark "*Ridiculum acri fortius et malius plerumque secat res.* Anvers, 1761." This title probably refers to a reprint of some portions of the encyclopaedia. Between 1758 and 1800, were placed upon the Index at intervals practically all of the works of Voltaire, but, excepting in Spanish Indexes, the term *Opera omnia* does not appear. In 1762, the treatise by Rousseau on education, entitled *Émile,* was prohibited by the Inquisition; and in the same year, the book was ordered by the Parliament of Paris to be burned. It was also censured by the Sorbonne and prohibited for France by the Archbishop of Paris. The work was also condemned by the Protestant authorities in Geneva.

In 1784, was prohibited, by a brief of Pius VI, a work issued under the title of *Recherches Philosophiques sur les Américains ou Mémoires intéressants pour servir a l'Histoire de l'Humanité.* The author was Cornelius de Paw, a canon in Zante.

In 1761, the Congregation prohibits the French version of the essay by David Hume, *A Treatise on the Human Understanding.* This edition had been printed in Amsterdam in 1758, twenty years after the appear-ance of the original.

Gibbon's *Decline and Fall of the Roman Empire,* printed in an Italian edition in 1776, was prohibited in 1783. The writings of Thomas Paine and Joseph Priestly escaped the attention of the compilers of the Roman Index, but the name of the latter author appears in the Spanish Index of 1806.

The writings of Frederick the Great of Prussia, as printed in Berlin, in 1750, under the title of *Oeuvres du Philosophe de Sans-Souci*, receive the compliment of prohibition by the Inquisition in 1760. The Spanish Index does not include the works but does find place for the *Mémoires pour servir à l'Histoire de la Maison de Brandebourg*.

25. Works on Philosophy and Natural Science, 1800–1880. —Among the works prohibited during the period in question in the department of philosophy and natural science, may be noted the following:

Villiers, Ch. de, *A Treatise on Kant*, printed in Paris in 1801, prohibited in 1817. An Italian edition of Kant's *Critique of Pure Reason*, printed (in Rome) in 1821, prohibited in the same year.

Buhle, J. G., *Geschichte der neuern Philosophie*, printed in Leipsic, 1800–1805, prohibited (in the French and Italian versions) in 1828.

Tennemann, *Grundriss der Gesch. der Philosophie*, printed in Leipsic in 1812, prohibited (in the Italian version) in 1837, prohibited again (in a Polish version) in 1865.

Bentham, Jeremy. Of this author practically all the works find place sooner or later in the Index, but the term *Opera omnia* has not been used.

Whately, Richard, *Elements of Logic*, printed in 1822, prohibited in 1851.

Mill, John Stuart, *Treatise on Liberty*, prohibited in 1851; *Principles of Political Economy*, printed in 1848, prohibited in 1850.

Darwin, Erasmus, *Zoönomy*, printed in 1794, prohibited in 1817. (*The Origin of Species* and the other treatises by Charles Darwin, the grandson of Erasmus, have, curiously enough, escaped the attention of the Index authorities.)

Draper, J. W., *History of the Conflict between Religion and Science*, printed (in New York) in 1874, prohibited (in a Spanish version) in 1876.

Condorcet, the Marquis, *Esquisse d'un Tableau historique du Progrès de l'Esprit humain*, printed in 1804 as a division in a series of works comprising in all twenty-one volumes, prohibited 1827.

Condillac, Abbé de, *Cours d'Étude*, printed (in Paris) in 1773, prohibited in 1836.

Ahrens, Henri, *Cours du Droit Naturel*, printed in 1838, prohibited 1868.

Cousin, *Cours d'Histoire de la Philosophie*, printed in 1827, prohibited in 1844. This is the only one of the long series of works by this author that finds place in the Index. Cousin was induced by his friends Sibour and Maret, for the purpose of preventing the threatened condemnation of his works by the Congregation of the Index, to write a letter to the Pope. He writes, under date of April 30, 1836, in substance as follows: " As Your Holiness has already been informed, I am myself a devout upholder of the Christian faith and I place all my hopes for the future of mankind upon the maintenance and extension of Christianity. I can but be troubled that my views have been placed in a false light and I have attempted to produce a philosophical treatise which should be entirely free from the possibility of reproach and in the preparation of which I have secured the counsel of scholarly divines. If it may be the case that, notwithstanding my own watchful care and the aid of these scholarly advisers, certain passages which could cause concern to Your Holiness have escaped attention, I will ask that these may be indicated to me. I am more than anxious to correct or to eliminate any expressions or statements that may be open to criticism from the point of view of the Church. My sole purpose is to do all that may be practicable to perfect the text of these modest writings of mine."

Comte, Auguste (†1857), *Cours de Philosophie Positive*, printed in Paris in 1864 with an introduction by Littré, prohibited in the same year. No one of the other works by Comte finds place in the Index. Littré had sharp controversies with Dupanloup in 1863, and was characterised by the Archbishop as an atheist, but no one of Littré's writings was formally condemned.

Taine, Hippolyte Adolphe, *Histoire de la Littérature Anglaise*, printed (in Paris) in 1863, prohibited in 1866. This work had, in 1864, been condemned by the French Academy as tending to undermine the belief in the freedom of the will, the sense of personal responsibility, and morality in general.

Legrand, Jacques, *Recherche des Bases d'une Philosophie Pratique*, printed in 1864, prohibited the same year.

Mangin, Arthur, *L'Homme et la Bête*, printed in 1872, prohibited the same year.

Figuier, Louis, *Le Lendemain de la Mort ou la Vie Future selon la Science*, printed 1871, prohibited 1872.

A collection of essays by Tyndall, Owen, Huxley, Hooker, and Lubbock, translated into French, together with certain papers by Raymond, edited by the Abbé Moigno, on the general subject-matter of science and faith, was printed in Paris in 1875 and prohibited in the same year. Connected with the prohibition is a statement that the notes of Moigno on Tyndall and the other naturalists meet the approval of the Congregation.

Leopardi, Giacomo, *Operetti Morali*, printed 1827, prohibited, with a *donec emendatum*, in 1850.

Spaventa, Bernardo, *Opera omnia*, printed between the years 1861 and 1874.

Vera, Auguste, *Opera omnia* in each and every version. These two writers had given instruction in the Hegelian philosophy. Vera's works had appeared in Italian, French, and English editions.

Ferrari, Gius., *Opera omnia*, prohibited 1877. The chief work of this author, *Essai sur le Principe et la Limite de la Philosophie d'Histoire*, had been printed as early as 1837 and had for forty years escaped condemnation.

Settembrini, Luigi (a third Neapolitan Hegelian) *Lezioni di Letteratura Italiana*, printed in 1868, prohibited in 1874.

Sicilinoni, Pietro (professor of philosophy in Bologna), a series of works printed between the years 1878 and 1887, placed upon the Index from year to year immediately after their publication.

Ranke, L., *Die Römischen Päpste, ihre Kirche und ihr Staat, im XVI ᵗᵉⁿ und XVII ᵗᵉⁿ Jahrhundert*, printed in 1835, prohibited in 1841.

Historical Works

Hume, David, *History of England*, printed in 1761, prohibited in 1823.

Robertson, William, *History of Charles the Fifth*, printed in 1762, prohibited (in a French edition) in 1777.

Goldsmith, Oliver, *History of England*, printed in 1770, prohibited (in an Italian edition), with a *d.c.*, 1823.

Roscoe, William. *Biography of Leo X*, printed 1805, prohibited, in both the English and Italian versions, in 1825.

Hallam, Henry, *View of the State of Europe during the Middle Ages*, printed in 1818, prohibited (in the Italian edition) in 1833. *Constitutional History of England*, printed in 1824, prohibited 1827.

Beugnot, A., *Histoire de la Destruction du Paganisme en Occident*, printed in 1835, prohibited in 1837.

Sismondi, J. C. L. S. de, *Histoire du Moyen-Age*, printed in 1812, prohibited in 1817. The prohibition covers, however, only the first eleven volumes. The sixteenth volume, which contains the noteworthy chapter on the pernicious effects produced on Italy by the casuistical morality of the Church of Rome, escaped condemnation.

Gregorovius, *Geschichte der Stadt Rom im Mittel-alter*, printed in 1859-1873, condemned in 1874, both in the German original and in the Italian version.

Mignet, F. A., *Histoire de la Révolution Française*, printed in 1824, prohibited 1825.

Ségur, Comte de, *Galerie Morale et Politique*, printed in 1817-1823, prohibited 1826.

Jobez, Alph., *La France sous Louis XV*, printed 1865-1867, prohibited 1868.

Le Bas, Phil., *L'Univers Pittoresque*, printed in 1851, prohibited in 1853. The reprehensible chapters in this descriptive work were those giving an account of the religions of the world

Munks, *La Palestine, Description géographique, historique, et archéologique*, printed 1845, prohibited in 1853.

Dictionnaire Encyclopédique de la France, edited by Le Bas and Rénier, printed, in twelve volumes, 1840-1845, prohibited (in a separate decree) in 1853.

The prohibitions of this period include a long series of French, German, and Italian encyclopaedias, universal dictionaries, gazetteers, etc., in addition to those specified.

Lalande, J. L. de, *Voyage en Italie*, printed in 1769, prohibited in 1820. It is possible that one reason for placing on the Index, so many years after the date of its appearance, this particular book was the association at a later date by the author with the *Dictionnaire des Athées* which was compiled by Maréchal. This latter work, however, curiously escapes the attention of the Index compilers.

Didier, Ch., *Rome souterraine*, printed in 1833, prohibited in 1835 It is proper to point out that this work has to do, not with the Catacombs, but with the secret societies of Rome.

Viardot, Louis, *Les Musées d'Italie*, printed in 1842, prohibited in 1865. A later work by this author on the Jesuits, the bishops, and the pope, apparently much more serious in its subject-matter, escapes attention.

Ciocci, Raffaelle, *A Narrative of Iniquities and Barbarities practised at Rome in the 19th Century*. printed (in a French version) in 1841, prohibited in 1845. The author was formerly a Cistercian and had been librarian of the papal College of San Bernardo. It is not surprising that his work failed to secure the approval of the Roman authorities.

La Châtre, Maurice, *Histoire des Papes; Les Crimes, Meurtres . . . des Pontifes Romains, depuis S. Pierre jusqu' à Gregoire XVI*, printed in 1842–1845, prohibited in 1848.

Among the noteworthy works under the heading of general literature may be cited the following:

Sue, Eugene, *Mystères de Paris*, printed in 1843,

prohibited in 1852; *Le Juif Errant*, printed in 1845, prohibited in 1852. Later in the same year, Sue's
name was placed upon the Index connected with the term *Opera omnia*. In 1864, the list of French authors all of whose works were prohibited includes the following names : Balzac, Champfleury, Dumas the elder and Dumas the younger, Feydeau, Murger, Sand, Soulié, and Stendhal. The name of Flaubert appears in the same year in connection with two only of his romances. The volume of the Abbé Michon, published anonymously under the title *Le Maudit*, was prohibited in the year of its publication, 1864, and the later volumes issued as by the author of *Le Maudit* were prohibited as they appeared. Since 1864, the compilers of the Index have given comparatively little attention to French fiction.

In 1834, the *Chansons* of Béranger were prohibited. Some of these had been printed as far back as 1815. Additional titles from French literature are as follows:

Lamartine, Alph. de, *Souvenirs d'un Voyage en Orient*, printed in 1835, prohibited in 1836.

Hugo, Victor, *Notre Dame de Paris*, printed in 1831, prohibited in 1834; *Les Misérables*, printed in 1836, prohibited in 1864.

The famous volumes by Ferd. Fabre, *Lucifer* and *L'Abbé Grand*, curiously enough escape condemnation.

The selections of this period from German literature are inconsiderable. They include:

Lessing, *Erziehung des Menschen-geschlechts*, prohibited 1835.

Heine, H., *Reisebilder*, printed in 1834, prohibited in 1836; *De la France*, printed in 1833, prohibited in 1836; *De l'Allemagne*, printed in 1835, prohibited 1836; *Gedichte*, printed in 1844, prohibited in 1845.

In 1855, Mrs. Stowe's *Uncle Tom's Cabin* was prohibited, under some special instruction, as far as its sale in the papal States was concerned. The title does not find place in the Index.

The small group of Spanish and Portuguese works includes the following titles:

Torres, *Quentos en verso Castilano del Remédo de la Melencholia*, prohibited 1824.

Tressera, *El Judio Errante*, prohibited 1864.

The long series of anti-clerical romances by Benito, Perez, and Galdós escape condemnation.

Stockler, *Poezias Liricas*, printed in 1820, prohibited in 1836.

The Italian list includes:

Foscolo, Ugo, translation of Sterne's *Sentimental Journey*, printed in 1817, prohibited in 1819; *La Commedia di Dante*, illustrated, printed in 1830, prohibited in 1845.

Zaccheroni, G., an edition of Dante's *Inferno* with notes, printed in 1838, prohibited (as far as the introduction and the notes are concerned) by the Inquisition in 1840. The larger number of the commentaries on Dante are condemned as printed.

Guerrazzi, Dom., *L'Assedio di Firenze*, printed in 1830, prohibited in 1837. His later romances, *Isabella Orsini* and *Beatrice Cenci*, were prohibited promptly on publication, the former in 1844, the latter in 1854.

Niccolini, G. B., *Arnaldo da Brescia*, printed in 1844, prohibited the same year.

Bossie, Conte Luigi, *Della Istoria d'Italia Antica e Moderna*, printed in Milan, 1819–1822, in nineteen volumes, prohibited in 1824. The same author produced a translation of Roscoe's *Life of Leo X,* which was promptly condemned some twenty years after the prohibition of the same work in the original.

Botta, Carlo, *Storia d'Italia del 1729 al 1814,* ten volumes, printed in 1824, prohibited in 1826. Botta had gained the name of "the Italian Tacitus." His son, Vincenzo Botta, was well known in New York as a man of letters, between the years 1850 (he was one of the exiles of '48) and 1880.

Rossetti, Gabrielle, *Sullo Spirito anti-Papale,* etc., printed in 1832, prohibited 1833; *Iddio a l'Uomo,* printed in 1836, prohibited 1837.

The Spanish and Portuguese group of general literature of this period includes the following titles:

Llorente, J. A., *Histoire Critique de l'Inquisition de l'Espagne,* printed in Paris in 1820, prohibited in 1822. The author, who was the Secretary-General of the Inquisition, had been banished from Spain in 1812 His history, written in Spanish, was translated under his own supervision.

Historia Completa des Inquisiçoes de Italia, Hispagnia e Portugal, printed (anonymously) in 1822, prohibited in 1825. This is probably a translation of the *Histoire de l' Inquisition* of Lavalée printed in Paris in 1809, and prohibited in 1819. The histories of the Inquisition, whether written from the Dominican point of view or from that of their opponents, found their way in great part into the Index.

26. The Synod of Pistoja, 1786.—In 1794, the conclusions arrived at by the Diocesan Synod held at Pistoja at the instance of Bishop Ricci, were condemned by the Bull *Auctorem Fidei* of Pius VI. In this Bull, were censured specifically eighty-five propositions. The Pope condemns and prohibits, under penalty of excommunication, the printing, distribution, or reading of any editions or translations of the acts of the synod and of all works written in defence of these acts. It is doubtless through oversight that this very sweeping condemnation does not find place in the Index. Certain publications reporting the conclusions of the synod had been already specifically prohibited; while certain further works, the subjects of which were connected with the issues raised by the synod, were prohibited in later years, in certain instances as late as 1817. For these later prohibitions, the statement was added that the works were already condemned under the Bull *Auctorem Fidei*.

27. The Festival of the Heart of Jesus.—In 1697 and again in 1729, the Congregation of Rites recalled the authorisation for a specific office for the Sacred Heart of Jesus; and in 1704, was prohibited the treatise by the Jesuit Croiset, written in defence of this office. Under Clement XIII in 1765, the office was again authorised, and under Pius IX, the festival in honour of the Heart of Jesus was made a general usage. This special act of adoration had originated with the Jesuits; those who opposed it were classed as Jansenists. The office came, however, into question with a good many Churchmen other than Ricci and his friends; and a number of the most important of the treatises written against it were published under Clement XIV in Rome.

28. Theological Writings of French, German, and English Catholics, 1758-1800.—But one important work of theology printed in France, *Theologia Lugdunensis*, came upon the Index during the last decade of the 18th century. From England, the single title of the same period covers a book of worship, and from Germany, were prohibited, in addition to the writings already referred to, a volume by Isenbiehl and several treatises by Stättler, Meyer, and Oberrauch. During these years, were published in England a number of works by Catholic authors which had to do with the controversies of the time, such as the Oath of Allegiance, the re-institution of the hierarchy of bishops, etc., but no one of these writings is recorded in the Index. The single English work above referred to was published in London, in 1767, under the title *The Catholik Christians' New Universal Manual, being a true spiritual guide for those who ardently aspire to salvation.* The book contains the entry, *Permissu superiorum,* which did not prevent its prohibition in 1770. On the other hand, the writings of Charles Dodd, J. Berington, Alexander Geddes, George Cooper, and Bishop Butler, the teachings of which would hardly have met the approval of the Holy See, escaped condemnation.

29. The French Revolution.—The *Constitution Civile* of the clergy, framed in 1780, and the Defence of the same issued a year later by the so-called Constitutional Bishops, were promptly condemned by briefs of Pius VI, but they do not find place in the Index. The acts of the national councils of 1797 and 1801 were condemned in like manner but these titles also escaped the attention of the Index compilers. The practice on the part of the Index editors in regard to the recording of legislative acts appears not to have been consistent. In 1817, for instance, a collection of the acts and declarations of the Italian bishops and chapters, which had been printed in 1811, was placed upon the Index although the subscribers and compilers of the same had made recantation of the opinions expressed.

The long series of revolutionary writings and of anti-Church writings which came into print in France after 1789 were in large part recorded by the Spanish Inquisition but in the Roman Indexes are represented by only a few titles.

In July, 1797, the Congregation of the Index publishes its last decree for the century. The authors whose books are condemned include Stättler, Oberrauch, Tamburini, and Zola; in addition to these, there is a series of German theological and juristical theses which the students of Freiburg had defended between the years 1786 and 1794. The last work prohibited by the Inquisition during the 18th century is a treatise by Guadagnini.

The first prohibition of the 19th century condemns a monograph by a Greek theologian, printed in Corfu in 1800. The Congregation of the Index resumed its activities in 1804 after a suspension of more than seven years. In decrees issued in 1804, 1805, 1806, and 1808 were condemned a number of French and Italian writings that had to do with the Revolution. The imprisonment in June, 1809, of Pius VII again brought to a close the operations of the Roman Congregations. The Pope returned to Rome in May, 1814, and in August, 1815, the Inquisition resumed its supervision of literature. The work of the Congregation of the Index was, however, not taken up till January, 1817. In this year, a list of prohibitions was issued covering a number of works that had been published in France and in Italy between 1796 and 1815.

The two briefs that Pius VI had issued in March and in April, 1781, for the condemnation of the so-called Civil Constitution of the French clergy, were declared by the "constitutional" party in the Church to be apocryphal. It was pointed out that the second brief, while dated in Rome, April 13th, was distributed in Paris April 14th, from which detail, it came to be known as the "Miraculous Brief." In a brief issued in 1792, the Pope calls attention to this statement as one of the insults coming from France. The Index of 1806 contains, printed as an appendix, a list of the books prohibited from 1804 to 1806. The more important names in this list are those of Voltaire, Rousseau, Diderot, Mirabeau, Dulaurens, and La Fontaine.

30. The French Concordat of 1801.—In August, 1801, a Bull of Pius VII records the provisions of the Concordat that had been arrived at between Napoleon and himself. Under the Concordat, the number of the French bishoprics was reduced from a hundred and fifty-six to sixty and a new division of the dioceses was provided for. In a brief bearing the same date, the Pope calls for the resignation of all the French bishops, and in November of 1801, he issues a second Bull, declaring those bishops who had not resigned to be deposed, and fixing the limits of the new bishoprics. In 1803, thirty-six bishops present a protest against these regulations. This protest was widely circulated and served as the text for a long series of monographs in which were brought into discussion various questions relating to the Concordat. In 1817, a second Concordat was put into force between the Papacy and Louis XVIII. In 1822, a long series of writings which took ground against the authority of this Concordat were placed upon the Index.

31. Protestant Theological Writings, 1750–1884.— The selections for condemnation, in the last years of the 18th century and during the first half of the 19th century, of works by Protestant theologians appears to have been made with no greater consistency and with no more assured principles than had been apparent in the selection of Protestant writings of an earlier date. The following titles may be noted:

Michaelis, J. D., *Introduction to the New Testament*, published in 1750, condemned in 1827.

Strauss, *The Life of Jesus (Das Leben Jesu)*, published in 1835, prohibited 1838.

Bauer, *Streit der Kritik mit Kirche und Staat*, published in 1844, prohibited in 1845.

Bunsen, *Hippolytus and his Age*, published 1852, prohibited 1854.

Maurice, F. D., *Theological Essays*, published 1854, prohibited 1854 (the entry in the Index is under the word "Denison").

Stroud, *The Physical Causes of the Death of Christ*, published 1847, prohibited 1878.

Morgan, Lady, *Italy*, prohibited 1822.

Waldie, *Rome in the Nineteenth Century*, published 1820, prohibited 1826.

Blunt, James, *Vestiges of Ancient Manners and Customs in Modern Italy and Sicily*, published 1823, prohibited 1827. The difficulty with Mr. Blunt's treatise was the connection made by him between certain ceremonies and practices of the Roman Church and the earlier Pagan usages.

Seymour, Hobart, *A Pilgrimage to Rome*, printed 1851, prohibited 1851. The title is entered under "Pilgrimage."

Whately, Archbishop, *Introductory Lessons on Christian Evidences*, an Italian version printed in 1850 and prohibited in the same year.

The treatise by John Poynde, *Popery in Alliance with*

Heathenism, the publication of which (in 1835) brought out some sharp controversial letters from Wiseman, escaped the attention of the Index compilers.

The more noteworthy of the French titles in the Indexes of this period are the following:

Bruitte, Edouard, abbé and professor of philosophy, *Mes Adieux à Rome*, published in 1844, prohibited in 1844.

Mourette, *Le Pape et l'Évangile*, published in 1844, prohibited in 1845. This latter was also prohibited in Paris.

Coquerel, Athanase, (†1868), *Le Christianisme experimental*, published in 1847, prohibited in 1850. No other of the series of writings by this famous Protestant preacher nor any of those of his son, Athanase Josue, find place in the Index.

Bugnoin, T. R., *Catéchisme de l'Église du Seigneur*, published in 1862, prohibited in 1863.

Martig, Emm., *Manuel d'Histoire religieuse a l'Usage des Écoles*, published at Geneva in 1877, prohibited in 1878.

D'Aubigné, *L'Histoire de la Réforme du Seizième Siècle*, printed, in an Italian edition, in 1847, prohibited in 1852.

The list of Italian and Spanish publications contains few names that would be familiar to English readers.

Bianchi, Angiolo, *Biographia di Fra Paolo Sarpi*, printed (in Brussels) in 1836, prohibited in 1844; *Del Pontificato di S. Gregorio il grande*, printed (in Milan) in 1844, prohibited in 1853.

Boni, Filippo de, *Del Papato*, printed in 1850, prohibited in 1852.

Castro, Adolpho de, *Historia des los Protestantes Españoles*, printed in 1851, prohibited in the same year.

32. Writings concerning the Eastern Church.—The larger number of the works under this heading the titles of which come into the Index of the 19th century, are the production of the "United Armenians." The addition of a group of monographs by Polish writers is doubtless due to the fact that during the reign of Pius IX. the consultor of the Congregation was a Pole, Peter Semenenko. The Bull issued by Pius IX in July, 1867, under the title of *Reversurus*, in which it had been ordered that the procedure of worship of the Armenians should be reconstituted, resulted in a schism in this division of the Church. Between the years 1872 and 1873, three monographs by Ormanian and one by Casangian, written in opposition to this Bull, are placed upon the Index. The list also includes the following:

Pichler, A., *Die kirchliche Trennung zwischen Orient und Occident.*

The Greek Church of Russia is represented in the Index of this time by but one or two titles:

Tolstoy, Dimitri, *Le Catholicisme Romain ou Russe*, published in 1864, prohibited in 1866. This work stands in the Index under the entry "Dimitri." The entry is connected with the reference *Opus praedamnatum ex reg. II. ind.* This entry indicates that, prior to 1870, the Russians were already classed as heretics.

Pociej, Joh. (Chancellor of the Cathedral at Chelm), *O Jezusie Chrystusie* (a study of the record of the early Christians), printed in 1852 (with the approval of the Church authorities at Warsaw), prohibited in 1857.

The record of the proceedings of a Synod of Melchites, held in 1810, in Beyrout, with the approval of the papal delegate, Gandolfi, was condemned in 1835 by a brief of Gregory XVI. The record had been printed in Arabic and was not likely therefore to have secured an extended circulation in Catholic States.

In 1851, was prohibited an Italian version of the *Critical History of the Greek and Russian Church* by Josef Schmitt,which had been published in Mayence in 1840. In 1868, was prohibited a work by the English writer, Edmund S. Ffoulkes, which had been published in London in 1865 under the title, *Christendom's Divisions, a Philosophical Sketch of the Divisions of the Christian Family in East and West.* The work had been sharply criticised by Manning, but it does not appear that Manning had made any formal denunciation of the same to Rome.

33. The Theologians of Pavia, 1774-1790.—In 1774, the Austrian Government instituted a theological faculty in the University of Pavia. In 1783, the Emperor Joseph II transferred to Pavia, for use in the newly instituted *Collegium Germanicum et Hungaricum*, the collections belonging to the old *Collegium Germanicum* of Milan. The divines of the theological faculty of Pavia came to be classed as Jansenists. The classification appears to have been based not so much upon their teaching of the Augustinian doctrine of Grace as upon their own sharp antagonism to the theories and practices of the Jesuits. These divines contended openly that the so-called Jansenist heresy was a phantom, and they also undertook the defence of the Church of Utrecht. They were, further, opponents of the doctrines taught by the Jesuits in regard to morality; they were in sympathy with the claims of the Gallican Church, and, finally, they maintained stoutly the necessity for reforms within the Catholic Church on the lines indicated by the Synod of Pistoja.

In the years succeeding 1781, were placed upon the Index the titles of a number of writings by these theologians and by others who had accepted their views. Among these writers may be mentioned the following: Pietro Tamburini, Giuseppe Zola, Count Th. Trautmannsdorf, Canon Litta, and G. B. Guadagnini. The treatise by Trautmannsdorf on Toleration, condemned in 1783, the author found desirable to disavow in order to secure his appointment as bishop.

34. French, Dutch, and English Writings, 1817-1880. —In 1825, a report was laid before the French Minister of the Interior concerning certain writings classed as irreligious or immoral which had been published between the years 1817 and 1824. The list included various editions of the complete works of Voltaire and of Rousseau, together with a number of issues of their separate volumes. There were no less than eight editions of the *Système de la Nature*, by d' Holbach, and four of the *Lettres Persanes*. It was complained that these pernicious books were being sold so cheaply that they were brought within the reach of the masses of the people and were bringing about widespread evil. The *Tartuffe* of Molière, sold for five sous, had at once reached a sale of one hundred thousand copies. In 1821, Étienne Antoine, Bishop of Troyes, in a pastoral letter writes: "We renew all the censorship orders issued, between the years 1782 and 1785, by the clergy of France, and the individual orders issued by the archbishops of Paris, in which these works were condemned as godless and sacrilegious, and as tending to undermine morals and the State. We prohibit, under the canonical law, the printing or sale of these books within the territory of this diocese, and we charge the vicar-generals to enforce this regulation and to see to the carrying out of the necessary penances for all who make confession of disobedience to these regulations." The authority of the Church of France appears to have been considered as sufficient for the control of the matter. No application was made to have these books again placed upon the Index.

Dupuis, Ch. Fr., *Origine de tous les Cultes*, printed 1794, prohibited, 1818. An abridgment of this work, printed in 1798 and reprinted in a number of editions thereafter, escaped condemnation.

Volney, J. F., *Les Ruines ou Méditations sur les Révolutions des Empires*, printed in 1799, prohibited in 1821. This book was also strongly condemned in the Spanish Indexes. An Italian translation, printed in 1849, escaped the Index.

Pigault, Le Brun, *Le Citateur*, printed in 1803, prohibited in 1820. This work contains some bitter assaults on the Bible and on the dogmas of Christianity. Reiffenberg states that, in 1811, Napoleon, in a state of irritation with a brief of Pius VII, gave instructions for the distribution to the public, free or at a nominal price, of ten thousand copies of *Le Citateur*, but there is no record that these instructions were carried out. A Spanish version of the book, printed in London in 1816, was prohibited in Spain in 1819.

Essai historique sur la Puissance temporelle des Papes, printed in Paris in 1818, prohibited in 1823. No author's name is connected with any of the several editions of this treatise, but the introduction to the original issue states that the work was translated from a Spanish manuscript found at Saragossa.

After the Restoration, negotiations were in train during a series of years for a modification of the provisions of the Concordat of 1801. A series of controversial publications bearing upon the Concordat were placed upon the Index as they appeared.

Constant, Benjamin, *De la Religion Consideree dans sa Source*, etc., printed in 1824–1831, in five volumes, prohibited in 1827.

Gandolphy, Peter, *A Defence of the Ancient Faith, or Exposition of the Christian Religion*, printed (in London) in 1813, prohibited in 1818. Gandolphy was a priest of the Catholic Church and at the time of this publication had charge of the Spanish Chapel in London. The book had been promptly condemned by Pointer, Apostolic Vicar in London. Gandolphy journeyed to Rome and succeeded in securing for his book the approval of the master of the palace and a certificate giving him the authority to state that his book had been approved by the Holy See. On the strength of this certificate, he placed copies again on sale. Pointer secured from the Inquisition instructions to confirm the prohibition, and as this was still ignored by Gandolphy, the latter was suspended. After some years of controversy, the difficulty was finally adjusted by the correction of the text according to the specifications of Pointer.

Earle, Charles J., *The Forty Days, or Christ between His Resurrection and Ascension* and *The Spiritual Body*. These were printed in 1876 and 1878 and were prohibited in 1880. Earle had in 1851 been converted to Romanism.

In 1857, an association was instituted in England "for the promotion of the unity of Christendom." Its special purpose was to bring together the members of the Catholic, the Greek, and the English Churches. The members of the society accepted the obligation to make a daily prayer to this end. Cardinal Patrizzi declared in the name of the Inquisition, in a letter addressed, September, 1864, to the English bishops, that Catholics were forbidden to take part in this association. In 1866, Archbishop Manning confirmed this prohibition. Patrizzi had condemned in his first letter the *Union Review*, which was the organ of the society, but the *Review* was not placed on the Index. A series of essays on the reunion of Christendom, written by members of the society, and edited by F. G. Lee, was placed on the Index in 1867.

35. **Writings of German Catholics, 1814–1870.**—During the 19th century, were placed upon the Index a larger proportion than in the earlier period of the writings of the Catholics of Germany, but the selection of the works so distinguished appears as heretofore to have been arrived at with no very definite policy or principle. It is evident that the books were not selected on the ground either of their relative heresy, of their scholarly importance, or of their popular influence. It seems probable that the condemnation of any particular work was dependent upon the accident of its title being brought to the attention of the Congregation. The names of a few of the more noteworthy authors in the list are specified below.

Wessenberg, Vicar-General of Constance, *Die deutsche Kirche*, printed in 1806, condemned by a brief of Pius VII, in 1814.

Dannemayer, *Institutiones Historiae Ecclesiasticae*, printed (in Vienna) in 1780, prohibited in 1820.

Rechberger, *Enchiridion Juris Eccles. Austriaci*, printed in 1809, prohibited in 1819.

Reyberger, *Institutiones Ethicae Christ.*, printed in 1805–9, prohibited 1834.

Bolzano Bernhard (professor of geology in Prague),

Stunden der Andacht, printed in 1813, prohibited in 1828. It was largely on the ground of this work, which was published anonymously, that Bolzano was deposed from his professorship. *Lehrbuch der Religions-Wissenschaft*, printed in 1813, prohibited 1838.

Brendel, Sabold, professor of law in Würzburg, *Handbuch des kath. und protest. Kirchenrechts*, etc., printed in 1823, prohibited in 1824. Brendel retained his professorship but was later ordered to give up instruction in canon law.

Theiner, Anton., *Die katholische Kirche in Schlesien* (published anonymously), printed in 1826, prohibited the same year.

Müller, Alexander, *Handbuch des kath. und protest. Kirchenrechts*, printed 1829–1832, prohibited in 1833. It would appear that very few of the treatises on canon law or ecclesiastical jurisprudence were so written as to meet the approval of the Index authorities.

Hirscher, J. B., a treatise on the mass, entitled *Missae Genuinam Notionem Eruere*, etc., printed in 1821, prohibited in 1823.

Drey, G. S. von, a treatise on confession, entitled *Diss. Hist. theol. Originem et Vicissitudinem*, etc., printed, in 1815, prohibited in 1823.

Gehringer, *Liturgik und Theorie der Seelsorge*, printed in 1848, prohibited in 1850.

Hermes, George, *Die philosophische Einleitung in die christ. katholische Theologie*, printed in 1819, prohibited in 1831. The other writings by this author, together with a long series of treatises by his followers, were for the most part prohibited. It was contended by the Hermessians, as it had formerly been contended by the Jansenists, that the specific errors on the ground of which the condemnations had been arrived at did not as a matter of fact exist in the writings of Hermes. In May, 1837, six years after the death of Hermes, Professors Braun and Elvenich journeyed to Rome for the purpose of securing a fresh examination of the works of Hermes and of establishing their orthodoxy, but after a series of conferences, they failed to secure the recall of condemnation.

Günther, A., *Peregrins Gastmahl, Janusköpfe für Philosophie und Theologie*, and a group of similar writings published between 1830 and 1843, were condemned together in 1857. The Congregation of the Index began in 1851 to give special attention to Günther. In 1852, instructions were given by Pius IX to the bishop of Wurzburg to prohibit the teaching of the theories that had become known as the philosophy of Günther.

Trebisch, Leop. (classed as a follower of Günther), *Die christliche Weltanschauung in ihrer Bedeutung für Wissenschaft und Leben*, printed in 1858, prohibited in 1859.

Frohschammer, J., *Ueber den Ursprung der menschlichen Seelen*, printed in 1854, prohibited in 1857. The work of Frohschammer was brought upon the Index by the influence of the Jesuit Kleutgen. It is recorded that the secretary of the Congregation asked Dr. Döllinger, who was at the time in Rome, to induce Frohschammer to submit himself and to recall his treatise, but no such action was taken by the author. His later treatises, *Einleitung in die Philosophie, Der Grundriss der Metaphysik*, and *Ueber die Freiheit der Wissenschaft*, were prohibited together in 1862. He was suspended from his functions in 1863, and in 1871, placed under excommunication. In the introduction to the papal brief of 1863, Pius writes that he had learned with great sorrow that a number of the theologians and instructors in philosophy having chairs in the Catholic institutions of Germany had permitted themselves to bring into their teachings an unwarranted license of thought and of expression. The works through which these teachings were distributed to the general public were in many cases carrying most pernicious errors. These works, in so far as they had been examined and reported upon, the Pope had therefore ordered to be placed on the Index.

Oischinger, Paul J. N., who appears to have belonged to the same theological group with Frohschammer, is recorded as the author of a long series of philosophical works, only one of which was placed upon the Index: *Die spekulative Theologie des H. Thomas von Aquin*, printed in 1859, prohibited in 1859. Oischinger maintains that Thomas had wrongly comprehended a number of the most important divisions of the dogma of the Church.

Pichler, Aloys, *Geschichte der kirklichen Trennung zwischen dem Orient und Occident*, printed in 1865, prohibited in 1866. *Die Theologie des Leibnitz*, printed in 1869, prohibited in 1870.

36. La Mennais.—The writings of Abbé La Mennais had, even before 1830, brought out in France some measure of criticism. They had, however, secured the approval of Leo XII. After the Revolution of July, 1830, the opinions of La Mennais and his associates were condemned in Rome as in more ways than one pernicious. In August, 1832, Gregory XVI, in the encyclical entitled *Mirari*, condemned the ecclesiastical and political opinions presented in the journal issued by La Mennais and his associates under the title *L'Avenir*. No one of the writers was mentioned by name, but in a letter by Cardinal Pacca accompanying the encyclical, they were informed that the condemnation applied to their work. They all submitted themselves to the authority of the Church. After some negotiations, La Mennais, in December, 1833, gave his signature to a formula which had been sent from Rome for the purpose. A few months later, however, he brought into print a monograph entitled *Paroles d'un Croyant*, through the declarations in which he made a direct breach with Rome. In June, 1834, he received, through a separate encyclical, sharp condemnation. A year later, the Congregation placed on the Index the treatise *Affaires de Rome* and the subsequent writings were prohibited promptly on their appearance. The earliest publication of La Mennais, issued in 1809 under the title *Réflexions sur l'État de l'Église en France pendant le XVIIIme Siècle et sur la Situation actuelle*, was promptly suppressed by the imperial police, but was not placed upon the Index. The *Essai sur l'Indifférence en matières de Religion*, published in 1817-1820, was sharply criticised in France but was not condemned in Rome. The monograph *De la Religion Considérée dans ses Rapports avec l'Ordre Politique et Civile*, printed in 1826, was condemned by a number of the bishops and the author was sentenced by the courts to the payment of a large fine.

The journal *L'Avenir*, previously referred to, had for its purpose the maintenance of the independence of the Gallican Church against the encroachments of the Ultramontanes, and also the final separation of Church and State. The publication of the journal was suspended by the Government in 1831, and Lacordaire and Montalembert journeyed to Rome to present the case of its editors. A *Mémoire* written by Lacordaire was delivered in February, 1832, to Cardinal Pacca. In this, the memorialists asked the pope to have thorough investigation made of their purpose and actions and to give permission for the continuation of their work. After some weeks, Pacca gave decision on behalf of the pope that, while the good service rendered in the past by the memorialists was fully acknowledged, he found ground for grave disapproval of their later actions in stirring up controversies which tended to bring the authority of the Church into disrepute. While the matter was under consideration, an appeal came to Rome from thirteen of the bishops of France, asking the pope to confirm the condemnation of *L'Avenir* and specifying fifty-six propositions which were in themselves sufficient ground for its condemnation. This memorial secured later the support of fifty further French bishops. In September, 1832, La Mennais and his associates sent to Rome an acknowledgment of the decision of the pope and made promise that the journal *L'Avenir* should no longer be printed. In May, 1833, the pope sent to the Archbishop of Toulouse a brief in which he made reply to the memorial of the bishops. He pointed out that in the encyclical he had presented the sound and final doctrine of the Church and that he had taken measures to prevent the further circulation of the pernicious opinions complained of by the bishops.

In August, 1833, La Mennais sent to the pope through the Bishop of Rheims a letter in which he protests against the strictures expressed in the papal brief. He professes himself prepared to give the fullest possible acceptance to all provisions of the Holy See which have to do with matters of doctrine and of morals. He asks the pope to indicate the expressions occurring in his writings which are open to condemnation. In October, 1833, the pope replies to the Bishop of Rheims, pointing out certain statements by La Mennais the purport of which tends to undermine the authority of the Church. La Mennais had taken the ground that he was not undertaking to interfere with purely ecclesiastical questions. While in such matters he gave the fullest acceptance to the authority of the pope, he was not prepared to accept the judgment of the pope in matters that seemed to him to be outside of the proper authority of the Holy See.

In 1834, La Mennais published, under the title of *Affaires de Rome*, a report concerning his correspondence and relations with the Holy See. This was duly prohibited by the Congregation in 1835. *Le Livre du Peuple*, printed in 1837, was prohibited in 1838. The same course was taken with his later writings, appearing between 1841 and 1846. La Mennais died in February, 1854. The set of his works in five volumes, published after his death, 1855–1858, does not appear in the Index.

37. The Roman Revolution of 1848.—The operations of the Index Congregation were not intermitted on the ground of the absence of Pius IX from Rome, from November 25, 1848, to April 12, 1850. During this period, three sessions were held in Rome and two in Naples, and judgment was passed upon a number of the more important of the publications of the day. Among those condemned the following titles may be noted:

Rosmini, Antonio, *Die fünf Wunder der h. Kirche*, and *Die Verfassung gemäss der socialen Gerechtigkeit.*

Gisberti, V., *Der moderne Jesuit.*

Ventura, G., *Discorso funebre dei morti di Vienna*, etc. (The three titles in German are recorded in Italian.)

A few months before the condemnation of the two

treatises of Rosmini, his name had been under consideration with the pope for appointment as cardinal. His theological and philosophical writings had been denounced by his theological opponents as early as 1841, but, in 1843, Gregory XVI had ordered the controversies concerning the doctrines of Rosmini to be brought to a close. In 1850, the denunciation of the writings of Rosmini was renewed. The Congregation of the Index caused an examination of the works to be made by a number of consultors and, in 1854, the judgment was given that they were not to be disapproved, *dimittantur opera* This continued controversy concerning the philosophical and theological teachings of Rosmini brought about, in 1880, an authoritative definition of the formula *dimittantur.*

In November, 1848, Pius IX took refuge in Gaeta. Rosmini followed the Pope thither, but finding that the influence of his opponent, Cardinal Antonelli, was still controlling, he returned without securing any personal consideration. A series of negotiations, controversies, and correspondence followed, but it was not until 1854 that his works finally secured quittance. The question then placed before the Congregation was whether, as the writings of Rosmini had been thoroughly examined and had been shown to be free from errors in matters both of doctrine and morality, the prohibition that had been placed upon them ought not to be cancelled. The Jesuits were still unwilling to give up their contest against the teachings of Rosmini. They pointed out that the Inquisition held higher authority than that of the Congregation, and that in a number of instances books which had been passed with approval by the Congregation had been condemned by the Inquisition. Cornaldi, in a treatise printed in

1882, contended that the philosophy of Rosmini was distinctly opposed to the doctrines of St. Thomas. Leo XIII, in a brief addressed, in January, 1882, to the Bishops of Milan and Turin, reproves the attempts to renew the controversies concerning Rosmini and calls attention to his encyclical in which he had indicated the way by which all devout philosophers could arrive at a harmony of conclusion.

38. Traditionalism and Ontology, 1833-1880.—In 1833, Abbé Bautain of Strasburg was responsible for the initiating of certain controversies, in part philosophical and in part theological, which appear to have turned upon the proper interpretation of the doctrines so-called of Traditionalism and Ontologism. In 1870, these controversies were revived in Louvain and in Paris with the result of bringing out certain condemnations from the Congregation and from the Inquisition. In 1840, Bautain was compelled to subscribe to certain propositions formulated by the Congregation, and in 1855 his associate Bonnetty took the same course. In 1861, the Inquisition declared seven propositions, selected from the writings of Ubagh and other French Ontologists, to be heretical. Ubagh was compelled to correct certain treatises of his own according to specifications laid down by the Index; and, in 1866, after lengthy negotiations, his friends in Louvain were obliged to declare their acceptance of the reproval and of the conclusions of the Congregation and of the Inquisition. Ubagh held in the University of Louvain the chair of philosophy and logic.

39. Attritio and the Peccatum Philosophicum.—In addition to the Inquisition's decrees in which whole series of propositions were condemned, certain decrees were issued in which consideration was given to one or two propositions. In May, 1667, Alexander VII issued a decree in which, while not undertaking to decide the issue that had arisen concerning the sufficiency of incomplete repentance to secure absolution, he prohibited any writings which maintained that one view or the other of the matter was in itself heretical. In August, 1690, a decree of Alexander VIII condemns the two propositions, first, that the love of God is not requisite for the leading of a proper life, and, second, the theory that a sin which has been committed by some one who does not know God, or committed during a moment in which the sinner is not thinking of God, (the so-called philosophical sin as distinguished from the theological sin) is not to be classed as a mortal sin. These two definitions of the Inquisition resulted in the prohibition of a number of writings upon the questions. The most important of these was the *Amor poenitens* by Johannes Mercassel, Bishop of Castro, which, after a long series of investigations, was finally condemned in 1690, with a *d.c.*

The Council of Trent[1] had declared that the perfect repentance which has its motive in the love of God (*contritio caritate perfecta*) can secure reconciliation with God before the sacrament of confession may be received, but it does not free the believer from the requirement for this sacrament. The instruction says, further, that the incomplete repentance, the so-called *attritio*, which arises from a consideration of the shamefulness of the sin or is produced by a fear of the punishment of hell and which is therefore connected with the will to refrain from sin with the hope for forgiveness, can not of itself and without the sacrament of confession, bring about a reconciliation with God. Such a con-

[1] S 14 sec. Poen., c.

dition in the believer places him, however, by means of the sacrament of confession, in a position to secure grace. The doctrines presented in these instructions were, as above indicated, the texts for a long series of writings, many of which failed to secure with the Index authorities approval as orthodox.

40. Communism and Socialism, 1825–1860.—The selections from the long lists of works of those classed as socialists are but inconsiderable and, as in the case of certain other important divisions of literature, it is difficult to trace any plan or principle upon which they have been based. Proudhon is distinguished by having his entire series of works included in the Index, while of Saint-Simon (†1825) not a single volume has been condemned. Of the works of Charles Fourier (1768–1837), one book only has been selected for prohibition, *Le Nouveau Monde, Industriel et Sociétaire*, printed in 1829, prohibited in 1835.

Étienne Cabet (1788–1856) is represented in the Index by one only of his long series of treatises, *Le Vrai Christianisme*, printed in 1846, prohibited in 1848.

Esquiros. H. A. (†1876), has, next to Proudhon, the longest list in the Index of works belonging to this class. Of these the most important is *L'Évangile du Peuple*, printed in 1840, prohibited in 1841 This is followed by three socialist tracts entitled *Les Vierges Martyres, Les Vierges Folles, Les Vierges Sages*, printed in 1841, prohibited in 1842.

Further titles in this group are:

Constant. L. A., *La Bible de la Liberté*, printed in 1841, prohibited in the same year. The author was condemned to imprisonment for his works.

Chevé, Ch. Fr., *Le Dernier Mot du Socialisme, par un Catholique*, printed in 1848, prohibited in 1852.

41. Magnetism and Spiritualism, 1840-1874.—From the year 1840, the Inquisition published a series of decrees or opinions in regard to the theory of animal magnetism, but did not undertake to lay down any final conclusions. Certain expressions of opinion were also given in regard to the theories grouped under the name of spiritualism, but for this subject also there is wanting from the censorship authorities any authoritative or final word of counsel. From the long list of writings by the spiritualists of the time, only about a dozen were formally condemned. The list includes:

Kardec, Allan, *Revue Spirite, Journal d' Études Psychologiques*, 1858-1864; *Le Spiritisme à sa plus simple Expression*, printed in 1862, prohibited in 1864; *Le Livre des Esprits*, printed in 1863, prohibited in 1864.

Guldenstubbe, L. V., *Positive Pneumatologie*, printed in 1870, prohibited in 1874

Under magnetism may be noted:

Cahagnet, L. A., *Guide du Magnétiseur; Le Magnétisme Spiritualiste*.

With this group may also be classed the Memoir of Swedenborg by the Protestant theologian, J. Matter of Strasbourg, *Swedenborg, Sa Vie, ses Écrits et sa Doctrine*, printed in 1863, prohibited in 1864.

42. French Authors, 1835-1884.—Among the more important of the books by French authors which are represented in the Index during this half-century may be noted the following.

Ségur, Mgr. L. G. de (1881), *La Piété et la Vie Intérieure*, printed in 1864, prohibited in 1869. The name of the author is not recorded in the Index and it is stated that the omission was due to personal consideration for him. Ségur states, in an article printed in 1860, that the monograph, before being brought into print, had been passed upon with approval by a number of devout scholars. He said, further, that seventeen thousand copies had been distributed and that during the five years since the publication no criticism concerning it had come to him. He yields himself now to the authority of the Holy See and recalls the work from circulation.

Cloquet, Abbé. This author comes into the Index in 1864, on the ground of a series of monographs having to do with the subject of indulgences.

Alletz, P. A. (†1785), *Dictionnaire Portatif des Conciles*, printed in 1758 and re-issued in 1822, first prohibited (with a *d.c.*) in 1859.

Caron, L. H., Abbé, *La Vraie Doctrine de la Sainte-Église*, printed in 1852, prohibited in 1856.

Siguier, Aug., *Christ et le Peuple*, printed in 1835, prohibited in 1836.

Marne, M. G. de la, *La Religion Défendue contre les Préjugés et la Superstition*, printed in 1823, prohibited in 1843.

Quinet, Edgar (1803–1875), *Ahasuérus*, printed in 1833, prohibited in 1835; *La Génie de Religion*, printed in 1842, prohibited in 1844; *L' Allemagne et l' Italie*, printed in 1839, prohibited in 1848; *La Révolution*, printed in 1865, prohibited in 1866.

Michelet, J., *Mémoires de Luther* (a translation from the German), printed in 1835, prohibited in 1840; *Du Prêtre, De la Femme, De la Famille, L'Amour, La Sorcière, La Bible, De l'Humanité*, printed between 1845 and 1864, prohibited promptly after publication.

Mickiewicz, Adam (1798–1855), *L'Église Officielle et le Messianisme*, printed in 1843, prohibited in 1848.

Renan, E. The writings of this author ought properly to have come into the Index under the specification

Opera omnia. The Congregation appears to have taken prompt action concerning each book as soon as information of the publication came to hand, but a few titles escaped attention. The more important of those recorded are the following: *Le Livre de Job, Étude d'Histoire Religieuse, Origine du Langage, Histoire des Langues Sémitiques, Averroés et l'Averroisme, Vie de Jésus, L'Antéchrist, Les Évangiles, La Mort de Jésus.* (These books appeared between the years 1858 and 1884.)

Péyrat, Alphonse, *Histoire Élémentaire de Jésus,* printed in 1864, prohibited the same year.

Soury, Jules, *Jésus et les Évangiles,* printed 1878, prohibited 1878.

Scholl, *Le Procès de Jésus,* printed in 1878, prohibited 1878.

Havet, E , *Le Christianisme et ses Origines,* printed 1873, prohibited 1878.

Aube, B., *Histoire des Persécutions de l'Église; Histoire de l'Église; La Polémique Paienne à la fin du deuxième siècle; Le Christianisme dans l'Empire Romain,* printed 1876–1880, prohibited as published.

Larroque, P., *Examen des Doctrines de la Religion Chrétienne; L'Esclavage chez les Nations Chrétiennes,* printed in 1859–1864, prohibited as published. Later writings by this author were also placed on the Index, apparently in so far as their titles were brought to the attention of the Congregation.

Jacolliot, L., *La Bible dans l'Inde; Vie de Jezeus Chrishna,* an identification of Christ with the Chrishna of the Hindus, printed in 1869, prohibited the same year. A group of later writings by this author were also promptly condemned.

Rodrigues, H., *Les trois Filles de la Bible,* printed in

1865; *Les Origines du Sermon de la Montagne*, printed in 1868; *La Justice de Dieu*, printed in 1869; *Histoire du Premier Christianisme*, printed in 1873. The above books were prohibited together in 1877 with the specification: "these works are condemned in accordance with the Constitution of Clement VIII, issued in 1592, on the ground of their presenting Jewish writings which contain heresies and errors tending to undermine Christian doctrine."

Lajollais, Mlle. Nathalie de, *Le Livre des Mères des Familles sur l'Éducation Pratique des Femmes*, printed in 1845, prohibited (with a *d.c.*) in 1846.

Gréville, Mme. Henri, *Instruction Morale et Civile des Jeunes Filles*, printed in 1882, prohibited the same year.

Bert, Paul, *L'Instruction Civile à l'École*, printed in 1883, prohibited the same year. The volume of Bert had been officially adopted for use in the schools of Paris and also in certain other of the large cities. The decree of the Index was published by the Archbishop of Albi and by the Bishops of Annécy, Viviers, Langres, and Valence. The ecclesiastical authorities were sharply reproved by the magistracy for their interference in the matter and for their undertaking to criticise the action of the Government in a matter which, as it was claimed, belonged to the temporalities. In May, 1883, Minister Ferry, speaking in the Senate, says:

"We will never recognise as binding in a matter of this kind the conclusions or judgments of the Congregation of the Index. We propose to maintain free from interference the Gallican and the French tradition of the independence of the civil power. How is it possible to conceive that a Frenchman would be prepared to accept conclusions of a body like the Congregation which has in past years seen fit to condemn and to attempt to repress great spirits of humanity like Descartes, Malebranche, Kant, Renan, Bouillet? . . . I understand that a manual by Compayré was condemned because the author says that it is more important for a child to know the names of the Kings of France than those of the Kings of Judea. . . . This Index decree is sent out over the heads of our ambassador in Rome and of the Papal Nuncio in Paris in such manner as to arouse needless antagonism in France."

43. Italian Writings, 1840–1876.—Of the works by Italian authors condemned during this period, the following may be noted as indicating the policy of the Congregation.

Lazzeretti, David. *Opuscula omnia quocumque Idiomate edita*, printed in 1876, prohibited in 1878. Lazzeretti represented a mystic school of thought. He had for a time been in favour with Pius IX.

Gravina, D. B., *Su l'Origine dell' Anima*, printed in 1870, prohibited in 1875.

Nuytz, G. N., *Juris ecclesiastici Institutiones*, printed in 1844, prohibited in 1851. In this condemnation, the critics have taken the pains to specify certain propositions which are considered pernicious.

Zobi, Ant., *Storia civile della Toscana*, 1737–1848, prohibited in 1856.

Amari, Mich., *Storia dei Musulmani in Sicilia*, volume one, printed in 1845, prohibited in the same year. The following volumes of this work escaped condemnation.

Rusconi, Carlo, *La Repubblica Romana del 1849*, printed in 1849, prohibited in 1850.

Leva, Jus. de, *I Jesuiti e la Repubblica di Venezia*, printed in 1866, prohibited in 1873.

Cantu, E., *Storia Universale*, printed in 1858, prohibited in 1860.

Torti, Giov., *Un Abisso in Roma*, printed in 1864, prohibited (by the Inquisition) in 1865.

44. American Writings, 1822-1876.—The first work by an American author which finds place in the Index is a monograph by W. Hogan, a priest in Philadelphia, having to do with a controversy that had arisen concerning the Church of Saint Mary which Bishop Henry Conwell proposed to have consecrated as a cathedral. The action of the Bishop was contested in some fashion by the trustees acting on behalf of Hogan who wanted to retain his pastorate. Hogan's pamphlet was condemned in 1822. Hogan finally gave up the contest and at the same time left the Catholic Church and married. In 1864, was placed upon the Index a translation, printed in New York, of a monograph by Fr. Hollick, entitled *Guia de los Cassados o Historia Natural de la Generacion*.

Draper, J. W., *History of the Conflict between Religion and Science*, printed (in New York) in 1874, prohibited (in a Spanish version) in 1876.

Canada is represented in the Index of this period by the titles of two year-books issued by a literary association in Montreal, which, printed in 1858-9, were prohibited in 1864. In the year 1858, at which time the association contained seven hundred members, a proposition, submitted at the instance of certain ecclesiastics in the membership, was brought up for consideration, under which all non-Catholic members were to be excluded and two Protestant journals were to be removed from the reading-room. This proposal was voted down, and on that ground and also on the further complaint that the library contained pernicious literature, the Catholic members were called upon to leave the association. One hundred and fifty left and instituted a Catholic French-Canadian institute. The majority of the original association issued a statement declaring that the library contained no unworthy books and that, in any case, the decision concerning its literature rested with the managers of the association. In April, 1858, Bishop Bourget issued a pastoral brief in which he reminded the members of the old association that the reading or possession of heretical books involved the penalty of excommunication, and that any books recorded in the Index were to be classed as heretical. The institute was instructed to recall its action, and if it refused, the Catholic members were ordered to resign, under penalty of excommunication. Two hundred Catholics disregarded the command of the Bishop and remained members. They explained that they did not assert the right to read forbidden books, but they did maintain their right to remain members of a society in whose collections such books might be contained. In 1864, these Catholic members took the pains to place before the Bishop a catalogue of the library with the request that he would indicate the books classed as pernicious and with the suggestion that these books should be placed in a separate collection. To this proposition the Bishop paid no attention, whereupon seventeen of the members made direct appeal to Pope Pius IX. From the Pope they received no reply, but in July, 1869, the Bishop, then in Rome, sent to Montreal a pastoral brief in which he reported that the Inquisition declared the work of the institution to be pernicious. He reported, further, that the annual volume of the Canadian institute for 1868 (in which volume were contained certain addresses on toleration and freedom of conscience) had been condemned and that any person possessing or reading this year-book

or remaining in the institute had come into mortal
sin and must be refused the sacraments.   Later in the
year, a second memorial was addressed to the prefect
of the Propaganda by the Catholic members of the
institute, in which they stated that they accepted
without question the condemnation of the year-book.
To this memorial no reply was received.   The Bishop,
however, declared in a report to the vicar-general that
the submission rendered in this memorial was inade-
quate because the writers remained members of an
institute in which was maintained the righteousness
of religious toleration.   In November, 1869, died a
distinguished Catholic member of the institute named
Guibord, a man whose life had been above reproach.
The pastor and the other authorities refused to make
burial of the body even without religious ceremonies.
The widow secured a provisional interment in uncon-
secrated ground.   She then instituted a suit demanding
the right of burial in consecrated ground.   The suit
continued until after her death in 1873.   In November,
1874, the judicial committee of the priory council in
London decided that the body was entitled to burial
in the consecrated ground of his pastoral church and
decided further that the Church authorities must
provide for the very considerable expenses of the suit.
The re-burial took place in November, 1875, after
the Church authorities had filed a protest and had
ordered faithful Catholics to take no part in the
ceremonies.   The record is of value in the history of
censorship proceedings as an example of the over-
riding by the authority of the State of a decision of
the Church, in regard to a matter which had heretofore
been held as belonging strictly within ecclesiastical
control, namely the right of burial in consecrated

ground. In 1870, a later annual giving the record of the conclusion of the process, was condemned by the Inquisition.[1]

The contributions to the Index from the literature of South America are for this period more considerable than those from the United States and Canada. The following titles indicate the direction of the censorship.

Vidaurre, Manuel Lorenzo de, *Proyecto del codigo eclesiastico*, printed (in Paris) in 1830, condemned in 1833. The author, a doctor of law of the University of Lima, was Chief Justice of the Supreme Court of Peru. His "project" proposed certain rather radical changes in ecclesiastical regulations. *Tratado sobre Denaciones*, printed (in Madrid) in 1820, prohibited in 1833. In the same year were placed upon the Index three monographs by Vidaurre, one on the Bishop of Rome and the condition of the Church, the second on Celibacy, and the third on Confession.

Vigil, Francisco P. G. de, *Defensa de la Autoridad de los Gobiernos y de los Obispos contra las Pretenciones de la Curia Romana*, printed (in Lima) in 1848, prohibited in 1851. The author was a priest and at the time of his death Curator of the National Museum at Lima. The work, issued in six volumes, octavo, gives consideration to almost every detail of the organisation of the Church. *Manual de Derecho Publico Eclesiastico, and Dialogos sobre la Existencia de Dios y la Vida futura, á la Juventud Americana*, printed (in Lima) in 1863, prohibited in 1864. Vigil died in June, 1875. He had declined to submit himself to the condemnation of the Church and he was therefore refused the last sacraments. The Congress of Peru directed, however, that he should have the honour of a public funeral.

[1] Reusch iii., 1201.

La Riva, J. F., *El Espiritu del Evangelio comparado con las Practicas de la Iglesia Catolica,* printed (in Lima) in 1867, prohibited in the same year.

Fotvárad, Carlos H. de, *O Casamento civil,* etc., printed (in Rio Janeiro) in 1858, prohibited in 1859. This monograph was written in reply to a treatise, published in Rio in 1858, by Canon de Campo. The author undertook to maintain the exclusive authority of the Church (as against the State) in all matters connected with marriage. *Las Biblias falsificadas,* etc., printed (in Rio) in 1867, prohibited in 1869. This was a further criticism of the utterances of de Campo.

D'Aranjo, M. R. (Bishop of Rio). *Elementos dé direito Eclesiastico publico,* etc., printed (in Rio) in 1857, prohibited in 1869. *Compendio de Theologia Moral,* printed (in Oporto) in 1858, prohibited in 1869.

Monte, Carmelo J. de, *O Brazil Mystificado na Questao religiosa,* printed in 1875, prohibited in 1876.

Mexico is represented in the Index of the period by a treatise entitled *Conducta,* the work of D. J. C. Portugal, Bishop of Michoachon, printed (in Mexico) in 1835, prohibited in 1840; and by two treatises of N. Pizarro, *Catecismo Politico Constitucional,* and *Catecismo de Moral,* printed in 1867, prohibited in 1869.

45. Periodicals, 1832–1900.—In 1832, the Congregation of the Index issued a declaration stating that the regulations of the Index of Trent (renewed in the succeeding Indexes) concerning ecclesiastical censorship, covered material printed in journals as well as that published in books. After the year 1848, however, the attempt to enforce in Rome ecclesiastical censorship, over the contents of journals as given up was impracticable. It was pointed out that no advantage could be secured in placing upon the Index journal issues of a back date, the reading of which had already been completed.

During the 18th century, however, various attempts were made to control the literary policy of journals the managers of which were within reach of ecclesiastical authority, and during the 19th century, censorship decrees were issued in regard to a number of journals which concerned themselves with ecclesiastical subjects. The only practicable measure to take against journals the articles in which are judged to be pernicious in their influence is to prohibit the faithful from reading or from possessing copies of the same. It has, however, been found convenient, in the cases in which such prohibitions appeared to be called for, to have the same issued and enforced, not by the Congregation, but by the local authorities.

After 1850, the Minister of the Interior in the papal States printed lists of the foreign journals the reading of which was forbidden.

1862. December. Adames, Apostolic Vicar of Luxemburg, declared in a pastoral letter that the publisher of the *Courier de Luxemburg* and his editors were excommunicated. The subscribers and readers of the journal were to be excluded from the sacraments on the ground that they were helping to support a work of Satan. The publisher took the matter into the courts, but the judges dismissed the complaint against Adames, taking the ground that his action was within his ecclesiastical and legal rights. (Vering, *Archiv*, X, 422, XII, 172.)

In 1863, the Patriarch of Venice and the ten Venetian bishops, in a pastoral letter, prohibited the reading of three journals specified.

1870. Melchers, Archbishop of Cologne, published

an instruction against the *Rheinische Merkur*, with which instruction the Bishop of Mayence and the Capitular-Vicar of Münster concurred. The Bishop of Paderborn issued an edict forbidding, as a mortal sin, the possession of a copy of the journal. No action appears to have been taken by the publishers, possibly because the circulation of the *Merkur* was not seriously affected by these episcopal fulminations.

1871. Under instructions of Pius IX, a circular letter was issued by Cardinal Vicar Patrizzi to the pastors or parish priests directing them to forbid to their parishioners the reading of certain Roman journals. The list included *La Libertà*, *Il Capital*, *Il Tempo*, *La nuova Roma*, *La Vita Nuova*, and six others. Disobedience to this order was to be classed as a grievous sin. In 1873, a papal brief gave certain general instructions in regard to journals. It pointed out that these were covered by rules 2 and 7 of the Index. Papers were to be considered sheet by sheet, simply as open books. Permission might be accorded to a person to whom the information was necessary, to read in heretical or dangerous papers the political or financial articles, but the permission should be strictly limited to these portions of the journal.

In 1882. September, the Patriarch of Venice prohibited in like manner the reading of *Il Veneto Christiano*, and of *Fra Paolo Sarpi*, as "godless, blasphemous, and heretical productions." The Patriarch declared that the publisher and those who read these journals with belief were excommunicated.

1885. February. The Archbishop Magnasco, of Geneva, condemned the *Epoca* Editor, publisher, distributor, and readers were alike condemned to excommunication. Whoever buys or reads a number, or gives it to another, has committed mortal sin.

46. The Roman Question, 1859-1870.—Between the years 1859-1861, a number of monographs and volumes, chiefly by French writers, were brought into print that had to do with the question of the political authority of the Papacy. These French theories brought out a full measure of criticism and condemnation. Among the works thus reproved was a treatise by La Guérronnière, *La France, Rome et l'Italie*, printed in 1861, in regard to which Cardinal Antonelli issued a specific condemnation. No single title of the group is, however, to be found in the Index. The monograph by La Guérronnière expressed, as was well understood, the views of the Emperor Napoleon III, and had probably been written at the Emperor's suggestion. A companion volume was published about the same time by Edmund About and this also was sharply condemned not only by Cardinal Antonelli but also by a number of the French bishops, including Dupanloup. The list of the Italian controversial publications on this question is also considerable. The earlier works had to do simply with the political authority of the pope, but since 1870, a number of writers have given attention to the desirability, on the ground of the welfare of Italy and also of that of the Church universal, of the reconciliation of the Papacy with the Government of the United Italy. These writings were met with sharp condemnation on the part of Pius IX and Leo XIII and of the supporters of the civil authority of the Papacy, but in only few instances was action taken in regard to them by the Congregation of the Index.

47. The Council of the Vatican, 1867-1876.—The conclusions reached by the council held in the Vatican in 1867 resulted in the publication of a number of controversial works of which certain titles found their way into the Index. The more important of these are the following:

Michelis, Fr., *Fünfzig Thesen über die Gestaltung der kirchlichen Verhältnisse der Gegenwart*, printed in 1867, condemned in 1868.

Renouf, Le Page, *La Condamnation du Pape Honorius*, printed in 1868, prohibited in the same year.

"Janus" (the name adopted for the moment by Döllinger) *Der Papst und das Concilium*, printed in 1869, prohibited in the same year.

Wallon, Jean, *La Vérité sur le Concile*, printed in 1872, prohibited in 1873.

Dupanloup, Archbishop, *Testament Spirituel de Montalembert*, and *La Cour de Rome et la France*, printed in 1871, prohibited in 1872.

Pressensé, *Le Concile du Vatican*, printed in 1872, prohibited in 1876.

In 1870, the general Congregation published a protest, signed by a number of members of the council, calling for the specific condemnation of a series of newspapers, articles, and pamphlets in which the work of the council had been criticised. The secretary of the Congregation of the Index reported, however, that it did not seem wise to take action. During the years 1871 and 1872, were, however, condemned by the Inquisition a number of periodical articles on the work of the council by such authors as Lord Acton, Berchtold, Friedrich, Ruckgaber, Schulte, Zirngiebl, and others.

48. Example of a License.—A license given by the inquisitor-general of Spain to Dr. Andrew Sall in June,

1652, states that he was permitted to keep and to read prohibited books for use in connection with the writing of any doctrinal or devotional books or treatises. The holder of the license was charged with the duty of giving information to his Grace of any censurable propositions that he might find in books, ancient or modern, which might not already have been comprehended in the expurgatory Index. The license was marked as duly entered in the record of licenses, the page (Number 138) giving indication of a considerable series of licenses outstanding. These instruments were renewed from year to year. Dr. Sall relates that with the second grant came a complaint that he had reported no censurable propositions. He had excused himself by saying that he had not had in his hands any Protestant books; but he gave specification of some perverse and apparently heretical doctrines he had found in certain books which were approved and were much in use with themselves. He gave as an example citations from the Commentaries on Esther by de Murcia:

Etiam Deus Op. Max. proposita ante oculos morte in meliora contendat; and

Etiam demon morte ante oculos constituta contendit in meliora.[1]

Sleumer gives the following example of the form in force to-day (1906) for an application for the permission to read forbidden books.

" To the very reverend Vicar-General of the diocese: The undersigned respectfully request permission for the reading of certain books which have been specifically forbidden in the Index or which in their class come under the general provisions of the Index. The requirement is based upon the following grounds: . . .

[1] Cited by Mendham, 138.

"The undersigned feels assured that the proposed use of this forbidden literature may be made by him on these grounds without any undermining of his faith or any interference with his conscientious duty to the Holy Church." [1]

[1] Sleumer, 39.

CHAPTER VIII

THE CENSORSHIP OF THE STATE AND CENSORSHIP BY PROTESTANTS

1. General.
2. Catholic States: Catholic Germany, France, Spain and Portugal.
3. Protestant States: Switzerland, Protestant Germany, Holland, Scandinavia, England.
4. Summary.

1. General.—In this chapter, I am undertaking to present, not any comprehensive summary of political censorship, a task which would in fact require many volumes, but merely certain noteworthy examples of regulations issued under civil authority which will serve to indicate the general character of the censorship supervision of literature that was attempted by the State.

I have grouped together here instances of Catholic censorship in which the ecclesiastics carried out their prohibitions under the authority of the State, or in which the State censorship regulations had been put into shape by the ecclesiastics. In the record of the so-called Protestant censorship, that is to say of the regulations adopted in Protestant States for the control of theological or religious literature, it is not practicable to separate the acts and utterances of the theologians from those emanating from the civil authorities, whether municipal or national. The larger number of the prohibitions of books having to do with theology or religion were naturally initiated by the divines, although even for this class of literature the civil authorities frequently did not hesitate to take into their own hands the responsibility of selecting the works to be condemned.

The chief distinction, however, between the censorship methods of Protestant communities and those which came into force in Catholic States was the fact that for the former the censorship authorities were dependent for the enforcement of the prohibitions and penalties upon the machinery of the civil authority. The Protestant divines had at their command no such dread penalty as the ban of excommunication by means of which the Catholic ecclesiastics were able to enforce upon the faithful obedience to the commands of the Church. In the Protestant States, it was necessary for the divines, first, to convince the rulers of the essential importance of their particular creeds or forms of "orthodoxy," in order to secure the enactment of the necessary laws or the issue of censorship edicts; and, secondly, to keep the magistrates up to the mark in the enforcing of the penalties prescribed.

It is true that in Catholic States, such as France, Austria, or Bavaria, the authority of the Crown and the machinery of the civil power were frequently utilised to carry out censorship regulations that had been framed by the ecclesiastics; but even with the citizens of those States (as far at least as they were Catholics) the most pertinent influence in insuring obedience for the prohibitions of the Index was the dread of being deprived of the rites of the Church. Excommunication meant that the adults were prohibited from marriage and their children were deprived of baptism; it meant that for the living there was no communion, for the dying, no absolution, and for the dead, no burial in consecrated ground. Life without the sacraments was full of fears, and with the deprival of absolution and of Church burial, death took on new terrors. These same influences were, of course, all-important also in securing the active co-operation even of the most worldly and most skeptical of the civil rulers in creating and in maintaining the machinery for controlling the operations of the printers and book-sellers and for enforcing adequate civil or criminal penalties against heretical delinquents who were not amenable to the authority of the Church.

In the States in which in this fashion the co-operation of Catholic rulers could be secured in support of the censorship policy of the Church universal, the administration of such censorship was, of course, more consistent, and it is fair to say less arbitrary (at least outside of Spain) than in the Protestant States in which the principles of prohibition changed from decade to decade with the changes of administration or as one theological faction or another secured influence with the rulers.

In 1904, the Jesuit Father, Joseph Hilgers, published, under the title *Der Index der verbotenen Bücher*, a treatise presenting, from the point of view of an earnest upholder of the authority of the Roman Church, an historical study of the Roman Index. The immediate text for the production of this treatise of the learned Father was the publication, in 1900, of the second Index of Leo XIII, of which Index the Father gives a comprehensive description and analysis. Father Hilgers takes the ground that it was impossible for the Church, without neglecting its manifest duty,

to avoid accepting the responsibility for the supervision and control of literary production and of the
reading of the faithful. The pope, says the Father,
is, as the head of the Church on earth, the direct representative of God. It is through him that God makes
known his wishes and the principles upon which the
life of the faithful is to be guided. It is for the shepherd
of the flock to preserve the flock from poison. The
shepherd is charged not merely with the right living
of his sheep during their earthly career, but with the
much larger responsibility of seeing that their lives
are so shaped that they shall secure a blessed hereafter.

In the historical sketch of the operations of the Index,
Hilgers touches but lightly upon the examples of inconsistencies or difficulties in the enforcement by the
Church of the control over literature. He makes no
mention of the many contests that arose between
the different ecclesiastical bodies. He hardly touches
upon the fact that the Index came to be from time to
time an expression of theological differences between
the great Church bodies or Orders such as, for instance,
the Jesuits and the Dominicans or the Jesuits and the
Franciscans. He has nothing to say about the instances
in which the utterances of successive popes came into
conflict with each other. He also barely makes mention
of the contentions, maintained in Spain as in France,
of the right of the national Church, acting in co-operation with the national Government, to decide what
principles should be maintained for the supervision of
the literature of the nation. His big treatise, comprehensive in many respects, is very curious in its
omissions. In dwelling upon the beneficent influence
of this Church censorship, he omits altogether the
record of the control of this censorship by the In-

quisition in Spain. He has nothing to say about the imprisonment or execution of Spanish heretics whose crime had consisted in the production, the selling, or the reading of books classed as heretical. If the reader had no other knowledge of the Index than that which came to him by the history as presented by Hilgers, he would have before him simply a record of an administration of fatherly beneficence on the part of wise advisers, of a pleading with the perverse that they should be saved from the consequences of their own perversity; of actions furthering all scholarship that was in itself wholesome and sound, and of the discouragement simply of such perverted intellectual efforts as tended to lead men away from their duty to their Creator and to undermine the moral conduct of their own lives.

Hilgers is not prepared to admit that any of the works repressed by the Church, or the repression of which was undertaken by the Church, could have constituted, if permitted free circulation, or do actually constitute as far as, in spite of the opposition of the Church, they secure such circulation, any additions of value to the intellectual life of mankind. He would probably, if the question had been put to him directly, have taken the ground that no intellectual gain could sufficiently offset the moral or spiritual loss. In maintaining the contention that any properly ruled community must accept a supervision of its literary activities, he naturally lays stress upon the long series of censorship systems which were undertaken by ecclesiastics or by the civil rulers of Protestant States. He calls attention to the series of so-called Protestant (theological) Indexes, and he adds a very considerable list of instances of political censorship. He is able to point out that the number of books which have come under condemnation through this Protestant censorship (including the censorship undertaken directly by the civil authorities) very much exceeds the books condemned in the whole series of Roman Indexes, although in this comparison he omits all Indexes which came into publication outside of Rome.

He does not take pains to present any results of the effectiveness of these Protestant Indexes. In omitting the record of the censorship of the Spanish Inquisition, he is able to avoid any reference to the fact that the censorship machinery put into force by the Inquisition was, for the territory controlled by it, thoroughly effective; so that if a book was condemned in Spain, it was the case, for the centuries in question, that, as far as Spanish territory was concerned, the editions were thoroughly suppressed and the production or distribution of copies was rendered impossible. He speaks of each of the censorship edicts of the German States as if they had effect throughout the whole of the territory of Germany. He omits to point out that the books condemned in one city or in one State promptly came into print and into circulation in adjacent territory in such manner that the circulation was practically unchecked.

He is able, however, fairly to make out his main contention, that for the century succeeding the Protestant Reformation, the will or desire on the part of the Protestants to establish a censorship of literature was just as emphatic as that of the authorities of Rome; and that if their efforts were only partially successful, it was through no want of conviction on their part that such efforts were required for the maintenance of what they considered to be the true Faith. He is able to make good the further contention that these examples

of Protestant censorship present a much larger series
of inconsistencies than could be found in the record of
the Index of the Church of Rome; even though one
should for the purpose of the comparison include under
the Church Index, in addition to those printed in Rome,
the Indexes that emanated from Madrid, Louvain, and
Paris. He also makes his point good in regard to
the political Index. He is able to show that, as far at
least as the edicts of the State were concerned, these
were more bitter, more comprehensive, and more regardless of literary interests than those of the Church.
What he does not emphasise is that these political
edicts were very much more spasmodic and tempor-
ary in their influence, and that, as a fact, they had
very little continued effect on the literary development of the communities which were responsible for
them.

A political censorship becomes of necessity the foot-
ball of political parties and is therefore not to be maintained with any measure of consistency or justice.
The multiplicity and changeableness of the religious
doctrines of the reformers gave to the so-called Protestant censorship an inconsistent and contradictory
character which is not to be paralleled under any epoch
of Roman supervision of literature. A censorship of
this kind is the natural product of the fissure of creeds.
Hermann Wagener, writing in Berlin in 1864, remarks
that all the measures of the State thus far attempted
to protect the public against pernicious influences from
the printing-press, are open to the criticism that their
action is purely negative. On the other hand, as he
points out, the censorship policy of the Catholic Church,
while on the one hand prohibitory, on the other asserts
positive and constructive principles for the literary and

intellectual development of the community by wholesome and wise methods.

It is true, says Hilgers, that the works of great writers
like Tasso, Molière, Châteaubriand, Vondel, Goethe,
Schiller, Grotius, and other leaders of thought have
come under the ban of censorship and that the publication or use of their works had been permitted only
after certain eliminations or purgations had been made.
The censorship regulations in regard to these authors
emanated however not from Rome but from the
authorities of France, Holland, Germany, and Denmark.
It was the case even with *Faust* that its production
could not be permitted on the stage of Berlin until
certain " dangerous " passages had been eliminated.

2. Catholic States.—The Edict of Worms of 1521,
which committed the Emperor Charles V to the support
Catholic   of the contentions of the Papacy, and threw
Germany   the great weight of the Holy Roman Empire against the cause of the Protestant reformers,
constituted the beginning of an imperial censorship, a
censorship which was confirmed and extended by the
Edict of Nuremberg of 1524 In the regions under
Lutheran influence, the only effect of the imperial and
ecclesiastical prohibition was, as noted, to increase
largely the circulation of the writings of the reformers.
In the districts into which the reform doctrines had
only begun to penetrate, the ecclesiastics were able,
in great part at least, to stop the further circulation of
the pamphlets, by taking prompt and harsh measures
against the colporteurs. From this time and until the
close of the Thirty Years' War, Church and State
(the imperial State) worked together (although not
always in harmony) against the freedom of the press,
on the broad ground that such freedom necessarily

resulted in heresy and in treason. In 1529, the persecution of the printers and of the Protestants in Austria was for the time relaxed because of the peril of Vienna from the Turks, an exigency which absorbed the full attention of the imperial authorities.

The Church and the Holy Roman Emperor finally took the ground that every writing that came from the pen of a Protestant author, even though it had nothing whatsoever to do with religion or politics, must be classed as libellous. In 1548, the Emperor issued a new series of most strenuous laws for the control of the press. The penalties were brought to bear at one point or another with full severity, but it proved to be impracticable to secure in the Germany of the time any uniformity of obedience. In Austria and in Bavaria, the penalties included the use of the rack for authors, printers, and sellers of publications that came under condemnation. In 1567, a *Flugschrift* was printed in Frankfort under the title of *Nachtigall,* which was at once interpreted as a libel on the Emperor. Fourteen hundred copies were sold within a few hours of its issue and there were various reprints within the next few weeks. The Emperor ordered the punishment not only of the printer, but of the magistrates of Frankfort. The former was placed in prison for two years and the magistrates were fined thirty thousand gulden, an enormous sum for those days.[1]

The Emperor Ferdinand was a more faithful, that is to say, a more bigoted, son of the Church than Charles, but he refused to admit that the control of the press was a Church matter. He took the ground that censorship was a matter pertaining to the State, that is, to the Crown, and that the bishops could

[1] Kapp, 548.

take part in it only as delegates of the authority
of the State. This was the contention asserted, and
finally maintained, in France by Francis I and his
successors.

In an official document of 1580, occurs the phrase,
"The regulation of books (*das Bücher-regal*) which has
for many years been within the control of the emperor."
Schurmann is of opinion that the authority for the
regulation of books was derived from, or connected
with, the rights reserved to the imperial authority
under the Golden Bull. A century after the issue of
the Golden Bull, at the time namely of the invention
of printing, the reserved powers (*Reserva-rechte*) of the
empire had become materially weakened, and were
being in large part exercised by the local authorities,
and the attempt of the emperor to enforce control
over literary production and distribution was from the
outset met by antagonism and protest on the part of
princes and of the municipal magistrates, and was also
opposed by the contention of the Church that such
supervision properly belonged to her. The question
was raised as to whether the decrees of the imperial
Diet contained any references to the imperial control
of book publishing. The omission was explained on
the ground that such control was exercised as a personal
right of the emperor. It was under such imperial
authority, for instance, that an approval or privilege
was given to the *Germania* of Aeneas Sylvius (afterwards Pius II), originally issued in Italy in 1464 and
printed in Germany in 1515.

In 1530, there came to Vienna a group of Jesuits
who did much to strengthen the machinery of censorship. The undertakings of the printers and of the
booksellers decreased in direct proportion with the

growth of the influence of the Jesuit advisers of the emperor. In 1523, the production and sale throughout the empire of the German Bible is prohibited. In 1564, the Elector of Bavaria orders that the work of the publishers must be restricted to printers whose Catholic orthodoxy has been duly tested. In this year, the Elector begins the issue of an annual list of books that were to be permitted. In 1569, the use in the schools of Bavaria of certain Latin classics, including the works of Virgil, Horace, and Ovid, was prohibited. In 1616, the Elector appointed Catholic commissioners of censorship for each town in Bavaria. The University of Ingolstadt became the centre of the work of the Jesuits, who, in Bavaria as in Vienna, had secured the direction of censorship.

In 1579, under Rudolf II, the Jesuits were called upon to put into shape a more effective censorship for the empire. Under the régime thus established, the standard of thought for the political action and for the religious belief of Germany was to be fixed in Rome and in Madrid. Under the direction of the Jesuit censors in the year 1579, no less than twelve thousand books in German and two thousand in Bohemian were burned by the public hangman in the town of Gratz.[1]

In the same year, an imperial commission was appointed, with headquarters at Frankfort, which was charged with the supervision of the book production of the empire. The operations of this commission were very largely controlled by the interests, real or imaginary, of the Catholic Church, and the personal supervision and arbitrary censorship of the ecclesiastics, had not a little to do with the disintegrating of publishing under-

[1] Kapp, 551.

takings in Frankfort and with the transfer, some years later, to Leipsic of the leadership in the business of book production and book distribution.

Hilgers, while admitting the influence of the Jesuits in the direction of State censorship in South Germany, denies that the results of their work were adverse to the development of literature ("sound literature") or to intellectual activity. Hilgers writes: "It may at once be admitted that the Jesuit Fathers were, during the 16th century, active in securing in Austria, Bavaria, and other States a censorship of literature. The Holy Ignatius, Father of the Order, had from the beginning of his active work insisted upon the responsibility resting with the Church and with the active workers of the Church for preserving the faithful from the poison of literature." [1] In 1550, and in the years following, Peter Canisius, at that time the head of the Order in Germany, took active measures for the enforcement throughout the empire of the regulations of the Index of Paul IV, and after the publication, in 1564, of the Index of Trent, the Jesuit Fathers in Germany had a large part in bringing about the enforcement of the regulations therein presented. Hilgers points out that, under Jesuit influence, there were issued in Bavaria during the years succeeding 1565 not only lists of books condemned and prohibited, but further lists of books commended for the reading of the faithful. These catalogues had been prepared by the Jesuit Fathers at the instance of Canisius and under the authority of Duke William V. They were distributed chiefly through the parish priests. Against the contention made by German historians that the influence of the Jesuits, particularly in South Germany, had

---

[1] Hilgers, 192.

served to restrict, and in certain instances practically to repress, literary production and publishing activity, Hilgers insists that in Germany, as throughout Europe, the influence of the Order had always been an intellectual influence; and that its efforts had furthered education and had advanced the interests of scholarly literature, of printing, and of publishing. He contends with some ingenuity that the elimination from literary production of activity in undesirable productions and the concentration of literary force in the channels in which such force could be directed to the best service of humanity, far from lessening intellectual or literary force, could but serve to strengthen this and to render it more effective.[1]

During the first half of the 16th century, there may well have been ground for a censorship of literature in Germany in connection with the long series of lampoons and libellous tractates and volumes that came into print. Even leaders of thought such as Luther and Reuchlin, were tempted into language that became not only unscholarly, but coarsely abusive. The more earnestly the community interested itself in religious convictions, the more bitter became the expression of hate and scorn for other earnest believers who had arrived at different convictions.

It is certainly not in order to hold the Jesuits responsible for the general censorship policy of Rome. The direction of the Roman censorship has never been in Jesuit hands. The first secretary of the Congregation of the Index was a Franciscan, while all the succeeding secretaries have been Dominicans. Hilgers does not mention one detail in regard to which this Dominican control of the Congregation has doubtless been import-

---

[1] Hilgers, 205.

ant: of the books on the Index which were the work
of members of the great Catholic Orders, those of the
Jesuits equal in number all of the others together.
One cause for this was probably the fact that this Order
included a larger proportion of educated workers. The
literary interests of the Jesuits were greater and so
also was the number of books produced by them.

During the second half of the 18th century, the
censorship commissions instituted by the State were
given powers under which the authority of the censorship bodies of the Church was materially modified
and restricted. In Austria, a number of Indexes were
compiled by these civil commissions, and in Bavaria
one such Index was published. These Indexes have
importance chiefly because they represent a claim made
on the part of the State to control certain matters which,
according to the ecclesiastics, properly belonged within
the exclusive domain of the Church.

In 1752, Maria Theresa, for the purpose of checking
the distribution throughout the Austrian dominions
of Protestant writings, issued an edict ordering all
Catholics to submit to their confessors the copies of
religious books in their possession. The confessors
were to retain all doubtful works and to return the
others duly certified with their signatures and with an
ecclesiastical seal. In 1756, the bookbinders were
instructed to deliver to the parish priests copies of any
Protestant writings placed in their hands for binding.

In 1753, the examination of books that were already
in print, together with the censorship of works submitted for the purpose of securing a printing permit,
was transferred from the University of Vienna to a
censorship commission which was charged with the
work both of censorship and revision. This commis-

sion was appointed under the imperial authority and remained in existence until 1848. It issued from time to time catalogues of prohibited books. Books were in part prohibited unconditionally, and in part with the restriction that they should be placed only in the hands of scholars who had secured from the police authorities a special permission for their use.

In 1754, was published the first Austrian Index. It bears the title *Catalogus librorum rejectorum per Concessum censurae*. After 1758, the lists bore the title of *Catalogus librorum a Commissione Aulica prohibitorum*.

Between the years 1758 and 1780, were issued continuations of the Aulic catalogues. Later, the system obtained of printing fortnightly lists of books which had failed to secure an *Imprimatur* or *Admittetur*, these lists being distributed to police magistrates, libraries, and booksellers. Every two months the same were classified and reprinted.

In 1768, was published in one volume the series of catalogues covering the prohibitions of the preceding seven years. The title reads: *Catalogus Librorum a Commissione Caes. Reg. Aulica Prohibitorum. Vienna mdcclxviii. Prostat. in officiana Libraria Kaliwodiana.* With this volume, are bound in supplements to a preceding Austrian Index, numbered from I to VI, comprising annual lists for the six years succeeding 1761. The work was reprinted in Vienna in 1774 with further annual lists. Similar issues were made, with annual supplements, in 1776, 1777, and 1778. These volumes contain lists only, with no prefatory matter and no reference to the authority under which the condemnations are made. The selections presented a much larger proportion of English books (including plays and novels) than have received attention in any other Continental Indexes. Of Melanchthon only two works are condemned. Mendham points out that the Aulic Council, which was undoubtedly the authority for the preparation of these lists of prohibitions, was at the time composed of an equal number of Romanists and Protestants. The Aulic Indexes are probably the only examples of prohibitions arrived at by the judgment of Catholics and Protestants working together under the authority of the State.

In 1788, was published in Brussels an Index for use in the Austrian Netherlands, under the title *Catalogue des livres défendus par la Commission Impériale et Royale.*

The *Enchiridion Juris Ecclesiastici Austriaci,* edited by Rechberger and printed in Vienna, in 1808, presents the ecclesiastical law of Austria at that date in force. Rechberger declares in his preface that the " Index of Trent has no force in the Austrian dominions."[1]

In 1816, was published in Vienna a general Index of German books under the title *Neues durchgesehenes Verzeichniss der verbotenen deutschen Bucher.*

In the earlier Vienna Indexes, are included the titles of certain works selected from the Roman Index, but it is difficult to arrive at the principle on which the selection has been made.

In 1769, under Max Joseph III, was instituted in Bavaria a "College of Censorship" comprising, in addition to the president, eight councillors. The subjects of theology and of ecclesiastical procedure were placed in the hands of three divines selected from the

[1] See also Appendix to the report from the Select Committee concerning the laws in foreign States respecting Roman Catholic subjects, 1816, cited by Mendham, 247.

theological faculty of the University of Munich and the other councillors included representatives from the philosophical faculty.

Municipal Censorship.—An early instance of the exercise of a city censorship occurred in Nuremberg, in 1527, in the case of a volume containing woodcuts illustrating the history of the Tower of Babel, for which cuts a rhyming text had been supplied by the cobbler-poet, Hans Sachs. The book had been printed without a license or permission from the magistracy. The magistrates decided that the book must be suppressed. They further cautioned Sachs that the writing of verses was not his proper business, and that he should keep to his own trade of shoemaking. The edict was simply an emphatic reiteration of the old proverb. "Shoemaker, stick to your last." The difficulty in this case appears to have been due not to the Lutheran tendencies of Sachs's rhymes, but to the lack of respect shown to the magistrates in issuing a book without a permit: and to the further breach of authority on the part of a man licensed only as a shoemaker undertaking also to carry on the avocation of a poet.

In France, the first State regulations for the control of the press date from 1521, and were directed against the works of the writers of the Protestant Reformation. While it was the case that the **France** theologians of the University and the bishops put into action certain measures against works of heresy, the larger proportion of the censorship regulations came directly from the Crown or from the Parliament. In 1735, Duplessis d'Argentré published, in three volumes, a *collectio judiciorum* which contained the most important of the acts and edicts in regard to censorship from the faculty of the Sorbonne, from the bishops, from the Parliament, and from the king up to the year 1735.

In 1757, the King (Louis XV) issues an edict prohibiting, under penalty of death, the publication and distribution of writings against religion.[1] There appears to be no record of the enforcement of this penalty. The policy of Malesherbes, who was director of censorship from 1750 to 1768, was lenient. One of the first acts of the revolutionary Government of 1789 was the repeal of the censorship laws of the old monarchy, but the new regulations, established by the revolutionists themselves for the control of the press, were still more severe and exacting than those that they replaced. It may be remembered, however, that these regulations, while in form universal, were as a matter of fact in force only in Paris and one or two other of the larger cities. Dupont, in his *History of Printing*, published in Paris in 1854, says that the press had been less seriously burdened under the persecutions of monarchical government than when it came under the control of the so-called "liberty" accorded to the community by the revolutionists of 1789. In form at least these revolutionists had shown themselves keenly interested in freeing the press from all burdens or restrictions. Under the Act of August, 1789, it was decreed as follows: "Article Two. Full exchange of thought and of opinion is one of the rights most precious to mankind. Every citizen is to be at liberty to speak, write, and print as he will, with the sole restriction that if the liberty be abused, he will be liable for any injury caused through such abuse." It appears that certain inconveniences resulted from this cancellation of all restrictions. In March, 1793, the convention

[1] R., ii, 908.

decrees as follows: "Whoever shall be convicted of having written or brought into print books or writings of any kind that assail the authority of the national representatives or that shall advocate the reëstablishment of royalty or that attempt to antagonise in any way the sovereignty of the people, shall be brought to trial before the special tribunal and shall, if convicted, be punished by death." As a result of this decree, there were brought to the scaffold within the next year twenty journalists and fifty other writers.

The "rights of man" continued, however, to be maintained, at least by decree, as unassailable. The constitution of the Jacobins, published in September, 1793, declares that there must be no interference with the right of expression of thought and of opinion whether by word of mouth or in printed documents. In the constitution of the year III (1795) it is ordered that no censorship shall be imposed on writings before publication and that no author shall be hindered from bringing into print what he will. By September, 1797, the pendulum had again swung in the other direction. Under a decree issued in the name of the Senate and of the Five Hundred it was ordered that sixty journalists and other writers and printers who had been charged with conspiracy against the Republic should be brought to trial. Bailleul, speaking in the name of the Council of the Five Hundred, declared that "the mere existence of writers of this class is a crime against Nature. . . . they constitute a disgrace for mankind. The star of freedom must be freed from their presence. Not only these writers but the printers who have aided them in bringing their infamies into print must be banished into the penal colonies." Fifty-five writers and printers were so banished.[1] In 1799, a new press law was enacted which brought the printing-press formally under the control of the police department. This system remained in force until the régime of the First Consul, when it was strengthened and the regulations were carried out more thoroughly. The censorship established under the empire is a part of the history of Europe. Fouché carried out with full measure of thoroughness the policy of Napoleon in regard to the operations not only of the journalists but of the printers, the book publishers, and the booksellers. The shops of the latter were placed under reiterated examination in order to avoid the risk that they might bring into the territory of France pernicious literature. The policy of the imperial censors concerned itself almost exclusively with works of a political character or which might, through criticisms of persons, by any possibility exert a political influence. The production and distribution of works in theology and religion had in any case been very much lessened, and during the consulate and the empire, there was but very little ecclesiastical censorship. But little attention seems during these years to have been paid to the protection of the morals of the community. Criticism of a book as *contra bonos mores* does not find place in any of the French censorship lists of the time. In June, 1806, it was ordered by an imperial edict that the director-general should instruct all the booksellers and printers to place with the minister, in advance of any sales, a copy of every book whether it was printed in France or was an importation. They were at liberty to accept books which belonged without question to the divisions of science and art. This was the time in which the

[1] Welschinger, 232.

battle of Jena was being fought and one might perhaps suppose that the attention of the Emperor would have been sufficiently engaged with affairs in Germany.

Under the imperial censorship, occurred instances of expurgations which recall the expurgatory Indexes of the Spanish Inquisition. In the *Athalie* of Racine, before a new edition was permitted to be printed, certain passages had to be cancelled because they contained allusions to "tyranny." Chénier had permitted himself in his drama *Cyrus* to present the following lines:

> "*Je ne commande point, j'obéis à la loi;*
> *Et je suis à l'État, l'État n'est point à moi.*"

These lines had to be cancelled before the performance of the play was permitted.[1] Kotzebue's *Souvenir d'un Voyage* was prohibited because the author had permitted himself certain favourable references to the late Queen of Naples and to the English Admiral, Sidney Smith ("that pirate," said Napoleon). Madame de Staël's *Corinne* was prohibited in 1807 and a bitter criticism of the work, printed in the *Moniteur*, is ascribed to the pen of Napoleon himself. Chateaubriand's *Les Martyrs* was, before being published, severely handled by the censors. After suffering a large amount of elimination, it was brought into print, but even then proved unacceptable and was prohibited. A reference to the court of Diocletian was held by the police to constitute a *lèse Majesté*. In November, 1809, Napoleon specified as the responsibilities of censorship, *Le droit d'empêcher la manifestation d'idées qui troublent la paix de l'État, ses intérêts et le bon ordre.* In the same year, Napoleon says: *Qu'on laisse donc écrire librement sur la religion, pourvu qu'on n'abuse pas de cette*

---

[1] Hilgers, 261.

liberté pour écrire contre l'État.[1] In 1810, the Emperor instituted the post of *directeur general de l'imprimerie et de la librairie,* with Portalis as the first incumbent. The system of inspection and repression established under this bureau continued until the close of the empire and was, in fact, renewed with no great change after the return of the Bourbons.

Peignot, writing in 1806, during the "strenuous" years of the First Empire and at a time when political censorship in France and in the great territories outside of France that were under Napoleonic control was most severe, is prepared to speak with full measure of respect of the importance and the necessity of censorship. He finds ground for criticism, however, in the cases in which the Roman Church has undertaken to interfere with the control over French literature which properly belonged to the bishops and to the civil government of France, but he is quite prepared to accept the judgments of the Church in regard to pernicious books provided that these judgments are kept subordinated to the authority of the State.

Peignot speaks of " the happy Europe of his time " (the Europe controlled by Napoleon),

"in which governments now rest on foundations conformed to natural law. Individual liberty maintains itself through nearly all the civilised world. The princes recognise that they command not themselves but men and that their own authority is so much more to be respected when they submit themselves to the laws of their State. The rapid progress of science and art has developed the human spirit and has freed it from the prejudices and from the immorality, the tyranny and anarchy which had in

[1] Welschinger, 307.

the last years of the preceding century shaken and confused Europe."[1]

Peignot includes in his lists of books condemned to be burnt not only the books which he finds recorded as condemned but certain further works which in his judgment ought to have been suppressed.

The Results of Jansenism in France.—The Jesuit Hilgers places upon the Jansenists the responsibility for the wave of heresy, of free thought, and of unrestricted passion which at the close of the 18th century undermined in France, Church, State, and the foundations of society. Hilgers writes (in substance) as follows:

During the 18th century, through the Jansenism which affected a large part of the community in France, place was being made for the free thought philosophy which later became responsible for the great Revolution, and the result was the burst of a storm of public opinion against the Jesuits. In 1761, the Parliament of Paris prohibited twenty-four works by Jesuit writers and a year later, in a fresh prohibition, condemned a hundred and sixty-three Jesuit treatises. The contention was made in these edicts that the prohibited works had had an exciting and pernicious effect, had served to undermine Christian morality, and had tended to demoralise the life and to impair the safety of the citizens; and it was further contended that the opinions presented in these writings constituted an assault against the persons of the princes. These pernicious and godless heresies of the Jansenists continued to gain strength; the Jesuit Order in France became one of the first victims of the heresy; the Revolution gathered strength and the Parliament issued a fresh series of orders; the

[1] Peignot, xxii.

sacred persons of the king and queen fell victims on the scaffold and the best of the citizens lost property and in many cases life; the moral law of Christianity was replaced by the law of man and the goddess of Reason was accepted as the divinity of the community, and at her feet were burned as sacrifices the books of religion and the pictures of the saints. History has recorded how extreme became the tyranny of this world of so-called reason under the laws of men. This tyranny naturally extended itself to the censorship of all literature. The Jacobins controlled with an iron hand journals and journalists; the censorship instituted by them enforced the strictest supervision over their printed and spoken words; and when the rule of the mob was replaced by that of the despot Napoleon, the regulations controlling the press became still more burdensome and the penalties still more severe. Under the rule of Napoleon, it was not only the press of France of which the freedom was crushed, but throughout the broad territories of Germany and Italy, under the hand of the despot, every utterance of the people was checked and repressed. No censorship ever attempted or established by the Church had equalled in severity, in arbitrariness, in its crushing influence that instituted first by the so-called people of France (or to speak more accurately, by the mob of Paris) and later that continued and developed by the product of the mob revolution, Napoleon the despot.

The above is a summary of the forcibly presented contention of the Jesuit Hilgers. He traces back to the unrestrained utterances of the Jansenists what he terms the free-will riot of opinion that took possession of France. He makes this the natural causation of the excesses of the Revolution and of the oppressions of Napoleon. It is easy to point out that the causation is not adequate. The fact that the teachings of Port Royal preceded the Revolution is not in itself sufficient to make Port Royal responsible not only for the Revolution but for Napoleon. As the response of a disputant to the criticism of Church censorship, the parallel presented by Hilgers is, however, deserving of consideration if only as indicating the state of mind under which a loyal Romanist interprets history.

"If," says Hilgers, "there is to be a sound and safe rule for the community, it is not possible to permit for men, whose understanding is at best but limited, an unrestricted freedom of investigation or of expression. To God alone, whose understanding is unrestricted and unlimited, can there be absolute freedom from limit for thought or for action. For man the sole safety lies in control." [1]

Voltaire was obliged in 1716 to make sojourn for a number of weeks in the Bastile on the ground of certain of his ribald *pasquilles*. Before this experience, he had already endured banishment on the ground of other rash utterances. Rousseau's *Émile*, which finds place in successive Indexes, was prohibited also by the civil authorities in Paris in 1762. The condemnation in Geneva was somewhat more serious; the book was burned by the hangman and the author was condemned to imprisonment.

In 1827, was printed in Paris (under Charles X) a State Index, under the title: *Catalogue des Ouvrages condamnés depuis 1814 jusqu'à Septembre, 1827, suivi du texte des jugemens et arrêts insérés au Moniteur.* The censures are specified as *conformément à l'article 26 de la Loi du 26 Mai, 1819.* The books condemned are for the most part classed as immoral.

Hilgers refers to the name of Mirabeau which stands

on the Roman Index connected with the godless and immoral essay on the Bible that was printed anonymously, but the authorship of which was identified. He points out that this same book, when later reprinted in Paris, was condemned in 1829, and again in 1868, and on these two occasions not by Rome, but by the censorship of the State.

Among the books which secured the distinction of condemnation by the civil authorities, may be cited the following:

d'Aubigné, Sieur, *Histoire Universelle*. This book was condemned and burned in 1667 immediately after its publication, under a decree of the Parliament and a sentence of the Provost of Paris. The ground for the condemnation was certain satirical references contained in the history concerning Charles IX, Henry III, and Henry IV.

Beaumarchais, Pierre Augustin Caron de, *Mémoire*. The book was condemned and ordered to be burned by the public hangman under a decree of the Parliament of Paris, February, 1774. It was described as containing scandalous charges against the magistracy and the members of the Parliament.[1]

To France had been accorded, since the time of Pepin, the title of "eldest son of the Church." It is France, however (or perhaps one should say consequently), that has found occasion to repudiate or to annul the greatest number of papal Bulls. I cite as follows certain of the more noteworthy of these acts of protest or of rebellion against the authority of Rome.

Papal Bulls Repudiated in France.—1300. Boniface VIII. A Bull was issued by the Pope against

[1] Peignot.

Philip the Fair in connection with the injunction imposed by the Pope upon the King to make a pilgrimage to the Holy Land, and more immediately as a result of the treatment accorded by Philip to the papal emissary, who had been imprisoned for threatening interdict against the King. The Bull of excommunication was replied to with a decree from the King headed: *Philippe, par le grâce de Dieu roi des Français, à Boniface prétendu pape, peu ou point de salut.*

1407. Benedict XIII (classed as an anti-pope). In this Bull the Pope excommunicates all those who undertake to prevent the peaceable settlement for which he was working and who opposed themselves to his designs as the University of Paris had already done. The Pope places under interdict the kingdom of France and the domains of the empire.

Charles II, the Parliament, the clergy, and the University of Paris issued in general council a decree stating that Benedict was not only a schismatic but a heretic.

1510. Julius II excommunicates Louis XII because the King had refused to deliver to the Pope certain cities over which the Curia claimed to have rights. Louis is reported to have said when learning of his excommunication: *Saint Pierre avait bien autres choses à faire que se mêler des affaires des empereurs sous lesquels il vivait.* The King appealed to the General Council of Pisa. The Pope, in confirming the interdict on the kingdom, relieved the subjects of Louis from their oath of allegiance. Louis in his turn excommunicated the Pope and caused to be struck certain pieces of money which bore on the reverse *perdam Baby-*

lonis nomen. The Council of Pisa refused to confirm the interdict of the Pope, who thereupon called the Council of the Lateran, but he died before this council had given a decision.

1580. The Bull *In Coena Domini,* issued by Gregory XIII. was publicly burned in Paris under decree of Parliament. This burning was the result of an attempt of the Pope to have the Bull published in France.

1585. Sixtus V issues a Bull against the King of Navarre, later Henry IV. The Pope declares the King, together with the Prince of Condé, to have been convicted of heresy and to be enemies of God and of religion. He decrees that the King shall be deposed from all rights in the kingdom of Navarre and in the principality of Berne, and shall forfeit his claim to the throne of France. This Bull gave satisfaction to the League in France, but had no political effect. The reply of Henry, copies of which were placed on the doors of the palace of the cardinals in Rome and even on the door of the Vatican, takes the ground that the declaration and excommunication on the part of Sixtus V, *soi-disant* Pope of Rome, are false and are based on falsehood. The Pope is declared to be anti-Christ.

1591. Gregory XIV publishes in Rome two Bulls by the first of which he declares Henry IV to be a heretic and to be excommunicated and deposed from his kingdom; by the second, he places under interdict all ecclesiastics who may render homage to the King. Henry replies by ordering the Bull of Gregory to be burned before the gate of his palace and declares this *soi-disant* Pope to be an enemy of the King, an enemy of France, and an enemy of peace and Christianity.

March, 1809. Pius VII issued a Bull of excommunication against his adversaries, this Bull being directed more particularly at Napoleon. Napoleon forbids the publication of the Bull in France and in the territories controlled by the French Empire and causes the Pope to be seized and taken from Rome to Savona and later to Fontainebleau. For a term of four years, during which he was practically a prisoner, the Pope refused to accept the instruction of the Emperor to cancel the Bull, but in January, 1813, he yielded, the Bull was recalled, and the *Concordat* was signed. This *Concordat* remained in force, at least in substance, up to 1906, in which year it was cancelled by the French Republic.

January, 1860. Pius IX issued a Bull (also described as an anathema) against those who had abetted the invasion of his dominions. This Bull was directed at Victor Emmanuel, who had, after the successful conclusion of the war with Austria, annexed the papal States, and at Napoleon III, through whose co-operation this annexation had proved possible. The Bull was, as far as France was concerned, suppressed by Napoleon III, who also suppressed the Paris journal (*Le Monde*) in which the Bull had been published.

The law of 1558, which continued in force until the publication, in 1812, of the Constitution of Cadiz, rendered the supervision of the press **Spain and** a process as cumbrous as it was thorough. **Portugal** Every manuscript for which a license was desired had to be passed upon by an examiner appointed by the Royal Council. After such examination, it was delivered to the corrector general, and when it had passed through the press, the manuscript as annotated by this official was returned to him with the printed copy for comparison. If the author was an ecclesiastic, a preliminary examination and approbation by his superior were also required. The book as printed carried on its front page a long series of official certificates, and the same process had to be repeated for each succeeding edition. The fees were provided by the author or printer and constituted, of necessity, an additional charge on the actual cost of production. As the system grew more complex, the fees and the fines were multiplied so that the total charge became for each publication a very serious matter indeed. The interests of the readers were guarded by accompanying the license with a *tassa* or specification of the price at which the book was to be sold, which price was determined by the Royal Council. This *tassa* was not abandoned until 1762, when it was taken off all books excepting what are called books of necessity, that is to say books of instruction, either secular or religious.[1] The charge assumed by the Spanish censors brought upon them, as was the case with the censors of other countries, an unavoidable responsibility for the soundness, orthodoxy, and morality of everything that, having succeeded in passing the official examination, was permitted to come into print.

In 1682, it was ordered that books on the several subjects "affecting the interests of the State" (a definition which was of course capable of a very wide range of application) should be submitted to a special

[1] Lea. 142.

council or the department to whose affairs they related.
The approbation of such department must be secured
before the license could be issued. For instance,
a book in regard to the colonies called for the approval of the Colonial Department, and one in regard to commerce or metals had to be submitted to
the Department of Commerce. As late as 1757, a
law issued by Ferdinand VI, and repeated in 1778 by
Carlos III, ordered that all books on medical science
must, before being published, secure the approval of a
physician selected by the president of the *Protomedicato*.
Printers and publishers, under the close supervision
of the host of officials who had charge of the printing-
offices and bookshops, were practically outlawed.
The only printers who had any measure of freedom
of action were those who carried on the printing-
offices in the religious houses. The Crown could
deprive its subjects of their civil rights, but it dared
not meddle with ecclesiastical privileges. In 1752,
under a royal decree, it is prohibited to import or to
sell any books in Spanish written by Spaniards and
printed abroad without special royal license; the penalty is death and confiscation. The death penalty
could, however, be commuted to four years of *pre-
sidio*. With this varied series of obstacles in the
way of printing and burdensome charges increasing the cost of publication, it is by no means surprising that the production of books in Spain was,
for the three centuries after 1560, inconsiderable as
compared with that of the other States of Europe.
As Lea says, Spain fell absolutely behind in the
development of literature, science, arts, and industry, when human thought seeking expression was
surrounded and rendered ineffectual by so many im-

pediments.   Carlos III, realising the disadvantage to the community of the hampering of the work of the printing-press, undertook, in 1769, to remove certain of the restrictions.   In 1778, he was able to congratulate himself on the increased prosperity of the printing business.

In 1782, the Inquisitor-General Bertram, following the instructions given in the Index of Benedict in 1756, recalled the prohibition of the printing and reading of Spanish versions of the Bible, a prohibition which had endured for two hundred and fifty years.   This action brought out sharp antagonism on the part of many of the ecclesiastics and after the revolutionary events of 1789, the Inquisition re-established the larger number of the old-time prohibitions and included in these a fresh prohibition for the reading of the Scriptures. The censorship activity of the five years succeeding 1789 was, however, particularly directed against the importation of political and so-called philosophical publications from France.   After the restoration of the Spanish monarchy under Ferdinand VII, the old regulations of the Index were again confirmed under an edict of July 22, 1815.   There were, later, certain modifications in these regulations, but in June, 1830, an elaborate law re-established the entire censorship system with its cumbrous machinery; every work contrary to the Catholic Faith or to the royal prerogative was forbidden under pain of death, and provision was made for the most elaborate supervision of books imported from abroad.

In 1768, Joseph I of Portugal declared that the *Bulla Coena* and the other Bulls of the Church having to do with censorship, and the series of Roman Indexes were not to be held as binding upon his subjects excepting in so far as they had been specifically confirmed by the State Government. Joseph instituted a commission to take charge of the matter of censorship; but this body did not produce any Index. In 1771, however, it issued a list of sixty books prohibited under the authority of the Church, this list being made up chiefly of treatises by Jesuits, Escobar, Mariana, Saintarella, etc. Fourteen further works were to be sold only when containing a printed notice in which were to be specified the condemned passages.

3. **Protestant States.**—The Roman procedure in censorship in Switzerland, and particularly in Geneva, presents close analogies to the **Switzerland** methods in force in Rome.

In 1525, the magistracy of Zurich established a so-called State Church. Under the regulations of this Church, no preaching could be permitted within the territory of the city other than the pure Gospel of Zwingli and his associates. The books of worship of the Catholics were ordered to be delivered and burned and a similar course was taken with the Lutheran Bibles and the Lutheran works of instruction of Melanchthon. A similar action was taken in Geneva under the direction of Calvin. The altars and altar pictures were destroyed and the Catholics were ordered to deliver for like destruction their books of worship, of song, and their catechism. The Inquisition established in Geneva assumed the authority to visit houses and shops and to confiscate for destruction all heretical books. In 1539, the magistrates ordered that no book should be printed until it had received a license from the authorities. This decree was renewed in 1556 and in 1560. The burning of Servetus, under the authority of the court instituted by Calvin, occurred in 1553.

In 1554, Calvin published his *Defensio Orthodoxi et Fidei de S. Trinitate contra Prodigiosos Errores Mich. Serveti Hispanii*, etc. This "Defence" bears, in addition to the name of the author, the subscriptions of fifteen of the divines of the Geneva Church. Later, Calvin called the theologians of Basel to account for permitting the publication of an anonymous monograph written as an answer to his "Defence," and demanded that the publishers of the same should be duly punished. Even after the death of Calvin (1564), the censorship system was renewed and continued.[1]

In 1580, Henricus Stephanus (whose father Robert had migrated to Geneva in order to free his printing-press from the censorship of the Catholic divines) was brought before the city council and formally reprimanded because, in a certain volume of *Dialogues du Nouveau Langage Français*, he had made additions to the text after this had been passed upon by the censors. He was reminded that he was already under reprimand in connection with his *Apologia Herodoti*, and was cautioned that, if he did further printing without securing a permit for the text as finally worded, he would lose his license. It was decided finally by the Consistorium that Stephanus was not obeying the regulations, and he was declared to be excommunicated, while the magistrates condemned him to a week's imprisonment. In 1559, knowledge came to the Church authorities in Basel that a certain heretical writer named David Joris had for some little time lived in the city unrecognised, and had died there in 1556. A formal process was entered into against the disinterred remains of Joris, and he was duly condemned (we may say *in absentia*)

---

[1] Stähelin, *Calvin*, ii, 316.

for heresy. His portrait and his books were burned by the public hangman. In 1563, in the process held in Zürich against Ochinus, it was made a charge that, without first securing permission from the city censors, he had brought into print, in Basel, a monograph on the Lord's Supper.[1] In 1562, Beza brought before the Synod of Geneva a book of Morelli de Villiers which he described as heretical. The synod, accepting Beza's view, orders the book to be prohibited and existing copies to be burned. One copy was burned in public by the hangman.

In 1566, Jo. Val. Gentilis was, in consideration of his repentance, spared from death but sentenced to walk through the street of Geneva in his shirt, barefooted, and with a burning candle in his hand, and, after doing penance in the church, he was, with his own hands, to burn his books. His march was to be preceded by trumpeters who were to specify his crime. Afterwards he was to be confined in Geneva for an apparently indefinite period. He escaped but was recaptured and was decapitated and burned.

In Basel, the first decree having to do with censorship emanated from no less an authority than Erasmus. In 1542, the magistrates issued an order prohibiting, under a penalty of a hundred dollars, the printing of any book until it had been examined and approved by the municipal censors.

An example is presented in Geneva, in 1645, of a prohibition or suppression of a book with a payment made to the author as consideration for his loss. The name of the author was Brios; the book was entitled *L'homme hardi à la France.* The amount paid was ten crowns. I do not find record of another instance of com-

---

[1] Hilgers, 232.

pensation in connection with the cancelling of a book.[1]

In certain of the States which had accepted Protest-antism, attempts were made at an early date to insti-
Protestant tute a censorship over the productions of
Germany the printing-press. There was, however, no central authority through which a permanent cen-sorship organisation could be maintained and it was not practicable to enforce any penalties for the pos-session or the reading of condemned books that could be considered the equivalent of excommuni-cation. No Protestant rulers took the ground that the reading of false or of erroneous doctrine constituted a mortal sin. The responsible authority for such cen-sorship as came into existence rested with the State. Action was taken by the State most frequently at the instance of the theological faculties of the universities, and it was to these bodies that was as a rule committed the task of supervising and examining the books that came into question. In the case, however, of works that were charged with assailing the rulers of the State or with any utterances *contra bonos mores*, the civil officials were accustomed to take the direction of the matter into their own hands. The German princes sometimes also assumed the authority to supervise matters of theology, a weakness that has been paral-leled as late as the 20th century by a German Emperor. Duke Ludwig of Würtemberg, in 1585, announced for instance that in his duchy no work of theology should come into print that had not been passed upon and approved by himself. He made no exception even for the writings of the divines of his own princpiality, the soundness of whose orthodoxy might, one should suppose, have been already tested.

[1] Heppe, *Beza*, 196.

In 1561, the Duke of Weimar appointed a consistorium, comprising four divines and four laymen, which was charged with the duty of examining all books offered for sale in the duchy, whether these were printed within the confines of Weimar or were importations. A book offered for sale without the approval of the consistorium (whose meetings took place only four times a year) was ordered to be confiscated. For a serious offence, such as a repeated disregard of the regulation, the printer or dealer was subject to a fine. The theologians of Jena promptly made protest against such a censorship, particularly in the case of imported books. They took the broad ground that the writing of books was a necessary responsibility of learning or of knowledge, and that any attempt to restrict the use of men's thinking power or the expression of their opinions was an attempt to place restrictions upon the Holy Ghost himself.[1]

The chief difficulty in the application of any censorship regulation within the Lutheran States was the existence of different schools of belief, the controversies between which soon became active. The control of the censorship machinery for any one State fell into the hands first of one set of controversialists and then of another, according to the activity of the respective leaders and to the influence brought to bear upon the local ruler. In the Lutheran States, such as Saxony, the prohibition against papistical writings was accompanied by an equally sweeping condemnation of the writings of the Calvinists; while the Calvinistic authorities of States like Brandenburg were prompt on their side to take similar measures for the protection of their own special tenets. This continued conflict

[1] Reusch, i, 422.

between the several groups of reformers had the necessary effect of bringing into disrepute and ineffectiveness the larger portion of the attempts at censorship control. Some attempts were made towards a more tolerant and a more practicable policy. Zwingli, for instance, insisted that his fellow-believers in Essling should follow the Christian example of the church in Zürich, which refused to interfere with the sale even of Anabaptist writings; but in Zürich itself this tolerant spirit was not long permitted to control.

The Elector of Saxony[1] prohibited, under a penalty of three thousand gulden, the printing of the *Corpus Doctrinae* of Melanchthon, and Frederick II of Denmark prohibited preachers and instructors, under penalty of the loss of their positions and (for persistency in misdoing) of further punishments, the use of the formula of the *Concordia.* Again, in 1574, the Elector of Saxony compelled the members of the University of Wittenberg to subscribe to an oath that they would neither purchase nor read the writings of the Sacramentists or of the Vermigli.

In 1439, Nicholas Wohlrab, who had, under the instructions of Duke George of Saxony and the Magistracy of Leipsic, brought into print the *Postille* of Wicels, was put into prison by Duke Henry, acting at the instance of the Elector John Frederick. Before he could secure his release, Wohlrab was obliged to take oath to bring no further works into print or into sale until these had received the censorship and the approval of the magistrates. The three other book-dealers of Leipsic were forbidden to print or to sell any books that had not secured approval of the censor appointed by the magistrates, and two deputy magistrates were de-

---

[1] Schmidt, P., *Vermigli*, 292.

tached to make a weekly inspection of the printing-offices and assure themselves that nothing was printed antagonistic to the teachings of the Gospel.[1]

There were from time to time schemes for a Protestant Index. In 1579, Duke Julius of Brunswick brought out a scheme for charging a general synod with the duty of compiling an Index of heretical books and of instituting measures for the censorship of the press; but the plan was not put into execution.

In 1593, Duke Louis of Würtemberg issued an instruction to the University of Tübingen which reads as follows:

"Book-dealers must be cautioned under sufficient penalties, neither to print, to possess, nor to sell, heretical or pernicious books, such as the abominable writings of the Jesuits. The preachers are directed to warn their hearers against the unclean literature. In order, however, that the instructors and preachers should be able to secure knowledge of the arguments of their adversaries and of the nature of their calumnies, printer George Gruppenbach is ordered to secure two copies of each of such books as are available and to deliver the same to the university. The preachers whose erudition and good judgment can be trusted to keep them from being led astray by pernicious doctrines, are to be permitted to read these heretical and sectarian writings, in order that they may be in a position to defend the true Faith. The superintendent appointed for the purpose is to keep a record of the pernicious books so distributed and is to secure reports as to the use made of them. The copies themselves are in any case to be returned to the university authorities, so that they may not be used to pervert the people. All this is done 'In order that the assaults of the hateful Satan (who in these last days has been permitted to work much evil upon the

---

[1] *Archiv des Deutsch Buchh.*, i, 22, 52.

Church of God) shall be withstood, and that for the people in this principality the true Faith shall be preserved and their souls shall be kept clean.'"[1]

Luther was, it should be remembered, thoroughly in accord with pope and with emperor in the belief that it was the duty of the faithful to destroy heresy. He only differed from the pope as to what constituted heresy. In 1525, we find him invoking the aid of the censorship regulations of Saxony and of Brandenburg for the purpose of stamping out the "pernicious doctrines" of the Anabaptists and of the followers of Zwingli. The Protestant princes were for the most part more than willing to establish and to maintain a censorship for the presses of their several localities, as such a system served in more ways than one to strengthen their authority, while it could be utilised also to head off undesirable criticism.

In 1525, Luther decides that a censorship ought to be established in the Protestant States. He asks the Protestant princes to co-operate in instituting the machinery for the purpose. The regulations established by the princes interfered seriously with the operations of the printers in the larger places. but proved ineffectual for securing any uniformity of religious publishing throughout the States of North Germany.

In 1532, Luther calls upon Duke Heinrich of Mecklenburg, for the sake of the Gospel of Christ and for the saving of souls, to prevent from coming into print a translation of the Gospels that had been prepared by the Catholic priest Emser. Melanchthon was fully in accord with Luther as to the necessity of repressing with sharpest and most effective censorship all books

[1] Hilgers. 287.

that were not in accord with the Protestant faith.

Zwingli and Calvin, acting each from his own point of view, established in their respective cities a censorship that was much more bitter and strenuous than anything as yet attempted under the authority of Rome. Hilgers points out that the Lutherans with their schools and their cliques, the Zwinglians, the Calvinists, the Anabaptists, the Mennonites, the Schwenckfeldians, the Weigelians, and the Socinians, contended with each other with full use of the weapon of censorship, and in censorship as in religion it was always the brutal power of the strongest that came into control. The princes, establishing with readiness a censorship machinery, changed the application of their penalties as they changed their faith, but the penalties themselves became, with each change, more severe.[1]

According to Gretser, the first article of the Calvinistic theologian stated that "the writings of Luther must be stamped out from the Church of God."[2] In Saxony, in the Palatinate, in Baden, in Würtemberg, in Brandenburg, and in Prussia after 1550, we find in full force a series of Protestant censorships directed sometimes spasmodically, but usually with no little bitterness, under the authority of the political power.[3]

The Jesuit Hilgers, who naturally makes use of Luther as a characteristic example of Protestant intolerance in censorship, writes:

"Luther, who characteristically enough began his notorious career with the burning of books, was by no means prepared to accept with patience any Catholic

---

[1] Hilgers, 289.   [2] Cited by Hilgers, 290.   [3] *Ibid.*, 297.

literature that stood in his way. What, nevertheless, made the Lutheran movement a radical revolution was the acceptance of the right of individual freedom of inquiry, a right that was to make each man the authority for his individual views of faith and doctrine against the accepted Catholic principle that the authority for the interpretation of doctrine and for the guidance of faith must rest with the Church. . . . Luther accepted as authoritative the teaching of the Scriptures, but it was his contention that this teaching could be ascertained by the individual understanding and without the guidance of the Holy Church. This very principle, however, of individual interpretation was almost immediately set to one side by Luther himself. He found that what he propounded as the true Faith could be maintained only through the protection of his faithful from the influence of pernicious literature; and he instituted promptly, to the extent of his own power, a censorship against not only the writings of the Catholics from whom he had broken away, but still more sharply against those of fellow-Protestants whose views of interpretation differed in any manner from his own. Luther became himself the first censor of the Word of God, and set up his individual understanding as a guide not merely for himself but for the misguided who were ready to accept the word of a single man rather than the authority of the Church universal. . . . Under the divine government, men have been placed in dependence upon each other. It is only through full recognition of this interdependent relation that State and Church can come into existence and can be maintained. No reasonable man will deny for a father the right and the duty to preserve son and daughter from the influence of pernicious companionship. One could more reasonably contend against the authority of the Lord in Heaven to impose upon Adam and Eve in Paradise certain prohibitions. That a still more seriously pernicious influence can be brought about by bad books than even by evil companionship can be denied by no thoughtful man. The evil is none the less because it may be brought about under the name of freedom and enlightenment. No father, with a proper consciousness of his own responsibilities, will permit a son who is still a youth to receive without restriction teachings, whether religious, philosophical, medical, or scientific, which have been shaped for the understanding only of older men. . . . The father must on his own authority restrict, direct, and select the literature upon which is based the instruction of his children. The authority of the State makes necessary a supervision of the action and influence of the printing-press. The Church includes in its responsibilities the relation of the father to the child and of the Government to the citizen. Its rulers must watch not only the matter of morality but that of sound doctrine and wholesome influence. If the ruler of a modern State finds it impossible to permit the circulation of writings which assail the character or the person of king or emperor, how much less is it possible for those who direct the government of the Church to permit the circulation of writings which assail the wisdom and the authority of the Lord of Hosts or of his Son. The realm of the Church is that of faith and of conduct, a realm which is of necessity directly influenced by the spoken word and still more by the word circulated in print. It is this realm that must be defended and protected against the invasion of the poison of pernicious and unsound writings. As in the modern State, a special system is required for the organisation of the defensive power represented by such bodies as the army and the police, so is it necessary for the Church, with the organisation of its own ecclesiastical army of bishops, priests, deacons, and soldiers of the Faith, to establish regulations for discipline, for defence, and, when the time comes, for assault upon the powers of evil. This system of the Church is expressed most logically through its control of thought and of literature, for the Church works through the mind with spiritual forces. The authorities of a city are prepared to prohibit, under the severest penalties, miscellaneous disturbances or a careless handling of dynamite; such precautions in regard to personal harm as the mayor finds necessary for the safety of his community, the bishop is under similar necessity of adopting for the preserving of his flock against spiritual assaults."[1]

In 1595, the astronomer, Johann Kepler, completed his first astronomical treatise, the *Mysterium Cosmographicum*, which was to be printed in Tübingen. Before the book could come into print, it was necessary to secure the approval of the senate of the university. The theological faculty gave permission for the printing only after cancelling the chapter in which the author undertook to bring the Copernican system into accord with the Scriptures. In Leipsic, the printing of the book was prohibited.

The great Elector of Brandenburg, in 1670, ordered that, for the purpose of avoiding religious strife and controversy, there should be a thorough censorship of all books, whether printed within his territory or imported from without, which were concerned with matters of theology or religion.

An order issued in Cologne in 1662 prescribes that the preachers shall engage in no disputations or conferences and shall bring into print no controversial writings, without the specific permission of the Elector himself.

In 1772, a Cabinet order prescribes that theological books for which privileges are demanded must be examined and, if necessary, revised by a consistorial commission comprised of certain Protestant ecclesiastics. The penalties imposed upon an ecclesiastic for printing any volume for which special permission had not been secured were particularly severe.

[1] Hilgers, 17 *ff*.

The persecution of Christian Wolff, who held for a series of years a professorship in Halle, is cited as a characteristic example of Protestant censorship and intolerance. The philosophic doctrines taught by the professor excited the indignation of Frederick II and in 1773, under a Cabinet order, Wolff was deprived of his post and was ordered to leave Prussian territory within forty-eight hours. Other instructors who had accepted the so-called Wolffian philosophy, such as Gabriel Fischer of Königsberg, were in like manner deprived of their offices and banished from the country. The various operations of royal censorship under the great Elector and his several successors, up to and including Frederick the Great, present examples of tyrannical inconsistency, inconsequence, unreasonableness, ignorance, and narrowness which have not been surpassed, and have possibly hardly been equalled, under any of the regulations of the Roman Index.

Frederick the Great developed the political censorship of Prussia into a system the influence of which persists under the German Empire of to-day. His censorship was directed more particularly against literature affecting the interests of the State, but it included the full control of theological utterances.

After the occupation of Silesia, an order was issued directing the Bishop of Breslau to submit for the approval of the royal censors, before publication, all edicts or utterances on the part of the Catholic Church.

In 1775, the King prohibited the publication in his dominions of the Bull of Clement XIV.

In 1784, Frederick the Great issued an edict prohibiting under serious penalties the acceptance by any of his subjects of Catholic doctrines. This edict being contrary to the conventions in force, he was obliged, however, to withdraw it.

In 1792, Frederick William issues an order for the systematising of the censorship of the kingdom. It is directed that all printing-offices, publishing concerns, and bookshops be placed under the strictest supervision, that no work shall come into print until it has secured the approval of the royal censors. The penalties included, in addition to fines, the cancellation of the editions, and in case of a persistent disobedience, the banishment of the delinquent. The university professors are also brought under close supervision for their utterances in lectures.

In 1794, in which year censorship in England was practically abandoned, the censorship system in Prussia under Frederick William II. became more severe and exacting than ever before.

In 1794, the *Allgemeine deutsche Bibliothek* is prohibited in Prussian dominions as constituting an influence against the Christian religion. This is an example of a long series of similar prohibitions. In 1816, the *Rheinische Merkür* of the poet Görres, who had done so much to arouse public opinion against Napoleon, was suppressed under a Cabinet order. The royal censorship was ameliorated under Frederick William but was again strengthened in 1848 and during the years immediately succeeding.

In 1844–5 was published at Jena a catalogue entitled *Index Librorum Prohibitorum*, giving the titles only of books prohibited in Germany.

In 1882, was published in Berlin what is probably the latest of the State Indexes. It is devoted to a list of works maintaining the principles of the Social Democrats, which works had been condemned and prohibited under the authority of an act of the Reichs-rath of 1878. The list includes several hundred publications, chiefly pamphlets.

The political censorship existing to-day throughout Prussia and the German Empire under the imperial control is of course familiar to all readers of the 20th century. Between 1878 and the close of the century, a very long list of Social Democratic writings, pamphlets, books, and journals came under condemnation and suppression. This policy was continued into the 20th century, although under present conditions its thorough enforcement is a matter of increasing difficulty.

Hilgers points out that the instances of Protestant political censorship against works which are purely literary or intellectual in their character. that is to say, which had no direct concern with either religion or politics, are far more numerous than under the action of the censorship authorities of Rome. Among other examples, he points out the action of Luther against the works of Erasmus and the writings of a number of the Humanists; the decree of the Duke of Weimar (acting at the initiative of Goethe) against *Isis*, and for the suppression of the epoch-making writings of the philosopher Fichte; the acts of Frederick the Great against Voltaire, and the measures taken by Bismarck against a long series of writings that came into print during the *Kulturkampf*.

An order issued in January, 1903, by the rector of the University of Berlin, prohibits the delivery of a lecture on Proudhon and Lasalle on the ground that it was necessary to take "all possible precautions for the protection of young souls from the pernicious and poisonous influence of sociological errors."[1]

[1] Hilgers, 93.

In November, 1902, in a convention held at Hamburg of the teachers of Germany, it was proposed to prohibit the use in schools of the catechism of Luther and of the Protestant Scriptures.[1]

The German *Goethe-bund* finds occasion to make protest, in 1903, against the *lex Heinze*: "In Berlin, we are not only under the burden of dramatic censorship which never sleeps and which causes perpetual irritation, but we have to endure the exacting regulations of the general press law under which are controlled not merely journals but publications of all kinds. For instance, in the three months from October to December, 1902, no less than seventy-seven works were condemned and their further publication prohibited; that is to say, in these three months the civil authority condemned more books than had been placed in the prohibitory Index of Rome during the ten years preceding." With such experience under the State control of the press, it is, claims Hilgers, absurd to make reference to " the pernicious interference with literature on the part of the Church censors."

Kant's *Critique of Pure Reason*, prohibited, in its Italian translation, in the Roman Index since 1827, had, years before that date, come under the condemnation of the royal authority of Prussia. In October, 1792, a Cabinet order contains a bitter characterisation of the work: "Our sacred person you have with your so-called philosophy attempted to bring into contempt . . . and you have at the same time assailed the truth of Scriptures and the foundations of Creed belief (*mich und Gott*). . . We order that henceforth you shall employ your talents to better purpose and that you shall keep silence on matters which are outside of your

[1] Hilgers, 94.

proper functions." The further circulation of the book was prohibited, but it is fair to remember that this prohibition proved entirely ineffective to suppress the book, even in Prussia.

The States General of Holland issued in 1581, and again in 1588, edicts prohibiting the printing, the reading, and the possession of certain condemned books, the lists of which were given with the edicts. These books were described as presenting " papistical superstitions." In 1598, certain Socinian books which had been printed in Amsterdam were condemned as heretical by the theological professors of Leyden. The editions were confiscated and the books were publicly burned in The Hague.

Holland

Among the noteworthy names included in the list of condemned authors may be cited those of Vondel, Grotius (who was certainly not to be ranked either as a Socinian or as an unbeliever, but whose form of Calvinism was not in accord with that of the authorities), Hobbes, and Spinoza. The poet Vondel, in 1641, went back into the Catholic Church and thereupon came under the proscription of the Synod of Delft as well as of the State. Before he accepted the Catholic Faith, he was accused of being an Arminian and a supporter of Olden-Barneveld. Later, his tragedy *Maria Stuart*, in which he declaimed against the murder of the Catholic queen, brought him again into trouble with the authorities.

Grotius suffered much more severely from the persecution of his fellow-historians than from any action on the part of censors of the Roman Church. His friend Olden-Barneveld had lost his life largely because of differences on theological matters with certain of his fellow-Calvinists. The same fate would probably have befallen Grotius if he had not succeeded in escaping from prison.

Hobbes, when instructor in the University of Cambridge, having undertaken to defend certain propositions concerning the law of nature, was prohibited from further teaching and was driven from the university. He betook himself to Amsterdam, but even here, the *Leviathan*, (printed in London, in 1651,) came under condemnation. The Roman censors are criticised (and with justice) for their prohibition of the writings of Spinoza, but the condemnation of Spinoza was much more severe among his own people than anything that had been proposed by the authorities of Rome. The ban uttered in the Jewish temple on the 27th of July, 1656, closes with the words:

"We order hereafter that no one shall have communication with Baruch Espinoza either by word of mouth or in writing, that no one shall render him any service, that no one shall remain under the same roof with or even accost him, that no one shall in any manner have communication with him."

The works of Spinoza and the *Leviathan* of Hobbes were brought under a series of condemnations under the authority of the Prince of Orange, the States of Holland, the synods of the Church, the local magistrates, the university authorities, and the Burgomaster of Leyden.

In 1668, Adrian Coerbach, a doctor of medicine of Amsterdam, was charged with having accepted the opinions of Spinoza and with having defended these before others. He gave evidence that he had never spoken with Spinoza and had not spoken publicly of his theories. He was, however, sentenced to be imprisoned for ten years and thereafter to be banished from

Holland for ten years. In 1678, the Synod of South Holland, in session at Leyden, gave fresh judgment concerning the pernicious writings of Spinoza. Between the years 1650–1680, there were in all no less than fifty similar edicts or judgments, in some instances accompanied by severe punishments, against the reading or circulation of the works of Spinoza. In many cases, under the same judgment was placed the *Leviathan* of Hobbes.

In Denmark, between the years 1537 and 1770, a severe censorship was maintained not only against works upholding the Catholic Faith, but against all books which were not in accord **Scandinavia** with the Lutheran doctrines that the Crown had established as the orthodox faith of the kingdom. Among books other than theological which came under condemnation, may be noted the *Werther* of Goethe, condemned in 1776. The severe prohibitions of the censorship law were not repealed until 1849 and 1866. In Sweden also, where the Lutheran creed had been established as the faith of the kingdom, a censorship was maintained against publications which were not in accord with the creed of Luther. In 1667, under a royal ordinance, the booksellers were directed to present from year to year to the censors a precise catalogue of all the books carried in stock and to secure permission for the sale of such books. The penalty was loss of license.

In 1764, was printed, at Upsala, an Index presenting a list of certain books which are held as prohibited in Sweden. It is to be classed as an historical tract and not strictly as an Index. The title reads as follows: *Historia librorum prohibitorum in Suecia; cujus specimen primum, consensu Ampl. Senat. Philos.*

Upsal. publica disputatione, submittunt Samuel J. Alnander, Philos. Magister, et Petrus Kendal, Stipend. Reg. Ostrogothi, Anno mdcclxiii, Upsaliae. The thesis recognises three sources of the power of prohibiting books, the royal Senate, specified in the title-page; the royal authority by edict; and the theological faculty of the University of Upsala. The lists are devoted mainly to works of the 17th century but there are a few titles from the 16th century. The books condemned are chiefly political. The volume has value chiefly as an indication of a system of censorship in a Protestant country and also (in connection with the meagreness of the lists) of the fact that such system was apparently neither comprehensive nor exacting.

In 1856, was printed in Gothenburg, in an edition comprising but sixteen copies, an Index bearing the title, *Elenchus Librorum in Suecia prohibitorum, saeculorum XVII et XVIII.*

The first censorship in England appears to have been made as a matter of Church discipline; the bishops **Censorship** assumed in these earlier cases the sole juris- **by the State** diction and the punishments were ecclesias- **in England** tical—penance and excommunication. In 1382, the State began to take action in matters of censorship. The occasion arose from the circulation of the doctrines of Wyclif, which, together with the teachings of the Lollards, were assumed to have had influence in bringing about the insurrection of Wat Tyler. The authorities decided that the bishops did not have the power required to suppress the inflammatory doctrines, because the preachers kept moving from one diocese to another and denied at the same time the jurisdiction of the ecclesiastical courts. In 1382, therefore, the Parliament passed an act directing the civil authorities to arrest all such preachers and to "hold them in arrest and strong prison until they will justify themselves to the law and reason of Holy Church." The mischief, however, continued and, in 1401, the more severe act known as "*de haeretico comburendo*" was passed. Dr. Shirley says that the first victim of this statute was W. Sawtree, preacher at St. Osyth's in the City of London. Sawtree was convicted of denying transubstantiation. Milman points out that the writ for the execution of Sawtree appears on the Rolls of Parliament before the act itself. It is possible, therefore, says Milman, that Sawtree suffered under a special act which had perhaps been proposed for the purpose of ascertaining, in advance of the consideration of the larger measure, the feeling of Parliament.

The last instances of execution for heresy in England occurred in 1612, in which year Bartholomew Legate was burned at Smithfield for holding Unitarian opinions. and Edward Wightman was burned at Litchfield for holding no less than nine "damnable heresies."

The papal Bull issued on June 19, 1520, for the destruction of the publications of Luther, Wolsey declined to enforce in England. It is probable that if the Cardinal had been left to himself, the cruel proceedings which characterised the reign of Henry VIII would not have been instituted. It is the opinion of Froude that with Wolsey, heresy was an error, while with More it was a crime.

A prohibitory Index was published in England in 1526, nearly twenty-five years before the issue of the first Index on the Continent, and thirty-three years before the first issue in the series of the Roman Indexes. In March, 1527, Tunstal, Bishop of London, gave to

Thomas More a privilege for the reading of heretical books in order that, following the example of the King (Henry VIII), More might be enabled to make good defence of the Catholic Faith against the new heresies. In June, 1539, the King gave his approval to an act of Parliament which was concerned particularly with the articles of faith. The first of these articles had to do with the real presence of Christ in the Sacrament. The act reads: "If any person writes, preaches, or disputes against this first article, he shall be punished with death as a heretic and his property shall be confiscated to the Crown."

In 1564, Queen Elizabeth issued an instruction to the Bishop of London to provide for an examination of the cargoes of all the vessels arriving, in order that pernicious and heretical books should be secured and destroyed. In 1571, an act of Parliament provided the punishment of treason against all who should secure from the Bishop of Rome any bull, brief, or other instrument or should undertake to make distribution of copies of the same. Under Elizabeth, it was ordered that any person should be treated as guilty of high treason and should be liable to sentence of death if he had in his possession a Catholic book in which was taught the doctrine of the supremacy of the pope. In 1582, an act of Parliament declared it to be felony to write, print, sell, distribute, or possess books, rhymes, ballads, letters, or writings of any kind which contained matter against the fame of the Queen or in any way injurious to the repute of the Government. Under this law, two ministers belonging to the sect of the Brownists, Thacher and Copping, were tried and executed. In 1575, Elizabeth approved a new act directed against the Anabaptists, the Puritans, the

Brownists, and the Catholics, under the provisions of which act a number of people were condemned and burned. Among the books prohibited under the same law, were certain writings of Henry Nicholas of Leyden which had been translated from the German. It was ordered that any persons possessing or distributing these writings should be punished. In 1583, a proclamation was issued by the Queen against the publishers, booksellers, or possessors of pernicious and schismatic literature. The Star Chamber, under the law of 1585, prescribed that each university should keep in activity but one press and prescribed from year to year the number of presses permitted for London. In 1593, Barrow and Greenwood, both Brownists, were executed as heretics. It is the view of the Jesuit historian Hilgers that throughout the whole of the reign of Elizabeth there was a persistent and bloody persecution against freedom of thought of any kind. In 1594, Adfield and Carter suffered death because the former had brought into England a Catholic book and the latter had had the same in his possession.

A sect that fell under the displeasure of Queen Elizabeth was the "Family of Love." The founder was a Dutch Anabaptist, born at Delft, called David George, but the leader whose influence was of the most importance was Henry Nicolai of Münster. Nicolai gave out that his writings were of equal authority with Holy Scripture. "Moses," he says, "taught mankind to hope, Christ to believe, but Nicolai taught man to love, which last is of more worth than both the former." The Queen ordered (in 1575) that all books and writings maintaining this doctrine should be destroyed and burned and that possessors of such books should be duly punished. In 1608, James I, in a proclamation concerning the supervision of literature, says: "For better oversight of books of all sortes before they come to the presse, we have resolved to make choice of commissioners that shall looke more narrowly into the nature of all those things that shall be put to the presse, either concerning our authoritie royall or concerning our government, or the lawes of our Kingdom."[1]

In July, 1637, the Star Chamber published an act for the regulation of literature which in the severity of its censorship can be compared only with a procedure under Napoleon. It was prohibited to import or make sale of any books the influence of which was opposed to sound faith or to the authority of the Church or to the authority of government or to any rulers or to the interests of the community, or in which there should be libels or attacks against any corporation or any individual person. The penalties prescribed included fines, imprisonment, and bodily punishment, the decision to be made under the authority of the Chamber. The printing of any book which had not secured the approval of the Chamber was forbidden under heavy penalties. Books in the department of jurisprudence must be approved by the Chief Justice or by some authority appointed by him; books on history and statecraft were to be approved by the Secretary of State; those on morals by the Lord Marshal; works on theology, philosophy, natural science, poetry, and general literature, by the Archbishop of Canterbury or Bishop of London or by the chancellor of one of the two universities. Licenses were to be issued for but twenty master printers outside of those appointed directly by the Crown and those allotted to the universities. No printer was to operate more

[1] Villers. 290 seq.

than two presses or was to have more than two apprentices. Should anybody undertake to operate a press without securing a license from the Chamber, he was liable to be placed in the stocks, to be flogged through the city, and, after judgment, to further penalties.

In 1638, Alexander Leighton was, under a judgment of the Star Chamber, condemned in connection with a book entitled: *An Appeal to the Parliament or Sion's Plea against the Prelacie.* He was sentenced to a fine of ten thousand pounds, to degradation from the ministry, and to be publicly whipped in the palace yard; he was made to stand two hours in the pillory, one ear was cut off, a nostril slit open, and one of his cheeks branded with the letters S.S. (Sower of Sedition). A week later, he underwent a second whipping and a repetition of the mutilation. He was then left in prison for three years but, in 1641, had the satisfaction of having his sentence reversed by the House of Commons. The book had declared the institution of Episcopacy to be anti-Christian and satanical and it accused the king with having been corrupted by the bishops to the undoing of himself and his people.

In 1633, Prynne was condemned by the Star Chamber to be fined five thousand pounds, to be placed in the pillory, to be deprived of his ears, and to perpetual imprisonment. The book on the ground of which this punishment was administered was entitled: *The Histriomastix, the player's scourge or actor's tragedies.* Lord Cottington, the Chancellor of the Exchequer, says in his judgment: "I do in the first place begin censure with Prynne's book. I condemn it to be burned by the hangman," etc. This is said to be the first instance in England in which a condemned publication was burned by the hangman. Prynne came again under condemnation, in 1637, in connection with a book called the *Flagellum Pontificis et Episcoporum Latinorum*, which was said to have been written in co-operation with J. Bastwick and H. Burton. I do not find the record of Prynne's punishment in this case, but Bastwick was condemned by the High Commission court to pay a fine of one thousand pounds, to be excommunicated, to be debarred from the practice of his profession (medicine), and to remain in prison until he recanted (and that is, he says, "until domesday in the afternoone").

The practice of burning books was continued by the Puritans, who also utilised for the purpose the services of the common hangman. One book so burned (in 1619) was the King's *Book of Sports*, issued by James in 1618, on the advice of Morton, Bishop of Chester. It had been ordered to be read in all churches throughout England. Copies were publicly burned in a number of the Puritan counties.

The regulations for the control of the press in England were more strenuous under the Commonwealth and the later Stuarts than before the death of Charles I. Between the years 1637-1681, more than two hundred books came upon the condemnation lists. Among the works condemned and prohibited by Cromwell was the *Areopagitica* of Milton, published in 1644. In 1646, was condemned the book by John Biddle (known as the father of modern Unitarianism) which bore the title: *Twelve Arguments from Scripture in regard to the Divinity of the Holy Ghost*. The author was imprisoned and the copies of the book burned. The censor of the press under the last two Stuarts was Roger L'Estrange The penalties in force at the time he assumed the office providing for the destruction of books, the imprisonment and in certain cases the death of the authors and printers, were, in his judgment, not sufficiently severe. He beseeched Parliament to give him authority to add to these penalties stocks, public whipping, the cutting off of the hand, the cutting out of the tongue, etc. A printer named Trogan, who came under the disapproval of the censor, was executed in 1686, with various revolting details.

In 1642, the Parliament condemned and ordered burned by the hangman five publications written by Royalists. In each succeeding year, similar action was taken with publications (mainly pamphlets) written in opposition to the control of Parliament. A more serious matter for the authors than the burning of the books was that of the fines. Joseph Primatt, for instance, in 1652, was fined five thousand pounds for the publication of a petition to Parliament, and Lilburne was in the same year fined seven thousand pounds. The first theological work dealt with by Parliament was a treatise by John Archer entitled *Comfort for believers about their Sinnes and Troubles*. This was published in 1645 and in the same year was, under the order of Parliament, publicly burned in four places. In September, 1650, a monograph by Lawrence Clarkson entitled *Single Eye, All light, no darkness*, was condemned to be burned by the hangman and Clarkson, after being imprisoned for a month, was sentenced to banishment for life. These instances are selected from a long series of similar condemnations merely in order to make clear that the theory of the Parliament in regard to the right and the duty of the Government to prevent the circulation of pernicious literature (that is to say, literature the opinions of which were not in accord with those of the existing authorities) differed in no way from that of the supporters of royalty. A similar series of condemnations, with burning of the books and fining of the authors, together with an occasional exposure in the pillory, was continued through the Restoration. In the year 1690, a treatise by Arthur Bury, rector of Exeter College, Oxford, issued under the title of the *Naked Gospels*, was ordered burned under the authority of the University of Oxford.

In 1698, a Scotchman named Aikenhead, who was at the time a student of but eighteen years of age, was hanged at Edinburgh, not on account of any heresies brought into print, but simply because in some wild talk he had referred to Christianity as a delusion. Under one of the statutes of Scotland, it was a capital crime to revile or to curse the Supreme Being or any person of the Trinity. The words used by the young man were not strictly within the definition of the statute, but this statute was, under the direction of James Stuart, Lord Advocate of Scotland, used to bring the boy to execution.[1]

The censorship laws were not repealed as an immediate result of the Revolution of 1688 but endured until 1695. The regulations then established maintained for the Crown the full authority to control the operations of the press, but the penalties were made much less severe. Among the books condemned under the new legislation were *Christianity not Mysterious*, by John Toland, *Thoughts concerning Human Souls*, by William Coward, and the *Fable of the Bees*, by Mandeville, in 1723. (The last had been published as far back as 1706). Mandeville's volume was made

[1] Macaulay's *England*, ix, 286.

the subject of a presentment by the Grand Jury of Middlesex. The book was described as "a public nuisance, having a tendency to the subversion of all religion, the undermining of civil government, and the impairment of our duty to the Almighty." No penalty was inflicted, or ordered, upon the author, nor was the book itself suppressed.[1]

Among the books condemned in the succeeding years were *The Doctrine of the Trinity*, by Samuel Clark, and the *Miracle of Our Saviour*, by Thomas Woolston. The author of the latter was fined twenty-five pounds and was then imprisoned until he could raise two thousand pounds. He died after four years' imprisonment.

In 1701, a treatise by John Asgill on the *Covenant of Eternal Life* was burned by the order of two Parliaments, English and Irish. In 1702, the famous essay by Defoe, *The Shortest Way with the Dissenters*, was burned by the hangman under order of Parliament and Defoe was sentenced to three days' punishment in the pillory, to a ruinous fine, and to a long imprisonment. The trial of Saccheverell brought about the burning, in 1710, of a long series of books, including his own sermons and works by both his supporters and adversaries. In 1707, the Grand Jury of Middlesex made a presentment characterising as a public nuisance the essay by Matthew Tyndale entitled the *Rights of the Christian Church*. Tyndale reflects that this proceeding will further "the wider circulation of one of the best books that have been published in our age among many people that would not otherwise have heard of it." It was burned by the hangman in 1710. In 1722, the Commons agreed with the resolution of the Peers to have burned at the Royal Exchange the declaration

[1] Stephen, *Free Thinking and Plain Speaking*, 279.

of the Pretender issued as the declaration of James III. In 1763, numbers of the *North Briton*, of John Wilkes, who was then himself a member of the House, were, under an order of the two Houses, condemned to be burned at the Royal Exchange. The author was expelled from the House, but secured, after a long contest, a re-election. A volume issued without name in 1775, under the title of *The present Crisis in regard to America considered*, was burned on the 24th of February of that year and is referred to as the last book which the English Parliament has condemned to the flames.

In 1795, Sheridan proposes to have publicly burned a treatise by Reeve entitled *Thoughts on English Government*, but his proposal was not supported. The press law, passed as late as December, 1819, imposed a penalty of transportation on the writers or printers of godless and revolutionary works. This law was repealed in 1837, and the legislation of 1869 finally secured an assured freedom for the press. It is the conclusion of Catholic writers, in summing up the history of what they call the exceptionally fierce and brutal censorship of England, that the responsibility for this rests with the original crime committed by the State against the Church universal; and with the continued and demoralising wrong caused by transferring the control of the Church to the civil authorities.

The history of political censorship, or of censorship by the State in England, is a large and complex subject to which in a work like this it is of course, possible only to make reference.

In 1877 was printed (privately) in London a catalogue which from the title has been classed with the Indexes: *Index librorum prohibitorum;* being notes bio-, biblio-, and icono-graphical and critical on curious and uncommon books, compiled by Pisanus Fraxi. This is, however, simply a list, probably prepared for commercial purposes, of obscene books.

4. **Summary.**—The instances cited are sufficient to show that the spirit of Protestantism, in each and all of the sects that came into power or influence in the State, has through the past centuries held it to be the right and duty of the Church, and of the State under the influence of the Church, to supervise and to control the productions of the printing-press and the reading of the people. The fact, however, that within the Protestant communion there were so many points of view, rendered it not only difficult but impossible to establish any consistent and continuing policy of censorship. There was also a lack of any effective machinery for carrying out, within these Protestant territories, such regulations as the censors of the Church might establish. In certain places and at certain times the civil authorities. like the magistrates of Geneva or the Elector of Saxony, were ready to utilise the force of the State for carrying out the decrees of the Church, but such co-operation and support were at best (or at worst) but intermittent and spasmodic. In Germany or in Switzerland. the authority of the State covered but a limited territory. If the censorship pressure became burdensome in one city, there was no essential difficulty in moving the composing-room and the press to some other place where the faith of the magistrates was not so "orthodox" or so strenuous. As a result, the Protestant writers, representing all schools of protest, found no continued difficulty in bringing their productions into print and in circulating these among sympathetic readers.

The Jesuit historian, while admitting that the condemnation of the Catholic Church has fallen upon certain works of unquestioned scholarly value, insists that the Protestant censorship of authors and books of similar standing has been, to say the least, no less severe. He maintains, further, that the Catholic policy and methods have been more consistent, more discriminating, more intelligent, and more moral in purpose and in effect than those of the Protestants. He emphasises the importance of distinguishing between the circles of readers for which different books are fitted, either to do service or to work injury. He writes: "The works of Grotius, Gibbon, and Guicciardini have a deserved repute with the scholars. We may admit, that scholars can derive from such works valuable instruction, but this does not make them suitable for the reading of the untrained or the half trained. The Church undertakes always to maintain this distinction "

The Father sums up his arraignment of the censorship of the State by a bitter reference to the methods pursued by the Protestant Government of Prussia with its Catholic subjects in Poland. What answer can an instructor make in a school in Posen when a child asks why he is forbidden to read the Polish Catechism? The instructor can only say that the modern State is all powerful, and that in the execution of its self-imposed task of crushing out nationality, it is willing to take the responsibility not only for the interpretation of science, but for the shaping of belief.[1]

"Whence," says Hilgers, "do the civil authorities secure the right to compel Catholic children to accept

[1] Hilgers, 192

instruction from heretical books; and to prohibit the use in Catholic families, outside even of the walls of the official institutions, the use of Catholic books and documents? Here is a censorship tyranny with which in the history of Rome there is nothing to be compared."

CHAPTER IX

THE BOOK PRODUCTION OF EUROPE AS AFFECTED BY CENSORSHIP

1. General. 2. The Universities. 3. Italy. 4. Spain. 5. France. 6. Germany 7 The Netherlands. 8. England. 9. The *Index Generalis* of Thomas James, 1627.

1. **General.**—Four men, Columbus, Luther, Copernicus, and Gutenberg, stand at the dividing line of the Middle Ages, and serve as boundary stones marking the entrance of mankind into the higher and finer epoch of its development.[1]   It would be difficult to say which one of the four has made the larger contribution to this development or has done the most to lift up the spirit of mankind and to open for man the doors to the new realms that were awaiting him.   The Genoese discoverer opens new regions to our knowledge and imagination, leads Europe from the narrow restrictions of the Middle Ages out into the vast space of Western oceans, and, in adding to the material realm controlled by civilisation, widens still more largely the range of its thought, and fancy.   The reformer of Wittenberg, in breaking the bonds that had chained the spirits of his fellow-men and in securing for them again their rights as individual Christians, conquers for them a spiritual realm and brings them into direct relations with their Creator.   The great astronomer shatters,

[1] Kapp, *Gesch.*, 231.

through his discoveries, the fixed and petty conceptions of the universe that had ruled the minds of mankind, and in bringing to men fresh light on the nature
and extent of created things, widens at the same time
their whole understanding of themselves and of duty.
The citizen of Mayence may claim to have unchained
intelligence and given to it wings. He utilised lead no
longer as a death-bringing ball, but in the form of
life-quickening letters which were to bring before
thousands of minds the teachings of the world's
thinkers. Each one of the four had his part in bringing
to the world light, knowledge, and development.

Before the beginning of the Reformation, the business
of printing books, which had originated among Germans,
had secured in the so-called Latin countries, Italy,
France, and Spain, larger development than in the
German lands. It is certainly the case that, irrespective of the facilities afforded by the printing-press,
the intellectual development in Italy was, during the
15th and the first portion of the 16th century, far in
advance of Germany and for that matter of the rest
of Europe. If the Reformation was not in itself an
important factor in the transfer of the centre of literary
activity, this period certainly coincided with such
transfer. After 1518, the centres of literary production
and intellectual activities are to be sought rather in
Germany and in Holland than in Italy or Spain.
France, on the other hand, appears to have been able,
while accepting a rather burdensome measure of censorship, to have retained an important intellectual position,
the influence of which is, of course, most closely associated with the university of Paris.

During the years immediately following the invention
of printing, the Church gave to the new art a cordial

welcome. The scholarly ecclesiastics were among the first to recognise the service that could be rendered by the printers in multiplying for general distribution the books of doctrine and of devotion. The Church felt secure in its hold upon the minds of the people and for three quarters of a century, at least, there was no apprehension that the people could be diverted from their allegiance to the true Faith. Many of the monasteries made space for printing-presses, while others placed funds at the disposal of printers who were needing co-operation. It was not only in the scholarly circles of the Church that the new art secured prompt recognition. The Brothers of Common Life, who for a century or more had taken upon themselves the work of teaching the people and who had utilised in this work manuscript copies of books of devotion, were among the first to make use of the printing-press in the work of education for the distribution of their books of devotion. Within eighteen years after the production of Gutenberg's Bible, the Brothers had printing-presses at work in Deventer (Holland) and in a number of their monasteries in North Germany. In Strasburg, Magdeburg, Nuremberg, and elsewhere before 1470, the monasteries of the Carthusians had established printing-presses.

The work of publishing material for popular circulation begins practically with the Reformation. It was with the great popular demand for instruction and information which had been developed through the work of the reformers, that there came to the people at large the realisation of the value to them of the invention of Gutenberg, and an understanding of its importance for the work of educating and of organising the people and for the securing the right of individual thought production against the oppression of Church and State. The system of censorship, ecclesiastical and political, a system which was to do much to hamper the development of literature and of publishing, dates in substance from the Reformation.

The effect of the censorship of the Church on the activities of publishers and on the production of books varied very materially, even in those States in which the regulations of the Church were, in form at least, accepted as authoritative. The States in which, during the 16th and 17th centuries, the work of the printer-publishers came into conflict, in one way or another, with the censorship edicts, and in which literary production and activity were influenced by censorship policy, were: Italy, France, South Germany, North Germany. Switzerland, England, Spain, the Spanish Netherlands, and Holland.

In Italy, the edicts of the Roman Inquisition and of the Congregation of the Index having to do with the prohibition or the expurgation of books were of course, at least in form, binding equally upon all the States and cities in which printing-presses were at work. As a fact, however, at no time, not even after the labours of the Council of Trent, did it prove practicable to secure any uniformity of procedure or of result in the enforcement of the censorship decrees throughout the territory of the Italian peninsula. The printers of Rome were under obligation to take immediate action in regard to the cancellation or withdrawal from sale of books condemned. Outside of Rome, or at least outside of the States of the Church, periods of from thirty to ninety days were allowed within which the printers were expected to secure knowledge of the prohibitory edicts. The Church authorities assumed

that these edicts were binding throughout the entire
Catholic world, but, outside of Italy, the printers,
booksellers, or readers were not under obligation to
have knowledge of the prohibitions until the edicts
had been published by the local bishops or the local
inquisitors. It was the case that from time to time
the local bishops were not in sympathetic accord with
the literary policy of Rome, and delayed indefinitely,
or declined altogether, to make publication of the
edicts. In certain of the Italian cities, of which
Venice is the most noteworthy example, the civil
authorities took the ground that no regulations concerning printing and bookselling could be considered as in
force unless and until such regulations had been confirmed by the civil authorities. The Church claimed
not only the right to prohibit pernicious literature,
but to authorise and to protect for sale throughout
the world the works which secured its approval.
The papal privileges conceded, in form at least, to the
printers to whom they were issued, exclusive control
not only within the States of the Church, but in all
the States of the world that acknowledged the authority of the Church. There was, however, practically
no machinery for enforcing the authority of the papal
privileges. The material advantage belonging to
such a privilege was that it carried with it the assurance
of the approval of the Church concerning the character
of the book. It constituted, namely, evidence that the
book had secured the approval of the Church censors and
(with an occasional exception) it preserved the book
from interference on the part of local ecclesiastical censors, whose prejudices were usually more bitter and
whose ignorant dread of heretical scholarship was greater
than was the case with the censors appointed directly

by the Congregation.   The fact that during the 16th and 17th centuries, Latin was the official language of scholarship and nearly universal as the language of literature, and that the great majority of publications of importance came into print in Latin, served to maintain a certain universality of learning, of literature, and of science and to build up a body of scholars who belonged not to any one State, least of all possible to the "country of origin," but to Europe as a whole, to the world of literature and learning.   The detail of smallest importance that occurs in thinking of the career of a Casaubon, Scaliger, or an Erasmus is the place of his birth.   This universality of language furthered also, however, during the same centuries, the operations of the ecclesiastical censors and the enforcement of the policy of censorship.   When there came to be a development of national literatures brought into print in the national languages, the difficulties of a standard of censorship and of a general enforcement of such standard, even through the States recognising the authority of the Church, became very much greater. It is evident, in fact, from the fragmentary additions of the lists of the later Indexes that the examiners, acting on behalf of the Congregation or of the Inquisition, had very little familiarity with literature that came into print in language other than Latin or Italian.

The art of printing was one which evidently could not long be restricted to any one locality.   It was speedily carried from Mayence to other communities in which literary interests or educational facilities could be furthered by its use.

In 1462, on the 28th of October, Archbishop Adolph of Nassau captured the city of Mayence and gave it over to his soldiers for plunder.   The typesetters and printers, with all the other artisans whose work depended upon the commerce of the city, were driven to flight and it appeared for the moment as if the newly instituted printing business had been crushed. The result of the scattering of the printers was, however, the introduction of the new art into a number of other centres where the influences were favourable for its development. The typesetters of Mayence, driven from their printing offices by the heavy hand of the Church, journeyed throughout the world and proceeded to give to many communities the means of education and enlightenment through which the great revolt against the Church was finally instituted.

An important influence in securing for the work of the early printer-publishers of Germany a greater freedom from restriction than was enjoyed by their contemporaries in France was the fact that, in Germany, the beginning of printing, or at least its development, took place, not in a university centre but in a commercial town and was from the outset carried on not by scholars but by workers of the people. This brought the whole business of the production and the distribution of books in Germany into closer relations with the mass of the people than was the case in France. The direct association with the university of the first printers in France (who were themselves the immediate successors of the official university scribes) brought the printing-press under the direct control of the university and rendered easy the establishment by the university authorities, and particularly by the theologians, of a continued censorship.

Hegel, in his *Philosophy of History*, refers to the renewed interest in the writings of the ancients which was brought about through the service of the printing-press. He points out, further, that the Church felt at the outset no anxiety concerning the influence of the pagan literature and that the ecclesiastical authorities evidently had no understanding of the new elements of suggestion and enquiry that this literature was introducing into the minds of men. It may be considered as one of the fortunate circumstances attending the introduction of the art of printing that the popes of the time were largely men of liberal education and intellectual tastes, while one or two, such as Nicholas V, Julius II, and Leo X, had a keen personal interest in literature and were themselves creators of books. The fact that Leo X was a luxury-loving, free-thinking prince rather than a devoted Christian leader or teacher, may very probably have been a favourable influence for the enlightenment and development of his own generation and of the generations that were to come. An earnest and narrow-minded head of the Church could, during the first years of the 16th century, have retarded not a little the development of the work of producing books for the community at large.

It was a number of years before the dread of the use of the printing-press for the spread of heretical doctrines, and of a consequent undermining of the authority of the Church, assumed such proportions in the minds of the popes in Rome and with the bishops elsewhere as to cause the influence of the Church to be used against the interests of the world of literature. As a result of this early acceptance by the Church of the printing-press as a useful ally and servant, the first Italian presses were supported by bishops and cardinals in the work of producing classics for scholarly readers, while at the other extremity of the Church organisation, and at a distance of a thousand miles or more from

Rome, the Brothers of Common Life in the Low Countries were using their presses for the distribution of cheap books among the people. Many citations could be made of the approval with which the scholarly ecclesiastics of the time regarded the new art. Felix Fabri, prior of the Dominican monastery in Ulm, says in his *Historia Suevorum*, issued in the year 1459, that "no art that the world has known can be considered so useful, so much to be esteemed, indeed so divine as that which has now, through the Grace of God, been discovered in Mayence." Johannes Rauchler,[1] the first rector of the Tübingen School, rejoices that through the new art so many authors can now be brought within the reach of students in Latin, Greek, and Hebrew, authors who are witnesses for the Christian faith, and the service of whose writings to the Church and to the world is so great that he can but consider "this art as a gift directly from God himself."

The favourable relations between the Church and the printers were checked by the Humanistic movement, which, a generation or more before the Reformation, began to bring into question the authority of the Church and the infallibility of the Papacy. The influence of the Humanistic teachers was so largely furthered by the co-operation of the printers that the jealousy and dread of the ecclesiastical authorities were promptly aroused, and they began to utter fulminations against the wicked and ignorant men who were using the art of printing for misleading the community and for the circulation of error. Ecclesiastics who had at first favoured the widest possible circulation of the Scriptures, now contended that much of the spread of heresy was due to the misunderstanding of the Scriptures

[1] Kapp, 62.

on the part of readers who were acting without the guidance of their spiritual advisers.   The Church now took the ground that the reading of the Scriptures by individuals was not to be permitted and that the Bible was to be given to the community only through the interpretations of the Church.   At the same time, the authority of the Church was exerted to repress or at least to restrict the operations of the printing-press and to bring printers and publishers under a close ecclesiastical supervision and censorship.   It was, however, already too late to stand between the printing-press and the people.   Large portions of the community had become accustomed to a general circulation of books and to the use without restriction of such reading matter as might be brought within their reach, and this privilege they were no longer willing to forego. In Spain, in Italy, and in France, the censorship of the Church soon became sufficiently burdensome to hamper and to interfere with publishing undertakings and to check the natural development of literary production. Even in Italy, however, the critical spirit was found to be too strong to be crushed out, and from Venice, which became the most important of the Italian publishing centres (because it was the freest from papal control) it proved possible to secure for the productions of the printing press a circulation that was practically independent of the censorship of Rome.

The importance of Frankfort as a centre of the trade in books began with the first years of the 15th century, when the dealers in manuscripts were present with booths at the Frankfort Fair.   The manuscript dealers came together once a year also at the fairs of Salzburg, Ulm, and Nordlingen, but the book-trade at Frankfort soon assumed a pre-eminence that it did not lose for two centuries. The earliest date at which is chronicled the sale at the Frankfort Fair of printed books was 1480. For these earlier sales of manuscripts and printed books, there was apparently no censorship or official supervision.

The manuscript trade in the Netherlands was more important both in character and in extent than that carried on in Germany, and it appears to have exerted a larger influence upon the general education of the people than the book-trade of the time in either France or Italy. In France and in Italy, the earlier book-trade, first in manuscripts, later in printed volumes, was connected with the work of the universities. In the Low Countries, on the other hand, and particularly in such centres as Ghent, Antwerp, and Bruges, there came into existence during the first half of the 15th century an active and intelligently conducted business in the production of books, both of a scholarly and of a popular character, the sale of which was made among citizens who were for the greater part outside of university circles. One reason why the trade in books found a larger development in Belgium than in Germany was the greater wealth of the working classes in the Low Countries. With the wealth, came cultivation and a taste for luxuries and among luxuries soon came to be included art and literature. Another factor in the early development of the book-trade was the freedom from the university censorship control which in Paris, Bologna, and other book-producing centres restricted the undertakings of the dealers.

A special characteristic of the literary undertakings of the 16th century is the practice of collaboration. Such works as the great dictionary of the Academy and the *Corpus inscriptionum latinarum* are instances of undertakings which would have been impossible for individual authorship. The Catholic reformation was also contemporary with an important development in literary form and in literary expression. It is fair to remember, however, that for this development the influence of the Italian writers of the Renaissance may be considered as chiefly responsible.

The Renaissance, the influence of which in Germany had been so large a factor in bringing about the Protestant Reformation, had not succeeded in Italy in revitalising paganism, but the Italian writers of the time broke away from the traditions of Christianity. Their Deity was no longer the sombre avenger invoked by Dante; or the consoler who, in the verse of Petrarch, reunites the souls that have been purified under suffering and have endured the separation of death. It was Art. The religion of Ariosto may be summed up as the development of literary perfection coupled with an indifference to moral ideas.[1]

The rule of Alexander VI (Borgia), 1492–1503, coincided with the beginning of the active work of the printing-presses in Venice, Florence, and in Rome. The influence of the Pope was, however, promptly brought to bear to discourage the undertakings of the printer-publishers. Venice was practically outside of his control, while even in Florence the printers were not prepared to accept dictation from the papal representatives. In Rome, however, the subjection of the press to ecclesiastical censorship, for the initiation of which the responsibility rested with Alexander, proved at once a serious limitation to its activities. It was undoubtedly this restriction which gave to the printers of Venice their great advantage over their early

---

[1] De Sanctis, *Storia della letteratura italiana*, ii, Chap. 13.

competitors in Rome. Venice was the leader among
the cities of Italy in resisting the censorship of the
Church, although even in Venice the Church succeeded
in the end in gaining the more important of its contentions. In Spain, the control over the printing-presses
on the part of the censors of the Church was hardly
questioned, but these censors represented the authority
not of Rome but of the local Inquisition. The Spanish
Inquisition was, for the longer period of its existence
under the direction of the Dominicans, and it was frequently the case that the decisions of the Spanish
inquisitors, in regard both to the literature to be condemned and to that to be approved, were in direct
opposition to the conclusions of the Papacy. In
France, after a century of contest, the ecclesiastical
control of the printing-press became practically merged
in the censorship exercised by the Crown, a censorship
which was in itself as much as the publishing trade
could bear and continue to exist. In Austria and in
South Germany, after the crushing out of the various
Reformation movements, the Church and the State
worked in practical accord in maintaining a close supervision of the printing-presses. In North Germany,
on the other hand, the ecclesiastical censorship never
became important. The evils produced by it were,
however, serious and long-enduring over a large portion
of the territory of Europe, and the papal Borgia,
although by no means a considerable personage, must
be held responsible for bringing into existence an evil
which assumed enormous proportions in the intellectual history of Europe.

2. **The Universities and the Book-trade.** The book-
dealers of Paris, beginning their work as part of the
organisation of the university, had their first quarters

in the immediate vicinity of the college buildings. The foundation of the College of the Sorbonne dates from 1257. The college had been instituted by Robert de Sorbon, chaplain to Louis IX, from whom it took its name. It was at once affiliated to the university, the work of which had begun about half a century earlier. The college assumed the control of the theological instruction in the university and the divines of the Sorbonne exercised from the outset a controlling influence over the general policy of the university. The theological faculty took charge, on behalf of the university, of the censorship of the Paris book-trade and of the productions of the Paris press. It based its authority for this censorship in part on the fact that the book-dealers had from the earliest manuscript period been under the direction of the university, and in part on the authority of the Church. The dealers who did not secure a license from the university occupied as their locality the precincts of Notre Dame on the island of La Cité. Throughout Europe, in fact, the earlier book-dealers carried on their business very frequently under the immediate shadow of the cathedral if not within its portals. In Cologne, for instance, the manuscript-dealers in the early part of the 15th century took possession for their shops or booths of various corners or angles of the cathedral building; while in Münster was allotted to them the court immediately in front of the cathedral. There is a reference as early as 1408, in one of the Strasburg chronicles, to the scribes who sold books on the steps of the Cathedral of Our Lady.

With the invention of printing, the universities (with the exception of Paris) lost their control over the business of book production, and there resulted necessarily a decrease in their influence and relative importance in the community. They continued to lay claim to the control of censorship but this claim could not be supported in the face of the direct action of the Church on the one hand, and that of the civil authorities on the other. Paulsen[1] writes: "The tradition of the universities, and, in particular, their method of instruction in the arts and in theology, were rejected with scorn by the new educator through its representatives, the poets and the orators," to whom the form and the substance of this teaching seemed alike to be barbarism. The *Epistolae obscurorum virorum*, published in 1516, was the work of a band of youthful poets working under the leadership of Mutianus at Erfurt; it expressed the hatred and detestation felt by the Humanists for the ancient university system. Within a few years from the publication of the *Epistolae*, the influence of the Humanists had so far extended itself as to have effected a large modification in the systems of study in all the larger universities. The ecclesiastical Latin was replaced by classical Latin; and the old translations of the Aristotelian texts were driven out by new versions representing more exact scholarship. Greek was taken up in the faculty of arts, and courses in its language and literature were established in nearly all the universities This change was coincident with the shifting of the authority for censorship from the hands of the university theologians to those of the direct representatives of the pope or of the State.

The strifes and contentions of the Reformation checked for a time the development in the universities of the studies connected with the intellectual movement of the Renaissance, and lessened the demand for the

---

[1] Paulsen, 41.

literature of these studies. The active-minded were absorbed in theological controversy, while those who could not understand the questions at issue could still shout the shibboleths of the leaders. As Erasmus puts it, rather bitterly: *ubi regnat Lutheranismus, ibi interitus litterarum.* The literature of the Reformation, however, itself did much to make good for the printing-presses the lessened demand for the classics, while, a few years later, the organisation in Germany of the Protestant schools and universities aroused intellectual activities in new regions and created fresh requirements for printed books. Within half a century of the Diet of Worms, the centre of the book-absorbing population of Germany had been transferred from the Catholic States of the south to the Protestant territories of the north and the literary preponderance of the latter has continued to increase during the succeeding generations.

Mark Pattison says[1]:

" If we ask why Italy did not continue to be the centre of the Humanist movement which she had so brilliantly encouraged, the answer is that the intelligence was crushed by the reviviscence of ecclesiastical ideas. Learning is the result of research, and research must be free and cannot co-exist with the claim of the Catholic religion to be superior to enquiry. The French school, it will be observed, was wholly, in fact or in intention, Protestant. As soon as it was decided (as it was before 1600) that France was to be a Catholic country and the University of Paris a Catholic University, learning was extinguished in France. France saw without regret and without repentance the expatriation of her unrivalled scholars. With Scaliger and Saumaise, the seat of learning was transferred from France to Holland.

[1] Casaubon, 453.

The third period of classical learning thus coincides with the Dutch school. From 1593, the date of Scaliger's removal to Leyden, the supremacy in the republic of learning was possessed by the Dutch. In the course of the 18th century, the Dutch school was gradually supplanted by the North German, which from that time forward has taken, and still possesses, the lead in philological science."

As early as 1323. the University of Paris was the most important in Europe for theological studies, as that of Bologna was the authority on jurisprudence, and that of Padua for medicine. The early development of theological studies in Paris was one of the influences that brought about the authority of the College of the Sorbonne in the censorship of the book productions of the kingdom.

An anonymous author of a polemical tract, written in the previous century for the purpose of pointing out the errors of some heretical production, says: *Is autem erroneus liber positus fuit publice ad exemplandum Parisiis anno Domini 1254. Unde certum est quod jam publice predicaretur nisi boni prelati et predicatores impedirent.* ("This heretical tract was openly given to the scribes to be copied in Paris in the year of our Lord, 1254. Whence it is evident what manner of doctrine would now be set forth to the public had not good priests and preachers interfered.")[1] By the beginning of the 16th century, the University of Vienna had taken a leading place among the centres of education in Europe. It is said to have contained at this time no less than seven thousand students and the work of the Humanists in furthering the revival of interest in the classic authors was in Vienna at this

[1] *Gesch. der Präger Universität*, viii, 8.

time particularly active. Within a quarter of a century after Luther had begun his protests, the Jesuits secured the controlling influence in matters in Vienna and from this time the relative importance of the university steadily declined.[1]

The jurist Scheurl writes from Nuremberg to Cardinal Campeggi, March 15, 1524: "Every common man is now asking for books or pamphlets and more reading is being done in a day than heretofore in a year."[2] In Nuremberg, as in other towns, it became the practice to read the books of Luther out loud in the market place. Erasmus complains, in 1523, that since the publication of the German New Testament, the whole book-trade seems to be absorbed with the writings of Luther, and to be interested in giving attention to nothing else. He says, further, that it is very difficult to find in Germany publishers willing to place their imprint upon books written in behalf of the Papacy. As an example of the kind of interest caused by the writings of Luther, it is recorded that the magistrates of Bremen sent a bookseller to Wittenberg for the purpose of purchasing for their official use a set of Luther's works. The citizens of Speyer are described as having the books read to them at supper, and as making transcripts of the texts. In hundreds of towns throughout Germany, Luther's writings were brought to the notice of the people by means of the very edict which had for its purpose their final suppression, and after the Diet of Worms, the demand for them rapidly increased. The preacher Matthaeus Zell writes from Strasburg, in 1523: "The Lutheran books are for sale here in the market-place immediately

[1] *Gesch. der Präger Universität*, viii, 8.
[2] Kapp 417.

beneath the edicts of the emperor and of the pope declaring them to be prohibited."

With the beginning of the 13th century, it was realised that the newly organised universities had become the centres of intellectual activity. The popes undertook promptly the institution of machinery for the supervision of the work done in the universities and of the literary productions that came from the instructors. It was the contention of the papal representatives that the appointments of the university officials having to do directly with the work of multiplying books, must rest with the theological faculty, that is to say with the immediate representatives of the Church. This contention was, in the main, sustained in such university centres as Bologna, Paris, Prague, Vienna, and Cologne. A brief, issued in 1479 by Sixtus IV, charges the rectors and the deacons of the university with the responsibility of censorship. The edict in 1486 by Berthold, Archbishop of Mayence, is to be classed not as an ecclesiastical act but as an expression of authority of a German prince. The Archbishop asserted the right on behalf not of the Roman Church but of his State. The censorship exercised by the University of Cologne terminated with the close of the 15th century. The representative of the Archbishop claimed authority, on the strength of the Bull issued in 1486 by Innocent VIII, directed against the printers of pernicious books, to take into his own hands the direction of censorship of the entire principality.

3. Italy.—The introduction of the printing-press into Italy was brought about under the initiative of Juan Turrecremata, who was Abbot of Subiaco, and who later became Cardinal. The Cardinal was a Spaniard by birth and his family name (in the Spanish form

Torquemada) was, later, associated with some of the most strenuous of the persecutions which the Inquisition brought to bear upon the printers. The great Spanish inquisitor was a nephew of the Cardinal. The Cardinal had been one of the confessors of Queen Isabella and is said to have made to her the first suggestion of the necessity of establishing the Inquisition in order to check the rising spirit of heresy. He did not realise what a Trojan horse, full of heretical possibilities, he was introducing into Italy in bringing in the Germans and their printing-press.

Turrecremata was a man of scholarly interests, and he felt assured that the new art could be made of large service to the Church. He provided funds for the establishment in Subiaco, in 1464, of the first printing-press in Italy, which was placed in charge of the Germans Schweinheim and Pannartz who had learned their art directly from Gutenberg. The two Germans later migrated to Rome and within a few years there was a large invasion of German printers into the capital. The first books printed in Subiaco under the instructions of the Cardinal were a *Donatus*, an edition of Lactantius, and an edition of the *De Oratore* of Cicero. Until towards the close of the century, when the Church authorities began to realise the risks that were to be incurred by the Church through the popular distribution of printed literature, the German printers found opportunities in Italy for successful and remunerative business.

In 1492, the printing art was introduced into Venice, where it speedily developed into one of the most important of the industries of the city. For nearly a century thereafter, Venice took place among the most influential of the European centres of publishing and literary activity.   There were various grounds on which

Venice   the productions of the Venetian presses aroused criticism and antagonism in Rome. After the beginning of the work of Aldus in 1495, the Venetian publishing lists included a number of productions by Greek scholars.   The majority of these books being editions of Greek classics, had of course nothing whatever to do with matters of doctrine or Church policy.   The Roman censors of the time had no knowledge of Greek, an ignorance for which they were hardly to be criticised, as, until the books of the Aldine press began to reach the university centres, it was an ignorance that was shared by all the scholars of Europe.   These ecclesiastics were, however, very apprehensive of the influence of the doctrines of the Greek Church.   They appear to have imagined that the text of Homer or of Aristotle, or the accompanying notes, might be made to carry the contentions of the Greek Church in regard to the old-time issues which had divided Constantinople and Rome.   As the censors were unable themselves to examine the texts, and were unwilling to accept the conclusions of any examiners who understood Greek, their only means of defence against this insidious attack on the orthodoxy of Italy was to prohibit the production and the circulation of any volumes printed in this heretical language.

The presses of Venice were dangerous not only because they were being utilised by the scholars of Greece, but because they were bringing into print also works in Arabic, in Hebrew, in Persian, and in Chaldean.   In the Index lists as printed in Rome, the term "Chaldean" is utilised to cover the entire group of Oriental tongues which came into print in one form or another

from the presses of Venice. The censors who were ignorant of Greek were not likely to have any knowledge
of Hebrew, while there was still less chance that they
would be able to secure an understanding of the character of the literature presented in other Oriental
tongues. The first Hebrew books issued in Venice
were editions of the Hebrew Scriptures, of the *Talmud*
and of the *Targum*, which were printed under the
directions of the rabbins and at the cost of a publication
fund, collected for the purpose from Hebrew congregations throughout South Europe. The doctrines presented in the long series of Talmudic commentaries
might very possibly, if they could have been read by
the censors in Rome, have been interpreted as antagonistic, at least by implication, to the authority of the
Church of Rome. It would have been difficult, however, to point out any measure of doctrinal antagonism
in the Arabic books selected for production in Venice.
These comprised treatises on mathematics, treatises on
medicine, and Arabic versions, with commentaries by
Arab philosophers, of certain of the texts of Aristotle.
The two or three Persian volumes printed in Venice during the first years of the 16th century included an exposition of the faith of Zoroaster, a memoir of Hàroun-
al-Raschid, and some specimens of the poets of the 14th
century. The actual Chaldean volumes, but one or
two in all, were devoted to astrology. It was the
repute that came to these volumes that brought about
the application of the term Chaldean as a description
of any works of divination or magic. Each of the
Roman Indexes, from 1559, down, reiterates the prohibition of "Chaldean books of magic." The date
of the publication of the first of the Roman Indexes
happened to coincide with the time of the greatest

activity of the publishers of Venice. If the censorship policy of Rome could be enforced in Venice, the Venetian printers would be driven out of business. The issue was one that had to be fought out. The victory finally secured by the printers was due, in the main, to the courage and the intellectual force of a priest, Paolo Sarpi.

In 1479, Pope Sixtus IV makes Jenson, printer-publisher of Venice, Count Palatine, the first nobleman among publishers. In 1503, the Venetian Senate charged Musurus (the friend and literary associate of Aldus and professor of Greek in Padua) with the censorship of all Greek books printed in Venice, with reference particularly to the suppression of anything inimical to the Roman Church. This constitutes one of the earliest attempts made in Italy to supervise the work of the printing-press. The action of the Senate was doubtless instigated by the authorities of the Inquisition. It was natural that the ecclesiastics should have dreaded the influence of the introduction into Italy of the doctrines of the Greek Church, while it was doubtless the case that the refugees from Constantinople brought with them no very cordial feeling towards Rome. The belief was very general that if the Papacy had not felt a greater enmity against the Greek Church than against the Turk, the Catholic States of Europe would have saved Constantinople. The sacking of Constantinople by the armies of the Fourth Crusade was still remembered by the Christians of the East as a crime of the Western Church. There were, therefore, reasons enough why the authorities of Rome should think it necessary to keep a close watch over the new literature coming in from the East, and should do what was practicable to exclude all doctrinal writings, and the censorship instituted in 1503 was but the beginning of a long series of rigorous enactments.

The censorship measures undertaken by the Government of Venice (as was true of the measures of other States in which the business of publishing became of importance) were more largely concerned with the supervision of the press for the safety of the State than for the interests of the Church. For the century between 1407–1528, this censorship in Venice was carried on without the aid of any general law, and was based simply upon a series of precedents evolved from the individual action taken by the Government in each instance as it arose. The responsibility for the censorship of the press rested with the Council of Ten, which, in its capacity of a standing committee, assumed a general charge of the morals of the community. An application from a printer for a privilege must, according to the usual routine, be accompanied by a certificate or *testamur* from the examiners who were willing to certify as to the soundness and the importance of the work in question.

In the year 1508, we have the first example of an ecclesiastical *testamur* being required by the Council of Ten as a condition for their own *imprimatur*. The work was the *Universalis animae traditionis liber quintus* of Gregoriis, and the ecclesiastical censor reported that he found in it nothing opposed to Catholic verity.[1] This is the first instance of a religious censorship exercised by the secular government. The case indicates the position the Government of Venice proposed to take in regard to supervision of books touching upon theological matters. The State had a personal interest in protecting the Church against

[1] Brown, 63.

the attacks of books likely to be subversive of the Faith, and the authorities were glad to secure the opinion of the Church in regard to the character or tendency of a doubtful work; it intended, however, to retain in its own hands the final decision as to the permission to print; and it contended that the interests of Church and State could be best protected by the State taking action for both. It was the conclusion that, while there should be a religious censorship, the censor should act only through powers delegated to him by the secular government.

In 1515, an order was issued by the Council of Ten which established a general censorship for the literature of the Humanists. It was worded as follows:

"In all parts of the world and in the famous cities not only of Italy but also of barbarous countries, that the honour of the nation may be preserved, it is not allowed to publish works until they shall have been examined by the most learned person available. But in this our city, so famous and so worthy, no attention has as yet been given to this matter; whence it comes to pass that the most incorrect editions which appear before the world are those issued in Venice, to the dishonour of the city. Be it, therefore, charged upon our noble Andrea Navagero to examine all works in Humanity which for the future may be printed; and without his signature in the volumes they shall not be printed, under pain of being confiscated and burned, and a fine of three hundred ducats for him who disobeys this order."[1]

This is the first Italian example of a general or prevention censorship, applied to a whole class of literature. The third class of censorship concerns itself with the morals of literature, political morality,

[1] Brown, 65.

the attitude of the writer or of the publisher towards the State, and the probable influence of the book upon decency and *bonos mores*. The political censorship was apparently more effective than the censorship of morals. It was certainly the case that the *imprimatur* was given to not a few books of a scandalous character. In 1526, the Council of Ten issued a general order decreeing that for future publications, the *imprimatur* should be given only to works which had been examined and approved by two censors who should make a sworn report that its character was satisfactory.

In 1544, the commissioners of the University of Padua were constituted the permanent censors of Venetian books submitted for the *imprimatur* of the council. The censorship of the commissioners covered all points excepting those relating to religion or theology, which were still left to be passed upon by the ecclesiastical censors. In 1548, the first catalogue of prohibited books was issued in Venice. In this year were instituted, as an addition to the regular executive, three commissioners on heresy, the *Savii sopra l'Eresia*, who were charged with the new publications having to do with matters of religion or doctrine and also with the examination of imported books. The Lutheran heresy was now being promulgated by means of the press, and the ecclesiastical authorities were especially suspicious of literature coming from Germany. The organisation in this same year, 1548, of the Venetian guild of printers and publishers had for an important part of its responsibilities the checking of the production or the importation of heretical books.

In September, 1573, the History of Venice, written by Justiniani, which had been examined and, to a considerable extent, corrected by the local inquisitor, having been brought into print, was required to submit to a further censorship on the part of the Roman examiners. Fra Marco, the first examiner, writes to Sirleto that he has already written so frequently in regard to this book that he is mortified to trouble him further. He points out, however, that the Venetians are in a state of irritation that the promised papal permission has not been secured, and he asks for a decision in a matter that has already been held up for a long period of months.

In 1547, occurred the first instance of a trial undertaken in Venice by the Holy Office for offence committed through the printing-press. The list is closed in 1730, with the trial of Giovanni Checcazzi. In the 16th century, there were one hundred and thirty-two trials by the Inquisition; in the 17th, fifty-five; in the 18th, but four. It is not clear whether the diminished activity of the Inquisition during the later years was due to the increasingly hostile attitude taken by the Government of Venice towards the Church of Rome after 1596, or to the fact that the vigour of the press prosecutions during the last half of the 16th century had effectively stamped out the publication in Venice of heretical and immoral publications.

It is in connection with the Index of Pope Clement VIII and the Concordat that the history of publishing in Venice comes for the first time into touch with general history. The claim of the Church to the control of all publishing undertakings soon became involved in the larger question of the relations between Venice and Rome. Paolo Sarpi, who became the champion of the cause of the independence of the State against ecclesiastical domination, comes into the history of literature as the upholder

Venice and the Pope

of the rights of authors and of publishers against the crushing censorship of the Inquisition. The problem presented to the Venetian Government was whether the Venetian press, supported in its liberty by the Government, should continue to maintain its character as one of the freest presses in Europe (and therefore one with the most active production): or whether it should be permitted, for want of the support of the Government, to fall under the repressive influence of the Inquisition and the Index. As early as 1491, Franco, Bishop of Treviso and Papal Legate, had issued a decree prohibiting any one from printing in Venetian territory or from causing or permitting, to be printed, any books treating of the Catholic faith or of matters ecclesiastical without the express permission of the bishop or of the vicar-general of the diocese. The Legate named at once two works. Rosselli's *Monarchia* and Miran-dola's *Theses*, which were absolutely prohibited, and all existing copies of which were to be burned in the cathedral or in the parish churches within fifteen days from the publication of the decree. There was no charge that these works were in any way immoral or scandalous. They were condemned simply on the ground of the unsoundness of their doctrine. The contention raised in this order on behalf of the Church was far-reaching. If it were heretical to discuss, in a sense at all hostile to the Curia, the relative powers of the pope and the emperor, there would be an implied right in the Church to censure and to condemn any political writings in which reference was made to the authority of the pope or to the responsibilities of the emperor. It became in fact the keystone of the ecclesiastical position that in the case of the Church no separation was possible between politics and ec-

clesiastical dogma. In July, 1693, Paruta, the ambassador of Venice at the Vatican, submitted to the
pope a vigorous protest against the publication of the
Clementine Index, which was then in readiness. Paruta
pointed out that the commercial importance of the
book-trade in Venice at that time exceeded that of any
city in Europe; that the book-trade was in itself
deserving of protection and consideration; that a sufficient censorship was already exercised by the *imprimaturs* of the Council of Ten, who utilised among
their examiners the inquisitor; that the publication of
this Index would destroy the property, and might cause
the ruin, of many who, believing themselves to be safe
as long as they kept within the regulations of the
Council of Trent, had published books which were now
to be prohibited in the Clementine Index; that the
new Index not only made many additions to the lists
of prohibited books, but proposed a radical change in
the standard of prohibition—a great number of books
were now, on the ground of some trivial expressions, to
be condemned although they were not at all concerned
with ecclesiastical or religious questions; that it was
important for the Church to keep well affected men
of learning throughout the world and that such men
would certainly be very much troubled with any measures that interfered with scholarly undertakings and the
distribution of the world's literature. The arguments of
Paruta and similar protests that came to Rome from
Germany and from Paris had the effect of convincing
the pope that some modification of his Index was
necessary. The Index, as finally published four years
later, was very much altered and diminished. Among
the omissions from the first lists were the titles of the
whole class of non-religious books printed in Venice,

in behalf of which Paruta had spoken. In 1596, the printers and publishers of Venice again found occasion to appeal to the Senate for support against the regulations of the Clementine Index. They found that the works that remained prohibited in the Clementine lists, in addition to those on previous lists the prohibitions of which were still in force, included many that had constituted an important staple in their trade and that this trade, particularly for export, was suffering severely. The Clementine regulations also undertook to take away from the Venetian printers the right to print Bibles and missals and to restrict the printing of such books to Rome. Negotiations between the Senate and the Papacy lasted for some months but in the end the pope gave way on the more important points complained of, and a declaration or Concordat was agreed upon which lessened as far as Venice was concerned the stringency of the most objectionable features of the Index. When this Concordat had been signed, the Senate authorised the publication of the Index. The most important clause in the Concordat was the seventh, which provided that the right of the bishops and inquisitors to prohibit books not on the present Index should refer only to books which attacked religion, or which were printed outside of Venice, or which were issued with a false imprint. This limitation of the ecclesiastical Inquisition to purely religious or theological questions constituted a most valuable precedent in the long fight between the Church and the secular authorities for the control of the press. The Concordat was the last arrangement arrived at until the year 1766 between Rome and Venice in regard to the supervision of the press. During the century and a half following the Concordat, the Venetian republic persistently refused to authorise the publication within its territory of an augmented Index. A list of later prohibitions was, however, finally accepted in 1766, *juxta formam concordatorum*.

The most prominent figure in this long struggle between Venice and the Papacy was Fra Paolo Sarpi. Cleric though he was, he contended vigorously that the Church was embarking upon a wrong course, and he held that the State was justified in resisting, in secular matters, ecclesiastical encroachments upon the rights of the sovereign. The fight made by Sarpi on behalf of the independence of the State, and particularly of the right of the State to supervise and control literary productions, was of first importance for the intellectual activities of Europe. The arguments used in Venice were repeated in Madrid, Paris, Zürich, and Oxford. Time was gained for authors and for printers, until, largely by means of the presses which the Church was endeavouring to throttle, the spirit of resistance to the domination of the Papacy, and the feeling of national independence against the right of Rome to lay down the law for Europe, had gathered so much strength that the claims of the Church had to be withdrawn or very much moderated.

In 1613, two books by the Englishman Thomas Preston, who wrote under the name of Roger Widdrington, *Apologia Cardinalis Bellarmini* and *Disputatio Theologica*, were placed on the Index by the Congregation. The Government of Venice, acting under the advice of Sarpi, refused to allow the provision to take effect in Venice on the two grounds that the theological doctrines taught by Widdrington were sound and orthodox, and that his arguments against the pernicious doctrine of the temporal authority of the pope over princes were eminently worthy of dissemination.

There were also instances of books that were approved by the Church but the publication of which was considered detrimental to the interests of the State, and their sale in Venice was accordingly prohibited. An example of this class was the *Recantation* of the Archbishop of Spalato, printed in Rome in 1623. The republic objected to the contention of the Archbishop that the pope had power in things temporal as well as in things spiritual. The republic also prohibited the History of the Council of Trent, by Cardinal Pallavicini, written in answer to the History by Sarpi, on the ground that the work contained sentiments obnoxious to the Government of the republic. In a report written to the Government by Sarpi, he takes the ground that the course of action of the Church during the past few years had produced a series of books whose doctrines were entirely subversive of secular government. The writers taught that no government but the ecclesiastical had the divine origin; that secular government is a thing profane and tyrannical which God permits to be imposed upon his people as a kind of trial or persecution; that the people are not in conscience bound to obey the secular law or to pay taxes; that the imposts and subventions are for the most part iniquitous and unjust, and that the princes who impose these have in many cases been excommunicated. In short, princes and rulers are held up to view as impious and unjust; subjects may have to obey them perforce, but in conscience they are free to do all that in them lies to break their yoke. Sarpi emphasises the importance on the part of the republic in retaining in their own hands the control of literary censorship. He pointed out that unless the burden of papal censorship could be lessened, literary production in Venice and elsewhere must cease. He contended that in the correction of books which are open to censure, it is not advisable to follow the practice of the Church of "raking through the entrails of an author" and altering the sense and the intention of a whole sentence so that the writer is made to say the reverse of what he had desired to say; first, because all the world stigmatises such action as falsification; secondly, because such conduct would bring upon Venice the infamous charge of castrating books; thirdly, because the court of Rome assumes for itself the sole right to alter passages in books. He submitted ten propositions upon which he recommended the Government to take action. The purpose aimed at in these propositions was the retention in the hands of the State of the final decision as to prohibition or expurgation, admitting that the civil authorities could very properly utilise in matters of doctrine the service of ecclesiastical censors. Sarpi insisted that in all Venetian editions of the Index, the Concordat should itself be printed.

It was evident in the course of the controversy that Venice was, ostensibly at least, as anxious as the Church could be for the purity of the press. In fact, judging from the Indexes, this point had not caused the Church any particular anxiety. The unsettled question was, which authority should exercise the censorship over the offences of libel, scandal, and obscenity—the Church or the State? It was the opinion of Sarpi that all such books should be absolutely prohibited. The risk, as emphasised by him, was that the Concordat might fall into desuetude, leaving the Venetian press, deprived of the bulwark which the

State had secured for its defence, placed completely under the control of the Inquisition. The future justified Sarpi's dread. The heat of the argument died away, and the Concordat was substantially forgotten. The Inquisition secured full control of the censorship. The press of Venice came under the influence of the Index and the Rules. Its losses were greater than those of the other presses that the Council of Trent had undertaken to regulate, for the reason that it had so much more to lose. From the middle of the 17th century, the printing-press of Venice, though not destroyed, ceases to hold pre-eminence in Europe. The last contest of Venice with Rome occurred in August, 1765, when the Senate issued a decree instructing the *Rifformatori* to publish and to circulate the Index of Clement and the Concordat, and providing further that the *Rifformatori* should appoint as an equal associate with the inquisitor an ecclesiastic who should be a subject of Venice, and whose *testamur* as to matters of faith and doctrine should have equal weight with that of the inquisitor.

A decree was at once issued by the papal court prohibiting the sale or circulation of all books licensed by the newly appointed Venetian officers and the nuncio demanded the withdrawal of the Venetian decree. The issue between the republic and the Papacy turned simply upon the selection of the authority that should decide what was heretical or dangerous. The republic was prepared to make use of ecclesiastical censors but insisted that these must be appointed by the civil government. The Papacy, on the other hand, maintained that the entire responsibility of keeping the faithful from poisonous food had been entrusted to the Church. The Venetian decree of 1765 was never withdrawn and the place of inquisitor as censor of books upon matters of faith was thereafter held by persons appointed by the *Rifformatori* of the university. As late as 1794, the commissioners of heresy secured an opinion from these university censors upon the *Institutiones Theologicae* of De Montazet, Archbishop of Lyons, which had been condemned at Rome in 1792. As a result of their report, the Government refused to sanction the decree of the Congregation of the Index. Such an instance can be accepted as an evidence that the press of Venice had at last secured freedom from the censorship of Rome. The revolutionary spirit which was agitating all Europe, and which in France had for the time completely overthrown both Church and monarchy, must have seriously weakened the control of the Papacy over the Italian States, and doubtless exercised no little influence in this final contest between the ecclesiastical censorship and the printing-press. The Venetian press possessed a greater measure of freedom than had been secured by the printer-publishers of any other Italian State and this was an important factor in its long-continued pre-eminence. The general course, however, of the legislation for the supervision of the press was similar in character to that of the other Italian cities in which attention was given to printing.

The city which undertook the task of at once purifying and revitalising the literature of the Christ-

Rome   ian world, has itself been curiously barren of literary producers. In examining the lists of the writers of Italy whose names and whose works have survived through the centuries, one is surprised to note how few are to be credited to Rome. It is Florence, Venice, Bologna, Ferrara, Milan, and Naples that are recorded as the birthplaces of the most illustrious of the writers of Italy, and it was also largely in these smaller cities rather than in the capital that their important work was carried on.

In artistic productions, the record of Rome is more important. There was, during the 16th and 17th centuries, a Roman school of art that had influence, while in Rome were produced many of the famous works by artists who were natives of Tuscany, of Venice, or of other regions outside of the States of the Church.

The vision of the cardinal's hat or of the tiara must have had a powerful effect in attracting to the papal capital the talent of the Christian world, and particularly, of course, of Italy; but the concentration of energies upon ecclesiastical aims and dignities may easily have had a depressing and restricting influence on general intellectual development, at least as expressed in literature or art.

Dejob suggests that the possession of the throne of St. Peter, held as the chief wealth of the country, may possibly have brought intellectual poverty to Italy as the mines of America had caused ruin to Spain.

It is the conclusion of Dejob that the crushing surveillance of ecclesiasticism, in connection with the demoralising influences that opulence had brought upon a society already corrupt, has been the chief reason why the States of the Church produced fewer writers and artists of note than are to be credited to the other Italian States; while the Roman writers whose names are known, such as Leopardi and Caporali, have in their work manifested an aversion rather than a patriotic sympathy for the spirit of their home government.[1]

[1] Dejob, 336.

An examination of the list of the popes shows how seldom the choice has fallen on any one not a native of Italy. Since Adrian VI, who died in 1523, no "foreigner" has been called to the headship of the "World's Church," while of the forty-one popes who have ruled the Church since Adrian, no less than twenty were born within the territory of the States of the Church. Dejob (writing in the time of Pius IX) is willing to ascribe greatness to but one pope since the 16th century, namely Sixtus V.[1]

This impresses me as too sweepingly pessimistic, at least if we are to consider the term greatness by the standard attained by the other monarchs of Europe. I should suppose for instance that Benedict XIV was entitled to a high relative position among the rulers of the 18th century for wisdom and for capacity.

In 1561, Pius IV calls to Rome Paul Manutius, son of Aldus, to take charge of the publication of the writings of the Fathers of the Church and of such other works as might be selected. Pius was impressed with the belief that the printing-press, under scholarly management, could be made of service to the cause of the Church in withstanding the pernicious influence of the increasing mass of the publications of the German heretics. These Protestant pamphlets and books were not merely undermining the authority of the Church in Germany, in Switzerland, and in France, but were making their way into Italy itself. The first issues of the Aldine press in Rome were the decrees of the Council of Trent, the writings of Cyprian, and the letters of St. Jerome. The press secured the continued support of Pius V and of Gregory XII.

Pius V, when he was Inquisitor of Como, had made

[1] Dejob, 335

one seizure of twelve bales of books characterised by him as heretical, which had been sent from the Valtelina to Como for distribution in Lombardy and Romagna. The books were detained at the office of the Inquisition, but the application for their release on the part of the bookseller to whom they were consigned, being backed up by the vicar and the chapter, the too zealous inquisitor was compelled to release the books, and escaped only with difficulty payment of damages to the importer whose business had been interfered with.[1] The same inquisitor, when stationed at Bergamo, made seizure of two chests of prohibited books, which were in the possession of a priest who was waiting for a favourable opportunity for their distribution. The inquisitor reports that the priest had become depraved by the reading of heretical literature.[2]

In 1614, the Milan guild of printers and booksellers secured a fresh edict confirming its authority and enjoined, under heavy penalties, strict obedience to its regulations. In the application for this decree, the guild no longer lays stress upon the necessity of upholding the dignity and honourable standard of the book-trade, but emphasises the risk to the Church and to the community of believers if permission to print or to sell books should be given to uneducated and irresponsible persons who could not be familiar with the lists of forbidden works. Experience had evidently made clear to the publishers that with a government like that of Spain (which might be described as a despotism tempered by the Inquisition) this class of considerations would be more influential than any thought of upholding the dignity of the

Milan

---

[1] Fuenmayer, *Vida de Pio V*, 89.
[2] Gabutius, *De Reb. et Gest. Pii V*, Rome, 1605, 12.

business of making and selling books. The confirmation of the authority of the guild under the direct control of ecclesiastics representing the Spanish Inquisition, had the effect of checking its business in publications outside of the classes of jurisprudence and medicine. These subjects were naturally less affected by ecclesiastical censorship.

A factor to be taken into account in considering the selections of books ordered to be condemned, was the **Discrimina-** patriotism of the Italian clergy, in whose **tion in** hands rested the control of the operations **Censorship** of the Congregation. They were as unwilling to characterise as pernicious noteworthy and representative books by Italian writers, as they were to place any one but an Italian on the throne of St. Peter. This partisan zeal for the literary glory of Italy must frequently have seriously interfered with the aim of securing a consistent and effective Index and have brought upon a conscientious pope not a little embarrassment. An example of the difficulty experienced by Rome in enforcing a consistent censorship in the face of Italian patriotism, on the part of ecclesiastics, no less than of laymen, is afforded by Dante and Petrarch. Of the former, was prohibited the *De Monarchia*, but the *Divine Comedy*, with all its bitter strictures of things ecclesiastical, escaped condemnation and even expurgation.

The *Canzoniere* of Petrarch were also left untouched by Rome, although the Inquisition of Spain had characterised them most severely in the Indexes of 1612 and 1667. It was not until 1667 that the *Satires* of Ariosto were placed upon the Index, while the *Comedies* of the same poet were never condemned although in these the poet had assailed fiercely the trade in indulgences, and had painted a vivid picture of the traffic carried on by the capital of the Christian world with the blood of the apostles and martyrs.

The example of independence set by Venice in its series of contests with the Church for the freedom of the press had a natural influence in other cities of Italy where conditions were favourable for publishing activity. In Florence, Pisa. Ferrara, Milan, and other cities in which scholarship had flourished during the manuscript period, the productions of the printing-press became, during the 15th and 16th centuries, of increasing importance. This work was frequently interfered with and sometimes seriously hampered by the censorship regulations of Rome and by the operations of the local inquisitors, but it was never entirely blocked even in any one city. The feeling of State and municipal independence and the individuality of the people were too strong to be crushed out by Roman edicts or by the threats of the Inquisition. In Italy as in Germany, the fact that there was not one government in the peninsula, but a number of independent States, helped to secure for the work of the printers some degree of opportunity, notwithstanding the censorship edicts of the Church and the repressive measures of the State. The presses of the day were small and in case of trouble in one city, they could easily be moved to another.

An instance of a book the censorship of which caused no little difficulty to the authorities of the Index is afforded by the *Decameron* of Boccaccio. The book had, under the instructions of Paul IV, been placed upon the Index of 1559, and the prohibition was confirmed in that of 1564. In response to an urgent requirement from the public, an expurgated edition was printed for the needs of the faithful by the Giunti in Florence in 1573, under a special privilege from the Duke of Tuscany and from Gregory XIII, who himself contributed a prefatory word. The volume includes further an authorisation from Manrique, Grand Inquisitor, and one from de Pise, Inquisitor-General of Florence. The introduction states that the work has been purged of its obnoxious passages. It appears, however, that the eliminations were confined almost exclusively to the passages which were tainted with heresy, and to the uncomplimentary references to the clergy and to monastic institutions. The amorous incidents are left untouched, but in all cases in which a monk or a cleric, an abbess or a nun is made by Boccaccio to play an undignified or unworthy rôle, the character is replaced by a citizen, a nobleman, or a bourgeoise.

The edition of the *Decameron*, revised under the instructions of Gregory XIII, did not prove satisfactory to Sixtus V, and the book was therefore replaced on the Index. The demand for copies on the part of readers, ecclesiastics and others, who were prepared to respect the prohibition of the Index, continued urgent, and the Pope authorised the production of a further expurgated edition, which was printed in Florence in 1582 and reprinted in Venice in 1588. The task of expurgation had been confided to two laymen, Salviati, known as a linguist, and Groto, a poet. This further revision still failed to satisfy the Pope and the book remained on the Index, but it continued in general reading, and the authorities appear finally to have decided to close their eyes to this particular instance of disobedience. The record presents a curious example of a book the vitality of which, persisting through the centuries, defied all efforts for its suppression. It is referred to by the historians as the first *chef d' oeuvre* in prose that had as yet been produced in Italy, whose literature was so rich in great poems.

One would suppose that the authority of the head of the Church ought to have been accepted in all cases as adequate to cover the permission re- **Papal Au-** quired for the printing and continued circu- **thorisation** lation of a book. It appears, however, that from time to time even the papal authorisations were disregarded or failed to receive continued consideration. Dejob refers to a history of Bologna by Sigone, the publication of which was suspended, owing to the malignancy of certain Bolognese, after the approval had been secured from the examiners appointed by the pope. Baronius, the defender of the most extreme claims for the supremacy of the Papacy, secured for his monograph on Sixtus V the approbation of the papal examiner and of the master of the palace. Notwithstanding this approval, the printing of the book was blocked through some cabal and the work was held up until Cardinal Caraffa intervened to secure its publication.[1]

In the year 1600, was completed, in thirteen folio volumes, the *Annales Ecclesiastici* of Baronius, the most comprehensive work which the controversies of the Protestant revolt had as yet produced. The series was continued by various writers until, in the edition issued at Lucca in 1738–1786, it had grown to thirty-eight folio volumes, a work of which purchase was difficult and perusal impossible.

A reply to Baronius was undertaken by Casaubon, who published in London in 1604 (as a fragment of the work originally planned) his *Exercitationes*, a volume

[1] Dejob, 57.

of eight hundred folio pages. For the great work of Baronius, the authorities of the Church interested themselves in securing through the Church machinery channels of distribution and such reading public as was practicable considering its compass and scholastic character.

The Roman idea of reforming and developing the intellectual life of the State was to follow a policy of official supervision with prohibitions and penalties. Ecclesiastical censors undertook to bring authors under a system of religious and theological obligations, and were willing to give their official approval only to works complying with their standards. Certain writers accept with docility the regulations imposed, but it is not those whose productions will live or will retain influence. The books that have not conformed to the ecclesiastical restrictions must be either reshaped or suppressed. It is not under such conditions, says Dejob, that a great literature can be produced.[1] And yet in spite of an ecclesiastical policy of restriction and repression enforced, or at least attempted, through centuries, the intellectual vitality of Italy was so great that it proved impossible to crush out its independence of thought, or even seriously to limit the expression of its spiritual and literary ideals. A scholarly Catholic of France writing in 1883 says (in substance):

The peculiar conception, that from the earliest times Italy had formed, of the Kingdom of God and of the way in which this Kingdom was to be reached, the astounding freedom of spirit with which (during the middle ages) it handled matters of dogma and of discipline, the serenity that it was able to maintain in the face of the great mystery of life and death, the mar-

[1] Dejob, 339.

vellous way with which it brought into accord faith and rationalism, its indifference for heresies and for the temerities of its mystical imagination, the ardent affection with which it accepted the highest ideals of Christianity, and finally, the indignation with which from time to time it denounced the feebleness, the violence, the corruption of the Church of Rome,— this is the religion of Italy, the faith of Peter Damien, of Arnold of Brescia, of St. Francis, of John of Parma, of St. Catherine of Siena, of Savonarola, and of Ochino; but it was also the faith of Dante and of Petrarch, of Giotto, of Fra Angelico, and of Raphael, of Vittoria Colonna and of Michael Angelo.[1]

4. **Spain.**—In Spain as in Italy, the Church did not at once realise the risks to orthodoxy that were to be associated with the work of the printers. German printers coming to Spain as early as 1474 were received with favour and found opportunities for profitable work. Even Hebrew printers were at the outset welcomed. Between the years 1499–1510, Cardinal Ximenes (following in the footsteps of Turrecremata) paid fifty thousand crowns for the production of a series of classics. It was not until 1510 that the Church began, through the organisation of its censorship, to hamper the work of the printers. Pütter is authority for the statement [2] that for a term of two years (1484–1486) Christopher Columbus served as a bookseller's apprentice and as a colporteur. An ecclesiastic named Bernaldes writes in 1487: "I have recently seen a man named Christofero Colombo who comes from Genoa and who is a dealer in printed books

[1] Gebhart, *Introduction à l'histoire du sentiment religieux en Italie*, etc., p. 2

[2] Pütter, 23.

that he has brought to this city (Cogolludo) from Andalusia."

The destruction of books classed as pernicious appears to have been, during the 15th century, within the province of any person of position and influence.[1] In 1490, Torquemada burned, under order of Ferdinand and Isabella, a number of Hebrew Bibles, and, later, he made at Salamanca an *auto-da-fé* of more than six thousand volumes described as books of magic or as infected with Jewish errors. Ximenes, while yet merely Archbishop, burned in the public square of Granada no less than five thousand Arabic books, many of them splendidly ornamented and illuminated. The only books spared from the collection were those on the subject of medicine, which were deposited in the University of Alcala.[2] In 1502, Ferdinand and Isabella enacted an elaborate law, which is referred to as the first of the kind in Europe, establishing a general censorship of the press. In this law, were laid down the principles on which were based nearly all subsequent enactments. To Spain thus belongs the honour of organising the system which was to exercise an influence so incomputable on the development of human intelligence.

" The Spanish people strove earnestly for the maintenance of the faith but it understood by this not the reform of methods of life and the correction of immorality, but the extirpation of heresy."[3]

" The uncompromising character of the Spanish temperament, which pursued its object regardless of consequences, saw at once what was elsewhere only

[1] Lea, 21.
[2] Gomez. Lib. ii. fol. 30. b.
[3] Dejob, 339.

perceived by degrees, that any endeavours to set bounds to the multiplying products of the press could be successful only under a thorough system of minute surveillance."[1]   It was ordered that no book should be printed or imported or exposed for sale without examination and license.   In some places, this duty was imposed upon judges of the royal courts and in others on the archbishops or bishops.   The examiners, men of good repute and learning, were to be appointed by these authorities and were to be adequately paid for their work.   After a work in manuscript had been licensed for printing, the printed sheets were to be carefully compared with the original to insure that no alteration had been made on the press.   Any book printed or imported or offered for sale without such license was to be seized and burned and the printer or vendor was declared incapable of longer carrying on the business.[2]   In this first enactment, no reference is made to the Inquisition as having any concern either with the investigation of books for heresies or with the punishment of delinquents; but the Inquisition had not long to wait before its jurisdiction over literature was established on an impregnable basis.

After the beginning of the Reformation in Germany, the operations of the censorship in Spain were carried on with renewed vigour.   Special efforts were naturally made to protect the faithful in Spain from contamination through the importation of heretical books from Germany.   A letter of June 25, 1524, written by Martin de Salinas, mentions that a ship from Holland bound for Valencia had been captured by the French and then recaptured and brought into San Sebastian.

[1] Lea, 22.
[2] *Nueva Recop.,* Lib. i, tit. vii.

In discharging the vessel, there were found two casks of Lutheran books which were publicly burned. Salinas writes, some months later, that three Venetian galleasses had arrived at a port in Granada, bringing large quantities of Lutheran books. The books were burned and the captains and crews arrested. An edict of the Supreme Council of the Inquisition, issued in August, 1530, urged the inquisitors to increased vigilance in connection particularly with the destruction of certain Lutheran writings that had been introduced under false titles or under the names of Catholic authors. The inquisitors were ordered to add to the Edict of Denunciations, published annually, a clause requiring the denunciation of all who possessed such books or of all who had read them.[1] In spite of the watchfulness of the inquisitors and of the customs officials, it is reported that, in 1570, no less than thirty thousand copies of a Spanish version of the *Institutes* of Calvin were brought over the frontier.[2]

It is the conclusion of Ticknor that by the end of the 16th century, bookselling in Spain, in the sense in which the term was used elsewhere in the world, was practically unknown, and the Inquisition and the confessional had often made most rare what was most desirable. In March, 1521, papal briefs were sent to Spain, warning the Spanish Government to prevent the further introduction of books written by Luther and his followers, copies of which had, it was believed, been penetrating into the country for about a year. These papal briefs were addressed to the civil administration, which still, in form at least, retained in its own hands the control of such matters. It was,

[1] Llorente, i, 457.
[2] Böhmer. *op. cit.*, ii. 78.

however, more natural and more in accordance with the ideas then prevalent, not only in Spain but in other countries, to look to the ecclesiastical power for remedies in a matter connected with religion. This was certainly the attitude of the great body of the Spanish people. In less than a month (as is evident from the date of the briefs in question) and possibly even before these briefs were received in Spain, the grand inquisitor addressed an order to the tribunals under his jurisdiction, requiring them to search for, and to seize, all books supposed to contain the doctrines of the new heresy. The measure was bold and proved successful.

In the meantime, the Supreme Council of the Inquisition proceeded with this work with a firm and consistent step. By successive decrees issued between 1521 and 1553, it was ordained that all persons who had in their possession books infected with the doctrines of Luther, and all persons also who failed to denounce the holders of such books, should be excommunicated and subject to severe punishments. These decrees gave to the Inquisition the right to inquire into the contents and the character of whatever books were sold and printed. They also relegated to itself the power to determine what books might be sent to the press. This assumption was made gradually and with little noise, but effectually.

While at first there was no direct authority for such action from either the pope or the Kingdom of Spain, it necessarily implied the assent of both, and was carried into effect by means furnished by one or the other. In certain works printed before 1550, the Inquisition began quietly and without any formal authority to take cognisance and control of books that were about to

be printed.   A curious treatise on exchange, by de Villa-
lon, entitled *Tratado de Cambios*, was printed at Valladolid in 1541.   The title-page declared that the book
had been "*Visto por los señores Inquisidores.*"   In the
Silva de Varia Leccion, of Pero, printed at Seville, in
1543, the title gives the imperial license for printing,
while the colophon adds that of the Apostolical inquisitor.   The author was evidently anxious to secure, in addition to a permission resting on law, one which rested
on the still more formidable authority of the Church.

A system which should effectually preserve the
faithful from the contamination of evil by keeping
from them the knowledge of its existence comprised two
functions; the first was the examination of all books
prior to publication, permitting only the innocent to
be printed; the second was the scrutiny of the books
that had come from the press and the condemnation
or expurgation of those containing errors which had
escaped the vigilance of the first examiners.   Under
the rigid institution of censorship in Spain, the first
of these duties was assumed by the State and the second
was confided to the Inquisition.   The first law in regard
to Spanish censorship was enacted in 1502 and forbade
the printing or importation of any book without an
examination and license.   The chancellor Gattinara,
writing in 1527 to Erasmus, says that in Spain no
book could see the light without a careful preliminary
inspection which was rigidly enforced.   This statement
is confirmed in 1540 by Hugo de Celso.   The Inquisition
had no legal status in the matter of preliminary licensing, but its growing influence caused its judgment to
be frequently appealed to in advance.   Ticknor makes
reference to books of 1536, 1541, and 1546 as bearing
records of examination by the Inquisition.

In 1554, an edict of Charles V confines to the royal council the function of issuing licenses for the printing of books of all descriptions. In the case of works of importance, the original manuscript was to be deposited with the council to ensure detection of any alterations made while the book was going through the press. In 1558, it is ordered under royal edict that no bookseller or other person shall sell or possess any books printed or to be printed which have been condemned by the Inquisition and that such books should be publicly burned. The penalty is death and confiscation of all property. The same penalties apply to the importing of any books in Romance which do not bear a printed license from the council. A later regulation specifies that, in order to prevent any alterations in the printing, the original manuscript shall be signed on every leaf by a secretary of the royal chamber, who shall mark and rubricate every correction or alteration in it and shall state at the end the number of leaves and of alterations. When the printing has been completed, these corrected leaves are to be compared with the printed sheets. The infection of heresy could be communicated by manuscript, and therefore the penalty of death and confiscation is decreed for all who own or show to others manuscripts on any religious subject without first submitting these to the council.[1] Lea goes on to say: "I am not aware that any human being was actually put to death for violating its provisions, unless the offence was complicated with heresy express or implied, but such violation remained to the end a capital crime. The only modification of this ferocious penalty occurs in a revision of the press law in 1752."[2]

[1] Lea, 61.
[2] *Ibid.*, 62.

It is not surprising that under restrictions of this character, the work of the Spanish printer-publishers during the 16th century was seriously hampered. As an example of the enforcement of the regulations of the Valdes Index of 1559, may be named the case of a French priest named Jean Fesque. He had handed to a bookseller named Trechel a volume without imprint, asking Trechel if he could say where it was printed. The book belonged to the condemned list, being a French version of the Psalms of David, translated by Marot and Bèza. Fesque stated that he had purchased the book from a boy in the street without knowledge of its character. He was brought before the Inquisition, and after five months' imprisonment and various examinations, he was put to the torture but was unable to give further evidence as to the history of the book. He was finally released after six months' incarceration, seriously disabled by the torture.[1]

The machinery of the Inquisition was effective even in the farther parts of the empire. In 1795, a priest in the settlement of Hopelcheen in Yucatan published a prohibition of the Inquisition warning his congregation not to read a certain book which had been described by the Inquisition as dangerous and to surrender at once all copies in their possession. The book was entitled *Disengaño del Hombre*, by Puglia, and bore the imprint (possibly fictitious) of Philadelphia. The congregation of Indians and half-breeds was hardly likely to have had knowledge of the book or to have been able to read it even if copies had reached Hopelcheen.[2]

The *Index expurgatorius* in its literal sense may be

[1] Lea, 70.
[2] *Ibid*, 73.

described as peculiarly a Spanish institution. In the Roman series, there is record of the publication of but one expurgatory Index, that of Brasichelli, and this was never republished and was in fact promptly recalled by the authorities. The inquisitors of Spain took upon themselves the task of preserving the faithful from contamination, and the successive expurgatory Indexes give evidence of the enormous labour expended by the examiners in the correction of the text of books which they were not prepared absolutely to prohibit, but the circulation of which they were ready to permit if the heresies could be expunged or corrected. The Roman prohibitory Index contained against many works the restriction *donec corrigatur*. This indicated that the book when corrected was to be permitted: the objectionable passages were, however, not specified, although the author could ascertain these on application. As an actual result, it was very rarely the case that it proved practicable to bring into publication an edition in which the corrections in question, having been ascertained from the authorities, could be made. The Spanish censors took credit to themselves for their liberality in securing the use of heretical works of value through the expurgation of the offensive passages. It is true that, under this system, permission was given for the production of the writings of authors like Erasmus, Casaubon, Bertram, and others who were absolutely prohibited in Rome. It does not appear, however, that as far as the publishers of Spain were concerned, this permission brought about for the greater portion of the books in question the production of corrected editions. It is in fact easy to understand how the heavy loss that must be incurred through the suppression of the original edition would have discouraged both author and printer from the task of risking a further investment in a second edition which might itself in like manner be prohibited until again revised. It may safely be concluded that the restricted prohibition in Spain had as far as the production and distribution of books were concerned practically the same result as the absolute prohibition in Rome. In fact, in Spain, the result was more effective simply because the regulations of the Spanish Inquisition were enforced, while for the similar orders of the Inquisition of Rome or of the Congregation of the Index, the enforcement throughout the States of Italy or outside of Italy was but vacillating and fragmentary. An example of the watchfulness of the Spanish examiners is given in the expurgation of a passage from the Second Part of *Don Quixote*. But a single sentence is cancelled. It reads: "Works of charity negligently performed are of no worth." In the *Divine Comedy* of Dante, the censors found but three passages for excision. Lea points out that for this work at least the examination can hardly be described as thorough.[1] In 1790, the history of the monastery of Sixena, by Varon, which had been published with the approval of the royal examiners in 1776, was prohibited until the following sentence had been expurgated: "When Philip the Second was despoiling the world to enrich his monastery of the Escorial." The Inquisition of Spain even assumed for itself the authority to revise and correct the utterances of the popes. The State utilised the censorship of the Inquisition not only for matters theological but for the suppression of writings that were purely political. Instructions of Clement VIII were accepted as the authority for

[1] Lea, 81.

the expurgation of teachings that were derogatory to princes and to ecclesiastics and contrary to good morals. In 1612, for instance, the works of Antonio Perez were placed on the Index because they were critical of Philip II.[1] In 1640, the Inquisition suppressed a manifesto addressed by the authorities of Barcelona to Philip IV, and, in 1642, it prohibited a further manifesto in which the Catalans accused the favourite, Olivares, of causing the misfortunes of Spain. In 1643, on the other hand, after the dismissal of Olivares, the Inquisition prohibited a pamphlet which had been issued in his defence.

Under an edict of 1602, commissioners of the Inquisition were stationed at all the ports with instructions to seize all books by new authors and all new and enlarged editions of new books as they **Book-trade and the Inquisition** arrived and to allow no one to handle these until they had been inspected by representatives of the supreme council.   Prohibited books were detained and burned. The regulations of the Inquisition had at this time rendered very difficult the carrying on of the printing and publishing business in Spain, with the result of very much decreasing the annual production of books. The requirements of scholars and readers could therefore be met only through the importation of books produced in France, Italy, or the Netherlands. The necessity, however, of securing for imported books, in addition to the inspection (onerous enough in itself) on the part of customs officials, an examination, volume by volume, by the representatives of the Inquisition, brought such serious burdens, expenses, and risks upon the business of the importers as to render this unprofitable. It is

[1] Lea, 83.

certainly the case that the circulation of books in Spain during the 17th century became very inconsiderable. An order issued in 1597 gives evidence of some consideration for the property of foreigners. When heretics came to trade, bringing books for their own use, the commissioner was instructed to examine these and to mark conspicuously and indelibly such as belonged to the prohibited list, so that they could be recognised by the faithful. The owners were warned, under heavy penalties, not to bring such books to the shore. In 1631, it was directed that "ships of England should be treated with gentleness so as not to cause offence."[1] The instructions for the examination of vessels, whether Spanish or foreign, to guard against the introduction not only of prohibited books but of heretics, and to punish any infractions of the faith that might during the voyage have been committed either by the crew or passengers, were very precise and exacting.

Under the fourth article of these instructions, a report is to be given as to what Christian doctrine and prayers of the Church have been recited at sea and what saints have been advocated and invoked in their necessities and perils. Under article six, it is ordered that all boxes and chests of the sailors and passengers were to be opened for evidence of heresy.

Henry C. Lea, in a letter to the writer (under date of October 31, 1898) in regard to the effect of censorship on the literary interests of Spain, says:

" I was chiefly interested in tracing the influence of censorship on the intellectual and political development of Spain, but in many instances a side light is thrown upon the

[1] Lea, 86.

resultant injury to the commercial interests involved,—as for instance the ruin of Portonares, the greatest Spanish printer, as a result of the censorship (*i. e* .the condemnation of the Vatable Bible.)   The business of bookselling was in fact crippled in every way.   I have met with one case in which a bookseller humbly petitions the Inquisition to come to a decision in regard to certain books which he had imported and which had been in the hands of the *Califi-cadores* (examiners) for four years.

" The *prima facies* was against all books; their innocence had to be proved before their circulation could be allowed and even after this they were still liable at any time to an adverse judgment.   Under these circumstances, commerce in books was necessarily crippled and the diffusion of intelligence was reduced to a minimum."

The books that were published during the 16th century, and indeed for a century later, bore everywhere marks of the subjection to which the press and those who wrote for the press were alike reduced. From the abject title-pages and dedications of the authors themselves through the series of certificates collected from their friends to establish the orthodoxy of works that were often as little connected with religion as fairy tales, down to the colophon supplicating pardon for any unconscious neglect of the authority of the Church or for any too free use of classical mythology, we are continually impressed with painful proofs, not only how completely the human mind was enslaved in Spain, but how grievously it had become cramped and crippled by what it had so long borne.[1]   Of the few dramatic pieces written in the earlier part of the reign of Charles V, nearly all except those on strictly religious subjects were laid under the

[1] Ticknor. i. 504.

ban of the Church; several in fact being now known to have existed only because their names appear in the *Index expurgatorius*; and others, like the *Amadis de Gaula* of Gil Vicente, though printed and published, being subsequently forbidden to be represented. [1]

Ticknor writes (with reference to the trial of Luis de Leon, in December, 1576):

"The very loyalty with which Luis bowed himself down before the dark and unrelenting tribunal into whose presence he had been summoned, sincerely acknowledging its right to all the powers it claimed, and submitting faithfully to all its decrees, is the saddest proof that can be given of the subjection to which intellects the most lofty and the most cultivated had been reduced by sinful tyranny, and the most discouraging augury of the degradation of the national character that was sure to follow." [2]

In 1676, was born Benito Feyjoo, who later became a Benedictine monk. While his life was spent in strict retirement (for forty-seven years he remained in the convent at Oviedo), the activity of his thought made him a fire in the community. He wrote a series of papers published, in 1726, under the title of the *Critical Theatre*. In these, he openly attacked the dialectics and metaphysics then taught everywhere in Spain. Few persons at the beginning of the 18th century were so well informed as not to believe in astrology, and fewer still doubted the disastrous influence of comets and of eclipses. The study of Copernicus was forbidden to be taught on the ground that it was contrary to Scripture. The philosophy of Bacon, with all the consequences that followed it, were unknown. In spite of the opposition of the Inquisition, before which

[1] Ticknor, ii, 49.   [2] *Ibid.*, ii, 96.

Feyjoo was more than once summoned, it proved to be impracticable to suppress his investigations or his publications. In 1742, he began a series of discussions published under the title *Learned and Enquiring Souls*. The series was finished in 1760. It was impossible for the Inquisition to assail the soundness of his faith. Fifteen editions of his principal works were printed in half a century. It is the conclusion of Ticknor that the quiet monk had done more for the intellectual life of his country than had been done in a century.[1]

Ticknor calculates that the number of *auto-da-fés* during the reign of Philip V exceeded seven hundred and eighty. It is believed that more than twelve thousand persons were, in different ways, subjected, under the authority of the Inquisition, to be punished and disgraced and that more than one thousand were burned alive. Charles III, with the assistance of his liberal ministers, was able so far to abridge the papal power that no rescript or edict from Rome could have force in Spain without the express consent of the throne. He restrained the Inquisition from exercising any authority whatever except in cases of obstinate heresy or apostacy. He forbade the condemnation of any book until its author or those interested in it had had an opportunity to be heard in its defence. Finally, deeming the Jesuits the most active opponents of the reforms he was intending to enforce, he expelled their whole body from his dominions all over the world, breaking up their schools and confiscating their great revenues. Certain abuses were, however, beyond his reach. When he appealed to the universities, urging them to change their ancient habits and to teach the truths of the physical and exact sciences, Salamanca answered

[1] Ticknor, ii, 73.

in 1771: "Newton teaches nothing that would make a good logician or metaphysician and Gassendi and Descartes do not agree so well with revealed truth as does Aristotle."[1]   The other universities showed little more of the spirit of advancement.   Under Charles IV, in 1805, the Inquisition, grown forcible in the hands of the Government as a political machine but still renouncing none of its religious pretensions, came forth with its last *Index expurgatorius* to meet the invasion of French philosophy and insubordination.   Acting under express instructions from the powers of the State, it instituted against men of letters, and especially against those connected with the universities, an immense number of denunciations which, though rarely prosecuted to conviction and to punishment, were still formidable enough to prevent the public expression of opinions on any subject that could endanger the social condition of the individual who ventured to entertain them.

5.   **France.**—Duke Philip Augustus in an edict issued in 1200, confirmed by St. Louis in 1229 and by Philip the

University of Paris

Fair in 1302, directed that the cases of university members be brought before the Bishop of Paris.   The university found disadvantages in being under the jurisdiction of the bishop (whose censorship later proved particularly troublesome for the publishers) and applications were made to replace the authority of the ecclesiastical courts with that of the royal courts.   In 1334, letters patent of Philip of Valois directed the Provost of Paris, who was at that time considered as the *conservateur* of the royal privileges, to take the university under his special protection, and in 1341, the members of the university were

[1] Ticknor, ii, 431 (note).

forbidden to enter proceedings before any other authority. This action brought the control of literary production in the university directly under the authority of the Crown and constituted a precedent for the contention, maintained through the 15th and 16th centuries, for the direct control by the Crown of the printing-presses. The claim on the part of the university, however, to control as a portion of the work of higher education the business of the makers and the sellers of books, while sharply attacked and materially undermined during the 17th century, was not formally abandoned until the beginning of the 18th. At this time, the Crown took to itself all authority to regulate the press, an authority which terminated only with the Revolution of 1789.

The first printing-office in France was established in 1469 by Gering, Krantz, and Friburger from Constance. At the request of two of the divines of the Sorbonne, space was given for the **Paris** printing-office in one of the halls of the college. An edict of Louis XII, issued April 9, 1513, confirms and extends the privileges previously acquired by booksellers as officials of the university. In this edict, Louis speaks with appreciation and admiration of the printing art, "the discovery of which appears to be rather divine than human." He congratulates his kingdom that in the development of this art "France takes precedence of all other realms."[1] A year later, the King places on record his opinion that dramatic productions and representations should be left free from any restrictions. In 1512, the King writes to the university requesting the theological faculty to examine a book that had been condemned as heretical by the Council of Pisa.

[1] Renouard. i, 25.

In place, however, of demanding that measures of severity should be taken against the writer, the King proposed that the professors should go over the book chapter by chapter and should present a refutation of any of its conclusions that seemed to them to be contrary to the truth. It was hardly possible that so fair a spirit of toleration should long continue. The spirit of the time was stronger than the power of any one king and it was impossible in the 16th century that the Church and the State could permit the free development and the unrestricted expression of thought.

In 1500, the publisher Badius, who had been selected by the theological faculty for printing certain of its censorial works, issued an edition of the *Regula S. Benedicti*, the famous Rule which had exercised so important and so abiding an influence on the literature and the intellectual development of Europe. The leading publisher in Paris between the years 1496 and 1520 was Henry Estienne. The so-called heretical opinions of Estienne rendered him obnoxious to the doctors of the Sorbonne and if it had not been for the special interference of Francis I, by whom his learning and his merits were held in high esteem, his life would more than once have been in jeopardy. His opponents succeeded, however, in procuring his expulsion from the university, and, driven from Paris, he was compelled to seek the protection of the Queen of Navarre. The case is one of a long series of instances in which the liberal views and scholarly interests of King Francis brought him into conflict with the doctors of the Sorbonne. In the end, however, the theological faculty, backed by the majority of the ecclesiastics of France and by the influence of the Papacy, proved too strong for the liberal tendencies of the Crown. With the triumph of Catholic orthodoxy in France, the leading publishers and their scholarly editors found so many difficulties placed in the way of their undertakings that these could no longer be carried on to advantage in Paris. The chief trouble was due to the ignorance and suspiciousness of the doctors of the Sorbonne. These doctors possessed at this period little or no knowledge of Greek and were inclined to imagine that any Greek sentence must contain or might contain some dangerous heresy.[1] Any critical analysis of Latin texts which, in some earlier, and usually imperfect or defective, form, had received the approval of the Church, also seemed to the divines likely to prove dangerous, and in any case, constituted a reflection upon the orthodox scholarship of the previously accepted versions. Their apprehensions became most keen and their indignation most active when the " new criticism " (as they probably called it) was applied to the text of the Scriptures, whether for the purpose of correcting the early clumsy Latinised versions of the New Testament or of securing more accurate rendering of the texts of the Hebrew books. During the first half-century of printing, however, the production of editions of the Scriptures constituted the most important division of publishing undertakings. It is not surprising, therefore, that the printers who were giving their time and their capital to the preparation of these editions, and who found themselves hampered and harassed by ignorant and bigoted censorship, came to the conclusion that the advantages of Paris as a literary and commercial centre were not sufficient to offset the continued difficulties and annoyances of such antagonism.

By 1540, the ecclesiastical control of the printing-

1 Greswell, i, 172.

press (exercised through the authority of the university) had become an established and an obstructive fact.   A necessary result of the antagonism of the Church to critical scholarship was to drive into the ranks of sympathisers with the reformers, if not into Protestantism itself, very many of the scholars who at the outset were not reformers and who were not keenly interested in the theological issues of the period, but who felt a natural indignation at the reiterated interference with scholarly undertakings on the part of very ignorant men.   The scholars engaged in preparing for the public critical editions of the world's literature asked to be let alone, but they asked in vain.

In 1546, the doctors of the Sorbonne secured the insertion in the prohibitory Index of Louvain of the edition of the Bible that had just been printed by Robert Estienne; but later in the same year, the King prohibited the printing or the circulation in France of the Index of Louvain.   The King also issued a brief ordering the divines to withdraw their strictures upon the Estienne Bible.   With the death of the King in 1547, the prohibition of the Bible was, however, renewed.   In 1552, Estienne, deprived of the protection of King Francis, is finally compelled to close his printing office and to remove to Geneva.   Estienne did not, however, find Protestant Geneva a place of liberal toleration.   The year after his arrival, he witnesses the burning, under the authority of Calvin, of the heretical scholar Servetus, and more than once during the later years of his work in Geneva, the Estienne publications came under the condemnation of the Calvinistic censorship.   Henry Estienne (the second) completed, in 1562, the publication of certain theological works which had been left unfinished in Geneva at the time of his father's death.   Among these, were an Exposition of the New Testament and an Exposition of the Psalms.   The editor, a certain Marloratus, a Huguenot minister at Rouen, was unfortunately, before the printing was completed, hanged as a heretic, under the direction of the Duke of Guise, but the books themselves were not suppressed nor was the publisher interfered with.   The faculty of the Sorbonne appears for the time to have suspended its censorious watchfulness over heretical publications, perhaps because it found its hands sufficiently full with the active work of suppressing, by fire, gibbet, and sword, the heretics themselves.   Henry found it later, however, good policy to divide his publishing undertakings, executing at Paris reprints of the classics and works in general literature, and reserving for his press at Geneva theological works which were likely to give offence in a period of "religious irritation."   This term is, I may mention, Maittaire's, and it is perhaps not too strong a description of a period in which a divine who had taken no part in politics could be hanged simply for editing a Protestant commentary.

In 1589, the city of Geneva was being besieged by the Duke of Savoy.   The city contained at the time a population of about 12,000 and was able to muster for its defence 2186 men capable of **Geneva** bearing arms.   Against this little force, the Duke brought up an army of 18,000 regular troops with the determination of destroying once for all this "nest of heretics."   The destruction of the city was earnestly urged by St. Francis de Sales.   The schools and the printing-presses were particularly pointed out by St. Francis as instruments of mischief.   The powers that determine events were this time not in accord with the saint.   The city survived a siege lasting for nine years, although at its close it had lost out of its little levy nearly three fourths. Casaubon tells us that in his time (he is writing in 1595) the ministers of Geneva exercised a strict surveillance over both the work of teaching and that of publishing. A professor in the academy was not permitted to publish until his book had passed through the censorship of the divines. It seems probable that the Calvinistic scrutiny in Geneva, during the last ten years of the 16th century, may easily have proved in its narrowness and persistency a more serious obstacle in the way of publishing undertakings and of scholarship than the censorship of the Catholic theologians of Paris.

Casaubon secured, in 1600, at the instance of his friend De Vic, appointment as Keeper of the Royal Library. This library contained at the time about nine hundred works, a large proportion of which were in manuscript. The collection of Greek manuscripts was said to be second only to that of the Vatican.[1] The new librarian found favour with the King although Henry IV was by no means a scholar. Scaliger says of him that he could not keep his countenance and could not read a book. The great minister Sully was, however, critical of any expenditure for literature. "You cost the King too much, sir," said Sully to Casaubon; "your pay exceeds that of two good captains, and you are of no use to the country."[2]

A letter from the papal nuncio at Paris, written in 1562 to Pius IV, makes reference to a statement made to the nuncio by Monsieur de Bourbon, to the effect that a few days earlier he had confiscated from

[1] Pattison, 182.
[2] Frith, *Life of Bruno*, 71.

a vessel a quantity of heretical books "of the most distressing character that can be conceived." These books were packed in wine casks and had been sent from Geneva. He had consigned them to the flames. No reference is made to the importer.[1]

Sacchino, historian of the Jesuits, writing in 1526, refers to the heretical city of Geneva as responsible for the introduction into Lyons of *vim infinitam librorum pestiferorum* ("a great mass of pestiferous literature,") prepared for circulation not only in France but in Constantinople. He states further, however, that owing to the efforts of the zealous Possevinus, the books were seized and burned (*Ut pestilentium illa farrago voluminum flammis aboliretur*).[2]

The interest of Francis in scholarship and the influence of Budaeus and other scholars led him to approve the scheme for a Royal College to be devoted more particularly to instruction in the ancient languages. The authorities of the university were, with hardly an exception, bitterly opposed to the plan of the new college. The argument on the part of the university was presented before the Parliament of Paris by Galliard. He urged that " to propagate the knowledge of the Greek and Hebrew languages would operate to the absolute destruction of all religion." "Were these professors theologians," he asked, "that they should pretend to explain the Bible? Were not, indeed, the very Bibles of which they made use, in large part printed in Germany, the region of heresy? Or at least were they not indebted for them to the Jews?" The rejoinder on the part of the new professors was made through Marillac. "We make no

[1] *Letters from the Nuncio of Pius IV at Paris*, i, iii.
[2] *Hist. Jesuit.*, vi, 44.

pretensions," said the professors, "to the name or the function of theologians. It is as philologists or grammarians only that we undertake to explain the Greek and Hebrew Scriptures. If you, who are criticising our teachings, possess any knowledge of Greek or Hebrew, you are at liberty to attend our lectures and, if you find any heresy in our instruction, to denounce us. If, however, you are yet ignorant of Greek and Hebrew, on what grounds can you base your fitness as censors or your claims to forbid us to teach in these tongues?" The victory rested with the scholars and the Collège Royal maintained its ground and increased in influence and importance.[1] Maittaire quotes in this connection the testimony of Heresbach, who says that, in 1540, he heard in a sermon delivered in Paris the following statement: "A new language has been discovered which they call Greek. Against this you must be carefully on your guard for it is the infant tongue of all heresies. There is a book written in that language called the New Testament. It is *un livre plein de ronces et de vipères*. As to the Hebrew tongue, it is well known that all who learn it presently become Jews."

In 1685, a royal edict was issued by Louis XIV, ordering the destruction of all heretical books and the punishment of those who should retain copies of the same. As a result of the edict, the Parliament of Paris issued a decree appointing the Archbishop of Paris to prepare an *Index prohibitorius* of books which in his judgment ought to be suppressed, an instruction which was carried out with all promptness. The list of the archbishop comprised the names of about five hundred authors. The books condemned were those of the Lutherans, Socinians, Arminians, and Greeks. In-

[1] Greswell, i, 219.

cluded with these were all versions of the Scriptures.
The Parliament published at once a decree enforcing the
prohibition and commanding a strict search to be made
for such books in the bookshops and printeries and also
in private houses.   Many books were burned, including a large number of copies of the Scriptures.   The
protection, or toleration, heretofore, in form at least,
extended to Protestants was during the same year,
1685, withdrawn by the Edict of Fontainebleau, repealing the Edict of Nantes.

The printers of Lyons succeeded in building up,
within a very few years after the introduction of printing
into France, a profitable business.   They had
the advantage of being well out of the way of   **Lyons**
both ecclesiastical and political censorship.   They were
quite prepared to take up promptly editions of books
which had been prohibited in Paris and in Rome, or
later in Geneva.   They were also among the earliest to
develop the art of what may be called piratical printing.
The great expense of the production of earlier editions,
more particularly of the classics, was the outlay for
scholarly editing.   The printers of Lyons promptly
discovered that they could make money by utilising
the expenditures of Aldus in Venice, or of the scholarly
printers in Paris, through the appropriation of editorial
material.   They brought out editions printed with the
text that had been shaped in Venice and in some cases
in direct imitation of the typography of these first and
so to speak authorised editions.   By the year 1495,
there were no less than forty printers doing active
work in Lyons, a number considerably in excess of
those who were then carrying on business in Paris.

In 1526, the university of Paris had authorised the

printing of certain dissertations written by the rector Noël Béda against Fabri and Erasmus. King Francis wrote to the Parliament directing it to cause the sale of these books to be prohibited. He added the general instruction that no books, even such as might have been written by members of the university, were to be printed or sold which had not first been examined and approved by the members of the court deliberating together. It would appear from the King's letter that he had sufficient sympathy with the reformers to be unwilling to have Erasmus attacked, and also that even in matters of theological doctrine, the final decision was entrusted, not to the faculty of theology, but to the court of Parliament. By 1531, however, the King had decided that, for theological questions at least, the responsibility for the control of literary production had better be left with the Sorbonne. In this year he gave a direct royal authorisation to the publisher Badius for the printing of the big treatise of Alberto Pio against Erasmus, which treatise had been duly approved by the divines. The fury of civil war and the bitterness of religious dissension gave a special character to the laws affecting printing and publishing and to the enforcement of these. In 1545, Etienne Polliot was sentenced for importing and selling heretical books. He was compelled to carry a bundle of his publications to the market-place, where he and his books were burned together. In 1546, the publisher Etienne Dolet, himself the author of a number of books, was burned in the Place Maubert, for his obstinate persistence in heresy. The ordinances of 1557 and 1560 punished with death, as guilty of treason, the printers, authors, sellers, and distributors of books which had been condemned as pernicious or libellous. The letters patent of 1563 fixed the penalty of hanging or strangling for the offence of printing a book without a royal authorisation. The ordinance of Moulins, of 1566, renews the same prohibition. Vitet[1] points out that the wars of the League had influence in securing a certain freedom for publishing. The government of the League did not undertake to free from restrictions the printing-presses of Paris. It prohibited them, however, only from such undertakings as seemed likely to prove of service to the enemies of the League. On the other hand, there was at Tours a government which was hostile only to such writings as were not royalist, and at Geneva another government the censures of which affected only that literature which was not Protestant. Through these three limited censures came into existence three fragments of publishing freedom. The power of the printing-press in influencing public opinion may, as far as France is concerned, be said to date from this period. Under the provisions of the Edict of Nantes, which bears date 1598, the production and sale of Protestant books were restricted to certain specified States and districts in which the public exercise of said religion was authorised. These Protestant books, while permitted to exist, are, however, classified as "libels and as inflammatory writings." It does not appear that any provision was made for the circulation of such publications between the cities in which they were permitted to be printed, as such circulation must, of course, have taken them across the "good Catholic" territory, within the boundaries of which the Protestant books were incendiary libels. The difficulties in the way of authors and publishers of such books must, therefore, at this time have been

[1] *De la Presse au Seizième Siècle.*

very considerable. In 1624, four royal censors were instituted by letters patent. The first four were all doctors of the theological faculty, but notwithstanding this selection of the board from the members of the Sorbonne, the university was dissatisfied with losing its ancient privileges of controlling directly the examination of religious literature. In 1629, it was ordered that works submitted for publication were to be passed upon by censors particularly designated for each work by the Chancellor or Privy Seal. It is probable that the volumes had to be put into type before the examiners were willing to give the time for examination. In 1702, an issue arose between the chancellor and the higher clergy on the question of certain general privileges in regard to printing which the bishops claimed to be still in force. It was the contention of the bishops that, being themselves the final judges of the doctrines of the Church, utterances made by them or utterances accepted by them could not with propriety be passed upon by others who were not authorities on points of doctrine. Madame de Maintenon gave the weight of her influence in favour of the bishops. The King dreaded exciting the ire of the Jesuits and dreaded also, says the chronicle, the risk of putting Madame de Maintenon into a bad temper. He avoided making a decision and an adjustment was finally arrived at in which the bishops withdrew their main pretensions. Bossuet made an indignant protest against what he called the attempt of the chancellor to control the utterances of the Church. It is not to be thought of, says Bossuet, that the Holy Church of Christ shall be compelled to submit, for the examination of magistrates, its decrees, catechisms, and spiritual teachings upon matters which should be confined strictly to the instructors of their flock. The King, influenced by the pleading of Bossuet, finally brought himself to decide that for the works which were at the moment in question, the authority should be left with the bishops.

The reports concerning the extent of the influence of censorship, from one authority or another, on the literary activities of France are, as we have seen, conflicting. The authority of the Sacred Office was, as stated, not accepted in France, and the work of the French writers of the 16th century was not seriously affected by the condemnations and expurgations, sometimes severe and sometimes indulgent, with which was supervised and restricted the literature of Italy. It is contended nevertheless (at least by French historians) that the productions of the French writers of the century, freer from the trammels of censorship as these writers were, represented a higher standard of morality and of refinement than characterised the contemporary literature of Italy.

During the 17th century, persistent attempts were made in France as in other Catholic States to enforce throughout the realm a policy of censorship. By one set of authorities, investigations are carried on in the bookshops and in public and private libraries, and copies of obnoxious or suspicious books are burned at the hands of the hangman; by another, St. Cyran is placed in prison and Arnauld and others of his group are driven into exile. The *Lettres Provinciales* of Pascal are indeed brought into print, but only by cleverly eluding the vigilance of the inspectors. It is nevertheless the case that at no time during the century did it prove to be practicable to keep in force, through the entire territory of the State, any consistent or effective policy. The authority to order proceedings against authors or to make condemnations of books is not, as was the case in Spain, in the hands of a special tribunal, all-powerful and irresponsible. In the place of an Index which preserves the record of a condemnation that has once been pronounced, we have individual edicts or orders which easily fall into oblivion; and in place of a Congregation or of an Inquisition, we find distinct authorities, and sometimes simple local authorities, the actions of which are more or less conflicting and lack permanency of influence. There is also throughout the century, as later, among the ecclesiastics themselves, a strong national feeling of protest against the exercise within the territory of France of censorship authority directed by Italians or Spaniards.[1]

While in Italy, the Church labours single-handed at the task of reforming the people, in France it is the entire nation, without distinction of ecclesiastics and laymen, that undertakes the reformation of itself. Frenchmen of the 17th century, equally assured of their devotion to the true faith and of their intention to maintain the virtues of Christianity, refuse to admit the necessity for submitting to a theocracy, a religious dictatorship, and for putting literature, so to speak, into a state of siege.

Dejob cites, on the authority of the Benedictine editors, a number of the absurdities introduced into the St. Ambrose text by the Roman editors, and concludes that " editorial methods so naïve and so unscrupulous were certainly in need of the aid of the Index in order to prevent, through the collation of their text with the work of more faithful scholars, the unmasking of their pious infidelities." "What," he

[1] Dejob, p. 89.

exclaims, "would have been the result for scholarship, for literature, and for the thought of the world, if the Inquisition had succeeded in establishing its domination throughout Europe, and in placing all the manuscripts of the Fathers under the keys of the Vatican?"[1]

Dom Petra, one of the learned editors of the *Acta Sanctorum*, writes in 1649: "If Rome condemns our books, the Jansenists will have a text for saying that this is brought about by intrigue and corruption. . . The Congregation [of the Index] appears to object to the work done by the editors of our *Acta* in the correction of errors; but the Congregation should understand that, rather than to confirm a record of impostures, we prefer to write nothing; the Congregation is giving an opportunity to the heretics to point out the unwillingness of the Papists to make corrections or to remedy abuses."[2]

Theophile Raynaud, in order to revenge himself for a condemnation issued against his books by certain Dominican inquisitors, undertook the defence, against the Dominicans, of the memory of Reuchlin and of Erasmus, victims, as he contends, of Dominican ignorance and calumny.[3]

Writing in 1661, in reference to certain copies of his books that had been seized in Italy, Raynaud says: "The sovereign pontiff gives authority, it appears, to his ministers to carry on robbery."[4]

The only portion of the writings of Rabelais that came under the ban of the French censors was the fourth book of the *Pantagruel*, which was prohibited by the divines of the Sorbonne.

[1] Dejob, 99.
[2] Dom Petra, cited by Dejob, 91.
[3] Cited by Dejob, 92.
[4] Raynaud's works, Cracow, 1669, xx, 267.

The writings of Montaigne were prohibited in 1576 by the Congregation of the Index but the prohibition was not confirmed in France. In 1595, an expurgated edition of the *Essays* was published at Lyons, from which was omitted, together with certain other passages, under the instructions of the censors, the fifth chapter of the third book. The twenty-ninth chapter of the first book, apparently equally reprehensible, escaped condemnation.

"I find," says Dejob, "no book of importance, excepting the *Tartuffe* of Molière, that the national authorities attempted to suppress. Molière, Racine, La Bruyère, were from time to time assailed, but there were always influences working on their behalf strong enough to prevent any serious or continued interference with their work. Once, it may be remembered, Richelieu *se ligua contre le Cid*, but the immediate protest of the public made clear to the minister that he was on a false track."[1]

It is certain that the authority of the Church exercised in France a much smaller influence over literature than either in Spain or in Italy. In fact, under Louis XIV, the Church found it necessary to resort to raillery rather than to discipline in the cases in which it found ground for criticism.

The learned historian of the Benedictines, Mabillon, brought himself into criticism on the part of the Papacy through proving that the bones taken from the catacombs, which were being distributed as relics for the faithful, had belonged neither to saints nor to martyrs.

Dejob is of opinion that the acknowledged superiority of the theological writers of France during the 17th century over those of Italy and Spain was

[1] Dejob 343.

chiefly due to the greater freedom possessed by the French scholars in carrying on their investigations and in bringing their books into print. [1]

The intellectual work of the orthodox clergy owes not a little to the feeling of obligation that rested upon them to offset the influence of the Huguenot controversialists and to secure for orthodox literature a prestige to balance that of Arnaud and of Pascal. It may fairly be claimed that the Church of France showed itself equal to the task Any nation may have been proud to produce within the term of a century five writers or scholars whose names could be compared with those of Bossuet, Fénelon, Bourdaloue, Malebranche, and Mabillon. No religion has counted among its ministers during any one generation men superior to these in intellectual force. Catholicism can refer to this group as an evidence that orthodoxy does not stifle originality of talent. It can claim further that the acceptance of dogma does not of necessity involve the renunciation of scientific and philosophical investigation. The lay writers of this famous century were hardly less influenced by the spirit of religion. It is this that inspired Corneille and Racine, not only in such creations as *Polyeucte* and *Athalie*, but in the moral conception with which they handle the subject of love; it is this which retains within wholesome limits the satirical verse of Boileau and of La Bruyère and which keeps within bounds even the bitter personalities of St.-Simon; it is this which raises far beyond the level of feminine curiosity and maternal egoism the writings of Mme. de Sévigné, and which imbues with eloquence the work of Mme. de Motteville. [2]

[1] Dejob. 90.
[2] *Ibid.* 347.

The religious spirit may be said to have influenced also the work of Molière, who uses his trenchant pen to emphasise our obligations to morality. Save in an occasional instance where the manners of the comedian get control of the pen of the poet, these obligations are set forth with the certainty of an infallible moralist, while the dramatist succeeds in securing for his readers (or hearers) full sympathy for those of his characters which show themselves faithful to wholesome ideals.

If it had been possible for the fathers who directed the work of the Council of Trent to have knowledge of this wonderful body of literature, which gave to Catholicism an incomparable intellectual éclat, they would surely have admitted that their pious expectations were surpassed. [1]

The classical literature of France retained, therefore, freedom of thought and of expression. The eulogies addressed to the rulers, even when extravagant in form, bore the stamp of sincerity. It was a saying of La Bruyère that the use of satire in really great subjects was denied to writers who were at once Frenchmen and Christians. But it is fair to remember that such an interdiction is confirmed by the opinion of the public itself, and also that to one who is himself a witness of great things, the dazzle of their brilliancy may easily prevent a clear perception of their blemishes. It is certain that the record of the work done by the great writers of France does not give any evidence of serious interference by the Church either for praise or for blame. Apart from the *Lettres Provinciales* (which after all secured a wide reading and a general appreciation), no work of the first importance was

[1] Dejob, 348.

brought under condemnation by the authorities either civil or religious. [1]

6. **Germany.**—Within half a century after the invention of printing in Mayence, the business of publishing was established in a number of towns, such as Frankfort, Strasburg, Basel, Cologne, and Nuremberg; and by the close of the 16th century, the work of the printers became important also in many towns of North Germany, such as Leipsic, Magdeburg, Wittenberg, etc. The development of the production of printed books followed very largely the lines of the trade in manuscripts which it superseded. The sale of manuscripts had, for the century before printing, constituted an important item in the business of the Fair at Frankfort, and after 1480, we find entries in the annual records of the Fair of sales of printed books. The organisation of the book-trade of the empire dates from about 1525. Frankfort was established as the centre or headquarters of this trade, and the Fair brought to the city twice a year representative publishers and dealers not only from the towns of Germany but from Italy, France, and the Netherlands.

The establishment of a centre or headquarters for the book-trade of Europe was, of course, of immediate advantage in furthering the knowledge and the distribution of the literature that came into print, and particularly of the books published in Latin. Latin was generally accepted throughout the world as the language not only of scholarship, but of literature, and it was therefore selected by the publishers of the time for the larger portion of the books brought into print. It is true that the work of the early printers of Germany was, unlike that of France and the Nether-

[1] Dejob, 343.

lands, carried on not in university centres, but, very largely at least, in commercial towns. The lists of these German printers contain a much larger number of books addressed to the general or unscholarly public than was the case with those of their competitors in Paris, Venice, or Leyden, but in Germany also the production of works printed in Latin, for the trade of the world, became each year of increasing importance.

For the operations of the general censorship of the Church, the organisation of the book-trade presented certain advantages or at least conveniences. The compilers of the earlier Roman Indexes utilised the bulletins and catalogues of the Book-Fair in securing for their lists information concerning new and forthcoming books of heretical writers or on controversial subjects. As is mentioned in the separate record of certain Indexes, the censors were not infrequently prepared to condemn a book without any examination whatever, simply on the repute of its author, or even on that of its publisher. It occasionally happened, as a result of this method, that a work was prohibited which never came into existence, some obstacle having prevented its completion or its publication after the title had been announced.

The first instances of books issued with *Imprimaturs* are two printed at Cologne in 1479 and sanctioned by the university, and a third printed at Heidelberg in 1480, under the authorisation of the Patriarch of Venice.

The earliest mandate of which there is record for the appointment of a censor of books was issued in 1486 by Berthold, Archbishop of Mayence. The Archbishop forbids the translation into the vernacular of any books from Latin, Greek, or other languages, or the sale of translations brought in from without, until these have been examined and approved by censors appointed for the purpose from the university of Erfurt.[1] He instructs the Burgomaster of Frankfort to make examination of all books at the Frankfort Fair before the permit should be given for their sale. In 1524, the Archbishop of Mayence claims, on the double ground of his position as High Chancellor of the empire and as a representative of the authority of Rome, the right to supervise the book-trade of the empire, and he makes immediate application of this authority to the control of the sale of books at the Frankfort Fair.

In 1648, the year in which the Thirty Years' War came to an end, the magistrates of Frankfort gave up formally the attempts to supervise the **Frankfort** book-production of the city. In 1662, the magistrates found occasion for protests against the imperial regulations for the control of the book-trade. The emperor, in his edict of March 18, 1662, was acting under the counsel of his Jesuit advisers. The magistrates were speaking as the representatives of the publishers, and, as they contended, for the interests of the community as a whole. In 1665, under some counsel which proved to be very ill-advised, the imperial commissioners undertook to fix the prices of the books presented for sale at the Frankfort Fair. It was contended that the commissioners who had been charged with the work of censorship had no authority to take upon themselves the determination of a business detail. It was very certain that they did not have the expert knowledge required for the task, but it was, of course, the case that no commissioners could have carried out successfully any such system. This price

---

[1] Beckman, *History of Inventions*, i, 89.

regulation proved to be one of the most effective of the various factors which caused the replacing of Frankfort by Leipsic as the centre of the publishing and bookselling interests of Germany.

In 1488, the city of Strasburg established under the directions of the emperor a local censorship supervised by the magistracy. The first book prohibited under this regulation was the *Germania Nova* of Murner, issued in 1502.

Strasburg

In 1501, Alexander VI publishes a bull prohibiting the printing, within the territories in question, of any books that have not secured an approval, in the form of a privilege, from the Archbishops of Cologne, Mayence, Treves, and Magdeburg, or from their vicars-general.[1]

By the year 1495, the book-trade of Leipsic had assumed very considerable proportions and was already beginning to rival that of Frankfort. The Booksellers' Association, organised (in Frankfort) in 1525, is at the present time, four centuries later, the most effective and intelligently managed trade organisation that the world has known. Leipsic publishers gave from an early period special attention to the printing of the controversial literature of the Reformation, and, as was natural from their close relations with Wittenberg, the sympathies of the larger proportion of the printers were in accord with the Lutherans. In 1524, Duke George, who was a Catholic, came to the throne and during his reign, which continued until 1533, the writings of the reformers were repressed by a rigorous censorship. The Duke utilised the machinery of the trade organisation for putting into effect the ducal regulations for supervision and

Leipsic

---

[1] Beckmann, *History of Inventions*, i, 99.

censorship, and two ecclesiastical censors, appointed under the ducal authority, secured the aid of the city officials in making examination of all the books printed and in confiscating or cancelling all heretical works found in the shops of either Leipsic or Dresden. The immediate result of these anti-reform operations of the Church and of the Duke was the practical destruction for the time being of the book-trade of Leipsic. Many of the printers transferred their presses to Wittenberg or Magdeburg.

In 1526, occurred in Leipsic an extreme instance of the application of Catholic censorship. Under the instructions of Duke George, Johann Herrgott, a printer and colporteur, was burned, with certain of his books, for the crime of distributing Protestant literature. In the next year, Hübmayer, the leader of the Baptists in Southern Germany, was burned in Vienna for a similar offence. In 1571, the Duke of Saxony ordered that the work of the printers should be restricted to three towns, Leipsic, Dresden, and Wittenberg. The purpose of this regulation was the facilitating of censorship control.

In advance of the aggressive Protestant measures of Luther, Wittenberg had already become an important place for book-production, having secured, among other favourable influences, **Wittenberg** the advantage of the transfer of certain of the printers and their presses from Leipsic. After 1515, Wittenberg was the most important of the centres from which were distributed throughout Germany the books and pamphlets (*Flugschriften*) of the reformers. It was in Wittenberg also that was brought into print the great Bible of Luther.

At an early date in the period of the Reformation, Magdeburg, in which the printing business had already secured an assured foothold, had taken an important place among the centres of distribution of Protestant literature. The work of the printers was interrupted for a time in 1518 by the repressive measures of the Catholic Albert of Brandeburg, but after 1528, the presses were again left practically free from civil authority, while the ecclesiastical influence in the city was never important. The book-trade was crushed out for the time by the destruction of the city by Tilly in 1631.

Magdeburg

The city of Münster was another centre for Protestant publications. The excesses of the Anabaptists, who, under John of Leyden and his associates, had possession of the town for a number of months in 1535–36, were, however, well-nigh destructive to its Protestantism and proved fatal to its publishing business. In 1562, an edict issued by the bishop ordered the destruction of all Protestant books in Westphalia and made it a misdemeanour to print, sell, or possess any such books.

Münster

The city of Basel secured at an early date an important position among the centres of publishing. The university, founded in 1460, brought to the city men devoted to scholarly pursuits many of whom took an early interest in the work of the printing press and were ready to give coöperation to the publishers. In 1501, Basel broke away from the imperial control. At that time, there were in the city no less than twenty-six important publishing and printing concerns.

Basel

During the most active period of its publishing interests, Basel had the advantage over the majority of the German towns in its comparative freedom from censorship either ecclesiastical or civil. The authority of Rome was permitted to exert practically no restrictions upon the productions of the printing-presses; while as a free imperial city, it had the right to claim exemption from any authority other than that of the emperor, whose examiners were too far distant to be able to bring their influence to bear, to any extent, upon the operations of the Basel publishers. It was this freedom that constituted the most important cause of the great development of the book-trade of the city during the 15th and 16th centuries. The leader among the great publishers of Basel, who ranked at the time with Aldus as one of the great publishers of the world, was Johann Froben, the publisher, friend, and close associate of Erasmus. It is the imprint of Froben that is associated with the most important of the volumes of Erasmus, including not only those that secured the approval of Leo X and of other of the Church authorities, but the group which brought the author into sharp criticism with the ecclesiastical censors. During the years between 1460 and 1500, the popes themselves sent to Basel for printing certain books which required more trustworthy work than could be secured in Rome.[1]

In 1523, the first application for censorship in the city of Basel was made by Erasmus in connection with the reprinting of certain French writings which he claimed to be libels of himself. The censorship of the city was under the direction of the magistrates. The magistrates forbade the printing of books in any other languages than Latin, Greek, Hebrew, and German. In 1598 the censors of the city required that there be placed in their hands catalogues of books that were

---

[1] Kapp, 125.

forthcoming in order that they might designate those calling for special attention.

Between the years 1520 and 1580, the presses of Zürich were busied with the production of the works **Zürich** of the Calvinist reformers. Froschauer, who was one of the first of the Zürich printers, was a close friend of Zwingli, whose special tenets he had adopted, and he placed at the disposal of the Zwinglians the machinery of his printing concern for the production and distribution of the Zwinglian treatises and tracts. Zürich presents also an example of early and strenuous Protestant censorship. Zwingli brought about a prohibition on the part of the civil authorities of Zürich for the sale within the city of the Lutheran publications.

The city of Augsburg occupied a similar place among the centres of Catholic book-production to that held **Augsburg** by Basel and Zürich for the works of the Protestants. The presses of the great publisher Koberger and his associates were devoted during the last third of the 15th and the first half of the 16th century to the production of editions of the works of the more scholarly of the Catholic theologians. The books were addressed to scholars and were comparatively high in price. The work of the German reformers had as one result the checking of the activities of the Augsburg publishers. In 1520, the civil authorities of Augsburg, at the instance of the local ecclesiastics, issued prohibitions for the sale in the city of the works of Luther and of Zwingli. It was the multiplicity of prohibitory authorities in the book centres of Germany that actually worked against the influence of the prohibitory system. There was also in these German cities a lack of any effective censorship machinery such as existed in Spain either for the examination of texts in advance of printing, or for the seizure of books and the punishment of printers after publication. There were, during the century after the Reformation, instances (aggregating a considerable number) of writers who on the ground of their heretical utterances had been punished in one way or another and some of whom had even suffered death, but there was no general or effective repression of literary production and distribution throughout Germany, either on the part of the Catholic censors working against Protestant writings or under the influence of the Protestant divines utilising for the prohibition of Catholic books the civil authority.

In Nuremberg, under a regulation of 1513, the printers were to be sworn each year as holding the orthodox Catholic faith and as agreeing to print no books contrary to that faith.[1] The magistrates **Nuremberg** issued in 1518 a special prohibition against the printing of the writings of the Hussites, and in 1521, a similar prohibition against the writings of Luther, Calvin, and Zwingli. This edict was withdrawn in 1535 when the magistracy of the city had become Lutheran. In 1527, the poet-cobbler, Hans Sachs, came under censorship for certain rhymes attached to an illustrated record of the Tower of Babel. In this case, the trouble appears, however, to have been not religious, but a matter of guild prejudice. Sachs, being licensed only as a cobbler, had no authority to do work as a poet. After 1535, when the control of Nuremberg had passed into the hands of the Protestants, there is a rapid development of the activity of its printing-presses and book-trade.

The works of Melanchthon were first printed in

[1] Kapp, 126.

Tübingen in 1511. Later, Melanchthon used for his
theological treatises and also for his long series of text-
Tübingen books the presses of Wittenberg. The statutes
Breslau of the University of Tübingen in regard to
the *Libelli famosi* were, in 1500, made binding throughout the electorate of Würtemberg. In 1557, an edict
of the Duke called for an annual visitation of the bookshops for the search for heretical publications. In 1593,
a ducal permission was given to one bookseller in
Tübingen, Gruppenbach, to buy for the use of the
professors two copies of any heretical books called for.
In 1601, an ordinance was published in Tübingen
prohibiting the sale of all sectarian or controversial
books, Catholic as well as Protestant. In the three
ecclesiastical principalities of Mayence, Cologne, and
Trier, the ecclesiastical censorship became, after 1525,
particularly rigorous with the result of a material
checking in the business of the printers and booksellers. In Silesia, Breslau became the centre of Catholic influence and the Protestant printers were, after
1577, largely driven out of business.

In Heidelberg, under an edict of the Elector of Baden,
the censorship control was, in 1651, placed in the
Heidelberg hands of the university and came under the
direction of the theological faculty.

The printing business in Vienna had during the first
years of the 16th century made a good start, but with
Vienna the beginning of imperial censorship under the
edict of Ferdinand, in 1523, the work of the
printers received a check. In this edict the printing, sale,
and possession of the books of Luther is prohibited
under heavy penalties. Ferdinand permitted the ecclesiastics to exercise directly (that is to say without reference of individual cases to the civil authorities) the

supervision of the work of the printers. These censors made effective opposition against scientific education and their repressive measures for literature other than theological was so far effective that, after the year 1560, the printing in Vienna of editions of the classics was brought to a close. In the year 1572, the printing-office and bookshop of Creutzer, who had for some years acted as the publisher of the university, was closed. In the year 1587, the book stock of Necker, who was at that time the leading bookseller in the city, was confiscated and in large part burned. By 1600, the control of the book business was placed almost exclusively in the hands of the Jesuits and as a result of their "supervision," the business practically came to a close.

Kapp points out that the prohibitory lists issued in Germany contained, in addition to the titles of the Protestant controversial writings and religious writings other than controversial, the titles of a number of books which were really in character *contra bonos mores*. The advantage of the advertisement given to the books deserving of existence was unfortunately shared by not a few volumes which were really scandalous in character.

The Thirty Years' War in Germany (1618–1648) may be considered as an extreme application of the principle of censorship. The power of the emperor and that of the Catholic princes who associated themselves with the emperor, was directed to the suppression of Protestantism in Germany and with this to the control under the direction of the Roman Church of German thought and of German intellectual development. This was, of course, an attempt to do something much wider than to control and restrict the printing-press, but the control and restriction of the operations of the printers constituted an essential part of the purpose of the pope, the emperor, and their allies the Jesuits and Dominicans. In so far as the Catholics held their own, succeeding in maintaining their control in the States of South Germany, the printers had to accept the continued authority of the ecclesiastics backed by the power of the State. The States of North Germany, on the other hand, with the all-powerful aid of Gustavus Adolphus and his sturdy Swedes, were able to maintain by force of arms their independence as citizens, and secured also the right to think and to speak, to print and to read for themselves, free from decisions to be arrived at by the Dominican Congregation of Italy or the Jesuit censors of Vienna. The waste of life and of treasure brought upon Germany through the thirty years' strife was enormous, but even as a matter of material advantage, the contest was for North Germany worth all that it had cost.

7. **The Netherlands**. The work of the printers in Holland was begun in Utrecht in 1473. The Dutch printers had from the outset the enormous advantage in their business of a practical freedom from interference by censorship, whether ecclesiastical or political. This was also true for a quarter of a century or more with the printing centres of Flanders, where, under the initiative of Mansion, Caxton, and their successors, the work of printing was begun, in 1474, in Bruges and in Louvain. In 1476, Caxton migrated from Bruges to London, setting up his first press in the courtyard of Westminster Abbey. The Dukes of Burgundy had, for several generations prior to the introduction of printing, been noted for their liberal interest in literature, and for their great collections of manuscripts, and this sympa-

thetic relation of the Burgundian rulers to literature continued through the first half-century of printing.

During the first three fourths of the 16th century, the Netherlands, with Antwerp as a centre, present the type of a most enlightened community. At the time of the great siege of 1585, Antwerp was at the height of its prosperity, and in the extent and the varied character of its commercial relations it was possibly the leading city of Europe. Antwerp possessed exceptional advantages as a centre of book-production and by the close of the 16th century, out of the sixty-five printers who were at work in the Netherlands, no less than thirteen were in Antwerp. The neighbouring University of Louvain supplied scholarly coöperation which was essential for all the publishing undertakings of the age, while not a few scholars, who, some years later, found themselves with the exiles in Leyden or in Amsterdam, were at this time resident in Antwerp, and were already largely associated with the work of the printing-press. In 1556, at the time of the beginning of the work of the great publisher Plantin, an entire quarter of the city was devoted to the making of books, a circumstance without a parallel among the cities of Europe. The result of the censorship of the Spanish Government was practically to crush out the book business of Antwerp. The presses were largely destroyed and the scholars and printers alike were scattered among the towns of Holland. Plantin placed his imprint upon a number of books of theology, for all of which it was necessary to secure the approval, with the "royal privilege," of the Duke of Alva and of the successors of the Duke who represented the Spanish Throne.

The ordinances issued by Philip II concerning books

were for the most part merely a confirmation, with some increase in severity, of the edicts of Charles V. The

Book Regulations, 1560-1570

modifications in these ordinances brought about by the States-General in 1566 provided that those books only should be prohibited that contained heretical or pernicious opinions; and that the responsibility for the examination and decision should be shared with the theologians by the scholars of the other university faculties; that instructors should be at liberty to utilise all books not on the prohibited lists; and that the visitation to the bookshops should be made only under the direct authority of the magistrates. Under Alva, the routine for such a visitation was to instruct the magistrates on a specific day (not announced in advance) to place seals on the doors of all printing-offices and bookshops; the examination of the books was then carried out by the suffragan bishop and the local head of the Franciscans. In the years 1566 and 1567, four printers were sentenced to banishment for from four to six years, one was sent to the galleys, and one was hanged.[1]

In 1570, Philip II instituted the office of "proto-typographer" or supervisor of printing for the Netherlands, and appointed as the first occupant of the office the printer Plantin. Master-printers applying to the supervisor for authorisation for a work to be printed must show the certificate of approval of the diocesan bishop or of his vicar, and also of the local magistrate. Printers were required to take an oath of conformity to the doctrines of the Church as set forth by the Council of Trent. No remuneration was attached to the office of proto-typographer, but the incumbent was freed from the duty of lodging soldiers. The im-

---

[1] Gachard, *Corr. de Philippe II*, ii, 9, 565.

portant service of the post for Plantin was, of course, the increased facility it secured for him in obtaining approvals and privileges for his own publications. The theologians of Louvain (through whom the ecclesiastical censorship for Antwerp was, in the main, carried on) were not likely to raise question concerning the undertakings of the literary representative of the King. It was suggested that one ground for his selection was the wish of the King to make good to Plantin the loss that had been caused to his business by his arrest in 1562 on a charge of heretical publishing, a charge which proved to be unfounded. It may also be recalled that Philip had promised, in 1568, to pay to Plantin the sum of 21,000 florins as a subvention for the polyglot Bible, edited by Montanus. This payment was, however, never made, and the failure to receive it was one of the causes that had, in 1570, brought Plantin into financial difficulties.[1]

Under the ordinance of 1570, the censorship is lodged with the council, the bishop, and the inquisitor. Each book that may secure their approval is to be referred to the stadtholder, by whom its selling price shall be fixed. Inspection of the printing-offices must be made from time to time by the bishop, the inquisitor, and the proto-typographer, and not less than twice a year by the magistrates. The booksellers must take oath that without permit from the censors they will bring in no book from abroad; that they will sell, except to a buyer with a written permit, no copies, printed in the vernacular, of the Scriptures or of controversial writings; and that they will faithfully obey all the regulations of these ordinances and of the Roman Index (that of Trent, printed as an appendix

[1] Putnam, *Books and Their Makers*, ii, 255.

to the ordinances); all packages of imported books are
to be opened only in the presence of the bishop or of
the inquisitor.

In 1573, it was ordered that of all the books printed
in the Netherlands, one copy should be delivered to
the royal library at Antwerp, and a second (to be paid
for) to the Escurial.

Henricus Hovius printed in Liège, in 1569, an edition of the Index of Trent in which (without any reference or specification) certain additional
names and titles have been inserted in the
alphabetical lists. The title-page states that
the Index has been prepared under the authority of King
Philip, and in accordance with a decree of the Duke of
Alva. The new titles, probably added at the instance
of the divines of Louvain, are for the most part repeated in the Antwerp Index of 1570. Reusch points
out that this Liège Index is very carelessly printed
and is full of errors.

1569. Liège
(Lüttich)

The prohibitions of the Trent Index were confirmed
under the authority of the diocesan synods of the
Spanish Netherlands. One of the diocesan edicts
required the printers and booksellers each year to take
an oath of fidelity to the faith of the Church, in default
of which the license to print was to be forfeited. In
1589, the Synod of Tournai prohibited the booksellers
from possessing a copy of the *Index librorum haereticorum*, a catalogue printed yearly for the use of the
Frankfort Book-Fair, which was based upon the lists
of the Index of Trent, but the titles in which were
from year to year brought down to date. The book-
dealers were already beginning to realise the value
for their business of the labour expended by the Church
in the preparation of bibliographies of the books which

were most likely to prove of interest to the active minded people of the world. This Frankfort catalogue of heretical books was the beginning of a series of such catalogues in which the work of the Congregation of the Index and of the Inquisition was taken advantage of (with material improvements in the accuracy of the bibliography) to emphasise the value and to further the circulation of the books which had been condemned by the Church. The edict of the bishops who met at Tournai in 1589 appears to have been the first expression of doubt on the part of ecclesiastical authorities as to the effectiveness of the condemnations of the Index in lessening the circulation and the influence of heretical literature.

In 1585, through the recognition of the independence of the Dutch Republic, the long contests in the Netherlands were brought to a close. The authority of the Spanish King was restored in Antwerp but the city was impoverished as to both men and resources. Irrespective of the loss of life in the great city, Antwerp had suffered the loss of some of the best and most enterprising of its citizens who had preferred to make their home in the Protestant communities of Holland. The departing Protestants took with them much of the intellectual life and literary activity in the city, while Amsterdam and Leyden, free from the hampering restrictions of Catholic censorship, presented many advantages for publishing undertakings. In 1585, there was but one book printing-press in activity in the city in which a few years earlier there had been no less than forty. Plantin's first publication for the new year was an official list of the books at that time under prohibition, the list comprising some six hundred titles.

It is not surprising, in view of the hampering regulations and restrictions above specified, that the book-trade of the Spanish Netherlands should have become demoralised and that the centres of publishing activities should have been transferred from Antwerp and Louvain to Amsterdam, Utrecht, and Leyden.

Among the Protestants who during this war period migrated from Flanders was Louis Elzevir, who removed from Louvain to Leyden and began there the business which developed later into one of the greatest publishing houses of the world. The coöperation of the scholars of the university, together with an absolute freedom from any censorship restrictions, gave to the new publishing concern advantages which were at that time possessed by no printer-publishers outside of Holland. The development of the book-trade of Holland was furthered thirty years later through the influence of the Thirty Years' War in Germany. During this period, 1618–1648, the territory of the Seven United Provinces was free alike from invaders and from civil strife. Much of the work of the scholars of Europe that had heretofore been brought into print through the presses of Frankfort or of Leipsic was now transferred to Amsterdam and Leyden. The theological discussions which became active in Holland, more particularly after the time of the Synod of Dort in 1618, furthered the work of the printing-presses. The Hollanders were also shrewd enough to realise the opportunity given to them for bringing into print the books which had been prohibited or cancelled in Spain, in France, or in Italy. With a few exceptions, these books had been written in Latin and the editions printed in Leyden or in Amsterdam were, therefore, available for the use of scholarly readers throughout Europe.

Andrea Schurius writes[1] that he has been told that the Amsterdam publisher of the *Bibliotheca Fratrum Polonorum* took special pains to secure the formal prohibition of his work, considering this to be the most effective means of bringing it into active sale.

During the 17th century, the press of the Dutch Republic continued this work free from restrictions which hampered publishing in all other States of Europe. The censorship measures in Holland were restricted to certain edicts and regulations issued by the States-General prohibiting the printing of libellous material or of works directed against princes or governments which were allied with the Republic. There is also an occasional edict against the circulation of publications classed as "irreligious" or "obscene." The machinery for the enforcement of these regulations appears, however, to have been very inconsiderable; and there is no record of any general inspection for the purpose of censorship of the productions of the printing-press. Among the earlier noteworthy publications of the Elzevirs were certain books that could not at that time easily have come into print elsewhere, such as *The System of the Universe* by Galileo and the *Defensio Populi Anglicani* of Milton. Galileo, writing in 1638, gave testimony to the excellence of the work done for him by his Dutch publishers. The list of scholars under censorship either ecclesiastical or political in their persons or in their books who had been exiled from their own countries and whose names are brought together on the catalogues of the Elzevir house is a long one. We may mention, in addition to Galileo, Scaliger, Hobbes, Pascal, Descartes, More, etc.

The Roman, Spanish, and French Indexes served as

[1] Epp., iii, 19.

guides to the Dutch printers for the selection of books likely to prove of interest and to secure circulation.   In not a few instances, the scholarly writers themselves who had been banished from Spain or from France in connection with their so-called heretical teachings, or who, irrespective of banishment, had decided that they could carry on their work to better advantage in a territory which was outside of the control of the Catholic Church, had taken up their residence in Holland. The influx of these scholars made Holland for a century or more the centre of scholarly activity in Europe and gave to the Dutch publishers, in the use of these scholarly pens for original work and for editorial work, an enormous advantage.   The ethics of publishing were at this time not recognised or certainly at least not recognised outside of national boundaries.   The Dutch publishers were quite ready, therefore, in the case even of books which had not been prohibited in the country of origin, to utilise texts that had been edited or shaped by competitors in Venice, in Paris, or in Frankfort, for the production of competing editions.   The printers of Holland secured for themselves a final advantage in developing after 1525 a better standard of typography, both for accuracy and for beauty, than had as yet been known in Europe excepting with certain of the issues of Aldus and of Froben.   The preëminence obtained under these several influences by the printers of Holland continued until the middle of the 18th century.

8. **England.**—The work of printing in England began with Caxton, in 1476.   His catalogue speaks of his books as being "printed in the Abbey of Westminster." His presses were as a fact placed in the almonry, a space within the Abbey precincts.   Sir Thomas More

has shown why Caxton could not venture to print a Bible in the vernacular, although the people would have greedily bought the Wyclif translation. Wyclif's translation was interdicted and More says: "On account of the penalties ordered by Archbishop Arundel's constitution, though the old translations that were before Wyclif's days remained lawful and were in some folks' hands, yet he thought no printer would likely be so hot to put any Bible in print at his own charge, and then hang upon a doubtful trial whether the first copy of his translation was made before Wyclif's days or since. For if it were made since Wyclif, it must be approved before the printing." This was a dilemma that Caxton was too prudent to encounter.[1]

In England, during the first half of the century, the printers, while having various other difficulties to contend with, such as lack of communication with a public, the small extent of the public that was ready to be interested in the printed book, and the serious interference that was caused to all trade by the events of the Civil War, were practically free from any burdens of censorship. Even if the ecclesiastics in England had been in a position to make their censorship troublesome, they would have had small occasion for interference with the first literary undertakings of the English printers. The lists included hardly any works having to do with theology, religion, or controversial subjects of any kind. Caxton and his immediate successors realised that at this period the interest of English readers could be depended upon much more safely for books of romance and for chronicles. It was nearly a century after the introduction of printing into England before any attempt was made to produce

---

[1] Knight. *The Old Printer*, 113.

English editions of the Scriptures. It was in Germany that during this period the attention of the printers was given largely to the production of Bibles, theological treatises, and controversial tracts. The lists of the printers of France were devoted mainly to classics, with some titles under the headings of romance and poetry, while in Italy the earlier lists were made up chiefly of classics and science.

The Stationers' Company received its charter by royal decree in 1566. two years after the marriage of Queen Mary (to Philip of Spain). It constituted an organisation of the publishing and printing trade of London which assumed to represent the publishing interests of the country. The basis of the authority of the Stationers' Company was the theory that all printing was the prerogative of the king. The Stationers' Company had, under its charter, summary rights of search. seizure, and imprisonment, and these powers were confirmed or renewed by the licensing acts. It seems probable that the purpose of the institution of the Company was not so much the furthering of the business of book-production, as the organisation of this business in such shape that it could be reached effectively and promptly by the censorship authorities of the Crown. No question appears to have arisen in England in regard to any conflicting authority on the part of the Church to control such censorship. The Crown utilised the services of bishops and of other ecclesiastics for the examination of works in the division of theology which came under the suspicion of heresy. The selection of the examiners and the decision concerning the disposition of the books so examined was reserved, however, for the direct action of the Crown or of the representatives of the Crown. Such censorship as came into action in England proved to be more important in connection with political literature than with works on religion or theology.   In 1644, the Long Parliament enacted certain regulations for the control of printing which provided that " No book, pamphlet, or paper shall be henceforth printed unless the same be first approved and licensed by censors that shall be thereto appointed."   Milton had been a persistent opponent of the policy of censorship and of licensing, and one result of the enactment was the publication of the famous *Areopagitica*, an oration in the form of a pamphlet, which presented with fierce eloquence a protest against the whole theory of the exercise by Government licensers of a supervision and control of literature, or of the delegation of such control to a commercial company (the Stationers' Company) which was the creation of Government.

9. **Oxford. Index Generalis. James. 1627.**—In 1627, Thomas James, the librarian of the Bodleian Library in Oxford, brought into print, under the title of an *Index Generalis*, a summary or catalogue which had been made up from the Church Indexes that had thus far come into print and of which James had been able to secure copies.   It was his purpose to present in this general catalogue the titles of the more important of the books condemned under the censorship of the Church, copies of which books it was, as he pointed out, important to secure for the Bodleian collection.   The so-called James Index came to be a working guide for book-buyers and its publication had a direct effect upon the circulation in England of the books specified.   It has, therefore, seemed in order to make reference to it in this chapter on the influence of censorship on the book-trade of England.

This catalogue of James was utilised during the succeeding years by English scholars generally, as a convenient guide to the literature condemned by the Church and which on the very ground of its condemnation might be assumed to possess interest and value for scholars who were not troubled by the dread of ecclesiastical penalties. The recommendation of James that copies of these works should be secured for the Bodleian has been carried out quite effectively. The copy of the James Index which has been preserved for the reference library of the Bodleian has been checked by successive librarians as copies of the books recommended have been secured and the list is now very nearly complete. The copies secured for the Bodleian represent in large part editions printed in Holland; as before pointed out, the publishers of Amsterdam, Leyden, and Utrecht had, from the date of publication in 1546 of the Index of Louvain, interested themselves in bringing promptly into print works condemned by Roman authorities and in furthering the distribution of these books throughout Europe.

The full title of James's Index reads as follows: *Index Generalis Librorum Prohibitorum a Pontificiis; una cum editionibus expurgatis vel expurgandis juxta serium literarum et triplicem classem. In usum Bibliothecæ Bodleianæ et Curatoribus ejusdem specialiter designatus. Per Tho. James, S. Theol. D. Coll. B. Mariæ. Winton. In Oxon. Vulgo. Novi dicti quondam Socium Oxonæ Excudebat Gulielmus Turner. An. D. 1627.*

I add a rendering of his preface (the original of which, according to the custom of the time, is in Latin) which is interesting as indicating the attitude of the Protestant scholar of the day towards the censorship of Rome. James includes in the volume of his Index an announcement (addressed to students of theology) of another work that he had in preparation which he entitles *A Universal Index of the Sacred Fathers of the Church*. He speaks of having published a sample of this and goes on to say,

"If my friends tell me that this sample which I have published is not displeasing to them, there will shortly after follow the other books of Scripture, if not in their own order, at least in a series which has the support of other authorities. My method of procedure will be as follows: The text before us will be the Vulgate, and no one who has read any of the works of Cyprian or Tertullian or of the other ancient Fathers of the Church, has ventured to say that this text is Hieronymian, and thus the various readings which do not agree with this Vulgate edition will be added, and the passages which have been disputed by Bellarmin and his school (of which there are more in this fifth chapter than in any other) carefully noted in the margin. By these means, the younger students to whom God has given the necessary leisure and inclination, may see whether the Fathers take the side of the Pontifical writers with their shrill unseemly clamour, or are ranged under our banners: for a careful inspection of the Company here drawn up will support opinions of the Eastern as well as the Western Churches one after another,—a support which is claimed falsely by the Papists, in direct opposition to the rules laid down by the Council of Trent, as they would see if they would but face the facts.

"If the opinion of those who have declared that these Books ought not to be published, or ought to be suppressed, wins the day, I shall not fall claiming to have championed in the struggle the fortunes of the Church or any great issue. No! but relying on conscience and on the conviction that I must promote the cause of God to the best of my poor ability,

Bull appended to the oath at the Council of Trent.—"I will never accept or interpret Holy Scripture except according to the unanimous opinion of the Fathers."

1 shall preserve my writings of whatsoever sort in my own house under my own roof; with the hope that if I can but present a willing and ready spirit I shall be not unworthy to serve the world, even though opportunities and resources fail; for has not the Poet said,

'In magnis est voluisse satis.'

" In everything I have tried to follow the counsel of S. Paul,—neglecting my own conscience, taking no care for my bodily health, not seeking your money, but yourselves, not trying to profit myself but to benefit the world.

" Finally, that there be no mistake as to the editions which I have used in the compilation, I have appended the following Index. Lest you experience difficulty in perusing it or strike upon the rock which has proved fatal to others, I would have you remember (being desirous of removing the obstacle which has long troubled many readers) that I have devised a way by which all future Editions may be referred to my pages, thus saving readers the expense and trouble of buying Edition after Edition. With these words of instruction, learned Reader, I would bid you farewell. May God direct and preserve us and our studies to the glory of His name and to the advancement of His Church.

" For the State and the Catholic Church of God these labours. TH. JAMES, D.D.

" OXFORD, 1627."

The preface to the Index itself reads as follows:

TO BE NOTED IN THIS CATALOGUE

"First, as regards the numerals 1, 2, 3, occurring throughout the book.

" 1. Denotes condemned authors, that is, authors whose religious opinions are orthodox and pious, but whose books are prohibited.

" 2. Denotes pontifical authors, in whose case caution or expurgation is prescribed.

"3. Denotes works of doubtful authorship which are prohibited.

" But it must be understood that the inquisitors (if one may say so) made a rather imperfect classification under these heads. For the authors Aventinus, Erasmus, Palingenius, Bruciolus, etc., were placed in the first class, whereas they belong rightly in the second; and on the other hand, Adolphus Metkerchus, Lavinus Lemnius, and others, who ought to be in the first class, are placed in the second. And the third class, which should consist of doubtful works, contains a good many known authors whose names and surnames are clear as day to any one looking at the title-pages with one eye. This appears plainly, for example, in the case of two books, *Bello Papali*, and another of which the title is, *Beliae, sive consolatio peccatorum.*

" Secondly, it ought to be clear to everybody that books prohibited by the *pontificii* (*i. e.* the Congregation of the Index, acting as the representatives of the Pope) ought to be sought with the more zeal and read with the greater avidity. For what the papists prohibit, God grants for our use and benefit, and the memory of those condemned by our adversaries is and should be blessed, since their names are doubtless inscribed in the Book of Life.

" Thirdly, a star(*) indicates editions or authors hitherto contained in the *Bibliotheca Oxoniensis*, which is to be set down as our gain since we need take no further trouble to make them known.

" Fourthly, the Greek letter denotes authors of the second class (almost all *pontificii*) who (unless they are emended and expurgated as the Indexes direct) set forth more clearly than the noonday sun the very doctrine of the Protestants, so that the *pontificii* do not venture even to mutter against it. This is doubtless the work of God's finger and of the inspiration of the Holy Ghost, who armed Midianite against Midianite, to their mutual slaughter.

" Fifthly, we have arranged all authors of whatever class in strict alphabetical order. Their names cannot be found so easily in the *Sandovillian* or *Roman* Index, in comparison with which other Indexes are rubbish.

" Sixthly, in this alphabetical revision are included books, written whether in Latin or in French, Italian or Spanish, chiefly on religious subjects, by men who were in their own day not subject to condemnation at the hands of either God or men, but who, if they were now alive, could hardly, or not at all, escape the Inquisition and damnation to the shades of deeper hell. Moreover (to speak more plainly and to make the thing clear by examples taken from this book) the *pontificii* are so far from being consistent that books hitherto praised and approved by worthy men are now transformed into prohibited books of the second or third class. In this way was treated even the *Evangelium Romanum prout a Clementis octavi manu Jacobs Davis Episcopo traditum est;* for after the book had (if the stories may be believed) worked miracles on the return of Perron to France, it was not only left neglected, but the possession of a copy was prohibited under penalty of excommunication.[1] Capucinus, inquisitor in the diocese of Naples, has his doubts about the Index of Quirogus (Madrid, 4vo, 1584), and for this reason he incurs censure in the Sandovillian Index, p. 365 (consult our catalogue) and the *Enchiridion Ecclesiasticum*, Ven., 1588 (see our catalogue) is by no means to be read unless *corrigatur*. In the same way, Gabriel Pentherbeus' book on The Destruction of Evil Books is not always free from the censure of others. What need of more examples? The Defence against the Re-

---

[1] The *Evangelium Romanum* was a Protestant satire on indulgences, printed in Leipsic, without the name of the author, in 1600. The book was as a joke ascribed to Jacques Davy, Bishop of Evreaux. Davy was better known under the name of Du Perron. He was a convert from Protestantism and was the Bishop selected to bring King Henry IV into the Catholic fold. The *Evangelium Romanum* was reprinted more than once and appears to have secured a wide circulation. Curiously enough, it did not find place upon the Index (Reusch, ii, 213).

formers, according to the principles of S. Francis, S.D.N., by Manfred (and, good God, what a man) is altogether prohibited, unless I have overlooked something. If so many and such men do not escape the hands, or rather the claws of their own party, who can guarantee safety to a book composed by any author whatever? Not Aesculapius himself, their God, their lord Pope, ventured to promise this, since Clement VIII changed the books of his predecessor, Sixtus V, with no consideration for the industry involved, on the ground of typographical errors, a most glorious lie. There are many more cases of this sort worthy of notice, but it has seemed best to mention but these few facts at present. Let the rest be left in the hands of the intelligent reader, or postponed to another time.

" Finally, it must be carefully noted that the censures sometimes recoil upon the censors themselves, for no law is juster than that the very inquisitors should be revised, corrected, and altered, under the rod. The complete works of Beatus Arias Montanus for one were most severely castigated by the first inquisitors and expurgators. This is done (strange but true) on page 55 of the Index Sandovilliano and on page 39 of the Roman Index, to say nothing of the Indexes named above. Are more instances wanted?"

CHAPTER X

EXAMPLES OF CENSORSHIP OF THE STAGE IN THE SIXTEENTH CENTURY

1. In Italy
2. In Spain
3. In France

THE scope and plan of this treatise do not permit any general consideration of so complex a subject as the censorship of the stage. In the present chapter, I am submitting merely certain examples of attempts at such censorship in Italy, Spain, and France in the 16th century, which it may be interesting to compare with the supervision that was being exercised in these countries at the same time over the production and distribution of literature.

1. **The Theatre in Italy, 16th Century.**—The action taken in regard to the censorship of the stage varied materially in the different localities. St. Charles Borromeo prohibited in Florence, in 1565, theatrical performances during the time of religious fêtes. Later, he secured the suppression altogether of the presentation of the drama of the Passion. Gregory XIII, as the result of an appeal made to him by St. Charles, prohibited dramatic performances in Rome on holy days. The influence of the saint secured similar action in Verona and in Bologna, and, in 1577, Venice banished the comedians altogether.

The Church as a whole, however, avoided being drawn into the consideration of the control of the drama; it made absolute prohibition of but two things: the presentation on the stage of ecclesiastical dress and the use of female actors.[1]

The Jesuit Ottonelli, writing in 1640, condemns "immodest" dramatic representations, of which he demands the complete suppression. He contends that there should be on the stage no scenes of love between a man and a woman left alone. He is willing to concede the communication, in connection with a proposition of marriage, by the father of the lover to the father of the girl, of the sentiments of the young man.[2]

2 The Theatre in Spain.—In Spain and in Italy the clergy undertook during the 16th century to repress or to restrict the license of the stage, and in Spain, at least, the clerical control of the drama was complete. The seven centuries of contest against the Moors had, among other results, served to associate indissolubly the Catholic faith with the cause of patriotism and nationality, and with the daily life of the people; and yet in Spain a large respect and an ardent devotion for the Church were not felt to be incompatible with a large indecency on the stage.

In Spain, the Inquisition, in place of being detested as in France, or dreaded as in Italy, was really a popular institution. Lope de Vega, who entered the priesthood after the birth of two illegitimate children which had come to him during his second widowhood, displayed at the head of his most indecent comedies his title of "Familiar of the Sacred Office." His

[1] See an edict of the Inquisition dated 1611, cited by Dejob p. 216.

[2] Ottonelli, *Memoriali*, etc., cited by Dejob, 218.

plays present alternate examples of passages of real piety and of verses the most obscene.

In 1548, however, as a result of a petition of the Cortes to Charles V, vigorous measures were taken against indecent performances; and between 1587 and 1600, such effective destruction was made by the clerical commissioners of dramatic productions that of a series of forty-three volumes, there remained copies of but ten.[1]

3. **The Theatre in France, 16th Century.**—The French Church of the 16th century did not manifest antagonism to the stage. The edict of 1548, which, for the purpose of protecting religion against indignities, ordered that dramatic performances should be restricted to subjects that were "profane, decent, and free from scandal," emanated not from the divines, but from the Parliament of Paris. The Church councils of the provinces restricted their interference to the prohibition of the use for such performances of consecrated buildings.[2]

[1] Ticknor, vol. ii, Appendix.
[2] Migne. *Nouvelle Encyclop. Théologique*, vol. 43.

CHAPTER XI

THE LITERARY POLICY OF THE MODERN CHURCH

1. The Indexes of Leo XIII.................. ......1881–1900.
2. Index Revision and Reform................. .....1868–1880.
3. The Index and the Liberal Catholics, "Romanus"
      and the "Tablet"......... ....1897.
4 The Present Methods of Roman Censorship ... .

1. The Indexes of Leo XIII, 1881–1900.

Rome, 1881, 1884, 1896.—*Index Librorum Prohibitorum sanctissimi Domini nostri Leonis XIII, Pont. Max. Jussu editus, cum appendice usque 1895, Augustae Taurinorum. Typog. pontif. 1896.*

Rome, 1900.—*Index Librorum Prohibitorum SSMI D. N. Leonis XIII, jussu et auctoritate recognitus et editus; praemittuntur Constitutiones Apostolicae de examine et prohibitione Librorum. Romae, Typis Vaticanis, 1900.*

The two Indexes issued by Leo XIII, the first compiled in 1881 and reprinted in 1884 and 1896 with supplements, and the second in 1900, constitute at the date of this writing (December, 1906) the latest expression of the censorship policy of the Church of Rome. It remains to be seen whether Pius X (who is not credited with any such measure of literary interests as characterised his scholarly predecessor) will undertake the production of any addition to the long series of Roman prohibitory Indexes. The first of the two Indexes of Leo is, bibliographically speaking, a fairly

379

creditable piece of work. The titles are, with few exceptions, correctly presented, and in this respect it makes a noteworthy exception to all the preceding Roman Indexes, excepting only that of Benedict, issued in 1758. Its typography is, however, undignified. The volume contains in all about 6800 entries. The number of separate works considered is, however, very much smaller, as in a large number of instances each book is entered twice in the alphabetical list, once under its own title, and again under the name of the author.

The volume of 1896 presents as front matter:

   I. The Preface (signed by Cajetanus Amatus) to the Index of Benedict... 1758
  II. The Address to the Reader, signed by Saccheri
 III. The Ten Rules of the Index of Pius IV (Trent) 1564
 IV. Observations on the Rules, from the Index of Clement VIII..................... 1585
  V. Observations on the Rules from the Index of Alexander VII.. 1664
 VI. The Instruction of Clement VIII..... ..
 VII. The Constitution of Benedict XIV. ....
VIII. The Decree *de libris prohibitis*, from the Index of Benedict 1758
 IX. The *Mandatum* from the Index of Leo XII 1825
  X. The *Monitum* of the Congregation of the Index 1828
 XI. The *Monitum* of the Congregation of the Index 1836
 XII. The Constitution of Pius IX 1869
XIII. The Declaration of Pius IX (in regard to the dogma of the Immaculate Conception) .. 1854

The Index of 1900 is very attractively printed, and is a credit to the work of the papal printing-office. It is the first of the Roman issues that can be so described. This second Index repeats, with a few omissions, the lists of the volumes of 1896, with the addition of certain titles selected from the publications of the intervening four years.

The prefatory matter of the volume of 1900 is made up as follows:

I   The Papal Brief. which bears the signature of Cardinal Macchi.

II. A Preface, with the signature of Esser, Secretary to the Congregation.

III. The Constitution of Leo XII.

IV. The *Decreta Generalia.*

V. The Constitution of Benedict.

I have thought it in order to present the full text of the first four of these documents as fairly representative of the literary policy of the Church at the close of the 19th century.

BRIEF OF LEO XIII

" The Roman pontiffs, to whom, in the person of S. Peter the chief of the Apostles, that great duty was committed of feeding the universal flock of Christ, have all been constant in preserving whole and inviolate the most precious deposit of the Faith, and in nourishing the Christian peoples of the world with the food of sound doctrine. Hence the fervent and provident care continually taken by them that, as good grain from tares, so sound and excellent books may be separated from the alloyed, the apocryphal, and the hurtful, lest Christian men, by using them incautiously or daringly, may injure the integrity of their faith and morals. Under this head, the pontiffs themselves or the councils have been ever careful to provide remedies suitable to the evils, changing these to suit the changes of time. When the invention, in the 15th century, of the new art of printing caused a great increase in the number of books and also a great spread of the pest of evil heresies, it was everywhere deemed necessary to take severe notice of evil writings, both to forestall danger and to repair evil already done. Therefore the Fathers of the Council of Trent, to whom our predecessor Pius IV had entrusted the matter, deemed that the great contagion of heretical books, or of books suspected of the crime of heresy, or of books hurtful to piety and morals, should be attacked in two ways: First, the scholars and theologians, chosen for this purpose by the authority of the same synod, made certain general rules so that it might be easier to decide of what books in general the faithful should beware; and secondly, they compiled an accurate and absolute exposition or Index of books of improper contents. When the synod adjourned, by its own decree, this Index, with the rules above mentioned, was shown to our predecessor, Pius IV, that it might, before publication, receive the support of the Apostolic sanction. The pontiff approved it after it had been worked over again with great diligence, and ordered its observance by all.

" In the nature of the case, his Index required additions as in the course of time new wicked and hurtful books appeared, and every one knows that the Apostolic Chair has attended to this again and again with zealous care. Thus Clement VIII and later Alexander VII and Benedict XIV, our predecessors, by the specification of those books which the popes had proscribed, by Apostolic letters, by the Roman Congregations, and chiefly by the Congregations of the Inquisition and the Index, revised and reshaped the Index proper so that it constituted practically a new compilation. Since (the issue of Benedict) there has been a long interval, almost a hundred and forty years, and the conditions seemed to call for something more comprehensive and more efficient for the present needs.   .   .

                 " (Signed),

                      " ALOIS. CARD. MACCHI.

" ROME, Sept. 17, 1900."

" PREFACE

" Behold, worthy reader, a new Index of the prohibited books, revised and published with the greatest care, by direction of His Holiness Leo XIII, P. M.; together with a syllabus of books to be avoided, there are published also the Constitutions of the Apostolic Chair by which the examination and proscription of bad books are at present governed: viz : the Constitution 'of Offices and Duties,' promulgated by Leo, Jan. 25, 1897, and the Constitution '*Solicita ac Provida*' by which Benedict XIV, on July 9, 1753, established clear and firm rules for the use of the Roman and universal Inquisition, and also of the Holy Congregation of the Index, in examining and judging books.

" As to the Constitution of Benedict XIV, it does not apply so much to the faithful in general as to those who are entrusted by the Holy See with the task of examining books. The Constitution of the present Pope has another object, since, revoking the rules of the holy Synod of Trent, 'it sets forth certain new general Decretals, which are to be obeyed religiously by Catholics everywhere.'

Furthermore, these general Decretals and the Index have this in common, that both exist for the purpose of teaching what books to avoid reading and owning. The Decretals, however, serve this end in one way, the Index in another. For the Decretals prohibit the greatest possible number, indeed almost all, of noxious and tainted books, the reading of which is strongly forbidden by the natural law itself; while the Index reviews and notes but a small part of these. By the Decretals, *genera* and classes only of bad books are proscribed; by the Index, individual books, each with its title and even the author's name. Hence it is plain how greatly they err who suppose the whole question of improper books to be decided by the Index alone, as though of the innumerable perverse and pernicious books which have appeared in the course of centuries, those only are prohibited which have been condemned by special decrees and noticed in the catalogue of prohibited books. In fact, any given book can only be safely declared lawful reading when these two conditions are satisfied: it must not occur in the Index nor be contained in any of those classes which are as a whole reprobated and condemned by the Decretals.

" It remains to consider what the character of the Index is and what the object was in planning and compiling it. For a catalogue of prohibited books does not go as far as to note each and every bad book. Obviously this would not be done, nor, if the principle of the Decretals be grasped, does it appear necessary. There must, therefore, be some special reason why the Roman Congregations black-list by special decree a book already included in those classes noted by the Decretals. This reason is furnished in most cases by denunciations, from a bishop or other of the persons specified in *Const. Off. ac Mun.*, vv. 27, 28, 29, recommending a given book to the Holy See for examination as destructive or dangerous. Following this clue, and not of set purpose choosing the worst among all the books in existence, the Holy See is very often led to examine other books not included by the Decretals. Therefore, it would be vain to seek in the Index either all noxious and wicked books or those distinguished as it were for wickedness in any department, or to demand that the books in the Index be dealt with in a fixed order based on either the argument or the matter. The only basis of the Index is then this, that it notes those works which for any reason have been prohibited by special decree during the last three centuries, whether by popes in Apostolic letters or by Roman Congregations, and especially the Congregation of the Index, so that neither oblivion nor ignorance may obscure the dangerous character of their contents.

" A few words are needed to explain the principle of the new edition and its chief points of difference from the earlier ones. The intention of the Pope in ordering a thorough revision of the Index was not only to temper the severity of the old rules but also, on behalf of the maternal kindness of the Church, to accommodate the whole spirit of the Index to the times. In the actual compilation of the list of prohibited books some material modification has been shown and the number of books formerly prohibited has been diminished. This can be seen in the first Decretal, by which all books prohibited before the year 1600 are declared to be henceforth expunged from the Index, although they are to be considered as much condemned to-day as they ever were, with the exception of those permitted by the new Decretal. Hence in the case of condemned authors hitherto described in Class I, all of whose works were prohibited, by the present Index those of their works are permitted which either *ex professo* do not treat of religion, or, if they do treat of it, contain nothing contrary to the Faith, unless they happen to have been prohibited by some general or special decree. And this mitigation may properly be extended to the case of non-Catholic authors whose complete works are expressly prohibited in the Index. This prohibition will not apply in future to those books which touch the Faith either not at all or only incidentally by the way, if these have not been noted by any general or special decree. Therefore the old distinction between 'all works' simply and 'all works treating of religion' might be cancelled as superfluous. For whenever the complete works of an author are prohibited, those works only are understood which either treat of religion or are proscribed by some general or special decree.

" Moreover, certain books, not a few in number, have been dropped from the Index, which, although they labour under certain defects or have some slight taint, yet have such a reputation for learning or such documentary value that their errors or views seem to be compensated by their usefulness.

" It was also thought best to delete a good many works which deal with the Immaculate Conception, soundly, it is true, but too intemperately or with some offence to adversaries. Again, a number in which domestic controversies and private quarrels were agitated with improper acrimony, to the injury of good feeling and with hardly any gain to truth; and some which deserved prohibition not by defective doctrine nor failure in charity, but by the indiscretion of the author in failing to obey the public injunction to silence for the sake of extinguishing private quarrels. These controversies having become extinct and the injunction to silence having been long ago removed, these books could be dismissed.

" Since certain books, otherwise harmless, had been placed on the Index because they contained offices and litanies of the Church which were disapproved and published contrary to prohibition, it seemed good to expunge these also, since to-day the power is entrusted to Ordinaries to publish litanies and prayers of this kind for the private use of the faithful.

" Certain minor works, frivolous, or absurd or superstitious, and such as cite false and apocryphal indulgences, are omitted. For superstitions and magic are sufficiently excluded by *Dec.* 12, 13, 16, and 17; while for the elimination of apocryphal indulgences, there is at hand for all the authoritative ' decree of the Holy Congregation in charge of Indulgences and Holy Relics,' published by command and authority of the Pope, and the decree 'concerning the discrimination between regular or normal indulgences and apocryphal,' published by the same Congregation on the 10th of Aug., 1899.

" It happened often that there were placed on the Index works of slight bulk, sometimes of only a few pages, which were full of venom and danger, but which have been so dispersed by the passage of time (as by the wind) that to-day copies are hardly to be found. These have not been placed on the new Index. Under this head are included a series of pamphlets, for the most part scholastic, which were transferred to the Index proper from the appen-

dices to the Indexes of Innocent XI and of Clement XI.
Theses, also, which were prepared for public academic
discussion, although not free from error and rightly and
justly placed on the Index on their first appearance, have
been thought fit for omission, the more as oblivion has
long ago blotted out most of them. But those prohibited
writings, however small in compass, which claim any part
in the historic evolution of Catholic theological doctrine,
are for this very cause retained in the Index.

" All those works were struck off which had been condemned only by the edicts of the *Magister Palatii* early in
the 17th century, and those in regard to which the Congregation itself decreed that they might or should be
omitted by the next decree, as well as certain old collections
of declarations, decisions, and interpretations of the Council
of the Congregation, which this body proscribed by its
decree of April 29, 1621. For although the decrees in these
collections are not to be considered authentic simply on the
ground of inclusion there, the collections are nevertheless
believed to be of some value to-day. Besides, the making
of such collections in future has been sufficiently guarded
against by *Dec. gen.* 33.

" It happened sometimes that the first volume or volumes
of a work were placed in the Index, the later volumes of
which followed the publication of the prohibition; or that
periodicals were proscribed which continued afterwards to
be published; also that all the works of an author were
proscribed, who, after the publication of the decree, produced other works. In all these cases, the volumes or
numbers published after the latest special decree, although
not mentioned in that special decree, are nevertheless held
suspicious and are justly presumed to fall under the prohibition of some general decree, unless there is evidence
of the author's change of heart.

" It remains to indicate in a few words, for the readier use
of the Index, the method used in arranging and describing
books. In order that the issue of Leo might be more correct

than its predecessors, and that all corruptions might be eliminated which, in the course of so many editions, (some of them prepared by private authority) had crept in, much zealous labour has been given to the investigation of the records of the Congregation of the Index and of the Inquisition, both Roman and general; and of libraries in Rome and abroad. Books whose authorship is declared in their titles are entered under their titles in alphabetical order, the author's name being subjoined when possible. These names are always entered in full, lest the omission of a syllable should lead to the confusion of similar ones. Assumed or fraudulent names included in titles are treated on the same basis as real names.

" Italian names prefixed by the syllable *De, Del. Di*, etc., which appears to be part of the name, always begin with that syllable in this catalogue. The same applies to *Van* etc., in Dutch names, and to *Des*, etc., and *St.* in French names; but names beginning with the two syllables *De la* are entered under *La*. When the syllable *De* alone begins a French name, it is placed after the name in this catalogue unless the name begins with a vowel.[1] . . ."

There follow certain further bibliographical details. The Preface bears the signature of "Fr. Thomas Esser, Ord. Praed. S. Indicis Congregationis a Secretis."

THE CONSTITUTION OF POPE LEO XIII, CONCERNING THE PROHIBITION AND CENSORSHIP OF BOOKS

" Of the duties and obligations which ought to be most carefully and faithfully performed in this Apostolic Office, this is the chief and most important matter, namely,— to watch zealously and make every effort that the integrity of the faith and morals of Christians shall not be impaired. If this were ever necessary, it is especially so in this age— when, in the midst of unbounded license of character and

---

[1] This detail is deserving of attention because the Index of Leo is the first which makes any attempt at bibliographical consistency or accuracy.

morals, almost all the teaching which Jesus Christ, the Saviour of Mankind, entrusted to the care of his Church for the salvation of the human race is attacked, with daily criticism and discussion.

" In this criticism, our opponents use various and innumerable stratagems and artifices for the purpose of causing injury; but especially dangerous is the lack of moderation in their writings and the influence of these pernicious writings among the people. For nothing worse can be imagined for contaminating the minds of men, both by making them despise religion and by suggesting many incentives to sin. Wherefore the Church, the guardian and protector of the integrity of faith and morals, in fear of this great evil, long ago came to the conclusion that measures must be adopted to guard against the danger. To this end, it made continued efforts to prohibit men, as far as practicable, from the reading of pernicious books, which are the worst kind of poison. Even the very remote age of St. Paul saw an eager zeal in this matter. And in like manner, every subsequent generation has witnessed the watchful care of the holy Fathers, the instructions of the bishops, and the decrees of the Church councils.

" Especially do the records of literature bear witness to the care and diligence shown by the Roman pontiffs to prevent the writings of heretics, a constant menace to the community, from making their way unnoticed into circulation. The earlier years are full of examples of this. Anastasius I condemned by a solemn edict the more dangerous writings of Origen; Innocent I did the same with all the works of Pelagius, and Leo the Great with those of the Manichaeans. There are known to be decretal letters about the same matter concerning the acceptance and the non-acceptance of certain books. For one of these letters Gelasius is responsible. Likewise, in the course of years, the decree of the Holy See has condemned the pestilent books of the Monothelites, of Abélard. Marsilius of Padua, of Wyclif, and of Huss.

" But in the 15th century, with the invention of the new art of printing, not only were prohibitions made against wicked books that had actually appeared, but efforts were also made to prevent the publication of any further such books. This foresight was demanded for that age not on any trivial grounds, but by the necessity for the preservation of the public integrity and safety: because an art. most excellent in itself. and the source of very great advantages, which had come into existence originally for the purpose of propagating Christian civilisation, had been speedily perverted by the action of many into a powerful instrument of evil. The great and pernicious influence of wicked writers had more serious and more rapid results because of this very increase in the extent of the circulation of literature. Therefore, by a most wise policy, both Alexander VI and Leo X, my predecessors, made regulations, adapted to the character of the times, to keep publishers in the path of duty.

" Later, as the evil was recognised as more serious, it became necessary to use strict and more strenuous measures to check the contagious spread of wicked heresies. To this end, the same Leo X, and afterwards Clement VII, positively forbade any one to read or to possess the books of Luther. But when, in accordance with the calamities of the age, the foul collection of dangerous books had increased beyond all bounds and had penetrated in every direction, the need of a more far-reaching and more immediate remedy was recognised. This remedy was first opportunely suggested by our predecessor Paul IV. namely, the publication of a list of writers and books, from the perusal of which the faithful were to abstain Not long afterwards, the Fathers of the Synod of Trent took further measures for checking the increasing license of writing and of reading. In accordance with their wish and instructions, directors and theologians chosen for this purpose took great pains not only in amplifying and perfecting the Index which Paul IV had published, but also in framing rules to be observed in the publishing, reading. and possessing of books. To these rules, Pius IV added the weight of the Apostolic authority

" But the needs of the public welfare, which in the beginning had caused to be framed the Rules of Trent, promulgated from the council, came in later years to call for further action. Therefore, the Roman pontiffs, and especially Clement VIII, Alexander VII, and Benedict XIV, with full understanding of the requirements and with thoughtful discretion, framed further decrees to explain these rules and to adapt their instruction to the later generations.

" This record shows plainly that the Roman pontiffs have always taken exceptional pains to protect human society from errors of opinion and from influences inimical to morality, and to combat those causes of disaster and ruin to the community which are engendered and distributed from pernicious literature. Good results attended this action as long as, in the administration of public affairs, the Divine law had control of the directing and the prohibiting, and as long as the temporal Rulers of States were in accord with the sacred Authority.

" As to what followed, no one is ignorant. When, in the progress of the ages, the conditions of society had gradually changed, the Church modified with discretion the application of its authority, because, with full understanding of the character of the times, it saw that these regulations were of assistance and service for the guidance of mankind. Several of the rules of the Index, which appeared no longer to be pertinent, were either abolished by decree, or the books therein forbidden were permitted under conditions and with wise judgment on the ground of the increasing importance of antiquarian researches. Of more recent occurrence is the action of Pius IX instructing the archbishops and bishops to modify materially the strictures of Rule V. In addition, in view of the approaching important Vatican Council, Pius IX confided to a group of learned men the task of making a fresh examination of all the rules of the Index with instructions to report as to what action might be necessary in regard to them. They unanimously agreed that certain changes ought to be made. The majority of the Fathers frankly avowed that they were of the same opinion and they submitted to the council a similar recommendation. There are extant letters concerning this matter from the bishops of France, whose opinion was unanimous as to the necessity for immediate action in order that these rules and the entire Index should be framed in an entirely different manner, which would render the regulations better suited to our age and easier to observe. Similar counsel was received from the bishops of Germany, who united in recommending that the rules of the Index should be submitted to a new examination and revision. A great number of the bishops in Italy and in other countries were in accord with this conclusion.

" If one considers the character of the times, and the condition of civil institutions and of popular morals, we must admit that these demands are just and reasonable, and are not out of accord with the purposes or the material affection of the Holy Church. In the rapid development of intellectual activity, there is no field of knowledge in which literature is not produced too freely, with the result of a daily accumulation of foul and of dangerous books. What is still more serious is that this great evil is not only connived at by the civil laws, but even secures under these a great freedom. As a result, therefore, unrestricted license is assured for reading anything whatever, and the minds of many are filled with religious doubts.

" Concluding, therefore, that we must now take measures to remedy these evils, we have decided that there are two things to be done in order that there should be a fixed rule of action in this class of matter, a rule that should be plain to every one. The Index of books forbidden to be read has been gone over again with the utmost care and this revised list shall be published as soon as it is in readiness. Furthermore, we have directed our attention to the rules themselves and have decided, without changing their general character, to make them more lenient, in order that unless a man be really depraved, he shall not find it a difficult matter to obey them. In this we not only follow the examples of our predecessors, but we also imitate the zeal of the Mother Church, which, with loving zeal, takes pains to spare the infirmities of her children.

" Therefore, after mature deliberation and after summoning the cardinals and a holy council to go over the lists of books, we have decided to publish the following general decrees, which are made part of this Constitution. The holy council will in the future make use of these rules only, and Catholics all over the world must obey them scrupulously. We decree that these only shall have the authority of law, and we abrogate the 'Rules' published by the order of the very holy Council of Trent, and the 'observations,' 'instructions,' 'decrees,' and 'precepts,' and every other statute or law concerning this matter which have been made by our predecessors, except only the 'Constitution' of Benedict XIV, which we decree shall remain in force in the future as it has done hitherto."

GENERAL DECREES CONCERNING THE PROHIBITION AND CENSORSHIP OF BOOKS

ARTICLE I

OF THE PROHIBITION OF BOOKS

I. OF THE PROHIBITED BOOKS OF APOSTATES, HERETICS. SCHISMATICS, AND OTHER WRITERS

1. All books condemned before the year 1600 by the Sovereign Pontiffs. or by Oecumenical Councils. and which are not recorded in the new Index, must be considered as condemned in the same manner as formerly: with the exception of such as are permitted by the present General Decrees.

2. The books of apostates, heretics, schismatics, and all writers whatsoever, defending heresy or schism, or in any way attacking the foundations of religion, are altogether prohibited.

3. Moreover, the books of non-Catholics, *ex professo* treating of religion, are prohibited, unless they clearly contain nothing contrary to Catholic Faith.

4. The books of the above-mentioned writers, not treating *ex professo* of religion, but only touching incidentally upon the truths of Faith, are not to be considered as prohibited by ecclesiastical law, unless proscribed by special decree.

II. OF EDITIONS OF THE ORIGINAL TEXT OF HOLY SCRIPTURE AND OF VERSIONS NOT IN THE VERNACULAR

5. Editions of the original text and of the ancient Catholic versions of Holy Scripture, as well as those of the Eastern Church, if published by non-Catholics, even though apparently edited in a faithful and complete manner, are allowed only to those engaged in theological and biblical studies, provided also that the dogmas of Catholic Faith are not impugned in the prolegomena or annotations.

6. In the same manner, and under the same conditions, other versions of the Holy Bible, whether in Latin, or in any other dead language, published by non-Catholics, are permitted.

III. OF VERNACULAR VERSIONS OF HOLY SCRIPTURE

7. As it has been clearly shown by experience that, if the Holy Bible in the vernacular is generally permitted without any distinction, more harm than utility is thereby caused, owing to human temerity: all versions in the vernacular, even by Catholics, are altogether prohibited, unless approved by the Holy See, or published, under the vigilant care of the Bishops, with annotations taken

from the Fathers of the Church and learned Catholic writers.

8. All versions of the Holy Bible, in any vernacular language, made by non-Catholics, are prohibited; and especially those published by the Bible Societies, which have been more than once condemned by the Roman Pontiffs, because in them the wise laws of the Church concerning the publication of the sacred books are entirely disregarded.

Nevertheless, these versions are permitted to students of theological or biblical science, under the conditions laid down above (No. 5).

IV. OF OBSCENE BOOKS

9. Books which professedly treat of, narrate, or teach lewd or obscene subjects are entirely prohibited, since care must be taken, not only of faith, but also of morals, which are easily corrupted by the reading of such books.

10. The books of classical authors, whether ancient or modern, if disfigured with the same stain of indecency, are, on account of the elegance and beauty of their diction, permitted only to those who are justified on account of their duty or the function of teaching; but on no account may they be placed in the hands of, or taught to, boys or youths, unless carefully expurgated.

V. OF CERTAIN SPECIAL KINDS OF BOOKS

11. Those books are condemned which are derogatory to Almighty God, or to the Blessed Virgin Mary or the Saints, or to the Catholic Church and her worship, or to the Sacraments, or to the Holy See. To the same condemnation are subject those works in which the idea of the inspiration of Holy Scripture is perverted, or its extension too narrowly limited. Those books, moreover, are prohibited which professedly revile the Ecclesiastical Hierarchy, or the clerical or religious state.

12. It is forbidden to publish, read, or keep books in which sorcery, divination, magic, the evocation of spirits, and other superstitions of this kind are taught or commended.

13. Books or other writings which narrate new apparitions, revelations, visions, prophecies, miracles, or which introduce new devotions, even under the pretext of being private ones, if published without the legitimate permission of ecclesiastical superiors, are prohibited.

14. Those books, moreover, are prohibited which defend as lawful duelling, suicide, or divorce; which treat of Freemasonry, or other societies of the kind, teaching them to be useful; and not injurious to the Church and to Society; and those which defend errors proscribed by the Apostolic See.

VI. OF SACRED PICTURES AND INDULGENCES

15. Pictures, in any style of printing, of our Lord Jesus Christ, the Blessed Virgin Mary, the Angels and Saints, or other Servants of God, which are not conformable to the sense and decrees of the Church, are entirely forbidden. New pictures, whether produced with or without prayers annexed, may not be published without permission of ecclesiastical authority.

16. It is forbidden to all to give publicity in any way to apocryphal indulgences, and to such as have been proscribed or revoked by the Apostolic See. Those which have already been published must be withdrawn from the hands of the faithful.

17. No books of indulgences, or compendiums, pamphlets, leaflets, etc., containing grants of indulgences, may be published without permission of competent authority.

VII. OF LITURGICAL BOOKS AND PRAYER BOOKS

18. In authentic editions of the Missal, Breviary, Ritual, Ceremonial of Bishops, Roman Pontifical, and other

liturgical books approved by the Holy Apostolic See, no one shall presume to make any change whatsoever; otherwise such new editions are prohibited.

19. No Litanies—except the ancient and common Litanies contained in the Breviaries, Missals, Pontificals, and Rituals, as well as the Litany of Loreto, and the Litany of the Most Holy Name of Jesus, already approved by the Holy See—may be published without the examination and approbation of the Ordinary.

20. No one, without license of legitimate authority, may publish books or pamphlets of prayers, devotions, or of religious, moral, ascetic, or mystic doctrine and instruction, or others of like nature, even though apparently conducive to the fostering of piety among Christian people; unless issued under license, they are to be considered as prohibited.

VIII. OF NEWSPAPERS AND PERIODICALS

21. Newspapers and periodicals which designedly attack religion or morality are to be held as prohibited, not only by the natural, but also by the ecclesiastical law.

Ordinaries shall take care, whenever it be necessary, that the faithful shall be warned against the danger and injury of reading of this kind.

22. No Catholics, particularly ecclesiastics, shall publish anything in newspapers or periodicals of this character, unless for some just and reasonable cause.

IX. OF PERMISSION TO READ AND KEEP PROHIBITED BOOKS

23. Those only shall be allowed to read and keep books prohibited, either by special decrees, or by these General Decrees, who shall have obtained the necessary permission, either from the Apostolic See or from its delegates.

24. The Roman Pontiffs have placed the power of granting licenses for the reading and keeping of prohibited books in the hands of the Sacred Congregation of the Index. Nevertheless the same power is enjoyed both by

the Supreme Congregation of the Holy Office, and by the Sacred Congregation of Propaganda for the regions subject to its administration. For the city of Rome this power belongs also to the Master of the Sacred Apostolic Palace.

25. Bishops and other prelates with quasi-episcopal jurisdiction may grant such license for individual books, and in urgent cases only. But if they have obtained from the Apostolic See a general faculty to grant permission to the faithful to read and keep prohibited books, they must grant this only with discretion and for a just and reasonable cause.

26. Those who have obtained Apostolic faculties to read and keep prohibited books may not on this account read and keep any books whatsoever or periodicals condemned by the local Ordinaries, unless by the Apostolic favour express permission be given to read and keep books by whomsoever prohibited. And those who have obtained permission to read prohibited books must remember that they are bound by grave precept to keep books of this kind in such a manner that they may not fall into the hands of others.

X. OF THE DENUNCIATION OF BAD BOOKS

27. Although all Catholics, especially the more learned, ought to denounce pernicious books either to the Bishops or to the Holy See, this duty belongs more especially to Apostolic Nuncios and Delegates, local Ordinaries, and Rectors of Universities.

28. It is expedient, in denouncing bad books, that not only the title of the book be expressed, but also, as far as possible, the reasons be explained why the book is considered worthy of censure. Those to whom the denunciation is made will remember that it is their duty to keep secret the names of the denouncers.

29. Ordinaries, even as Delegates of the Apostolic See, must be careful to prohibit evil books or other writings published or circulated in their dioceses, and to withdraw

them from the hands of the faithful. Such works and writings should be referred by them to the judgment of the Apostolic See as appear to require a more careful examination, or concerning which a decision of the Supreme Authority may seem desirable in order to procure a more salutary effect.

ARTICLE II

OF THE CENSORSHIP OF BOOKS

I. OF THE PRELATES INTRUSTED WITH THE CENSORSHIP OF BOOKS

30. From what has been laid down above (No. 7), it is sufficiently clear what persons have authority to approve or permit editions and translations of the Holy Bible.

31. No one shall venture to republish books condemned by the Apostolic See. If, for a grave and reasonable cause, any particular exception appears desirable in this respect, this can only be allowed on obtaining beforehand a license from the Sacred Congregation of the Index and observing the conditions prescribed by it.

32. Whatsoever pertains in any way to Causes of Beatification and Canonisation of the Servants of God may not be published without the approval of the Congregation of Sacred Rites.

33. The same must be said of Collections of Decrees of the various Roman Congregations: such Collections may not be published without first obtaining the license of the authorities of each Congregation, and observing the conditions by them prescribed.

34. Vicars Apostolic and Missionaries Apostolic shall faithfully observe the decrees of the Sacred Congregation of Propaganda concerning the publication of books.

35. The approbation of books, of which the censorship is not reserved by the present Decrees either to the Holy See or to the Roman Congregations, belongs to the Ordinary of the place where they are published.

36. Regulars must remember that, in addition to the license of the Bishop, they are bound by a decree of the Sacred Council of Trent to obtain leave for publishing any work from their own Superior Both permissions must be printed either at the beginning or at the end of the book.

37. If an author, living in Rome, desires to print a book, not in the city of Rome but elsewhere, no other approbation is required beyond that of the Cardinal Vicar and the Master of the Apostolic Palace.

II. OF THE DUTY OF CENSORS IN THE PRELIMINARY EXAMINATION OF BOOKS

38. Bishops, whose duty it is to grant permission for the printing of books, shall take care to employ in the examination of them men of acknowledged piety and learning, concerning whose faith and honesty they may feel sure, and that they will show neither favour nor ill-will, but, putting aside all human affections, will look only to the glory of God and the welfare of the people.

39. Censors must understand that, in the matter of various opinions and systems, they are bound to judge with a mind free from all prejudice, according to the precept of Benedict XIV. Therefore they should put away all attachment to their particular country, family, school, or institute, and lay aside all partisan spirit. They must keep before their eyes nothing but the dogmas of Holy Church, and the common Catholic doctrine, as contained in the Decrees of General Councils, the Constitutions of the Roman Pontiffs, and the unanimous teaching of the Doctors of the Church.

40. If after this examination, no objection appears to the publication of the book, the Ordinary shall grant to the author, in writing and without any fee whatsoever, a license to publish, which shall be printed either at the beginning or at the end of the work.

III. OF THE BOOKS TO BE SUBMITTED TO CENSORSHIP

41. All the faithful are bound to submit to preliminary

ecclesiastical censorship at least those books which treat of
Holy Scripture, Sacred Theology, Ecclesiastical History,
Canon Law, Natural Theology, Ethics, and other religious
or moral subjects of this character; and in general all
writings specially concerned with religion and morality.

42. The secular clergy, in order to give an example of respect towards their Ordinaries, ought not to publish books,
even when treating of merely natural arts and sciences,
without their knowledge.

They are also prohibited from undertaking the management of newspapers or periodicals without the previous permission of their Ordinaries.

IV. OF PRINTERS AND PUBLISHERS OF BOOKS

43. No book liable to ecclesiastical censorship may be
printed unless it bear at the beginning the name and sur-
name of both the author and the publisher, together with
the place and year of printing and publishing. If in any
particular case, owing to a just reason, it appears desirable
to suppress the name of the author, this may be permitted
by the Ordinary.

44. Printers and publishers should remember that new
editions of an approved work require a new approbation; and that an approbation granted to the original
text does not suffice for a translation into another
language.

45. Books condemned by the Apostolic See are to be
considered as prohibited all over the world, and into whatever language they may be translated.

46. Booksellers, especially Catholics, should neither sell,
lend, nor keep books professedly treating of obscene subjects. They should not keep for sale other prohibited
books, unless they have obtained leave through the Ordinary from the Sacred Congregation of the Index; nor sell
such books to any person whom they do not prudently
judge to have the right to buy them.

V. OF PENALTIES AGAINST TRANSGRESSORS OF THE GENERAL DECREES

47. All and every one knowingly reading, without authority of the Holy See, the books of apostates and heretics, defending heresy; or books of any author which are by name prohibited by Apostolic Letters; also those keeping, printing, and in any way defending such works; incur *ipso facto* excommunication reserved in a special manner to the Roman Pontiff.

48. Those who, without the approbation of the Ordinary, print, or cause to be printed, books of Holy Scripture, or notes or commentaries on the same, incur *ipso facto* excommunication, but not reserved.

49. Those who transgress the other prescriptions of these General Decrees shall, according to the gravity of their offence, be seriously warned by the Bishop, and, if it seem expedient, may also be punished by canonical penalties.

We decree that these presents and whatsoever they contain shall at no time be questioned or impugned for any fault of subreption or obreption, or of Our intention, or for any other defect whatsoever; but are and shall be ever valid and efficacious, and to be inviolably observed, both judicially and extrajudicially, by all of whatsoever rank and preëminence. And We declare to be invalid and of no avail, whatsoever may be attempted knowingly or unknowingly contrary to these, by any one, under any authority or pretext whatsoever; all to the contrary notwithstanding.

And We will that the same authority be attributed to copies of these Letters, even if printed, provided they be signed by the hand of a Notary, and confirmed by the seal of some one in ecclesiastical dignity, as to the indication of Our will by the exhibition of these presents.

No man, therefore, may infringe or temerariously venture to contravene this document of Our constitution, ordination, limitation, derogation, and will. If any one shall so presume, let him know that he will incur the wrath of Almighty God, and of the Blessed Apostles Peter and Paul.

Given at St. Peter's in Rome, in the year of the Incarnation of Our Lord one thousand eight hundred and ninety-seven, on the 25th day of January, in the nineteenth year of Our Pontificate.

A. CARD. MACCHI.

A. PANICI, Subdatary.

Visa.

De Curia: J. DE AQUILA VISCONTI.

L. ✠ S.

Registered in the Secretariat of Briefs,

I. CUGNONI.

THE LISTS OF THE WORKS CONDEMNED

In the lists (as was the arrangement in the earlier Index of Leo) the date of the decree under which the work was condemned is connected with the title of the book. For the works (a considerable proportion of the entire series) which are entered both under the title and under the name of the author, cross references are given. The number of entries in the second Index of Leo is about 7000, practically the same as that in the earlier volume. Of the publications of the last ten years of the 19th century, 131 works, representing 82 authors, are selected for condemnation. These books of recent date comprise 60 Italian volumes, 47 French, 16 Spanish and Portuguese, 4 German, and 4 English. This selection may be considered as indicative of the lack of familiarity of the examiners with the language or with the modern literature of Germany or of England.

As these two Indexes represent the latest authoritative expression of opinion in regard to the present literary policy of the Church of Rome, it is in order to present with some detail the character of the books selected for examination.

It is with the Leonine Indexes, as with all those

that preceded, difficult to arrive at the principle that
has guided this selection. The lists include no works
of the heresiarchs, and in fact no titles back of the
17th century. Place has been found, however, for
reprinting a number of the prohibitions of the early
17th century, as well as for those of the 18th. The
Leonine decrees confirm those of the Indexes of Pius
IV (Trent), 1564, of Clement VIII, 1596, and of Benedict XIV, 1758, and the lists in these cover, of course,
all the important heretical literature from the earliest
date of printing. It is not clear on what principle
have been selected the works of the 17th century
which in the judgment of the Leonine editors were
important enough to warrant a reiteration, three
centuries later, of the original condemnation. Still
more difficult for these editors must have been the
selection from the great mass of fiction and of current
literature of the past century, and more particularly
of the last half of the 19th century, of works that
impressed them as sufficiently pernicious in character
and abiding in their influence to call for specific condemnation. The result of this selection impresses
the student as curiously disproportionate, and in fact
as almost haphazard in its character. The fiction
which has been condemned is for the most part classed
under the description of *fabulae amatoriae*.

I have noted the titles of certain works which seem
to be in one way or another typical or which would
be likely to prove of interest to the English-speaking
readers of to-day.[1] It is doubtless the case that the
Italian literature (which constitutes the very large
proportion of the lists) possesses for the purposes of the

[1] These titles are transcribed in the precise form in which they are
printed in the Leonine schedule.

indexer a distinctive importance of its own, but these books are, I judge, less likely to be familiar to the readers who will be reached by my treatise. The dates placed against the titles are those, not of publication, but of the decrees, these decrees being in some cases as far as a century later than the date of the original issue.

Abrégé de l'histoire ecclésiastique de Fleury. Decr. 1769.

ACTON, LORD. *Zur Geschichte des vaticanischen Conciles; Sendschreiben an einen deutschen Bischof.* 1871.

ADDISON, JOS. *Remarks on Italy.* 1729.

ALBERTUS MAGNUS. *De Secretis Mulierum.* 1604.

Alciphron, by Berkeley. 1742.

Anglica, Normanica, etc., *a veteribus scripta,* etc. *d.c.* By Walsingham, etc., edit. Camden. 1605.

> These chronicles are, it is to be noted, to be permitted when corrected; but for such corrections they have already waited for centuries.

Apologie de Jansénius, évesque, etc. 1654.

> There are no less than sixteen entries under the term "Apology."

ARNAULD ANTOINE (*fils*).

> Seventeen works are entered under the name of this Jansenist writer. The decrees are of date 1656–1659.

Arrest de la cour de Parlement.

> Under this term are six entries, covering acts of the Parliament of Paris from 1680–1744, the condemnation of which it is considered important to confirm 250 years later.

Augustinus. Janseni. 1654.

> A condemnation that recalls a long and bitter doctrinal contest.

BALZAC, *oeuvres de.* 1841, 1842, 1864.

BARONIUS, VINCENTIUS.

> Three works. 1672.

BAYLE, PIERRE. *Opera omnia* 1698 to 1757.

> This is followed by entries of four separate works of the same author.

BENTHAM, JEREMIE.
>Four works, of which two are entered in the French editions. 1819–1835.

BÉRANGER. *Chansons.* 1834.

BERT, PAUL. *L'Instruction Civile.* 1882.

BLACKWELL, GEORGE, Archpriest of England. Letter to Clement VIII. 1614.

BOILEAU, JACOBUS. *Historia Flagellantium.* 1668.

Book of Common Prayer. London. 1714.

BOSSUET, ÉVESQUE. *Résponse à M. de Tencin.* 1745.

BROWNE, THOMAS. *Religio Medici.*

BRUNO, GIORDANO. *Opera omnia.* 1600.

BUNSEN, C. C. J. *Hippolytus and his Age.* 1853.

BURNET, GILBERT. *The Reformation of the Church of England.* 1714.
>"   "   *History of his own Times.* 1731.

CAMERARIUS, JOHANNES. *Opera omnia.* 1654

CASAUBONUS, ISAACUS. *De Rebus Sacris,* etc. 1614.
>"   "   *Epistolae.* 1640.

Catechisme, Catechismo, and *Catechism.*
>Under this heading and that of Katechism there are twenty-five entries in the four languages, under dates from 1602 to 1876.

CHARRON, PIERRE. *De la Sagesse.* 1605.

COLLINS, ANTHONY. *On Free Thinking.* 1715.

COMBE, GEORGE. *Manuel de phrénologie.* 1837.

COMTE, AUGUSTE. *Cours de philosophie positive.* 1864.

CONDORCET. *Tableau historique du progrés de l'esprit humain.* 1827.

CUDWORTH, RALPH. *Intellectual System of the Universe.* 1739.

DARWIN, ERASMUS. *Zoönomia.* 1817.

DESCARTES, RENATUS. *Meditationes de prima philosophia.* 1663.

DIDEROT. *Encyclopaedie raisonnée des sciences.* 1804.

Discovery of a New World. Wilkins, John. 1701.

DRAPER, JNO. WM. *History of the Conflicts between Science and Religion.* 1876.

> The much more comprehensive and incisive work on the same subject by Andrew D. White escapes attention.

DUMAS, ALEXANDRE (*pater*). *Omnes fabulae amatoriae.* 1863.

DUMAS, ALEXANDRE (*filius*). *Omnes fabulae amatoriae.*

EARLE, JOHN C. { *The Spiritual Body.* } 1878.
{ *The Forty Days.* }

ENFANTIN, BARTHÉLEMY P. *Science de l'homme.* 1859.

ERIGENA, JOHANNES SCOTUS. *De divisione naturae,* etc. 1684.

FÉNELON. *Explication des Maximes des Saintes,* etc. 1665.

FERRI, ENRICO. *Sociologia criminale* [and four other treatises]. 1895–6.

FERRIÈRE, ÉMILE. *Le Darwinisme* [and seven other treatises]. 1892–3.

FEYDEAU, ERNEST. *Omnes fabulae amatoriae.* 1864.

FONTENELLE, B. L. *La république des philosophes,* etc. 1779.

FOURIER, CHAS. *Le Nouveau monde industriel et sociétaire.* 1835.

FREDERIC II (of Prussia). *Oeuvres du philosophe de Sans-Souci.* 1760.

FROHSCHAMMER, JACOB. *Ueber den Ursprung der menschlichen Seelen* [and five other treatises]. 1857–1873.

GANDOLPHY, PETER. *A Defence of the Ancient Faith,* etc. 1818.

GIBBON, E. *The Decline and Fall of the Roman Empire.* 1783.

GOBLET D'ALVIELLA, E. *L'idée de Dieu d'après l'anthropologie,* etc. 1893.

GOLDSMITH, OLIVER. *Abridged History of England,* etc. 1823.

GREGOROVIUS, F. *Geschichte der Stadt Rom,* etc. 1874.

GROTIUS, HUGO. *Opera omnia theologica* [and five other works, comprising practically *Opera omnia*]. 1757.

GUICCIARDINI, F. *Loci duo ob rerum*, etc.   1603.

HALLAM, H *Constitutional History of England.*   1833.

"   "   *View of the State of Europe.*   1833.

HERBERT DE CHERBURY. *De Veritate*, etc.   1633.

Histoire, Historia, De Religione, etc.

> Under these terms are entered thirty-six different works.

History of the Devil, as well ancient as modern.

> Defoe, Daniel.   1743.

HOBBES, THOMAS. *Opera omnia.*   1703.

HUGO, VICTOR. *Notre Dame de Paris.*   1834.

"   "   *Les Misérables.*   1864.

JACOB (*filius*) *Chaviv.*, etc.   By Rabbi Jehuda Arje de Mutina.

> The title is reprinted in Hebrew.

JACOBUS I. *Rex Angliae.* Βασιλικὸν δῶρον.   1606.

"   *Meditatio in orationem dominicam* [and two other treatises].   1619.

JANSENIUS, C. *Augustinus*, etc.   1641, 1642, 1654.

KANT, I *Kritik der reinen Vernunft.*   1827.

LAMARTINE, A. *Souvenirs*, etc., *d'un voyage en Orient* [and two other works].   1836.

LAMÉ FLEURY, J. R. *L'Histoire Ancienne* [and five other histories].   1857.

LAMENAIS, H. F. R. *Paroles d'un croyant* [and six other works].   1834.

LANFREY, PIERRE. *Histoire politique des papes.*   1875.

LANG, ANDREW. *Myth, Ritual, and Religion.*[1]   1896.

LAUNOY, J. *Veneranda romanae ecclesiae circa simoniam traditio* [and no less than twenty-six other works by this much condemned author].   1688.

LEIGH, EDWARD. *Annotations upon the New Testament,* 1735.

LESSING, G. E. *Religion Saint Simonienne*, etc.   1835.

---

[1] The author. in a letter to the *Athenaeum* (Feby. 25. 1905), states that his book is concerned solely with savage and classical beliefs, and that he had been unable to secure a reply to his inquiry (submitted through one of the English Catholic bishops) as to the grounds for the condemnation.

Lettre, Lettura, Letter, and *Lettres.*

> Under these headings are seventy-eight titles.

LIMBORCH, P. *Historia inquisitionis,* etc. [and two other books]. 1694.

LIPSIUS, J. *Orationes,* etc. 1613.

LOCKE, J. *Essay on the Human Understanding.* 1734.
"   *The Reasonableness of Christianity.* 1737.

MACCRIE, TH. *History of the Reformation in Italy.* 1836.

MALEBRANCHE, N. *Traité de la Nature et de la Grâce* [and six other treatises]. 1689.

Mandement.

> Under this heading are fourteen entries, dating from 1667 to 1729.

MANDEVILLE, B. DE. *The Fable of the Bees,* etc. 1744.
"   "   *Thoughts on Religion.* 1732.

MANSFELD, R. *Diatriba theologica.* 1690.

Manual, the Catholic Christian's New Universal, etc. 1770.

MARMONTEL. *Belisaire,* etc. d.c. 1767.

MARVELL, A. *The Growth of Popery and of Arbitrary Power in England.* 1730.

MAURICE, F. D. *Theological Essays.* 1854.

Mémoire and *Memoria.*

> Under this heading are thirty-four entries, dating from 1667 to 1817, including several having to do with the Bull *Unigenitus,* the Gallican Church, etc.
> Under this title is entered the *Mémoires de la vie du Comte de Grammont,* which was not condemned until 1817

MERLE D'AUBIGNÉ, J. H. *Histoire de la Réformation,* etc. 1852.

MICHELET, J. *Bible de l'humanité* [and five other works]. 1840–1896.

MILL, J. S. *Principles of Political Economy.* 1856.

MILTON, JOHN. *Literae pseudo-senatus anglicani,* etc. 1694.

MIVART, ST. GEORGE. *Happiness in Hell.* 1892–1893.
> From "Nineteenth Century."

MOLINOS, M. DE. *Opera omnia.* 1687.

MONTAIGNE, M. DE. *Les Essais.* 1676.

MONTESQUIEU, C. de S. *Esprit des lois.* 1751.

    "   "   *Lettres persanes.* 1751.

MORGAN, LADY S. *Journal of Residence in Italy.* 1822.

MURGER, H. *Omnes fabulae amatoriae.* 1864.

PASCAL, B. *Pensées.* 1789.

POZA, J. B. *Opera omnia.* 1628–1631.

       This condemnation represents the confirmation or re-assertion on the part of Leo of the position taken by his predecessors three and a half centuries back, against the contentions of the Spanish Jesuits and of the Spanish Church.

PRESSENSÉ, E. de. *Le Concile du Vatican.* 1876.

PUFFENDORF, S. VON. *De jure naturae et gentium* [and four other treatises]. 1711.

QUESNEL, P. 1708–1720.

      A series of works comprising practically *Opera omnia.*

QUINET, E. *Le génie des religions.* 1844.

RANKE, L. *Die Römischen Päpste.* 1841.

RENAN, E. *Vie de Jésus* [and nineteen other works]. 1859–1892.

      This entry could more conveniently have been made *Opera omnia.*

RICHARDSON, S. *Pamela.* 1744.

ROCABERTI, H. *Vida y Dottrina* [and eleven other treatises]. 1688.

ROSCOE, WM. *Life of Leo X.* 1825.

ROSMINI. *Enciclopedia di science e lettere.* 1889.

ROUSSEAU, J. J. *Le Contrat Social* [and four other works]. 1766.

SABATIER, P. *Vie de S. Francis d'Assisi.* 1894.

SAINT-SIMON, C. H. *Science de l'homme.* 1859.

SAND, GEORGE. *Omnes fabulae amatoriae.* 1840–1863.

SARPI, PAOLO. *Historia sopra gli beneficii ecclesiastici,* [and three other treatises]. 1676.

SCALIGER, J. *Epistolae d.c.* 1633.

SISMONDI, J. C. L. *Histoire des républiques italiennes,* etc. 1817.

SPINOZA, B. DE. *Opera posthuma.* 1690.

STENDHAL, H. B. DE. *Omnes fabulae amatoriae.* 1864.

STEPHANUS, R. *Ad censuras theologorum parisiensium,* etc.
    1624.

STERNE, L. *A Sentimental Journey.* 1819.

STRAUSS, D. J. *Das Leben Jesu.* 1838.

STROUD. WM. *The Physical Causes of the Death of Christ.*
    1878.

SUE, E. *Omnes fabulae amatoriae.* 1852.

SWEDENBORG, E. *Principia verum naturalium,* etc. 1738.

TAINE, H. A. *Histoire de la littérature anglaise.* 1866.

Testament, le nouveau (printed at Mons), 1668, [together
    with three other editions in French, one in Dutch, and
    three in Italian, 1709–1820].

THOMAS KEMPISIUS. *De imitando Christo.* 1723.

TILLOTSON, JEAN. *Sermons, traduits de l'anglois.* 1725.

VOLNEY, C. F. *Les ruines, etc., des empires.* 1821.

VOLTAIRE, F. M. A. *Oeuvres.* 1752.

> This entry is followed by thirty-eight separate titles of
> the books of Voltaire which called for special con-
> demnation.

WHATELY, R. *Elements of Logic.* 1851.

WHITE, THOMAS. *Opera omnia.* 1655–1663.

WILKINS, J. *Discovery of a New World.* 1701.

ZOLA, É. *Opera omnia.* 1894–1898.

ZWICHER, G. *Monks and their Doctrine.* 1898.

2. Index Revision and Reform, 1868-1880.—Pom-
ponio Leto reports[1] that Pope Pius IX had instituted,
in addition to the six existing commissions of the council, a seventh commission placed under the direction
of Cardinal de Luca, which was to be charged with the
consideration of biblical material and of the revision
of the Index. It appears, however, that this commission held but one or two sessions in 1868 and after 1869
was not again called together.

From time to time suggestions have been submitted

[1] Reusch, ii, 26.

for the reform of Index proceedings.   In 1870, eleven French bishops took the ground that no work by a Catholic writer should be condemned by the Congregation unless and until the author had had an opportunity of being heard in its defence and of replying to criticisms of any special passages.   It seemed to these bishops outrageous that, possibly on the ground of the lack of correct understanding of certain individual passages, important books, representing the serious labour of devout scholars, should be placed under the same class of condemnation as that applied to godless and heretical writings or to books *contra bonos mores*.[1]

The bishops of Germany joined in the demand for a reshaping of the rules of the Index for which in a number of territories it had not been practicable to secure obedience.   They also demanded that in the future no book by a Catholic writer should be condemned until a hearing had been given by the bishops to its author. It was contended that by means of such direct action the injury of an official censorship would in a large number of cases be avoided.   In a number of monographs printed in 1869 and 1870, the contention was maintained that there should be either a discontinuance of the operations of the Congregation of the Index or a thoroughgoing reform in the whole method of Church censorship.[2]

Segesser says, in his monograph entitled *Am Vorabende des Conciliums* : "We do not admit that the Roman Index as now carried on fulfils the purpose for which it was instituted.   It seems to us that the present censorship system, together with the method of securing from repentant authors 'retractions' and

---

[1] Martin, *Omnium conc. Vat. documentorum, collectio*, 159, 170.
[2] Friedrich, *Vat. Koncil* , ii, 288, 289.

'submissions,' leads only to serious misapprehensions and confusions of judgment. . . . The responsibility ought to be left to the bishops to take action, each for his own diocese, concerning the books produced within the territory for which he is responsible." One of the editors of the *Mainzer Katholik*, writing in 1869, says[1]: "We accept the view which is now being presented very generally throughout the Church, that the reconstitution of the organisation and methods of Roman censorship is essential in order to meet the very great changes in the conditions of literary production which have come about since the time of Benedict XIV." Writing again later in the year, the same writer says:[2]

" It may well be doubted whether it is practicable, under the present social conditions, to enforce any prohibition in regard to the reading of books and whether, therefore, such prohibitions are not pernicious rather than helpful. . . . We are inclined to the belief that it would be wiser, in place of leaving the books to be passed upon in Rome, to place the responsibility for their examination in the hands of the bishop of the diocese. . . . We do not recommend that the Index should be abandoned, but it should certainly be revised in order to meet the new conditions of the present time. We submit with all deference the suggestion that a theological literary organ might properly be published in Bonn, and similar journals, speaking under the authority of the Church, in such centres as Munich and Tübingen. Such journals would, with their conclusions, criticisms, and recommendations, carry weight and wholesome influence among all faithful readers in the Church. A central organ of literature, speaking with all the authority of the Holy See and Church universal, should be published in Rome. In such a journal should be presented the record of theological literary activities throughout the whole world.   The conclusions and criticisms issued under the official authority of Rome would in themselves constitute a standard of theological orthodoxy and of literary form. . . . For such an undertaking, the support and the interest of devout Catholics throughout the world would be assured.   Its influence would have the effect of an Index or censorship of literature.   Such a journal should serve as a guide and an inspiration towards a true Catholic life."

A periodical which was in existence for a few years during the last decade of the 18th century appears to have had some such purpose as this writer considers important.   The *Giornale Ecclesiastico*, a weekly journal published in Rome from July, 1785, to June, 1798, presented, together with Church news and general information, a weekly review of books.   The journal included further the decrees issued, during this period of fourteen years, by the censorship authorities of Rome, against the books selected for condemnation. The first volume recorded in these decrees is a treatise entitled *Was ist der Pabst?* published anonymously but identified as the work of Eybel.   It receives the honour of a condemnation, not in the ordinary form, but in an elaborate "constitution" printed over the signature of Pope Pius VI.   The treatise had been issued at a critical time when the Pope found ground for alarm at the reformations announced by Joseph II. One of the works condemned in the later decrees was the *Pensées* of Pascal, with Voltaire's notes.

The criticism has been made more than once on the part of Protestant historians of the Index that the record of the conflicting decisions given by successive popes in regard to literary productions itself constitutes a substantial argument against the reasonableness of the doctrine of infallibility. This doctrine became officially one of the dogmas of the Church at the Council of the Lateran in 1870. It is the under- **The Infalli-** standing that, while the declaration of the **bility of the** dogma was made this year for the first **Pope** time, under the necessary interpretation of such dogma, it would be held to apply to the utterances of all the popes preceding Pius IX. The orthodox interpreters of Catholic doctrine point out, however, that the claim for infallibility does not cover all classes of papal utterances. Father Searle, for instance (writing in New York, 1895), makes the following statement in regard to the orthodox interpretation of this dogma:

" The special prerogative which Catholics now universally believe to have been conferred on the Pope by the Divine Founder of Christianity has a very special and limited range, although certainly quite complete within its proper domain. It consists in the Pope's ability to decide questions concerning religion about which there may be room for doubt in the minds of Christians, on account either of the large number of adherents or of the apparently plausible arguments on both sides of the question. . . . It should be clearly understood that it is not the office of the Pope to act as one inspired or to receive or give to the world any new revelation. It is merely to decide what the original deposit (as we call it) of faith was, as committed by Christ to his Apostles; or in other words to repeat the decision which the Apostles themselves would have made in regard to the doctrines of Christianity. Still less is it the office of the Pope to settle matters of science or ordinary questions of fact. Not but what the domains claimed by science and the domains claimed by faith may sometimes overlap; this may be the case for instance to some extent in the matter of evolution, especially if evolution is supposed to apply to the human soul, or it may apply in the cases in which science asserts that matter existed from all eternity. . . . And even questions of historical fact may belong to faith by being necessarily connected with some of its dogmas, or by forming part of the inspired record of Holy Scripture. There would, for instance, be a conflict of history or of geology with the Church, if it should be asserted in the name of either of these branches of learning that the account of the Deluge was simply a myth. But conflicts of this sort are rare. Practically no Catholic is impeded in any kind of study or investigation by any fear of papal condemnation. . . . The impression of Protestants that we Catholics believe the Pope to be incapable of error, no matter what he is speaking about or under what circumstances he expresses his thought, is of course without foundation. . . . The Catholics do, however, believe that the Pope is able to make infallible decisions with regard to morals as well as to faith. . . . But it by no means follows that because the Pope can solemnly instruct the faithful infallibly, he always or on all occasions holds or gives utterance to correct views with regard to right or wrong. . . . We hold simply that God assists the Pope in a special way to prevent him from making a decision at all if the way is not reasonably clear to it; or if God allows the decision to be made, to insure that this decision shall contain nothing contrary to the truth."[1]

It seems probable from the position taken by Father Searle that in the cases in which the utterances of the Papacy have by later events been shown to be based upon error or have even directly been recalled or corrected by later papal utterances, the Catholic of to-day would take the ground that these erroneous utterances did not belong to the class for which infallibility was claimed. Under this class of exceptions would doubtless be placed the condemnation of Galileo, and also the

[1] Searle, 36, ff.

condemnation of certain Catholic books maintaining doctrines not accepted at the time as dogmas of the Church but which later secured official acceptance.

3. The Index and the Liberal Catholics, in 1897. " Romanus " and " The Tablet."—In October, 1897, after the promulgation of the first Index of Leo XIII and at the time when announcements concerning the scheme of the second Index were being made, a writer in the *Contemporary Review* undertook to present views in regard to the literary policy of the Church of Rome and its responsibilities towards the intellectual development of the century The writer subscribes himself " Romanus " and writes as a faithful and conscientious member of the Catholic Church. He claims to be expressing the apprehensions of a large body of educated Catholics in England and on the Continent as to the probable loss of influence on the part of the Church and of the weakening of its hold on men possessing both education and conscience, in case its present rulers should persist in maintaining a mediaeval policy in regard to intellectual matters. " Romanus " insists that the Church must accept and abide by all of the conclusions of modern science the foundations of which are shown to be thoroughly assured, and that unless the Church may make science its own, it must of necessity lose influence with conscientious students throughout the world.

I cite below some of the more noteworthy utterances in this article.

" Leo XIII," says " Romanus," " has inspired respect and sympathy even among men who are strongly opposed to Catholicism." He goes on to speak of Leo as that " gentle, cultured, conciliatory pontiff, the promoter of historical research, the friend of the

French Republic." The main purpose of his article is to show that "liberal Catholicism," so far from having ceased to exist, has only been transformed into a much more "formidable movement."

"Liberal Catholics," says "Romanus," "are fully aware that the enormous power of the Church for good would be fatally impaired by an injury to its organisation, and they would regard as intrinsically absurd and unscientific any attempt to reverse the process of development. Their desire is, therefore, not to destroy, but to strengthen the authority of the Church by diverting it from proceedings detrimental to its own welfare. . . . They are profoundly convinced that the Catholic Church is the one great influence for promoting the spiritual welfare of humanity. They believe that there exists no power comparable to it for the promotion of virtue and of all that is highest, noblest, purest, and most self-denying and generous among mankind. They are convinced that it is the most complete—the only complete—organisation for bringing about among all classes, all nations, and all races, obedience to, and fulfilment of, Christ's two great commandments wherein lay all the law and the prophets—love of God and of our neighbour.

" Such Catholics also believe that the Church supplies, to our minds, as no other yet existing organisation can supply, means of access and address to their Creator through a worship such as the world has never before known— traditional, majestic, soul-satisfying, and, above all, profoundly spiritual, wherein the divine and human meet and *cor ad cor loquitur*.

" By its sacraments, every stage of human life is elevated and sanctified, the wounded conscience renovated and strengthened, the broken and contrite heart comforted and consoled, the various afflictions of life mitigated and its joys, as well as its sorrows, refined and consecrated. . . . These liberal Catholics not only look upon Catholicity as the special home and the most effective aid to what is good, but also as an influence making for beauty and the culture of art. Its influence with respect to philosophy they regard as of priceless value, nor do they think lightly of its service to literature. Profoundly influenced by such convictions, the adherents to 'Liberal Catholicism' must evidently desire to maintain unimpaired that wonderful organisation of which Rome is the head. . . . Liberal Catholics declare themselves to be devoted to the discovery, the promulgation, and the establishment of truth in every field of knowledge, historical, critical, and scientific, especially in what bears upon religion. Sincere Theists, they are profoundly convinced not only that the God of truth can never be served by a lie, but that the cause of religion can never be promoted by clever dodges, by studiously ambiguous utterances, by hushing up unpleasant truths, or (when such can no longer be hidden) by misrepresenting or minimising their significance—trying by a series of clever devices to disguise the consequences which logically follow from them. As St. Paul strenuously opposed himself to the circumcision of the flesh, so would the Liberal Catholics oppose themselves to the circumcision of the intellect. These believers are not so foolish as to be blind to the fact that a body so vast and complex in structure as the Catholic Church must move slowly. It neither surprises nor shocks them that new astronomical, geological, or physiological truths should not be accepted with alacrity or that discoveries as to the Old and New Testaments and startling facts with respect to the organisation of the Church in the first two centuries should not be welcomed with enthusiasm and loudly proclaimed. . . . What liberalism does not understand, what it vehemently protests against and deems fatal to the welfare of the Church, is not reticence, but declarations hostile to and condemnatory of ascertained scientific truth. No one in authority would probably now venture to affirm in so many words that Catholics must regard as historical facts such matters as the legend of the Serpent and the Tree, that of the formation of Eve, Noah's Ark, the destruction of Sodom, the transformation of Lot's wife, the talking ass, or Jonah and his whale; nevertheless (not only from what is popularly taught, but from what has been put forth in the name of the Supreme Pontiff) it would seem as if Reuss, Welhausen, and Keunen had never written at all, instead of having transformed our whole conception of the Hexateuch. Liberal Catholics need demand no formal disavowals. What they do most strongly deprecate are needless declarations freshly made in the full light of modern science, physical, physiological, historical, or critical, yet futilely hostile thereto. The well-known Syllabus of Pius IX afforded a memorable instance of what is thus objected to. . . . It was so worded as to make plain men believe that their reasonable liberties had been condemned, and many tender consciences were greatly troubled thereby. A year or two back, Leo XIII, in a letter concerning the Bible, afforded a most amazing example of misleading ambiguity. . . . It is understood that for this letter he was not personally to blame, his will having been overborne by the influence of the Jesuits of the *Civiltà Cattolica*. This letter contains, to be sure, a certain recognition of modern science; but it broadly declares that the Bible contains no error. . . . English Catholics have been played with of late in the matter of a new Index in a singularly inept and absurd manner, owing to the fact that the players at Rome are so densely ignorant concerning the state of things in England.

" The old Index was never supposed to be binding on English Catholics and, indeed, its provisions were such that it was practically almost a dead letter on the Continent also. . . . The new Index is, however, formally declared to be applicable to all countries, and great has been the distress which through its publication arose in the minds of a multitude of timid and scrupulous believers. . . . Pressure was brought to bear upon Rome, which was forced at last to learn something of the condition of affairs in England, and finally supreme authority has had to draw in its horns and suffer it to be spread about in England that the new reformed Index does not apply here, and that in this happy country every condemned publication can be read, and any work on morals or religion published and circulated, without ecclesiastics having the power to prevent it. . . . Since the affair of the Index, however, a yet more monstrous act has been perpetrated. Any one who has taken any interest in Scripture knows that for many years past the text in the Epistle of St. John about 'the three witnesses' (the Father, Son, and Holy Ghost in heaven) has been regarded as a spurious addition. An application was lately made to Rome to know whether the authenticity of this well-known text might safely be called in question. The reply was that it might neither be denied nor called in question. Thus authority, in this last act, has shown an utter contempt for historical and critical truth, and that it desires its spiritual subjects should be left to believe that an absolutely unauthentic passage is an inspired statement written 'by the finger of God.'. . . We live in a critical period. Dogmatic statements require special care when, thanks to the labours of such men as Harnack and Weiszäcker, so much light has been thrown on the genesis and history of dogma and the earliest condition of the Christian Church. But the diffusion of any such knowledge is but little perilous if only authority will refrain from self-destructive affirmations. . . . The advance of physical science necessarily carries with it changes in religious belief, as astronomy and geology unquestionably show. But changes in moral science and consequent modifications in human sentiment produce changes of far greater moment. . . . It is then above all things necessary that ecclesiastical authority should help in the elevation of popular ethical ideals, instead of trying, as the Catholic Church has in many cases already done, to retain these at a lower stage of development. . . . The scientific teaching now current about the Old and the

New Testament, the history of dogma and of the beginnings of the Church, must doubtless disturb the minds of many faithful Catholics now as future discoveries in the field of physiology will disturb the minds of persons who are to come after us. We are and we wish to remain in sympathy with the Church of centuries long gone; but surely we should also wish and strive to pave the way for the triumph of the Church in ages yet to come. We emphasise the importance of attention to past changes and the necessity of great consideration and accommodation on the part of authority at the present time and yet more in the future. We urge this because we are devoted to the cause of the Catholic Church; we urge this as humble followers of the great Apostle of the Gentiles, in the name of Him who was the first great teacher of 'accommodation' and who, as the great opponent of pharisaic narrowness, emphatically deserves the honourable title of the first 'Liberal Catholic' of the Universal Church of Christ."

The criticism of "Romanus," speaking on behalf of the Liberal Catholics, was promptly taken up by an "orthodox" Romanist, evidently a strong opponent of Liberal Catholicism, who is prepared to accept without question the authority and the policy of Pius and Leo in regard to the supervision of literature and the direction of the intellectual life of the Church. The reply of the defender of the papal policy appears in the *Tablet* (which may, I suppose, be considered as the official organ of the Church in England) in December, 1897. The following extracts will give the main conclusions of this upholder of papal authority.

" The article in the *Contemporary Review* which claims to represent the views of 'Liberal Catholicism' is not entitled to any serious attention on the part of educated Catholics. Its matter and its spirit are well known to them *ad nauseam*, and they easily recognise one and the other as a part of the stock-in-trade of certain writers who not unnaturally conceive that they can attack the Catholic Church more plausibly by affecting to stand within her pale, and while masquerading (anonymously, of course) under the name of Catholic.   The only passage in the *Contemporary* article which is deserving of any present attention is that relating to the modification of the recent Constitution of the Index.   In January last, the Holy See was pleased to simplify, and in many respects to modify, the provisions of the Index, and issued a Constitution to that effect.   Like all legislation of a general kind, it was issued to the Church as a whole.   The Holy See, following its most wise tradition, frames its general law upon the needs of the bulk or majority of its subjects, and makes such law, for the time being, the standard of the community, knowing that if its provisions, in whole or in part, should, owing to peculiar circumstances, become inapplicable to the minority or should press unduly upon them, their case can easily be met either by local modification, or by personal dispensation where they affect an individual or a class   A good deal of cheap rhetoric is often wasted upon the narrowness and intolerance of the authorities of the Index. We are concerned with the law itself and with the principles which underlie this law and with the reasons which justify it.   The measure of discretion (or of indiscretion) which characterises the action of the authorities in the administration of the law and in its application to this or that book or opinion deserves separate consideration. . . . It may safely be asserted that not a little of the ordinary criticism of the regulations of the Index is due in many cases to insularity.   Probably out of every hundred Englishmen or Americans who rail against the restrictions of the Index, not a tithe has any direct acquaintance with, or takes any due account of, the flood of bitterly anti-Christian literature, often infidel, immoral, and blasphemous, and almost always insidiously polemical, which is poured over Italy and the Continent generally, by the masonic and anti-clerical press. It is in great measure this degrading abuse of one of the noblest faculties of civilised society, and the need of duly protecting the minds of the masses that the provisions of the Index are specially designed to meet. It is simply a measure of Catholic sanitation. In fact, were a representative collection of such continental literature translated and put into the hands of the average English father, we conceive that he would promptly improvise himself into a domestic Congregation of the Index and take pains to see that all such vehicles of infection were rigidly excluded from his family. . . . That the Catholic Church, which is necessarily an authoritative and a teaching Church, should be equally solicitous about the members of her family, and that from her standpoint she should extend her solicitude, not only to manifest evils but to assaults upon the faith which she believes to be the logical substructure of morality, is a principle which assuredly need not excite our surprise. However much we may feel that, in times like our own, when our best triumphs promise to be gained by guiding, rather than by limiting human liberty, and when necessarily much must be left to the discretion of the conscientious, the practical application of the principle is a matter which calls for the exercise of that generous and tactful delicacy that the Catholic Church knows so well how to use in teaching her children. . . . No one who looks upon the face of Christendom to-day can fail to note that there exists a clearly marked difference between the whole set of social and political circumstances which obtain in the English-speaking lands and those which obtain in the various countries of the Continent. This difference applies particularly to the very circumstances which most affect the use and application of the provisions of the Index. . . . We maintain that in English-speaking countries there does not exist upon any large or popular scale such bitter and active propaganda against Christianity and Christian morality as are unhappily at work abroad, nor is there that widespread prevalence of aggressively anti-

Christian and pornographic literature which the infidel and anti-clerical press pours forth like a pestilential sewer in certain continental countries. The Church has wisely taken into account the special character and circumstances of Catholics in the English-speaking countries, and the significance which as expressing the more modern development of social and political life they promise to possess in the future. For centuries, the provisions of the Index in their more rigid sense have not been practically applied to these countries, and to a very large measure these provisions have been left in abeyance with the perfect knowledge of the Supreme Authority. . . . The Constitution published by the Holy See, in January last, was naturally issued to the Church at large, and when it appeared in the Catholic press of England it necessarily elicited from both clergy and laity the question whether this new Constitution was or was not intended to supplant the *status quo* which had hitherto existed among us. The reply to the enquiry addressed to Rome by the Cardinal Archbishop and bishops of England, conceded the most ample powers for dispensation, so that, owing to the 'special circumstances of the country,' the bishops in England were fully authorised 'to modify the rigour of the law by their prudence and counsel according as the case might demand.' Rome's reply was thus as ready and as liberal as could well be desired. . . .

" No Catholic forgets or can ever allow himself to forget that the Index is at most an institution which has been called into existence by the practical prudence of the Holy See to safeguard and to hedge around with specific regulations the observance of a moral law that is as old as Christianity itself and that, even if the regulations of the Index were abolished to-morrow, would remain in all its force in the Catholic Church. If the faithful Catholic in the course of his reading finds by experience that a given book is of a kind to undermine his faith or to work injury to his morals, he knows that he is bound by the very fact to deal with it as he would with a proximate occasion of sin, and to cast it aside. Christianity by its very condition means discipline. In it the unbridled freedom of thinking, saying, reading, and doing what we like is exchanged for the higher and holier freedom of union with the mind and with the life of Christ. The moral law of the Church is everywhere and always with us and every good Christian carries about with him inside of his own conscience a Constitution of the Index. . . ."

This article may, I judge, while now eight years old, fairly be accepted as an authoritative utterance on the part of the thoroughly orthodox Romanists of England, that is to say, of those who accept without question the decisions and the regulations from Rome. The writer in the *Tablet* declines, or, to speak more precisely, contemptuously refuses, to meet any of the specific criticisms of "Romanus" in regard to this or that text or to the relations of the Church with the conclusions of scientists. He bases his conclusions upon a general and implicit acceptance of the final authority of the Church in all matters and he apparently holds that only in such reverent acceptance and obedience can there be a religious sanity in this world or hope for the world to come.

4. The Present Methods of Roman Censorship.—The Papal Consistory may be considered as a direct successor or at least a continuation of the chancellery of the Roman Empire. When (in 328), the Emperor Constantine moved the court to Byzantium, he left the chancellery in Rome and the authority or organisation of this chancellery came to be associated with the authority of the Bishop of Rome.

The term Curia or Holy See is used to represent the Church organisation or final authority of the Church considered more particularly in its relations with foreign States or with outside bodies.

The Congregations date in their final organisation from Sixtus V (1585). The series now comprises eighteen. These Congregations might be compared in the nature and in the exercise of their functions to the standing committees of the United States Senate; excepting that their decisions do not have to be referred to any general body for action. These decisions are final unless disapproved by the pope. The pope retains for himself the official headship of the Congregation of the Index on the ground that the work of this Congregation has to do directly with matters of doctrine. The working body of the Congregation of the Index comprises ten to twelve members with votes, including always a group of cardinals. In addition to these voting members, there is a varying number of *consultores* (advisers) who are called in as experts in different divisions of knowledge, but who have no votes in the decisions arrived at. The Congregation which bears the name Propaganda is charged with the responsibility of receiving and sifting miscellaneous business, referring each division of such business to its appropriate Congregation. The Congregation of the Index has from the outset been conducted under the influence and under the practical control of the Order of the Dominicans. The secretary, who bears the name "commissarius" and who is always a Dominican, has the general responsibility for the selecting and the shaping of the business of the Congregation. It is to the commissarius that suggestions are submitted by ecclesiastics or others concerning books which, in their judgment, call for the consideration of the Congregation. The commissarius is also himself under obligation to submit titles of doubtful books of which he has personal knowledge. The exceptional influence of the Jesuits in statecraft and in personal relations with the popes and with other of the authorities of the Church is considered as constituting some measure of offset to the influence that the Dominicans have, in their control of the Index, been able to exert concerning the acceptance (or the reprobation) of literature presenting the special doctrines of the Jesuits. The method of thought and of reasoning of the Dominicans is, it is to be borne in mind, based upon the teachings of Thomas of Aquinas and of the Thomists. The Franciscans are described as the commemorators of the mystical spirit of Duns Scotus. The leadership in intellectual activity in the Church is said to rest to-day, as it has rested through the centuries, with the Jesuits. The great Order of the Benedictines and that of the Cistercians are still referred to as making some of the largest and most important contributions to literature that come from Catholic sources.

It is to be remembered that the bishop possesses in his own diocese a very large measure of independent authority, authority which may be considered as increasing in direct proportion to the distance of the diocese from Rome. This local authority is utilised in connection with literary censorship as for other matters affecting the action of believers. This censorship of the bishops is naturally of special importance when it has to do with books originating in languages other than Italian or Latin, as such books are less likely to be brought to the attention of the censorship authorities in Rome.

In regard to the literary policy of the Church to-day as expressed in the Index, the opinion of the Jesuit Father Hilgers is of interest. In reply to the enquiry, "What is the Index?" Hilgers presents (in the treatise before referred to) the following statement, the text of which I have somewhat condensed: "The Index of prohibited books does not contain or undertake to present the entire regulation or body of the enactments of the Church concerning the supervision of literature and the specification of prohibited books. This body of Church law is to be found in the general Decrees or Regulations (*Decreta Generalia*) of the Constitution, known as the *Officiorum ac munerum*. It is of course to be understood that the editions of the Index are controlled by the general prohibitions (that is to say, by the prohibitions which, in place of specifying individual works, express a general literary policy) and also by what may be called the law of nature. . . It is not safe for a believer to say, 'as this book is not found in the Index, I am at liberty to read it.' It should be understood that the book in question or any similar work may fall under the prohibition of the general rule or may under the law of nature be classed as pernicious. It is undoubtedly the case that many books which are pernicious for faith or for morals are not to be found in the Index. It would of course be a physical impossibility to include in any current lists all of the books of bad character or of bad influence which each year are being brought before the public. The Index is to be considered as itself a portion of the general Church prohibitions. It is not even to be admitted that the most dangerous or pernicious have with certainty found their way into Indexes, either the earlier or those that are now in force. The books which are undeniably bad should so reveal themselves to the conscience of the believer and are in any case clearly indicated by the law of the Church. This is the answer to the criticism that has more than once been made that the Congregation of the Index has concerned itself with the trivial or petty things, leaving without consideration books which are of most serious moment, for instance works belonging to the emphatically bad group. Examples of such are—in literature: those of Carl Gutzkow and Conrad Ferdinand Meyer; in natural science, those of Haeckel and of Krause (Carus-sterne); in philosophy, the writings of Feuerbach and Büchner; in theology, the works of F. C. Baur and of Bruno Bauer, etc. Against names like these, the caution of specific condemnation in the Index ought not to be required by any intelligent reader. There are to-day so-called philosophers whose representative works can be recognised as dangerous by the reason of each intelligent person, and these works it has therefore not been thought necessary to place in the Index. The very fact that the total number of books appearing in the Index is so inconsiderable is to be accepted as evidence that there has been no attempt to make specific condemnation of the whole mass of pernicious literature." According to the calculation of Hilgers, the Indexes of the last three hundred years contain an average of sixteen new titles only for each year; and these sixteen titles represent the total of the selections made from the literatures of all the countries of the world, principally of course of those of Europe.

The Index presents for us a collection of the utterances of the Church authorities concerning specific condemnations of individual books. It may be said to bear the same relation to the general censorship decrees as that borne, for instance, by a collection of the judgments of a criminal court to the provisions of criminal law. It is the business of the court to arrive at a judgment in each individual case and in each case to determine whether the law has been broken. The Index condemnations, like the court judgments, may be accepted as representative in the one case of the general policy or principles by which the Church is guided and in the other case of the principles and of the provisions of the law. In the Constitution *Officiorum ac munerum*, section I, chapter 10, is the instruction: "While it is the duty of all believers, and particularly of the educated Catholic, to bring to the attention of the authorities of the Curia or of the bishops, books believed to be dangerous, this responsibility rests more particularly upon the nuncios, the Apostolic delegates, and the rectors and associates of the higher schools." The word denunciation has a serious sound and yet such a word may be, applied as describing the duty of any magistrate acting under the law of the land. " The Index is not, continues Hilgers, " and never has claimed to be, a systematic and comprehensive collection of the titles of each class of prohibited books. It is no more just on this ground, however, that the Index should be charged with lack of system, plan, or consistency than that the civil authority should be criticised because, under the actual working of the law, there may not be each year examples of the imposition of penalties for all the offences specified. . . . It is further to be borne in mind that the influence of any particular work is naturally not the same during different periods or under different con ditions: a book which at the time when certain issues were pending might have exercised a seriously pernicious influence, could for later generations, under different conditions, be studied safely simply as an historical record. It is the purpose of the Index as of the *Decreta Generalia* to protect and defend the true Faith, sound morality. and wholesome conduct. The censorship prohibitions constitute one means by which those to whom has been confided the care of the flock of the faithful may be enabled to fulfil their responsibilities."

"In case there may be question of the accusation of any person for heretical doctrine the examination of the matter or the control of the case is held not under the direction of the Congregation of the Index, but under that of the Roman Inquisition. The condemnation of the book does not in itself carry with it a condemnation of the individual."[1]

The Reverend Spencer Jones, in his treatise *England and the Holy See*, printed in London, 1902, remarks that, in such cases, "when a teacher is silenced and his books have been placed upon the Index a large proportion of the public are apt to entertain pity for him, which is natural; but feel little concern for those on whose behalf the Church has interfered, which shows want of sympathy and contempt· for the authorities, which is for the most part unjust; the assumption being that because they judge it right to stay the treatise, they therefore wish to stop the truth."[2]

A further criticism has been made against the Index on the ground of the indignity caused to works of science and to productions of literature of thought in associating these under condemnation with vulgar erotic romances or with the passing pamphlet of the moment. The Catholic answer is very simple: the Church is responsible for the correction of error in whatsoever form such error may take. Such action in regard to an

---

[1] Hilgers, 70-73.   [2] Cited by Hilgers, 74.

error, whether this be a thought or form of expression, does not of necessity imply that the writer is himself unworthy. The Church may properly honour and does honour a faithful believer and great thinker like Fénelon, and may at the same time, in its watchfulness over sound thought and precise expression, find it necessary to correct some single utterance of Fénelon. The true Faith has to do not only with understanding but with the preservation of the purity of the soul and of right feeling.

It may be at once admitted that the regulations of the Congregation of the Index do not claim for themselves an infallible authority concerning matters of doctrine. The book prohibitions, while approved by the pope, do not (unless with rare exceptions) emanate directly from him and do not, therefore, partake of the infallibility of his Office. The pope can of course, in the cases in which it seems to him right so to do, decide with his own infallible judgment that the doctrine of a book is heretical and such a decision must carry with it full weight. The general prohibitions of the Index are, however, to be considered as simply an expression or conclusion concerning dogma in the narrower sense of the word. Such prohibitions may be considered as coming from the ecclesiastical court before which the book in question has been under trial and through such judgment the book is either condemned or passed upon as not a subject for disapproval.[1]

Hilgers calls attention to the method of procedure under which the successive Indexes collected into their lists the titles of books that had been condemned (in certain cases many years before) in specific decrees.

[1] Hilgers, 75.

The Index authorities have, he says. been criticised for bringing into condemnation books having to do with controversial questions, years after these questions have been practically adjusted or were no longer vital matters.   The answer is that the literature was considered at the proper time under a separate decree and the Index merely presents a summary of such decrees. The Index of Leo XIII makes clear in its record of condemnations of earlier date the immediate source for each condemnation; whether this took the form of a papal brief or bull or whether it was arrived at through the decision of one of the papal Congregations.   The books which have been condemned under a separate Apostolic edict (brief or bull) comprise in all a hundred and forty titles and these have been printed in each Leonine Index with a cross.   During the three centuries between 1600 and 1900, the Congregation of the Holy Office, that is to say, the Roman Inquisition, has issued in all nine hundred book prohibitions.   These are entered in the Leonine lists with the words: *Decr. S. Off.*.   During the same period, the Congregation of Rites has prohibited in all but three books.   The Congregation of Dispensations has issued two condemnation decrees.   It is clear from the above reference that each Congregation has been charged with the supervision of the literature belonging to its own special subject-matter.   The Congregation of the Index, however, is concerned with the books in every division of literature because its subject is the examination and determination of works classed as suspected.   The entries for which the Congregation of the Index is responsible during the three centuries in question aggregate about three thousand.   As before stated, the power rests with the pope to examine and to pass judgment upon any book without the intervention of any one of the Congregations.

The Leonine Index repeats but two prohibitions back of the date of 1600. The first, bearing date 1575, makes entry of the title of the *Chronicon* of Conrad of Lichtenau, and the second, under the date of 1580, the title of *Il Salmista secondo la Bibbia*, etc. During the above specified period, covering three centuries, the lists comprise some four thousand titles, but this number includes a hundred and eight authors whose entire writings (under the entry of *Opera omnia*) came under condemnation. If the works of these writers were added separately to the schedule, the titles would aggregate about five thousand. Of these titles, some fifteen hundred belong to the 17th century, twelve hundred to the 18th, and thirteen hundred to the 19th; while from the publications of the last decade of the 19th have been selected but one hundred and thirty-one titles. This last group includes, however, the *Opera omnia* of Zola. The writers of the 19th century who have been distinguished through the condemnation of their entire works comprise the following: Sue, 1852; Dumas (father and son), 1863; Sand (Dudévant), 1863; Balzac, 1864; Champfleury (Fleury-Husson), 1864; Feydeau, 1864; Murger, 1864; Soulié, 1864; Hume (David), 1827; Morado, 1821; Plancy, 1827; Proudhon, 1852; Spaventa, 1856; Vira, 1876; Ferrari, 1879; Zola, 1895.

The omission from the Leonine Index of a long list of names, which appeared in earlier Indexes connected with the term *Opera omnia*, is to be understood as giving permission to the faithful for the use of such books of these writers as do not appear under specific condemnation or as cannot at once be classed under the general prohibitions. All of the books of writers of this first class which do not antagonise either the true Faith or good morality are now free for Catholic readers. This exception would of course continue to rule out the writings of the leaders of the original Reformation, Luther, Calvin, Melanchthon, and the rest, although the names of these writers do not find place in the Leonine lists. The Index of Benedict (who from the liberal character of his convictions and policy was sometimes spoken of as the free-thinking Pope) strengthened the prohibitions against some fifty authors. The names of these authors, which had previously been connected only with specific books, are entered in the Index of 1758 with *Opera omnia*. Hilgers emphasises the greater liberality of Leo XIII in recalling these authors from the *Opera omnia* classification and in leaving condemned only certain specific works. He gives as another example of the liberality of Leo the freeing from condemnation of the famous treatise by Grotius, *De Jure Belli ac Pacis*. This had previously been condemned with a *d.c.* but the objectionable portions had never been specified and no corrected edition had ever been attempted. Another work of this class, previously condemned but now left free by Leo, is the *Paradise Lost* of Milton, and a third author whose condemnation has in like manner been cancelled is Leibnitz.

The Index of Leo concerns itself, further, with the correction of certain condemnations that had been made, under general decrees, of books having to do with questions that had finally been adjusted through some later utterances of the Church. In 1661, Alexander VII had condemned in a general decree all writings having to do with (either for question or for defence) the doctrine of the Immaculate Conception. In 1854, this doctrine was accepted by the Church as a dogma and the decree of Alexander was thereby cancelled. The Index of Leo recalls the prohibition of the books previously condemned which had defended the doctrine.

The great number of Italian books which swell, in the Leonine Index, the list of modern publications, are very largely concerned with the issues, that have been fought over and that are not yet adjusted, which arose from the development of the Kingdom of Italy. The condemnation in 1871 of two essays by Lord Acton was due to the approval given by Acton to the doctrines of the group of Catholic reformers led by Döllinger. The comparatively small selection that has been made in this Index and in those that more immediately preceded it of works from the countries outside of Italy was due to the fact that the examiners of the Congregation have felt under responsibility to pass upon only those books which were directly brought to their attention.

"The Index," says Hilgers, "has never given consideration to the person or authority of the author. The decision has always been arrived at purely on the basis of the influence, bad or good, of the book. It has not hesitated to condemn utterances of the theological faculty of the University of Paris on the one hand, or acts of the Parliament of Paris on the other It was ready to condemn ordinances of Duke Leopold I of Lorraine, the treatises of James I of England, and the works of the ' Philosopher of Sans-Souci.' It would be difficult in fact to contend that the material contained in these last was not likely to exert a pernicious influence. The royal writer of Sans-Souci scoffs at the immortality of the soul and, with his leader Voltaire, defends a religious nihilism. He who is concerned with maintenance whether of the throne, the altar, or the State, who feels a responsibility for the welfare of the people, will hardly guide his actions by the philosopher Voltaire." [1]

In December, 1901, a journal printed in Rome for English-speaking readers, under the title of the *Roman World*, prints the following comment on the Index of Leo, a copy of which had, as the writer of the article reports, been placed in his hands by a book collector of New York:

" One of the great book collectors of New York has recently secured from his foreign agent a copy of the new edition of the Index *Librorum prohibitorum* issued under the directions of Leo XIII. It is seldom that a copy of an official Index or record of books, the perusal of which is prohibited to Catholics, comes into the hands of an outsider. The copies printed are reserved for the use of the readers of the Church. It is necessary in order to secure a copy, to pay a high price. This particular copy, for instance, was estimated as worth from $40 to $50, while a little later, in connection with the greater difficulty of securing copies, it might easily have cost $400. The history of the famous Index is interesting. Its intellectual originator was the Emperor Charles V of Spain whose production bears date about 1550. In 1554, the Pope Paul IV took into his own hands the matter of the supervision of literature. This has since been retained under the direct control of the pope. Many hundreds of books which are not specified and mentioned in the catalogue are prohibited under the general decrees, which decrees, first issued by Benedict XIV in 1744, from that date on are repeated in the succeeding Indexes. It is well known that no Catholic ventures, under penalty of excommunication, to possess or read books which are contained in the Index unless he may secure a specific

---

[1] Hilgers, 141.

privilege or permission. It is not so well known that the catalogue is itself three centuries old and that it contains thus far the name of no single American writer, not even Thomas Paine or Robert Ingersoll. There are, however, in the lists dozens of works of the English classics and hundreds of French books which belong to the world's classics. Here for instance are to be found Bossuet and Pascal. The latter always believed himself to be a good Catholic. Among the English names placed under the ban are Gibbon, Hume, Hallam, and Goldsmith." [1]

Hilgers amuses himself, and with justice, with the mass of errors that have been crowded into the few paragraphs cited from the article. It is his conclusion that if an American writing in the city of Rome could be so thoroughly ignorant of matters that were easily within his reach, the impressions of Americans elsewhere and of Protestants generally concerning the purpose, the history, and the nature of the Index are probably equally erroneous.

The conclusions of the German Jesuit concerning the literary policy of the Church of Rome as expressed in its latest Index, may conveniently be supplemented by a statement (written in November, 1898) by a scholarly American priest, on the present policy and methods of the Roman censorship. This statement comes in a personal letter to myself and I am, therefore, not at liberty to bring into print the name of the writer.

" The action of the Index is meant to be both preventive and repressive. Its preventive action is exercised through the diocesan censor, that is, there is in every well constituted diocese an officer known as the *censor deputatus*, to whom the bishop can hand over, before they come into print, all

---

[1] Hilgers, 170.

works written by Catholics which deal with religion or morals. This officer gives his opinion in writing to the bishop, who thereby issues an *imprimatur* (permission) or a *nihil obstat* (no reason to the contrary). There is, moreover, at Rome a similar censorship on a somewhat wider scale which is to-day, as through the past centuries, exercised through the master of the sacred palace. This official continues to be a Dominican friar The greater part of the works submitted to this censor are of course books printed in the city of Rome or at least within the territory of the old papal States.

"As far as the repressive action of the Index is concerned, this is performed by the Congregation itself. I may recall, however, that at the Council of the Vatican, many bishops from France, Germany, and Italy asked that the 'Ten Rules of the Index' be revised. They asserted that the changed social and literary conditions in these countries made it impossible to continue to enforce these 'Rules' with the former strictness. The further request was made public that books should no longer be censured (condemned) at Rome until the local episcopal authorities had been heard in the matter so that the author might have his errors pointed out, and that, if he were writing in good faith, he might thus be afforded an opportunity of recalling his erroneous statements and thus save himself from the disgrace that from a Catholic point of view would of necessity have come upon him through the condemnation of his book. The text of this document may be found in the *Acta Sacrorum Conciliorum Recentiorum, Collectio Lacensis*, volume viii, 843–844. On pages 11, 79, and 780 will be found a petition of certain Catholic laymen for the abrogation of the Index.

" The application of the legislation of the Index is made by the refusal of the permission to print, or by condemnation of the printed book and the insertion of its title on the catalogue of prohibited books. This latter act is accomplished by means of special decrees in which one or more works may be specified. . . . As far as the positive legislation of the Index goes, it may be said that this is, as a matter of principle, everywhere obligatory in that it emanates from the supreme ecclesiastical authority. Nevertheless, it may in certain places be modified by use or by non-use. Sometimes it is not strictly applied or insisted upon ; still, it does not lose its binding force although the consciences of Catholics may thereby to some extent be relieved. In certain countries, and undoubtedly in English-speaking countries, the Index legislation has not been strictly observed. I must say, however, that within the last year (1898) a formal enquiry having been sent to the Roman authorities as to whether in these English-speaking countries the legislation of the Index was to be considered as in force, an affirmative reply was returned to the questioners.

" Publishers and booksellers, if they be Catholics, are in like manner bound to the observance of this ecclesiastical legislation. Inasmuch as the legislation is preventive, it is looked upon by them as a security and moreover in general it offers a *présomption d'innocuité* [presumption of innocuousness] to the book, which is of importance for those who furnish the capital for its publication. [This remark of the American Father is, it may be pointed out, in line with the conclusion submitted sixty years earlier by the Englishman Mendham to the effect that if a book were not included in an Index of its period, those interested in its publication had a right to assume that it contained nothing considered as objectionable by the authorities of the Church.]

" The repressive action of the Index may of course from time to time occasion losses to writers, publishers, and to booksellers. An author whose book has been placed upon the Index is under obligation to withdraw the book from circulation or to modify its text. [It is of course the case, although the Father does not mention it, that any modification of the text of the original edition calls for the cancellation of the copies of this edition and involves the outlay of printing further copies with the revised text]. Publishers and booksellers, if they be Catholics, are bound, as is the author, by the action of the Index authorities. If they be not Catholics and do not pay any attention to ecclesiastical legislation, they may still, in case the work has been written by a Catholic and is addressed to a Catholic reading public, expect to see its sale blocked or diminished through the censorship. . . .

" It may be said in general that the Index legislation, as formulated by Leo XIII, is no longer as severe as formerly; it has been modified in the sense of mitigation For example, a book written by an American for the purpose of education or instruction for instance in the Scriptures, is no longer *ipso facto* forbidden. As far as the Index is concerned, such books may be freely read by Catholics who may need them. . . . The famous 'Ten Rules' of the Index issued under the authority of Pius IV (1564) are to be interpreted to-day by the Constitution '*Apostolicae Sedis*' issued by Pius IX, a Constitution which reformed considerably the well-known system of censures, excommunication, and the like, and which is to-day the juridical source of general ecclesiastical censures of all kinds. In the *Compendium Juris Ecclesiastici ad usum cleri*, written by the Austrian Bishop, Simon Archner, Bishop of Brixen, (the sixth edition of which was printed in 1887), you will find (on page 521) the following passage:

"' The ecclesiastical prohibition of books, whether placed *nominatim* on the Index or forbidden by its general rules, whether forbidden by the natural law or by the positive law, remains still intact. Therefore, such prohibited books cannot be printed, read, or kept *sine peccato*. But, at the same time, certain modifications of these prohibitions remain also in force, modifications which have doubtless been introduced in various regions through legitimate custom. As to Germany, authors of authority mentioned by the Council of Vienna have maintained that profane books written by heretics, on special subjects, as law, medicine, philosophy, history, etc., although they may contain one or more heresies scattered throughout the text, heresies held by the authors *obiter tantum*, do not fall under the ecclesiastical prohibition. They say the same of those writings of Catholic authors, otherwise worthy books, which contain one or more doctrines that are not entirely in accord with Catholic theology, the sacred canons, and the constitutions of the popes, and which in certain matters may exceed the proper limits in comment on subjects that the writers ought not to touch. This moderation is extended also to the rules of the Index which are scarcely anywhere received in their entirety, and which still less can be republished in this century *ex integro*. Finally, in Germany, even those writings of non-Catholics may, generally speaking, be safely read by Catholics which speak of religious matters in a manner conformable to the doctrine of the Church: and especially is this the case with the works of writers who may seem to be nearing conversion to the Catholic religion. On the other hand, no such license can be given to writings which treat of obscene matter, superstitions, magic, incantations, and the like; such works, even though written by Catholics, are forbidden in Germany, and rightly so. It is further to be noted that even bishops can issue and are under obligations to issue positive precepts by which, even under pain of censure, they may forbid the reading of books if they are satisfied that such reading would bring danger of perversion. In such case, they will declare that the reading of the works in question is forbidden under the law of nature. In regard to this point, Pius IX on the 24th of August, 1868, renewed the injunction of Leo XII, urging the bishops to proceed in this matter not only by their own episcopal rights but also as delegates of the Apostolic See.'

" The work of the Congregation of the Index is continued at Rome practically under the same routine as in former centuries, modified only by the late legislation of Leo XIII. . . . The prohibitions of the Index are, as a rule, made known by being published in the *Osservatore Romano*. I am not able to say how the individual author learns of the condemnation of his work and whether it is customary to write a letter to the bishop of his diocese or whether the publication in the *Osservatore* is looked upon as sufficient; nor can I say whether there is any earlier or more juridical means of promulgation than that mentioned. As a matter of fact, such condemnations are first more widely published by means of the Catholic press; but there is no law or usage compelling further publicity than that specified. Indeed, I doubt whether the fact of the condemnation of a book by a decree, or the fact that it has been placed on the Index, is always known to the Catholic world in general or even to those Catholics who speak the language in which the book is printed. . . . It may be well to remember that, in practice, the condemnations of the Index probably affect very much less than is generally imagined the actual sale or distribution of the books condemned; partly because of ignorance of the condemnation, which is often very general, partly because of the accepted and increasing modification of the legislation, and partly because the persons for whom such books were chiefly intended are often by privilege or by dispensation provided with the authority to read the same."

At the time of the completion of the proof-reading of this division of my treatise (March 1907), there does not appear to be any prospect of the production, under the direction of Pius X, of any later issue of the Index. Books that are brought to the attention of the Secretary of the Congregation, or of the Master of the Palace, are, however, condemned from time to time by separate decrees. Among other recent similar condemnations. may be cited: Schell, Hermann (of Wurzburg), *Treatise on Catholicism*, (and three other works) 1899. Loisy, the Abbé, *L' Évangile et l' Église*, 1903. Horitin, the Abbé, *La Question Biblique chez les Catholiques*, etc., 1903.

The writings of these three authors gave rise to fierce controversies during the years between 1898 and 1903. Schell and Loisy submitted themselves. The treatise by Ehrhart, *Catholicism and the Twentieth Century*, published in 1901, and that by the Protestant, Harnack, *What is Christianity*, published in 1900, escaped condemnation. In July, 1906, a condemnation was made of *The Saint (Il Santo)* by Senator Antonio Fogazzaro. The author, who is reported to be a devout Catholic, is said to have "submitted himself" in regular course, but his submission could not prevent the continued sale of the book in the Italian as well as in the foreign editions.

I am informed by the publishers of the American edition that the prohibition by the Roman authorities was duly respected by the publishers of the leading Catholic papers of America, which declined to accept advertisements of the book.

CHAPTER XII

IN the earlier periods of the Index, the Curia had, in form at least, taken the ground that the prohibitions and condemnations as published in Rome were, without further action, to be held as binding upon all the countries in which the Church itself was recognised. This contention, as has already been noted, failed to secure acceptance in countries like France, Spain, Germany, and Belgium. In fact even in certain divisions of Italy, and conspicuously in Venice, the regulations of the Index were put into force only if, and when, the local authorities had confirmed the same. During the latter half of the 19th century, however, there came to be a change in the nature of the consideration given in Catholic countries to the censorship regulations of Rome. A series of provincial councils and a number of theologians and divines have taken the ground that the Index decrees were entitled to general acceptance and should be enforced with uniformity throughout all Catholic States. The protests and controversial opinions in regard to the condemnation or supervision of literature which, during the 17th and 18th centuries, had been so frequent had during these later decades become more and more exceptional. These earlier protests concerning certain individual books or individual writers developed, as we have seen, in quite a number of instances into general controversies, controversies many of which had an abiding influence on the opinions of believers and on the final policy of the Church. We may recall in this connection the results that arose through the action of the Roman authorities in regard to the works of such writers as the Jesuits Poza and Daniel, the Dominican Serry, the Jansenists Arnauld and Quesnel, the liberal Churchman Fénelon, etc.

It appears to-day to be the general practice in Catholic circles to speak of the purpose and operations of the Index with a fair measure of respect, and the authors of this later period permit themselves even to give specific commendation to the work of the Church in supervising and controlling, for the use of the faithful, the character of literary productions. Curiously enough, side by side with this increasing respect for the institution, or at least with the very considerable lessening of criticisms, protest, and antagonism against the working of the institution, there is evidence of an increasing ignorance of the details of the regulations of the later Indexes, those that are supposed at this time to be in force. The scholarly divines of the latter years of the last century had in not a few instances given evidence that they were by no means familiar with the present Index regulations or with the lists of books placed under condemnation. As late as 1890, Bishop Rass brought into print in Rome a volume by Justus Lipsius which had been condemned in two preceding Indexes; during the same period, Bishop Malou caused a new edition to be printed of a prohibited work. The vicar-general of Lorenzi printed in 1883 a treatise by Geiler von Keisersberg, oblivious of the fact that the name of the author remains in the first class of the Index. It is probably the case that there is under present conditions no such constant reference to the Index lists as guides for reading and for study as could secure for their regulations the authority which properly belongs to them under the theory of Church control. It is a question for the casuist to decide how far ignorance of the fact of condemnation of a book may serve as an extenuation of the sin of reading a volume, for which sin the penalty has been prescribed in successive Indexes of excommunication *latae sententiae*.

In 1862, under decision of the Quinquennial faculties, it was ordered that bishops had authority to extend permission for the reading of prohibited books only to priests who were actually engaged in the care of souls. Laymen desiring to secure such permission must make application direct to the Holy See. This is in line with the order issued, in 1853, by the Congregation of the Index under which the Ultramontane bishops had authority to extend to ecclesiastics of assured scholarship and piety permission to utilise, during their lifetime, prohibited books having to do with matters of religion and doctrine; but no such permission could be given for books *contra bonos mores*. In every permission issued by a bishop it must be specifically stated that the authority comes from the Holy See.

After the middle of the 19th century, there began to be a change in the relations of the ecclesiastics of France to the authority of the Index. In *La Revue Ecclésiastique*, an article printed in 1866 says: "If, twenty years back, the question had been put as to whether the authority of the Index was recognised in

France, the answer would simply have been a laugh or a word in derision. To-day, such recognition is assented to without serious question. The formula *Index non viget in Gallia,* heretofore printed in books the titles of which had come upon the Roman Index, is now no longer to be seen." Councils of the 19th century of the French Church in which the authority of the Roman Inquisition or of the Congregation of the Index to control literature in France had been accepted in substance, as cited in this article, are these : Paris and Rennes, 1849, Lyons and Clairmont, 1850, Avignon, 1849, Albi, Toulouse, Bordeaux, and Sens, 1850, La Rochelle, 1853, and Rheims, 1857.

Among the councils of this period, outside of France, which placed themselves on record as specifically accepting the authority of the Index, are those of Prague, 1860, Colocsa, 1863, Utrecht, 1865. A council held in Venice, in 1859, orders that the Roman prohibitions are from year to year to be printed in a diocesan calendar. This is a very different attitude from that taken by Venice during the 17th and 18th centuries.

In 1852, Bishop Baillès of Luçon writes in a pastoral instruction : " The prohibition of a book by the Holy See is binding upon believers throughout the Church universal. The lists issued by the authorities of Rome of condemned and prohibited books are securing from year to year a fuller authority and a wider recognition. . . . Only heretics, schismatics, and Gallicans at this time contest the general authority of the Index."

In Germany, the world-wide authority of the Index is asserted by such critics as Heymans and Phillips in their treatise on ecclesiastical law (issued in 1872) and by the editors of the Münster *Pastoral Blatt,* writing in 1879.   A modified view is expressed by the editor of the *Katholik*, writing in 1859, who says: "The Index, considered as a moral law, is to be accepted as authoritative throughout the world.   There may be ground for question, however, as to the general obligation to accept its penal regulations."   A little later, however, the editor of the *Katholik*, writing in 1864, says:

" The faithful throughout the world are under obligations to accept the authority of the censorship tribunals, the Inquisition and the Congregation of the Index, not only in regard to the prohibition of the use of prohibited books but also with reference to the conclusions reached by these censors concerning the soundness of doctrine or general fitness for devout reading of the literature contained in such books. . .   The history of the Church has secured for the wisdom of the work of the censorship authorities an assured, even a brilliant confirmation."   "The only utterance," continues this writer, "in which the Congregation of the Index can be convicted of a serious or decisive error of judgment is that of the decree issued in 1616 against the writings of Copernicus. . . . While the history makes clear (what in fact no one has ever denied) that the Roman Congregations are in their judgments not infallible, the evidence is overwhelming as to the wisdom and effectiveness with which the work of these scholarly and devout censors has been carried on through the centuries; and it would be an act of very gross presumption for individual believers to undertake to question the validity and substantial value of their conclusions."

In 1865, an article in the official *Civiltà Cattolica*[1] in regard to a treatise of the Bishop of Treviso, says:

" The infallibility of a prohibition or condemnation of a book which has been expressed through a papal Bull, a papal

[1] 4. 1, 446.

brief, or under a decree of the Congregation which has been issued under specific instructions from the pope, cannot be questioned. The ordinary decrees of the Congregation cannot be said to possess the same full measure of infallibility as these rest not upon the direct authority of the pope but merely upon the general authority under which the Congregation has been constituted. A book that has been condemned by the Congregation must, however, be considered as having been condemned by the Church of which the Congregation is for this purpose the authorised representative."

As before pointed out, the influence of the Dominicans in the operations of the Congregation of the Index has been continuous and all powerful. As a result, the theological writers whose books have been condemned included a large proportion of Jesuits, and the literature presenting Jesuit doctrines has from the outset been handled with special severity. In the cases in which occasion has been found for reproving the books of Dominican authors, the censorship has been comparatively mild, and if the books were prohibited, the entry was usually made with the reservation *d.c.*[1] Father Hilgers, of the Order of the Jesuits in Germany, whose treatise on the Index (issued in 1905) is referred to elsewhere. is one of the few of the scholarly Jesuits who have found it practicable to take a favourable view of the policy of the Index. The Jansenist view of the authority of the Index has not unnaturally been still less approving than that of the Jesuits. Arnauld, for instance, writing in 1656, says:

" In France we do not trouble ourselves very much concerning the censures of the Index. . . . We know on what

[1] G. Daniel, writing to Serry in 1724, *Oeuvres*, ii, 365.

grounds certain of the condemnations have been arrived at It is assuredly true that the prohibition of a work constitutes no evidence that it is really pernicious. . . If a pope who has such devout purposes as characterised Innocent XI, in coming under the evil practice of Rome, finds it impossible to avoid the condemnation of really devout and scholarly books, it is easy to understand what the results of censorship must be when the authority comes into the hands of popes who are less pious and less fair-minded. . . . One may await only bad results from the book censorship of Rome so long as the practice obtains of listening only to those who denounce the books and of giving no opportunity to the authors themselves to make clear the writing or precise character of their text.   In this way it has come about that books of most importance for scholarship and of religion have been condemned and cancelled on the ground of two or three sentences which have failed to be understood by careless or unscholarly examiners."

Writing again in 1693, under Innocent XII, Arnauld says:

" Our good Pope is labouring in praiseworthy manner for the abolition of abuses.   He has, however, not yet realised that one of the reforms most called for is to avoid appointing as members of the Inquisition cardinals who have no more trustworthy knowledge of the matters there to be considered than a shoemaker has of astronomy.   The 'qualificators' (the examining scholars) have only a vote for counsel.   It is with the cardinals that rest the deciding votes and these unfortunately are not weighed but simply counted.   How many and serious have been the blunders committed through decisions of the Inquisition (or of the Congregation) in matters of doctrine of which the majority of the cardinals are frankly ignorant !"

As an example, on the other hand, of an unquestioning acceptance of the wisdom and authority of the Church in this matter of censorship, may be cited St. Francis of Sales, who writes (in 1608):

" We pray our Catholic readers, in order to protect themselves from the contagion of evil influences, to accept without question the book prohibitions of the Holy Church. We may say that we ourselves have always given the strictest obedience to the Church regulations in regard to the reading of condemned books. In no other way can we manifest the full honour in which we hold its authority and our obligations as believers to accept this authority." [1]

Macchiavelli (writing about 1500) observes that if the princes of the Christian States had maintained religion in the form in which it was delivered by its Founder, these States would be more united and happier than they are. He adds, *ne se può fare altra maggiore conjettura della declinatione d'essa, quanto è vedere come quelli popoli che sono più propinqui alla Chiesa Romana, capo della Religione nostra, hanno meno Religione. Et chi considerasse i fondamenti suoi, e vedesse l'uso presente quanto è diverso da quelli, giudicherebbe esser propinquo senza dubbio, ò la rovina ò il flagello. Habbiamo adunque con la Chiesa e coi Preti noi Italiani questo primo obligo. d'essere diventati senza Religione e cattivi,* which Mendham interprets, "the more of Rome, the less of religion." [2]

Sir Edwin Sandys, whose *Europae Speculum,* printed at The Hague in 1629, was translated (from English) into Latin by Francus, gives in this a summary of the literary policy of the Church of his time. He writes:

" But the Papacy at this day, taught by woful experience

[1] Cited by Hilgers, 348.
[2] Cited by Mendham, 9

what damage this license of writing among themselves hath done them and that their speeches are not only weapons in the hands of their adversaries, but eyesores and stumbling blocks also to their remaining friends; under show of purging the world from the infection of all wicked and corrupt books and passages which are either against religion or against honesty and good manners, for which two purposes they have several officers who indeed do blot out much impiousness and filth, and therein well deserve both to be commended and imitated (whereto the Venetians add also a third, to let nothing pass that may be justly offensive to princes), have in truth withal pared and lopped off whatsoever in a manner their watchful eyes could observe, either free in disclosing their drifts and practices, or dishonourable to the clergy, or undutiful to the Papacy. These editions only authorised, all other are disallowed, called in, censured; with threats to whosoever shall presume to keep them; that no speech, no writing, no evidence of times past, no discourse of things present, in sum, nothing whatsoever may sound aught but holiness, honour, purity, integrity to the unspotted spouse of Christ and to his unerring Vicar; to the Mistress of Churches, to the Father of Princes. . . . and they brought forth in fine those *Indices Expurgatorii* whereof I suppose they are now not a little ashamed, they having by misfortune lit into their adversaries' hands from whom they desired by all means to conceal them."[1]

D'Aguesseau, in a *Mémoire* written in 1710, says: "It is well understood that the Index possesses in France no authority. It is sad to understand that it is still permitted to control literature in certain countries which have not known, as has France, how to uphold the freedom of a national Church. The Index has in fact been so misused as a power that it makes

[1] Sandys, 127–132.

prohibition of not a few books which are by no means deserving of so much honour."

In an essay by Villers on the *Spirit and Influence of the Reformation of Luther* (which obtained the prize offered in 1802 by the French Institute for the best treatise on the question) the author finds ground for no little indignation concerning the restrictions upon books by a pope who, while issuing fulminations against Luther, gave full license to Ariosto. The writer goes on to say:

" In Spain, in Italy, and in Austria, the prohibitions and censures went much further, and in those countries heavy shackles have been imposed on the liberty of writing and of thinking." The writer complains that " in public libraries in these countries, the works of Rousseau, of Voltaire, of Helvetius, of Diderot, and of other *esprits forts*, are kept under lock and key with the order that they shall not be communicated to any persons excepting to those who shall engage to refute their doctrines."

He makes reference to the dismissal from office, in 1780, of a professor of a Bavarian university who had requested that a copy of Bayle's *Critical Dictionary* should be placed in the common library.

" In those countries is still maintained as far as possible the policy of the Middle Ages, under which the minds of men are to be kept on certain subjects in complete stupidity or in a state of emptiness so that they may later be filled with convenient doctrine or may be kept free for superstition.[1]

Mendham points out that

" It is not going beyond the truth to say that an almost

[1] Villers, 290 *seq*.

perfect library might be formed from the books condemned by the papal Indexes, perfect indeed for all purposes of absolute and abundant utility. It would need only to have added to it a few Benedictine editions of the Fathers, histories and accounts of modern Roman affairs and the collection of the Bulls, Councils, etc. . . . It would also be somewhat lacking in English books, prolific as this island is in offensive and formidable heresy. The fact is, that the literary productions of England have come into contact or collision with the Italian only by means of translations. It is in this that we find in the Indexes the works of Swift, Tillotson, Sherlock, Robertson, Gibbon, and others. . . . There is a further detail, that these prohibitory and expurgatory instruments could only be put into execution among subjects of papal government. . . . Any attempt to enforce them in other States would have provoked hostilities with their heretical community with no prospect of advantage and with much risk of disadvantage to the Roman power."[1]

Mendham contends that under the general policy of the Church, as expressed in its Indexes, the inference is legitimate that what the Indexes do not condemn they approve and sanction. It therefore follows that the authority from which those Indexes issue (an authority which is the highest in the Church) must be understood as approving and even sanctioning all doctrines or assertions presented by writers of her own communion which her condemning decrees have failed either to proscribe or to expurgate. (This contention is, it must be remembered, denied absolutely by the Jesuit Hilgers, writing in 1905.) In the examination held in 1825 on the state of Ireland, the Rev. M. O'Sullivan stated in one of his answers that in the

---

[1] Mendham, 270.

case of an author of authority, such as Cardinal Bellarmin, the omission of criticism on the part of the authorities amounted to an approbation. The questioner drew the immediate inference: "Then you understand by the Index, not only a negative condemnation of all the books specified, but a positive affirmation of the doctrines or principles of all the books by Catholic writers not condemned." Against this inference the witness was reported as making no protest. With respect to Bellarmin, it may be noted that his name was entered in the Index of Sixtus V because he had failed to affirm the direct power of the pope in matters temporal, an entry which may be considered as supporting the above inference.

That the works appearing under the form of Indexes, catalogues, etc., however various, still all belonging to, or coming from, Rome, are at least uncommon and extensively unknown, requires no proof more elaborate or unquestionable than the not only ready but forward declaration of ignorance by the very persons who should be presumed to be best acquainted with them, by well informed members of the ecclesiastic community which promulgates and enforces them. Charles Butler, writing in 1824, says: "Few of the Roman Catholics know of the existence of the *Index expurgatorius*." [1] Dr. Murray, the Roman Catholic Archbishop of Dublin, states before a committee of the House of Commons, in 1825:

Ignorance of the Indexes

" The *Index expurgatorius* has no authority whatever in Ireland; it has never been received in these countries [*sic*] and I doubt very much whether there be ten people in

[1] Letter to C Blandell, prefixed to the *Vindication*, lxxxiv, cited by Mendham, 14

Ireland who have ever seen it; it is a sort of censorship of books established in Rome and it is not even received in Spain, where they have a censorship of their own. In these countries, it has no force whatever."[1]

Mendham trusts that "no equivocation lurks under the ambiguity of the epithet *expurgatorius*."

Dr. Slevin, prefect of the College of Dunboyne, says (in 1826):

"Our Catholics will respect the prohibitions of the Congregation of the Index."

In a work entitled *Church History of the English from the year 1500*, published under the name of Dod, (according to Mendham the real name of the author was Tootell), mention is made of a Council of Reformation. In chapter ix, pages 94 and 95, an extract is given from certain regulations framed by this council during the last decade of the 16th century. The wording is as follows:

" Publick and private libraries must be searched and examined for books, as also all bookbinders, stationers and booksellers' shops; and not only Heretical Books and Pamphlets but also prophane, vane, lascivious and other such hurtful and dangerous poysons, are utterly to be removed, burnt and suppressed, and severe order and punishment appointed for such as shall conceal these kind [*sic*] of Writing; and like order set down for printing of good things for the time to come."

"The earlier editions of the Index expurgatory," says Mendham, "were distributed with the utmost caution and were intended only for the possession and the inspection of those to whom they were necessary for the execution of the provisions. The reason is obvious. It certainly was little desirable that the dishonest dealings with the

[1] Mendham, x.

authors here censured should be known, either to those who were injured by them and to whom they would offer the opportunity of justifying themselves; or to the world at large whose judgment they must know would in many instances be at variance with their own. And evidently it was not to their interest to discover and to point out those very passages and writings, not only of reputed heretics but of reputed Catholics, which exposed the most vulnerable parts of their own system." [1]

" The *Indices Expurgatorii* are very good commonplace books and repertories, by help of which we may presently find, what any author (who has fallen under censure) has against them [*i.e.* the Catholics]. We are directed through the Index to the book, chapter, and line, where anything is spoken against any superstition or error of Rome; so that he who has the *Indices* cannot want for testimonies against Rome." [2]

In an article printed in 1861, in the *Katholik* of Mayence, the writer says:

" We are prepared to place upon any inquirer the responsibility of determining whether the Congregation of the Index in the whole series of its operations has ever committed an essential blunder. . . . The policy and method of ecclesiastical censorship as carried out through the Index is the most moderate, the most tolerant, and the wisest that could be conceived. . . . The Congregation of the Index secures in the shaping of its judgments the service of the scholarship and of the consciences and capable labour of wise and devout counsellors; and its decisions may be accepted as the conclusions of a scientific Areopagus which is entitled to the fullest respect and the most implicit obedience; and he who does not render such obedience is a stranger to, and an opponent of, the spirit of the Church.

[1] Mendham, x.
[2] *Remains* of Bishop Barlow, 1693, 70, 71.

. . . It is through the Index that the Holy See exercises one of the most important of its functions."[1]

In 1868, in an article having to do with the Council of the Vatican, the *Katholik* says:

" The sting of the Index (to its critics) rests in this, that it represents a judgment exercised by the highest authority in matters of faith over individual knowledge. It is the sting of infallible truth. . . . The Index has from the beginning been the most trustworthy teacher of sound theology and defender of true Faith."

Bishop Baillès of Luçon, writing in 1864, says:

" The Index contains no single book the condemnation of which was not arrived at under general rules. . . . It may be considered as itself one great book in which are characterised with more or less precision all the errors, heresies, and schisms of the ages—a book which for all devout scholars may be accepted as a trustworthy chart on which have been marked with a skilled and trusted hand all sunken rocks and other perils of the deep. The Index is the incomparable master work of the wisdom of the Church." Baillès says further: " No bibliographical work can be considered as complete until it has been collated with the Index. . . . The date of the prohibition of a book, taken in connection with the date of its first publication, indicates the time during which it has become more pernicious. . . The Index is to be classed as the most essential of critical bibliographies, one which no library should be without."

Bishop Plantier of Nismes, in a pastoral letter of 1857, describes the Congregation of the Index as " the throne of good sense, the magistracy of truth, and a tribunal each utterance of which constitutes an indispensable service to true philosophy."[2]

---

[1] II, 710.
[2] *Rev. des Sc. eccl.*, 1866, iii, 374.

Minister Jules Ferry, speaking in the French Senate, May 31, 1882, says:

" We will never recognise the decrees of the Congregation of the Index. We propose to maintain the traditions of the French State and of the Gallic Church. Where would the State be if the decisions of the body which has placed its interdict upon the great spirits of mankind, such as Descartes, Malebranche, Kant, Renan, and has even condemned the Dictionary of Bouillet, should be accepted as the law of the land? . . . The ground that has been assigned for the condemnation of the Handbook of Compayré was the statement contained in it 'that it was more important for the French child to know the names of the Kings of France than those of the Kings of Judea.'. . . The Index-decree went over the head of the Ambassador in Rome and of the Nuncius in Paris, in order to start a conflagration in our State.

"In a manual by André Berthet, published in 1882, (which did *not* find its way into the Index), stand the following questions: 'What is God? I know not. What becomes of us after death? I know not. Are you not ashamed of your ignorance? One need not be ashamed not to know what has not yet been known to any one.'"

Father Searle (writing in 1895) maintains that the Church does not prohibit Catholics who are competent to undertake scientific investigation, from so doing. She places absolutely no obstacle in **The Church** the way of their penetrating into all the facts **and Science** of nature as it stands or of their considering the probable indications as to its past history or of their weighing actual historical testimony. . . . The Church forbids, as against reason, common-sense, and the welfare of man, liberty of thought on matters, whether in the material or spiritual order, which have been clearly demonstrated and definitely ascertained; she refuses to abandon it on those matters which are still open to reasonable question, as is the case with certain scientific hypotheses not as yet proven.[1]

Such a statement, if accepted to-day as authoritative, would make it evident that the policy of the Church in the 20th century has changed very materially from the policy that was in force, with some strenuousness, in the 16th and 17th centuries.

Hilgers points out that the Church is naturally much more concerned with the protection of the morality and of the spiritual nature of the people than with any formal intellectual development such as is to be secured from the study of the so-called classics. If a classical work, for instance, teaches that suicide is praiseworthy or is defensible, it is the duty of the Church to keep such work out of the hands of the believers. In like manner, the Church prohibits writings of any kind which make defence of the propriety of divorce or which make reference to divorce as if it were a necessary condition of society. The Church can further give its approval either formally or tacitly to no work which attacks the inspiration of the Scriptures or the binding force of scriptural doctrine, and must bring its condemnation upon any writer, however great he may be, whether Catholic or Protestant, historian or litterateur, philosopher or theologian, whose utterances tend to undermine faith in the word of God.[2]

There are, however, not a few expressions of opinion from Catholic sources which are by no means in accord with the conclusions reached by Father Hilgers as to the wisdom and beneficence of the literary policy of

[1] Searle, 281–297.
[2] Hilgers, 378.

the Church of Rome. These critics have pointed out that the censors, whether in Rome, Madrid, or Paris, had been so seriously concerned with matters of doctrine, that they had given small measure of attention to publications of a scandalous character, and the influence of which was *contra bonos mores*.

A volume published in Osnabrück (Hanover) in August, 1906, may be cited as an example of cordial support given to the present censorship policy of the Roman Church by a loyal Catholic of North Germany. The author is Albert Sleumer, Doctor of Philosophy, and his book, issued under the title of *Index Romanus*. claims to present a complete record of all the German publications which have been placed upon the Roman Index, together with the titles of books other than German which have been condemned since 1870. Dr. Sleumer's volume is issued with the approval of Hubert, Bishop of the historic diocese of Osnabrück. Sleumer's volume had been originally issued in 1901 and now appears in a later revised edition. The contentions submitted by him in regard to the necessity of the Index, and as to the wisdom with which, from the beginning, the censorship of the Church has been conducted, are substantially in line with the position taken by Father Hilgers, whose larger and more important treatise has already been referred to. Sleumer is, like Hilgers, interested in citing examples of censorship by the State which are less consistent in principle and more extreme in application than similar actions by the authorities of Rome. He quotes, for instance, Thiers (whom he describes as "a well-known free-thinking author of France") saying, in 1830, that there could be no danger to the community in giving unrestricted freedom to the press.

" Truth alone," says Thiers. " can have abiding influence; that which is false can do no harm and in the end brings its own refutation and no government can ever be injured by libellous publications."

In 1834, Thiers takes a different ground:

" The representatives of the People are having their influence impaired by the falsifications of the Press. . . . The wickedness and lack of responsibility on the part of the Press have brought grave misfortunes upon the community. . . . It is essential for the safety of the State that there should be a close supervision of the Press.

We may remember that, between 1830 and 1834, the Bourbon government of Charles X had been overthrown and that Thiers was now a leader of influence under the administration of Louis Philippe.

Sleumer has himself no doubt that the press has to-day become " the most important expression of the ' Evil One.' " [1]

" Who could," he says, " deny to the State the right to control, with all the authority that has been confided to it, the development and the influence of a power that can undermine the authority alike of the family, of the government, and of the Church? But if such authority is necessary to maintain the foundations of the State, who shall deny an equal right and duty to those who are responsible for maintaining the foundations of the Church? " [2]

In presenting the lists of the German books condemned, Sleumer points out that it is of course an

---

[1] *Index Romanus,* 7.   [2] *Ibid.,* 9.

impossibility for the Congregation of the Index to compile with any measure of completeness the titles of all the books deserving condemnation. He contends however, that the books selected may be accepted as fairly typical of the classes calling for condemnation and that the Index schedules can, therefore, be utilised by the more intelligent of the faithful for their own guidance and by the confessors who have the responsibility of directing the reading of their flocks.

It is interesting to compare with the implicit acceptance given to the censorship policy of the modern Church by the scholarly Jesuit Father Hilgers and by the good Dr. Sleumer, the more discriminating and more critical analysis of **Tyrrell on the Index** this policy by a scholarly Jesuit in England, Father George Tyrrell, whose monograph entitled *A Much Abused Letter*, comes into print while this volume is passing through the press. Father Tyrrell had, it seems, been applied to for counsel by a devoted friend in the Church (since identified as St. George Mivart) who, in middle life, in connection with certain scientific pursuits and investigations. had found himself in perplexity as to the foundations of his faith. The friend had not been able to bring into accord the conclusions which he had arrived at through his scientific investigations with the latest utterances of the Church authorities having to do with the matters at issue. Seriously troubled at the thought of being forced out of relations with the Church in whose communion he had grown up, he had asked Father Tyrrell for advice as to his present duty. The Father had in his reply (which in compass and character constitutes an essay on the relations of faith with intellectual pursuits) taken the ground that there was nothing in the scientific conclusions that his friend had accepted which made it necessary for him to abandon the communion of the Church.   It was the Father's judgment that the spiritual relations of the believer were to be considered quite apart from his scientific opinions or intellectual development.   The letter, which was intended to be purely personal and which had for its purpose the saving to the Church of a valued member, through some inadvertency came into publication, and, as a result, Father Tyrrell was dismissed from the Order of the Jesuits.   The unauthorised publication of the letter had presented an incorrect, not to say a garbled, text, and the Father now felt at liberty to print the corrected text with some commentary on his own relations to the matters at issue.   The document is of decided interest as an expression of the spiritual and intellectual status of a scholarly Catholic of to-day.   The selection of opinions of Catholics on the present policy of the Church runs the risk of being unduly extended, but I think it in order to make one or two citations from the volume of this earnest English Jesuit.

" The express purpose of the Confidential Letter was to dissuade my friend from a breach with the Church which would mean an assertion of individualism and a denial of authority and corporate life. . . . My whole line of argument was to insist that the reasonable and moderate claims of the Church over the individual were not invalidated by any extravagant interpretation of those claims. . . . The heroes of moral romance sail serenely through life's darkest storms, cheered by the certainty of their rectitude and by the hearty applause of a thoroughly satisfied conscience. But in real life, it seems to me that such serenity, and the undoubted force and energy which it secures, are the privilege not so much of the heroic but of the unreflective.[1] . . Only when we take the word 'faith' in its ethical and evangelical sense, is it true to say that loss of faith necessarily implies some moral weakness or imperfection. But the saying is palpably false when faith is made to stand for theological orthodoxy, for assent to a dogmatic system. It is admitted on all hands that such faith as this may, and often does, go with the most extreme moral depravity—with sensuality and cruelty, with injustice, with untruthfulness and hypocrisy, prejudice and superstition. Temporal and selfish interests of one sort or another, or more commonly still, an absolute lack of all sympathetic and intelligent interest in their religion, will keep the great majority of such men in the paths of orthodoxy as long as orthodoxy is in public fashion and favour.[2] . . . For one reason or another theologians have, for generations, been letting their accounts get into disorder: they have trusted to the one general principle of 'authority' for the quieting of all possible doubts and have paid less and less attention to particulars. They have forgotten that, by a necessary law of the mind, the claims of authority will *de facto* inevitably be called in question as soon as the reasons on which those claims rest are cancelled or outweighed by those which stand against the particular teachings of authority; that though a Catholic as such cannot consistently call this or that Catholic doctrine in question, he can consistently call his Catholicism in question.[3] However unwilling a man may be to raise doubts in his own mind, he cannot live in an age and country like yours [England] without these being thrust upon his attention. In Mediaeval Spain, where index and inquisition were practically workable methods of protection, it was otherwise. There and then one needed only not to think in order to be at peace; here and now one needs also not to see or hear or read or converse or live.

---

[1] George Tyrrell. *A Much Abused Letter*, pp. 18, 21.
[2] *Ibid.*, 39.   [3] *Ibid.*, 41

There is now no educational grade so low as to be exempt entirely from the spirit of criticism, whose influence is of course still more strongly felt as we ascend to the higher grades.[1]... Turning to the clergy, we find a great readiness on the part of individuals to disclaim the honour [of having authoritative knowledge] and also a curious vagueness as to the precise depositaries for the final authorities [on intellectual difficulties]. Taken individually, they frankly say that they are themselves incompetent to deal with such problems, but they imply that they have an unbounded confidence in their own collectivity, or in certain persons (unknown and unknowable) whose specialty it is to adjust the claims of sacred and secular knowledge. Thus the responsibility, divided over the whole multitude of the Church's children, is shifted from shoulder to shoulder, and comes to rest nowhere in particular;[2] ... The conservative positions (in the Church) are maintained by ignorance, systematic or involuntary. ... The close historic study of Christian origin and development must undermine many of our most fundamental assumptions in regard to dogmas and institutions. ... The sphere of the miraculous is daily limited by the growing difficulty in verifying such facts, and the growing facility of reducing either them or the belief in them to natural and recognised causes.[3] ... If the intellectual defence of Catholicism breaks down (as far as the individual is concerned) does it straightway follow that he should separate himself from the communion of the Church? Yes, if theological 'intellectualism' be right; if faith mean mental assent to a system of conceptions of the understanding; if Catholicism be primarily a theology or at most a system of practical observances regulated by that theology. No, if Catholicism be primarily a life, and the Church a spiritual organism in whose life we participate, and if theology be but an attempt of that

---

[1] George Tyrrell. *A Much Abused Letter*, p. 42.
[2] *Ibid.*, 44.   [3] *Ibid.*, 48.

life to formulate and understand itself—an attempt which may fail wholly or in part without affecting the value and reality of life itself.[1] . . . Must we not distinguish between the collective subconsciousness of the 'People of God' and the consciously formulated mind and will of the governing section of the Church? May not our faith in the latter be at times weak or nil, and yet our faith in the former strong and invincible? . . . Let us recognise that. in spite of its noisy advertisements, this self-conscious, self-formulating Catholicism of the thinking, talking, and governing minority is not the whole Church, but only an element (however important) in its constitution.[2] . . . Faith is the very root and all-permeating inspiration of life. Not the faith of mere obedience to authoritative teaching, which is at best a condition of spiritual education . . . not the faith of merely intellectual assent to the historical and metaphysical assertions of a theology that claims to be miraculously guaranteed from errancy. After all. your quarrel is not with the Church, but with the theologians [we are to bear in mind that Tyrrell is still addressing his friend whose scholarship has brought him into doubt]; not with ecclesiastical authority, but with a certain theory as to the nature and limits and grades of that authority, and of the value, interpretation, and obligation of its decisions.[3] . . . Who formulate these decisions, determine their value, interpret them to us; who have fabricated the whole present theology of authority and imposed it upon us, but the theologians? Who but the theologians themselves have taught us that the concensus of theologians cannot err? These are, however, mortal, fallible, ignorant men like ourselves."[4]

May not Catholicism, like Judaism, have to die in order that it may live again in a greater and grander form? Has not every organism its limits of develop-

---

[1] George Tyrrell. *A Much Abused Letter*, p. 51.
[2] *Ibid.,* 59.   [3] *Ibid.,* 67.   [4] *Ibid.,* 87.

ment after which it must decay, and be content to survive in its progeny? Wine-skins stretch, but only within measure; for there comes at last a bursting-point when new ones must be provided.

Another volume expressing the views of scholarly Catholic believers in regard to the present intellectual **Briggs** policy of the Church comes into print in **on** 1906 while these pages are going through the **Censorship** press. It bears the title of *The Papal Commission and the Pentateuch* and is the work of two authors, the Reverend Charles A. Briggs, Professor of Theology and Symbolics, of the Union Theological Seminary of New York, and Baron Friedrich von Hügel, at present of Cambridge, England. The work and career of Dr. Briggs are, of course, familiar to all who have knowledge of the issues of later years between the creeds and dogmas of the Churches and of the difficulties of the great scholars of the present generation who have been investigating the texts and records upon which these creeds and dogmas have been based. Of these scholars, Dr. Briggs is known as one of the most authoritative and conscientious and also as one possessing the greatest reverence for the purposes and the spiritual power of revealed religion. Dr. Briggs, now a member of the Episcopal Church, has from time to time brought into expression certain ideals in regard to the development of the Church Universal. If one understands him aright, he looks forward to the reconstruction, under the new conditions of the twentieth century, of a world's Church or Church Universal, which was so nearly realised under the very different conditions of the fifteenth century. He is, therefore, sympathetically interested in the policy of the Church of Rome and he is in close personal relations with not a few of the scholarly leaders of that Church. He has united with his friend Baron von Hügel in the production of a monograph made up of two letters, one from himself and one from Baron von Hügel, which have for their purpose the analysis and criticism of the conclusions arrived at by the recent Papal Commission in regard to the origin and the history of the Pentateuch. The report of the Commission (of the text of which I have no direct knowledge) appears to have taken strong ground against the results of the so-called higher scholarship, that is to say, of the latest investigations concerning the origin and the formation of the writings going to make up the Pentateuch. Dr. Briggs cites from the record of the Papal Commission the statement that

"certain faulty readings in the text of the Pentateuch may be ascribed to the error of an amanuensis concerning which it is lawful to investigate and judge according to the laws of criticism. . . . But in so doing 'Due regard must be paid to the judgment of the Church.' It is admitted [says Briggs], (by the Papal Commission) that investigation and judgment must be 'according to the laws of criticism.' If this is so, then it necessarily follows that the laws of criticism must determine the entire investigation, and not merely any definite part of it." [1]

The Baron's division of the monograph applies, of course, more directly to the subject of the present chapter as an expression of the views of a scholarly Catholic on the present intellectual policy of the Church. He writes as follows:

Von Hügel on Censorship

'For you cannot teach whom you do not understand,

[1] Briggs and Hügel, *The Papal Commission and the Pentateuch*, p. 18.

and you cannot win the man with whom you cannot share certain presuppositions. . . . The cultivated non-Roman Catholic world is, in part unconsciously, often slowly yet everywhere surely, getting permeated and won by critical standards and methods. A system cannot claim to teach all the world and at the same time erect an impenetrable partition-wall between itself and the educated portion of that world.[1]. . . This opinion of the Biblical Commission is surely but one link in a chain of official attempts at the suppression of Science and Scholarship, beginning with Erasmus and culminating with Richard Simon and Alfred Loisy, but never entirely absent, as witness the lives of countless workers, well-known to their fellow-workers. . . . When and where has Rome finally abandoned any position however informal and late its occupation, and however demonstrated its untenableness? Where, in particular, is the case of its permission to hold critical and historical views even distantly comparable in their deviation from tradition to those here presented by us? But if no such cases can be found, then, surely, Rome stands utterly discredited. . ." [2]

The Baron recalls that, on January 13th, 1897, there appeared,

"approved and confirmed by Pope Leo XIII, a Decree of the Holy Office, in the highest Roman tribunal next after the Pope himself, and which, unlike the Biblical Commission, claims directly doctrinal authority, giving a negative answer to the question, 'Whether it is safe to deny, or at least to call in doubt, the authenticity of the text of St. John, in the First Epistle, chapter v, verse 7, "For there are three that give testimony in heaven: the Father, the Word, and the Holy Spirit, and these three are one."'"[3]

[1] *The Papal Commission and the Pentateuch.*
[2] *Ibid.*, 54.	[3] *Ibid.*, 59.

The Baron closes his letter (which is addressed to his friend Dr. Briggs) with the words:

" That we can and ought, both of us, to pray, to will, and to work that the advisers of the chief Bishop of Christendom, in the manifold mixed subject-matters which they have to prepare and to bring before him, may have a vivid realisation of the difficulty and complexity, the importance and rights and duties of those other departments of life—Science and Scholarship—lest these forces, ignored or misunderstood, bring inevitable obstruction and eclipse to those direct and central interests and ideals which are the fundamental motives of all spiritual life, and the true mainspring and impregnable citadel of the Christian, Catholic, and Roman Church."[1]

I can but feel that these utterances of sane and reverent Catholic believers of to-day are expressions of a state of mind with which the Church of Rome will have to reckon in the near future unless the realm of its believers is to be restricted to those who are the less sane and less scholarly and, to those who, to put it frankly, have a smaller measure of intellectual integrity.

It may be concluded that the general regulations of the Index and the insistence on the part of the Church of the right and the obligation of supervising the output of the printing-press and of **Conclusions** controlling and directing the reading of the faithful, did exert a restrictive influence on the production and distribution of literature. This influence was, however, limited to the territories in which the machinery of the Inquisition was in active existence. In the regions north of the Alps and the Pyrenees, the Index regula-

[1] *The Papal Commission and the Pentateuch*

tions brought about but a spasmodic and inconsiderable interference with the distribution of the works of Protestant writers. Outside of the lands of the Inquisition, the Church had no other means of hindering the reading of heretical books than to declare the same to be deadly sin and to threaten the delinquents with such penalties as excommunication. The records of applications for dispensations present, as Reusch points out,[1] evidence that scholarly Catholics made frequent opportunity for infringing the censorship prohibitions. It would in fact be difficult to specify any territory in which the Index regulations were accepted cheerfully and thoroughly. It is certain that, even in the most faithful of the Catholic communities, bitter complaints arose from time to time on the part of the scholars in regard to the destruction of valuable literature and the resulting interference with scholarly work. There were also complaints of a different kind. Those who were interested in preserving the true faith from being undermined by heretical doctrine, came to the realisation of the fact that heretical books were, through the operations of the Index, brought to the attention of many who otherwise would never have known of their existence.

In 1549, Gabriel Putherbeus, writing to Theotimus, complains that the books prohibited by the Paris divines were being read by people to whom they would never have become known excepting through the censorship lists.[2] Gratianus Verus writes that the Index of Paul IV had had a most pernicious influence in making known to Catholic readers a long list of Protestant writings. Protestant scholars utilised the

---

[1] ii, 599.   [2] Theotimus, 238.

catalogues in the Index very largely as recommendations of books that were deserving of consideration. The more thoughtful Catholics were ready to recognise that, as an offset to the importance of protecting the faithful from the influence of heretical doctrines, the publication of the Index-lists brought serious disadvantages. The reading of the Scriptures was rendered unduly difficult for many to whom the instruction therein contained should prove of service. The study of the Bible, of the works of the Fathers of the Church, and of much of the literature of scholarship, was seriously hampered even for devout scholars. The pursuit of scientific studies by Catholic students and instructors was placed under great disadvantages through the prohibition and cancellation even of such works of reference as lexicons, when these bore the names of Protestant compilers. The opportunity of utilising such lexicons when specific permission had been secured from bishops or from inquisitors could not sufficiently meet the difficulty. The possibility of securing expurgated editions of books the original and complete text of which had fallen under condemnation, proved in practice to be too slight a dependence. The printer-publishers, who had been subjected to loss, and often to very serious loss, through the cancellation of the original edition, were as a rule not encouraged to make the further investment required for the printing of the "corrected" and expurgated text. It was also the case that these expurgations were frequently made very heedlessly, and with a full measure of ignorance of the subject-matter of the book, and of the precise purport of the original text. As a result, if the eliminations ordered by the censors were carried out with precision, the text as it remained presented no adequate sense.   On the other hand, the insertion of any changes whatsoever, or of any new material in the expurgated text, subjected the reissue to a further censorship and to the risk of a second cancellation.

In the States in which, as in Spain and Portugal, the entire control of the censorship was left with the Inquisition, the scholars and students were practically deprived of the use of foreign literature.   Writers like Pallavicini congratulate themselves that the dread of the Index (that is to say, of course, of the penalties of the Index regulations) has had the effect of checking very largely the printing and the distribution of books, and must, according to his view, have served to discourage the writing of books.   It is evidently his point of view that the possible advantages from active literary production are more than offset by the resulting evils.

The difficulties for students and readers were of necessity increased by the lack of any consistency or uniformity of policy on the part of the Congregation of the Index, of the Inquisitions (whether in Rome or in Spain), or of the *Magister Palatii*.   In fact, with the inevitable change in the personnel of these authorities, it is difficult to see how any absolutely consistent policy could have been maintained through a term of years.   The men representing different Orders were, as Jesuits, Dominicans, Franciscans, etc., committed to differences of dogma and of interpretation which seemed to them to be vital.   As the opportunity came into their hands, it was inevitable that they should do what was in their power to discourage the production and to lessen the distribution, not only of the works of avowed heretics, but of the books of writers of different schools of thought and of faith within the communion of Rome. The contests between the Orders were carried into the work of censorship and found their expression in the varying lists of the Indexes of successive decades or of different centres of Church authority. There may be ground for wonder, not that the interference with the literature of these Catholic countries was so considerable, but that the Catholic scholars of the 16th and the first half of the 17th century were able, under such hampering restrictions, to leave any literary monuments of continued value. The results of the censorship system can of course also not be measured by what may be termed the direct action, the value of the scholarly books destroyed, the interference with the work of scholarly readers, the property losses caused to the printer-publishers and the booksellers, and, through them, to the community. We must bear in mind also the restrictive influence on literary production and on intellectual development. Many works that might have stimulated and enlightened the world were undoubtedly, after some sharp activities of the censors, destroyed in manuscript rather than, in being brought into print, to bring risk to their authors of loss of position, of banishment, or of excommunication. In other cases, writers of individuality and distinctive force decided to cancel their proposed books in the initial stage of lecture notes, rather than, in bringing the material to completion and into print, to risk loss of position, banishment, or excommunication. In the States that accepted the authority of the Index, and particularly in the territories in which this authority was exercised by the Inquisition, the existence of the Index and the machinery of the censorship acted as a blight on literary production and distribution and constituted a serious bar to the interests of higher education and to intellectual development. Such a restriction on the natural operations of the mind, enforced through a long series of years, must have had a repressing effect also on character and individuality, besides tending to the development of deceit and the impairment of manliness.

"In concluding my summary of the influence of the Church on the literature of Europe, I find myself," says Dejob, **Dejob on the** "considering one hypothesis. What might the **Papacy.** result have been for the Church and for Europe, if the college of Cardinals, in place of considering the nationality only of candidates for the tiara, had made its selections purely on the basis of merit and capacity? What might have happened if, for instance, the papal throne had been filled by a series of Popes from France? . . . Imperial Rome had the wisdom to select its successive rulers from the diverse provinces that came within its rule, and in so doing, it unquestionably widened and strengthened the foundations of the Empire. Christian Rome might assuredly have secured similar results from a similar worldwide policy. A Bossuet or a Massillon selected for the pontificate would certainly have governed the Church with a spirit at once more serious and more comprehensive, and would have rendered enormous service to the interests of Catholicism and of Europe. The spirit of Popes of such calibre would have kept within bounds the continued disputes on smaller matters of doctrine which have wasted the force and narrowed the intelligence of so many excellent Christians. They would not have been able to prevent the diffusion of philosophical ideas, but I feel confident that faith, as represented and defended by them, would have been assailed with less bitterness and with less effectiveness. . . . The Church, like France itself, should have been able to remain serious without becoming Puritan; and to develop intellectual brilliancy without any compromise of the foundations of faith or of morality.

" I may admit that we have here only an hypothesis but it is fair to remember, in thinking how the influence of France might have served the highest ideals of the Church, how large an evidence during the past two centuries the French spirit has given of earnestness, of moral discipline, of wholesome force. It has preserved with a hatred of hypocrisy, an aversion for servility, a large liberality of thought, and it is such a combination of qualities that should have been made of the largest service to the Church and to the world." [1]

As has been indicated in the preceding narrative, there has been through the centuries not a little varying in the policy of Roman censorship and in the enforcement of its regulations according as one or another Order or school of thought secured the control of the Papacy, or of the machinery of the Inquisition and of the Congregation of the Index. This control, however, has remained, not only for the Papacy, but also in great measure for the Roman Inquisition and for the Congregation of the Index, in the hands of Italians. The result has been, of necessity, from generation to generation, to force into a conformity with local Italian standards the literary activities, and the intellectual development, of the faithful throughout the world. There is certainly ground for the conclusion that under this policy, the Index (including under this term the whole system of censorship) came to constitute one of the more important of the influences which have worked through the centuries towards the narrowing of the Church Universal (the magnificent ideal of the Middle Ages) into the organisation known in our twentieth century as the Church of Rome.

[1] Dejob, 351.

SCHEDULE OF INDEXES

SCHEDULE OF INDEXES WHICH WERE ISSUED UNDER THE AUTHORITY OF THE CHURCH, OR WHICH, HAVING BEEN COMPILED BY ECCLESIASTICS, WERE PUBLISHED UNDER THE AUTHORITY OF THE STATE.

1526, London, Henry VIII, the Archbishop of Canterbury.

1543, Paris, the Sorbonne.

1544, Paris, the Sorbonne.

1545, Lucca, the Inquisition.

1546, Louvain, Theol. Faculty, Emperor Charles V.

1549, Cologne, Synod.

1549, Venice, Casa.

1550, Louvain, Theol. Faculty, Emperor Charles V.

1551, Valentia, Inquisition.

1552, Florence, Inquisition.

1554, Milan, Arcimboldi.

1554, Valladolid, Inquisition.

1554, Venice, Inquisition.

1558, Louvain, Theological Faculty.

1559, Valladolid, Valdés.

1559, Rome, Paul IV.

1564, Trent, Pius IV.

1569, Antwerp, Theological Faculty of Louvain.

1570, Antwerp, Theological Faculty of Louvain.

1571, Antwerp, Theological Faculty of Louvain.

1580, Parma, Inquisition.

1583, Madrid, Quiroga.

1584, Toledo, Inquisition.
1588, Naples, Gregorius.
1590, Rome, Sixtus V.
1596, Rome, Clement VIII.
1607, Rome, Brasichelli.
1612, Madrid, Sandoval.
1617, Cracow, Szyskowski.
1624, Lisbon, Mascarenhas.
1632, Rome, Capsiferro.
1632, Seville, Zapata.
1640, Madrid, Sotomayor.
1664, Rome, Alexander VII.
1670, Clement X.
1682, Innocent XI.
1704, Rome, Innocent XII.
1707, Madrid, Volladores.
1714, Namur and Liège, Hannot.
1729, Königgrätz, Bishop.
1747, Madrid, Prado.
1754, Vienna, Archbishop and Emperor.
1758, Rome, Benedict XIV.
1767, Prague, Archbishop.
1790, Madrid, Cevallos.
1815, Madrid, Inquisitor-General.
1835, Rome, Gregory XVI.
1841, Rome, Gregory XVI.
1865, Rome, Pius IX.
1877, Rome, Pius IX.
1881, Rome, Leo XIII.
1895, Rome, Leo XIII.
1900, Rome, Leo XIII.

No two schedules of Church Indexes or even of papal
Indexes could be prepared that would be in precise

accord with each other. An Index of one date would be reissued some years later with a later date, but sometimes without change of text; in the majority of instances, these later issues carried with them supplements in which were summarised the prohibitions of the years succeeding the original issue. The above schedule, which may be taken as approximately complete, is intended to cover only those Indexes which were issued under the authority of the Church or under the joint authority of the Church and the State, and which, having included, in addition to the classified lists of books condemned, separate "constitutions," decrees, or briefs, may be accepted, at least for purposes of reference, as constituting each a separate Index publication.

The form at present in use for the application, to be addressed to the Pope himself, for a permission, to remain in force during the life-time of the applicant, for the reading of prohibited books is as follows :

Beatissime Pater,

N.N., magister [praeceptor, professor . . .] diocesis N. ad pedes Sanctitatis Vestrae provolutus devotissime petit, ut sibi ad conscientiae suae tranquillitatem in studiis et pro munere suo implendo (vel in honestorum studiorum subsidium) concedatur facultas legendi omnes libros a S. Sede prohibitos, etiam ex professo contra religionem tractantes.

Et Deus. x x x

Ad Sacram Congregationem Indicis,
Romae
Concillaria Apostolica

INDEX

A

Abbadi, Jacques, ii, 2

Abélard, i, 65

About, Edmond, and the Roman Question, ii, 201

"Acceptants," the, and the Bull *Unigenitus*. i, 363 *ff*.

Acta Pauli, i. 1

Acta Sanctorum of the Bollandists, ii. 36, 343

Acton, Lord, writings of, ii, 202, 405, 437

Adames and the censorship of periodicals, ii, 199

Adams, *Vitae Germanorum*, i, 296

Addison, writings of, ii, 405

Adfield, execution of, ii, 259

Adolph, Archbishop of Nassau, ii, 275

Adrian VI, and van der Hulst, i. 94; and censorship, i. 104; adds to Bull *Coenae Domini*, i, 113; and Erasmus, i, 331: ii, 306

Aenaeus Sylvius on the Index, i, 336

d'Aguesseau, and the authority of the pope, ii, 83; on censorship, ii, 454

Ahrens, writings of, ii, 159

Aikenhead, execution of, ii, 264

Albert, Archbishop of Mayence, and censorship, i, 82; and von Hütten, i, 110

Albert of Saxony and Leo X. i, 83

Albert, Elector of Brandeburg, ii, 352

Albert V, Duke of Bavaria, and censorship, i, 216 *ff*.

Aldine Press, the, in Rome, ii, 306

Aldus, Manutius, work of, ii, 290

Aleander and Erasmus, i, 331 *ff*.

d'Alembert, Cyclopædia of, ii, 156

Alexander IV, Bull of, i, 24; and the Inquisition, i, 121

Alexander VI, and Pico della Mirandola, i, 89; Bull of, *Inter Multiplices*. i, 80; and censorship, ii, 281; Bull of, on printing (1501), ii, 350

Alexander VII, Index of, 1664, i, 307 *ff*.; and the five propositions, i, 348 *ff*.; and Oriental literature, ii, 79; and the Gallican Church, ii, 104; and mariology, ii, 141; and the Immaculate Conception, ii, 142; and Attritio, ii, 187

Alexander VIII and the Doctrine of Grace, ii, 4

Alexandria, Council of, i, 60

Alexius, Bishop of Malfi. and Leo X, i, 83

Allen, Cardinal, on Queen Elizabeth, ii, 115

Alletz, the writings of, ii, 190

Alva, Duke of, and censorship, i, 203, 229; ii, 359, 360

Amatus. Cajetanus, ii, 380

Amaury (Amalric), of Chartres, i, 65

America, Spanish censorship in, i, 105

American writings, prohibition of, ii, 67

Anabaptists. the. and censorship, ii, 244, 245, 258; and Münster. ii, 352

André, Ives, on the 101 propositions, i, 370

Anfossi and Settele, i, 314
Antoine, Etienne, Bishop, ii, 175
Antonelli, Cardinal, and the Roman Question, ii, 201
Antonio, St., of Padua, ii, 36
Antwerp, privileges secured by, i, 96; Indexes of, 1569, 1570, 1571, i, 226 ff.; the book-trade of, ii, 359: siege of, ii, 359, 363
Apostolic Brothers, the, i, 67
"Appellants," the, and the Bull *Unigenitus*, i, 363 ff.
Aquinas, Thomas, in Paris, i, 67; writings of, ii, 39, 428
Arabic literature, ii, 291
Aragon, earliest censorship in, ii, 22
d'Aranjo, Bishop, writings of, ii, 198
Arcadius, the emperor, edicts of, i, 59
Archer, John, condemnation of, ii, 263
Archirota and Sirleto, i, 212
Archner, Simon, ii, 442
Arcimboldi, Index of, i, 152
Areopagitica, the, of Milton, i, 54
Aretino in the Index, i, 202
d'Argentré, Duplessis, the *Collectio Judiciorum* of, ii, 221
Ariosto, writings of, ii, 281, 308
Aristotle, and Gregory IX, i, 66; and Descartes, ii, 127; and the Humanists, ii, 284; editions of, ii, 290
Arius, the *Thalia* of, i, 59
Arnauld, and Jansen, i, 346; writings of, i, 358 ff., ii, 405; and the decree of Alexander VIII, ii, 5; on censorship, ii, 451 ff.
Arnold of Brescia, i, 65
Arnold of Villanova, i, 68
Arundel, Archbishop, i, 70
Asgill, John, writings of, ii, 265
Askew, Anne, and the Sistine Index, i, 250
Astrologists, writings of, in the Index, ii, 129 ff.
Astrology and magic, works of, in the Index, i, 202 ff.
Athanasius and the Index, i, 287
Attritio, ii, 186
Aube, writings of, ii, 191

d'Aubigné, Merle, writings of, ii, 172
d'Aubigné, Sieur, History of, ii, 230
Augenspiegel, the, condemned by the universities, i, 83 ff.
Augsburg, Diet of, i, 106; the book-trade of, ii, 354
Augsburger Pact, the, i, 107
Augustine and the Index, i, 287
Augustinus, Thomas de, *Elenchus* of, 1655, 1658, i, 268
Aulic Indexes, the, ii, 219 ff.
Austrian Index, the first, ii, 219
Austrian Netherlands, the Indexes of, ii, 220
Authors, form of "submission" of, to censorship, ii, 64 ff.
Autpert and Stephen III, i, 63
l'Avenir, ii, 182

B

Bacon, writings of, ii, 128 ff.
Badius, publisher, ii, 330
Baillès, Bishop, on censorship, ii, 449, 460
Bailleul on censorship, ii, 223
Baillie, Robert, on the Index, ii, 7
Bailliet, the biographies of the saints, i, 352
Bailly, Louis, writings of, ii, 119
Ballerini, writings of, ii, 151
Balzac, writings of, ii, 85, 164, 405, 435
Bañez, writings of, ii, 39
Barambio and the Regalists, ii, 100
Barclay, John, writings of, ii, 116
Barclay, William, writings of, ii, 116
Bardain, A. A., ii, 61
Barker, Richard, the Bible of, ii, 31
Barlow, Bishop, in the Roman Index, i, 13
Barnes, John, i, 130
Baronius, the *Annales Ecclesiastici* of, ii, 311; and the Catholic Reformation, i, 208; and censorship in Spain, ii, 98; on indulgences, ii, 137; writings of, ii, 405
Barrow, J., execution of, ii, 259
Basel, the book-trade of, ii, 352; censorship in, ii, 239; Council

of, and the Immaculate Conception, ii, 142

Bastwick, J., condemnation of, ii, 262

Bauer, Bruno, writings of, ii, 171, 430

Baur, F. C., writings of, ii, 430

Bavaria, censorship in, ii, 215; College of, censorship of, ii, 220

Bayle, writings of, ii, 405

Beaumarchais, de, P. A. C., writings of, ii, 230

Becanis, Vidal de, Inquisitor, i, 99

Becanus, writings of, ii, 41

Beccatelli and the Index of Trent, i, 181

Béda, Noël, *Confessio Fidei* of, i, 101; and the Scriptures, ii, 21; and Erasmus, ii, 338

Belgian Indexes, 1695–1734, i, 319 *ff.*

Bellarmin, Cardinal, and Galileo, i, 310; on state censorship, ii, 108; on the temporal power, ii, 117; on monarchy, ii, 120; and the Index, ii, 457

Benedict, St., the Rule of, ii, 330

Benedict XIII, and Hebrew writings, i, 73; and the Bull *Unigenitus*, i, 364, 372; ii, 231; and Gregory VII, ii, 109

Benedict XIV, the Index of, i, 14; ii, 49 *ff.*; and the *Augenspiegel*, i, 84; and the Copernican theories, i, 129, 313; and the Congregation of the Index, i, 131; and the writings of Quesnel, i, 366; and the Jesuits, ii, 40, 47; issues Bull *Sollicita ac Provida*, ii, 70; and the Scriptures, ii, 32; regulations of, ii, 74; and Alexander, ii, 108; and Ottieri, ii, 111; and Garrido, ii, 112; and the Freemasons, ii, 131; and the writings of the clergy, ii, 109; and the marriage of converts, ii, 110; and the Roman ritual, ii, 136; and indulgences, ii, 137, and the assumption of the Virgin, ii, 143 *ff.*; and the doctrine of probability, ii, 151; and usury, ii, 152

Benedictines, the, and literature, ii, 428

Bentham, Jeremy, writings of, ii, 158, 405

Benzi, writings of, ii, 151

Béranger, writings of, ii, 164, 405

Berengar of Tours, i, 65

Berg, Adam, publishes Bavarian edition of Tridentine Index, i, 217

Berington, Joseph, on church and state, ii, 113

Berkeley, writings of, ii, 405

Berlin, Index printed in, 1882, ii, 250 *ff.*

Berruyer, writings of, ii, 42 *ff.*

Bert, Paul, writings of, ii, 192, 405

Berthet, André, writings of, ii, 461

Berthold, Archbishop of Mayence, and censorship, i, 78; ii, 348 *ff.*; edict of, ii, 288

Bertram, Inquisitor-General, ii, 236

Beugnot, writings of, ii, 162

Beza and censorship, ii, 239

Bianchi, A., writings of, ii, 172

Bible, the first, printed in England, ii, 31

Bibles, in Germany, ii, 12 *ff.*; Hebrew, ii, 12; in the Index, i, 154–156; Lutheran, censorship of, ii, 237

Bible-Society, the, of Great Britain, and the Scriptures in Spain, ii, 27

Biddle, John, writings of, ii, 262

Bishops, book prohibitions by, ii, 79 *ff.*

Bismarck and the *Kulturkampf*, ii, 251

Blunt, James, writings of, ii, 171

Boccaccio, *Decameron* in Index, i, 168, 200; ii, 309

Bodleian Library, ii, 369 *ff.*

Bodley, Thomas, and the Index of Quiroga, i, 239

Boehme, Jacob, writings of, ii, 129

Boethius, the *de Trinitate* of, i, 65

Bohemian Indexes, 1726–1767, i, 322 *ff.*

Boileau, writings of, ii, 345

Bollandists, the *Acta Sanctorum* of, ii, 36

Bologna, Index of, 1618, i, 267; University of, and Honorius, i, 120

Bolzano, B., writings of, ii, 178

Bonagratia of Bergamo, i, 68

Boniface VIII, Bull of, 1300, ii, 230

Book-Fair of Frankfort and the Index, i, 228 *ff.*; ii, 58

Book-prohibitions, publication of the, ii, 81 *ff.*

Booksellers and the Index of 1546, i, 143 *ff.*

Book-trade, the, of Europe, and the cathedrals, ii, 283; and the Inquisition, i, 123; ii, 323 *ff.*; of France, ii, 328 *ff.*

Books, approved, catalogues of, ii, 86 *ff.*; the burning of, i, 13, ii, 314 *ff.*; the production of, and censorship, ii, 270 *ff.*; recommended for the faithful, ii, 216

Borromeo, St. Charles, and the censorship of the stage, ii, 376

Borrow, George, and the Scriptures in Spain, ii, 27

Bossuet. and the authority of the pope, i, 299; ii, 83; on the Belgian Index, i, 321 *ff.*; and censorship, ii, 340 *ff.*; and Fénelon, ii, 149; and the Gallican controversy, ii, 104; writings of, ii, 405; Life of, by Bauset, ii, 18

Botta, C., writings of, ii, 166

Bourges, Council of, i, 97

Bourget, Bishop, and the Montreal Association, ii, 195 *ff.*

Bower, Archibald, on the papacy, ii, 122

Boyle. Robert. on the Index. ii, 7

Brandenburg, censorship in, ii, 241; the elector of, and censorship, ii, 248

Brasichelli, Index of, 1607, i, 270 *ff.*; ii, 321

Brendel, S., writings of, ii, 179

Breslau, book-trade of, ii, 356

Briggs, Charles A., on the Papal Commission, ii, 470 *ff.*

Brios, writings of, ii, 239

Broedersen on usury, ii, 152

Brothers of Common Life. the, and education. ii. 278; and publishing, ii, 272

Broughton, Hugo, writings of, ii, 84

Browne, Sir Thomas, writings of, ii, 405

Brownists, the, ii, 258

Bruges, first printing in, ii, 358

Bruno, Giordani, i, 266; writings of, ii, 405

Brussels, Privy-Council of, on the difficulties of censorship, i, 298

Bücher-Regal, das. ii, 214

Büchner, writings of. ii, 430

Budaeus, and Erasmus, i, 339; and the Royal College, ii, 335

Bull *Auctorem Fidei,* 1794, ii, 232; *Ad Extirpanda* of Innocent IV, 1252, i, 121; *Contra Impressores,* 1487, i, 108; *Decet Romanum,* 1521, i, 110; the Golden, ii, 214; of Gregory XIII, 1572, i, 221; *Immensa,* 1587, i, 133; *Inter Solicitudines,* i, 82; of Julius III, 1550, i, 215; of Julius III, 1550, for control of book-trade, i, 124; of Leo X, 1518, i, 109; of Leo X, 1520, i, 120; of Paul III, 1542, re-organises Roman Inquisition, i, 122; of Paul IV, 1558, of Pius IV, 1564, of Paul V, 1612, of Gregory XVI, 1623, of Urban VIII, 1627, i, 215; *Reversurus* of 1867, ii, 173; of Sixtus V, 1587, for the regulation of libraries. i, 216

Bull *Coenae Domini,* i. 111 *ff.*. 214 *ff.*: analysed by Ferraris, i, 112; modified by Pius IX, i, 112; publication of, prohibited by various rulers, i, 113; later comments on the, i, 115

Bullinger and the Index of Paul IV, i, 177

Bunsen, writings of, ii, 171

Burgundy, the dukes of, and the early printers, ii, 358 *ff.*

Burke, works of, in the Spanish Index, i, 303

Burnet. Bishop. on the Index, ii, 7; writings of, ii, 405

Burnett, Thomas, *The Sacred Theory of the Earth*, i, 315

Burton, H., condemnation of, ii, 262

Bury, Arthur, condemnation of, ii, 264

Butler, Charles, on the Index, ii, 457

Butler, J., on the Church and the Scriptures, ii, 18

C

Cabbala, the and the Inquisition of Rome i, 75

Cabet, Étienne, writings of, ii, 188

Cagliostro and the Inquisition, ii, 133

Cahagnet, L. A., writings of, ii, 189

Cala, Johannes, ii, 148

Calvin, John, and censorship. ii. 237; on the Diet of Ratisbon, i, 155; the *Institutes* of, a Spanish version of, ii, 316; and Servetus, ii, 332

Calvinistic Church, the, of Holland, and the Copernican System, i, 315

Camden, William, and persecutions under Elizabeth, i, 251

Canada, writings of, in the Index, ii, 194, *ff.*

Canello and the Catholic Reformation. i, 207

Canisius, and censorship in Bavaria, i, 220, ii, 216

Canterbury, Convocation of, and the Scriptures, i, 68, 70

Cantu on Copernicus and the Index, i, 314

Capellis on exorcising, ii, 135

Caporali, writings of, ii, 305

Capucinus, Index of, 1588, i, 241

Caraffa, and the Index of Paul IV, i, 171; and the Inquisition. i, 123; writings of, ii, 144

Carbonari. the, and the Index, ii, 132; writings of the, ii, 64

Carlos III. (of Spain), and the Inquisition, ii, 101; on papal authority, ii, 100

Caron, Abbé, the writings of, ii, 190

Carranza, and Paul III., i, 214; trial of, i, 221 *ff.*; and Valdes, i, 163

Carter, execution of, ii, 259

Casa. Index of. 1549, i, 148

Casaubon and Baronius, ii, 311 *ff.*; and Geneva, ii, 334; in Paris, ii, 334; and the Index, i, 286; on the Index, ii, 7; and State censorship, ii, 108; writings of, ii, 275

Castiglioni, Bernardo, and the Index of Trent, i, 916

Castro, Alphonso de, on the Index, i, 20

Castro, L. de, and the Scriptures, ii, 21

Casuists, the, and the Index, ii, 45 *ff.*; the propositions of. and the Index, i, 374 *ff.*

Catalani, on the oath of allegiance, ii, 113

Catalans, the, and censorship, ii, 323

Catalogus Haereticorum, i, 23

Cathari and the Scriptures, ii, 22

Caxton, William, ii, 358 *ff.*, 366 *ff.*

Caylus, Bishop, writings of, i, 366

Cazalla, Maria, and the reading of the Scriptures, ii, 24

Cecco d'Ascoli. i, 68

Celso. Hugo de, and censorship in Spain, ii, 318

Censorship, to what authorities committed, i, 137 *ff.*; of the Church, the beginnings of, i, 1 *ff.*; damages incurred under, i, 138, 139; and the distribution of literature, i, 32 *ff.*; in the early Church, i, 58; in England, ii, 367 *ff.*; regulations in Bavaria, 1561–1582, i, 216 *ff.*; decrees, 1624–1661, i, 279 *ff.*

Cervantes, writings of, ii, 131
Cevallos, and the authority of the pope, ii, 99; Index of, 1790, i, 299
"Chaldean" literature, ii, 290 *ff*.
Chancellery, the, of Rome, ii, 426
Charles III (of Spain) and censorship, ii, 327 *ff*.
Charles IV (of Spain) and censorship, ii, 328
Charles V, Emperor, ii, 212; and Bull *Coenae Domini*, i, 113; censorship edicts of, i, 95 *ff.* 116; and censorship in Spain, ii, 319; and the censorship of the stage, ii, 378; censorship under, i, 93 *ff*.; and Erasmus, i, 332 *ff*.; and the Index of 1551, i, 153; and Leo X., contract between, i, 85
Charles X (of France), Index of, ii, 229
Charron, writings of, ii, 109, 406
Chateaubriand, edict of, i, 100–103; writings of, ii, 212, 225
Checcazzi, G., trial of, ii, 296
Chénier, André, and censorship, ii, 225
Chevé, C. F., writings of, ii, 188
Chinese usages, the, in the Index, ii, 146
Christopher of Padua and the Index of Paul IV, i, 174
Chrysostom, St., and the Index, i, 288
Church and State, issues between, ii, 90 *ff*.
Churches of the East, writings concerning the, ii, 122 *ff*.
Ciampini, Cardinal, ii, 76
Ciocci, writings of, ii, 163
Cistercians, the, and literature, ii, 428
Civil power, the, and censorship, ii, 206 *ff*.
Civiltà Cattolica, the, on censorship, ii, 450 *ff*.
Clarke, Samuel, writings of, ii, 265
Clarkson, Lawrence, condemnation of, ii, 263

Claudius, i, 64
Clement IV and Hebrew writings, i, 73
Clement VI and d'Autrecourt, i, 69
Clement VIII, and Bellarmin, ii, 42; cancels Sistine Index, i, 253 *ff*.; Index of, i, 253 *ff*.; and the Congregation of the Index, i, 133, 253; and the Casuists, ii, 45; and censorship in Spain ii, 97, ii, 322 *ff*.; grants dispensation to scholars, 1591, i, 216; and Hebrew writings, i, 25, 75; the Index of, in Venice, ii, 296; and Molina, ii, 69; and the printing of Bibles, i, 190, ii, 299; and Suarez, ii, 46
Clement IX, and the five propositions. i, 349 *ff*.; the "Peace" of. i, 357 *ff*.
Clement X, and the Congregation of the Index, ii, 77; and the Immaculate Conception, ii, 142; Index of, 1670, i, 324; and the Jesuits, ii, 40
Clement XI, Index of, 1681, i, 324; and issues with the State, ii, 110; and the 101 propositions, i, 361 *ff*.; and Quesnel, i, 360 *ff*.
Clement XII, and the Freemasons, ii, 131 *ff*.
Clement XIII, and the Duke of Parma, ii, 114; and Helvetius, ii, 80; and the Jesuits, ii, 40, 43
Clement XIV, and the bishops, ii, 81; and the Bull *Coenae Domini*, i, 114; and Hebrew writings, i, 76; and the Jesuits, ii, 43
Cloquet, Abbé, writings of, ii, 190
Cock, Theodor, and the church of Utrecht. i, 359 *ff*.
Codde, Peter, and the church of Utrecht, i, 359 *ff*.
Coerbach, A., and censorship, ii, 254
Colbert, Bishop, writings of, i, 366
Collins, A., writings of, ii, 406

Cologne, censorship in, ii., 248; an early *imprimatur* in, ii, 348; Index of, 1629, i, 269; the printers of, i, 77; Synod of, i, 106; University of, and censorship, i, 77, 109; and Luther, i. 342: and the Scriptures, ii. 11; and the beginning of printing, ii, 11; and Sixtus V, i, 77

Colonto, Abraham, printer of Bibles, ii, 12

Columbus, Christopher, as a bookseller's apprentice, ii, 313 *ff.*

Combe, George, writings of, ii, 406

Comes, Natalis, and the Index of Paul IV., i, 177

Comendon, Cardinal, sent as Catholic missionary to Germany, i. 216

Communism, ii, 188 *ff.*

Como, book-trade of, i, 126

Comte, A., writings of, ii, 160, 406

Concina, writings of, ii, 151

Concordat, the French, of 1801, of 1817, ii, 170; the, of Napoleon, ii, 233; the, of Venice and the pope, ii, 296 *ff.*

Condillac, writings of, ii, 159

Condorcet, writings of, ii, 159, 400, 406

Congregatio de Propaganda Fide, the, ii, 77

Congregation of the Index, i, 5, 116 *ff.*, 131; ii, 134, 169; and Benedict XIV, ii, 70 *ff.*; and Pius V, ii, 96; and Gregory XIII, ii, 96; organisation of the, ii, 427

Congregation, the, on usury, ii, 153 *ff.*

Conrad of Lichtenau, writings of, ii, 435

Constant, Benjamin, writings of, ii, 177

Constant, L. A., writings of, ii, 188

Constantine, the Emperor, ii, 420

Constantinople, the sack of, ii, 292

Contemporary Review, the, and censorship, ii, 417 *ff.*

Convention, the, of 1793, and censorship, ii, 222 *ff.*

Conwell, Bishop H., and the Index, ii, 194

Copernican theory, condemnation of the, i, 309 *ff.*

Copernicus, and censorship in Spain, ii, 326; and the Inquisition, i, 128 *ff.*; writings of, ii, 74

Copping, execution of, ii, 258

Coquerel, A., writings of, ii, 172

Cordier, M., in the Index, i, 160

Cornaldi on Rosmini, ii, 185

Corneille, writings of, ii, 345

Corpus Juris Canonici, i, 225

Cortes, the, and the liberty of the press, ii, 27

Cosmo, Duke of Tuscany, and the Index of Paul IV, i, 178

Coton, writings of, ii, 42

Council of Alexandria, 1, 60; of Basel, i, 70; of Constantinople, i, 62; of Ephesus, i, 60; of Trulla, i, 62; of Rome, i, 62, of the Lateran, i, 66, 108; of Narbonne, 1227, i, 118; of Nicaea, i, 59; of Ten and censorship, ii, 293; of Toulouse, 1229, i, 119; of Trent, the, and *attritio,* ii, 187; of the Vatican, 1867, ii, 201; of Vienna and Segarelli, i, 67

Councils of the French Church in the 19th century, ii, 449

Cousin, writings of, ii, 159

Coward, Wm., writings of, ii, 264

Cracow, Index of, 1617, i, 289 *ff.*

Cranmer, Thomas, the Bible of, ii, 31

Creighton, Robert, on the Greek and Latin churches, ii, 122

Cremonini, Cesari, i, 130

Creutzer, condemnation of, ii, 357

Cromwell, Oliver, and censorship, ii, 262 *ff.*

Cromwell, Thomas, and the Scriptures, i, 88

Curia, the, ii, 426

Cyclopaedists, writings of the, ii, 81

D

Dalmeida, Index of, 1581, i, 235 *ff*.

Dal Pozzo on Catholicism in Austria, ii, 113

Dannemayer, writings of, ii, 178

Dante, in the Index, i, 200; writings of, ii. 281, 308: and John XXII, ii, 200

Darwin, Erasmus, writings of, ii, 159, 406

Daubenton, and Fénelon, ii, 75; on the writings of Quesnel, i, 368 *ff*.

David of Dinant, i, 66

Davy, Jacques, ii, 374

Decreta Generalia of Benedict XIV, ii, 50 *ff*.

Defoe, condemnation of, ii. 265: writings of, ii. 131. 408

Degola, T. A., ii, 61

Dejob, and the Council of Trent, i, 204 *ff*., ii, 106; on the editions of the Fathers, ii, 342 *ff*.; on Italian literature, ii, 312 *ff*.; on the literature of France, ii, 344 *ff*.; on the Papacy, ii, 478 *ff*.

De Marca, ii, 102

Denmark, censorship in, ii, 255

Denunciation of books, the, i. 137

De Placette on the doctrines of Jansen, i, 348

Descartes, on the Belgian Index, i, 319; writings of, ii, 127, 406

Deventer, printing in, ii, 272

De Vic, ii, 334

Diderot, the Cyclopaedia of, ii, 156; writings of, ii, 170, 406

Didier, writings of, ii, 163

Diet, of Nuremberg, i, 106; of Augsburg, i, 106; of Speyer, the, i, 107

Directorium Inquisitorium. i. 23, 85

Dispensations, Congregation of, ii, 434

Divine Comedy, the, expurgation of, ii, 322

Dod, the *Church History* of, ii, 458

Dolet, Estienne, condemnation of, ii, 338

Döllinger, doctrines of, ii, 437; writings of, ii, 202

Dominic, St., first *Magister Palatii*, i, 134

Dominicans, the, and censorship, i, 137. ii, 44 *ff*., 217, 427 *ff*.: and the Jews, ii, 44; and the doctrine of probability, ii, 151; and Gregory IX, i, 120; and the Immaculate Conception, ii, 141 *ff*.; and the Inquisition i, 119, 127

Dominis, M. A. de, i, 130

Don Quixote, the expurgation of, ii, 322

Dort, Synod of (1618), ii, 364

Drama, the, of Spain, and censorship, ii, 325 *ff*.

Draper. J. W., in the Index, ii, 159, 194, 407

Dublin Review, the, and Aquinas, i, 67; and the condemnation of Galileo, i, 314

Ducal commission of censorship in Bavaria, 1566, i, 217

Dumas, A., (fils), writings of, ii, 407, 435

Dumas, A., (père), writings of, ii, 85, 164, 407, 435

Dunoyer, Mme., writings of, ii, 131

Dupanloup, Bishop, and the Roman Question, ii, 201; writings of, ii, 202

Dupin, writings of, ii, 107, 119

Dupont, *History of Printing*, of, ii, 222

Dupuis, C. F., writings of, ii, 176

Duvoisey, Bishop of Exeter, and censorship, i, 86

E

Earle, C. J., writings of. ii, 177, 407

Eastern Church, writings concerning the, ii, 173

Eck, Chancellor, and the Index of Bavaria, i, 217

Eckart, the Dominican, writings of, i, 68, 69

Education and the Church, i, 10

Edward VI and censorship, i, 90

Ehrhart, the *Catholicism in the 20th Century* of, ii, 445

Elizabeth of England, censorship edict of, i, 93; and censorship, i, 92 *ff.*, 274, ii. 258 *ff.*; and Sixtus V. ii. 115

Elzevir, Louis, publishing undertakings of, ii, 364

Enfantin, B. P., writings of, ii, 407

England, censorship in, i, 86 *ff.*, ii, 256 *ff.*; the Scriptures in, ii, 29 *ff.*; and the Papacy, ii, 115 *ff.*

English statute *De Heretico Comburendo*, i, 121; theologians and the Index, ii, 6 *ff.*; oath of allegiance, ii, 116 *ff.*

Epistolae Obscurorum Virorum. i, 85, ii, 284

Erasmus, in the Index, i, 166, 197, 284, 287, 328 *ff.*; *Adagia* of, authorised by Gregory XIII, i, 225; the New Testament of, ii, 14 *ff.*; writings of, ii, 275; and censorship in Basel, ii, 239; and Froben, ii, 353; and his opponents in France, ii, 338; and the Reformation, i, 46; ii, 285; and Richelieu, ii, 44; on Luther, ii, 287

Erfurt. University of. i, 78

Erigena (Johannes Scotus), writings of, ii, 407

Erskine, Cardinal, and the Bull *Coenae Domini*, i, 115

Escobar, writings of, ii, 237

Espen, van, on the Belgian Index, i, 321

Espencé and censorship, i, 103

Esquidos, H. A., writings of, ii, 188

Esser, Thos., ii, 388

Estienne, (Stephanus), Henry ii, 330 *ff.*

Estienne, Henry (the second), in Geneva, ii, 332 *ff.*

Estienne, Robert, in Roman Index, i, 173; Bibles of, i, 102; New Testament of, ii, 15 *ff.*; in Geneva, ii, 332 *ff.*

L'Estrange, Roger, and censorship, ii, 262 *ff.*

Eugenius IV and Favorini, i, 70

Eunomians, books of the, i, 59

Excommunication, forms and penalties of, i, 114; a weapon of censorship. ii, 206 *ff.*

Exorcising, manuals for, in the Index, ii, 134 *ff.*

Expurgation of books, the, i, 19

Eybel, von, *Was ist der Pabst?* i, 326, ii, 114, 414

Eymeric, Nicholas, i, 23, 69, 85, 121, ii 23; *Directory of Heresy* of, i, 85

F

Falcioni. writings of, ii, 134

"Family of Love," the, ii, 259

Fanus, V., i, 308

Fathers, the, corruption of the text of, i, 277 *ff.*

Faure, on excommunication, i, 114; writings of, ii, 151

Favorini the Eremite, i, 70

Fénelon, and the authority of the pope, ii, 83 *ff.*; and Daubenton, ii, 75; on the Bull *Unigenitus*, i, 369 *ff.*; on the reading of the Scriptures, ii, 17; and the Roman Index, i, 325 *ff.*, ii, 149, 407; and Louis XIV, ii, 145

Ferdinand, Emperor, and censorship, ii, 213, 356: and Erasmus, i, 334 *ff.*

Ferdinand VII, of Spain, censorship under, ii, 236

Ferdinand and Isabella and censorship, ii, 314

Ferrara, publishing in, ii, 309

Ferrari, writings of, ii, 161

Ferraris, analyses prohibitions in Bull *Coenae Domini*, i, 112

Ferri, E., writings of, ii, 407

Ferry, Jules, on censorship, ii, 192, 461

Fesque. Jean. condemnation of. ii, 320

Feuerbach, writings of, ii, 430

Feydeau, E., writings of, ii, 407, 435

Feyjoo, Benito, and censor-
ship, ii, 326
Ffoulkes, E. S., writings of, ii,
174
Fichte, writings of, ii, 251
Figuier, writings of, ii, 160
Fischer, Gabriel, and censor-
ship, ii, 249
Fisher, John, in the Index, 155
Flaubert, writings of, ii, 162
Flemish Index, an early exam-
ple, i, 22
Fleury, writings of, ii, 108
Florence, Index of, 1552, i, 150;
publishing in, ii, 309
Fludd, writings of, ii, 128 ff.
Flugschriften, the, of Witten-
berg, i, 44
Fontainebleau, edict of, ii, 337
Fontanelle, writings of, ii, 407
Foscarini, and the Copernican
doctrine, i, 312; and the Inqui-
sition, i, 128 ff.
Foscolo, writings of, ii, 165
Fotvárad, writings of, ii, 198
Fouché, and censorship, ii, 224
Fourier, Charles, writings of,
ii, 188, 407
Fox's *Acts and Monuments*,
i, 89
Fox, John, and Dante, i, 201
France, censorship in, i, 16, 26,
30 ff., 96 ff., ii, 282; pub-
lishing in, ii, 276 ff.; and the
Index of Trent, 195; and the
Papal authority, ii, 83 ff.
Francis I, censorship edicts of,
i, 97 ff.; and the early printers, ii, 330 ff.; and Erasmus,
i, 332 ff.; and Estienne, ii, 15
ff.; and Paul IV, appoint
Inquisitors, i, 102; and the
Royal College, ii, 335; and
the University of Paris, ii, 338
Francis, St., de Sales, on censorship, ii, 453
Francis, St., Sons of, ii, 35 ff.
Franciscans, the, and censorship in the Netherlands, ii,
360; and censorship, ii, 428
ff.; and the Inquisition, i, 119
Franco, Niccolo, Bishop of Treviso, and censorship, i, 79, ii,
297

Francolinus, B., writings of,
i, 375
Francus, Daniel, writings of,
ii, 134
Fraudulent literature in the Index, ii, 147
Frankfort, and censorship, ii,
215; Book-Fair of, ii, 58, 347,
362 ff.; and the Index of 1570,
i, 228; and the book-trade,
ii, 279 ff.
Frankfort Fair, the, and the
Sistine Index, i, 249; cata-
logues of the, ii, 76
Frederick II (of Prussia), writings of, ii, 158, 407; and Vol-
taire, ii, 251
Frederick II (of Denmark), and
censorship, ii, 242, 249
Frederick II, the Emperor, and
the Inquisition, i, 119–120
Frederick William of Prussia,
and censorship, ii, 250
Freemasonry, writings on, in the
Index, ii, 131 ff.
French Revolution, the, writ-
ings on, ii, 168 ff.
Frevorius, writings of, ii, 114
Fride, life by, of Mary Ward,
ii, 38
Froben, J., ii, 13 ff., 353
Frohschammer, J., writings of,
180 ff., 407
Froschauer, Christ., and Zwin-
gli, ii, 12; and the printing of
Bibles, ii, 12; and Zwingli, ii,
354
Froude, on censorship, ii, 257
Fust, Johannes, and the print-
ing of Bibles, ii, 12

G

Galileo, and the Inquisition, i
128 ff.; the condemnation of,
i, 309 ff.; writings of, ii, 365
Galliard, and the Royal College,
ii, 335
Gallican Church, controversies
concerning the, ii, 101 ff.
Gandolphy, writings of, ii, 68,
177, 407
Garrido, writings of, ii, 112
Gassendi, writings of, ii, 127

Gattinara to Erasmus, ii, 318

Gelasius I, decree of, i, 61

Gemara, the Babylonian, condemned, i, 72

Geneva, censorship in, ii, 237, 333 *ff.*; journals of, in the Index, ii, 200; publishing in, ii, 332 *ff.*; siege of, ii, 333 *ff.*

Gentilis, condemnation of, ii, 239

George, David, ii, 259

George, Duke, of Saxony, and censorship, ii, 350 *ff.*

Gerberon, and censorship, i, 357 *ff.*; and the decree of Alexander VIII, ii, 5

Gering, ii, 329

Germany, the book-trade of, ii, 347 *ff.*; censorship in, i, 38, 105 *ff.*, ii, 240, *ff.*; and the Index of Trent, i, 195

Gesta Romanorum, i, 165

Ghisberti. V., writings of, ii. 184

Ghislieri, Cardinal. burns Hebrew books, i, 74; and the case of Carranza, i, 223 *ff.*; and the Inquisition, i, 123; Inquisitor at Como, i, 126

Giannone, writings of, ii, 111

Gibbon, Edward, the history of, ii, 157, 407

Gieseler, on the 101 propositions, i, 369 *ff.*

Giornale Ecclesiastico, the, ii, 414

Giunti, the, in Florence, ii, 310

Goethe. writings of. ii. 212. 251, 255

Goethe-Bund, the, and censorship, ii, 252

Goldsmith, writings of, ii, 161, 407

Gonzalez, T., on the morality of the Jesuits, i, 374 *ff.*

Görres, writings of, ii, 250

Gothenburg, Index of, ii, 256

Gottschalk, i, 64

Grace, the doctrine of, ii, 2 *ff.*, 39

Gratian, Emperor, decree of, i, 61

Gravina, writings of, ii, 193

Greek, the study of, in France, ii. 335 *ff.*; literature and censorship, ii, 290

Greenwood. execution of, ii, 259

Gregorovius, writings of, ii, 162, 407

Gregory VII, and the Immaculate Conception, ii, 142; and the Patriarch of Aquileia, ii, 113

Gregory IX, condemns the Talmud, i, 25, 72; and Aristotle, i, 66; and the Dominicans, i, 120; and the Inquisition, i, 120

Gregory XI., condemnation by, i, 69

Gregory XII, and the printing-press, ii, 306

Gregory XIII, Bull of 1572, i, 221; Bull of 1580, ii, 232; adds to Bull *Coenae Domini*, i, 113, and the Bible of Plantin, ii, 20; and Boccaccio, ii, 310; and censorship, i, 221 *ff.*; and the censorship of the stage, ii, 376; and the Congregation of the Index, i, 131 *ff.*; and the *Corpus Juris Canonici*, i, 225; and Erasmus, i, 333

Gregory XIV, and Henry of Navarre, ii, 232

Gregory XV, and the Congregation of the Index ii, 77; and the Council of Trent, ii, 78; *Monitum* of, on the Scriptures, ii, 33; *Monitum* of, ii, 64; and La Mennais, ii, 181; and the Melchites, ii, 173; and Rosmini, ii, 184 *ff.*

Gregory of Hamburg, excommunicated, i. 71

Gretser, on the prohibition of Bertram, i, 18; on Protestant censorship, ii, 245; and Paul IV, i, 169

Greville, Fulke, *Life of Sir Philip Sidney*, i, 301

Greville, Mme. Henri, writings of, ii, 192

Grimaldi, writings of, ii, 127

Grotius, writings of, ii, 6, 85, 212, 253, 407, 435

Gruppenbach, and censorship, ii. 356

Guadognini. writings of, ii. 169

Guerrazzi, writings of, ii, 165

Guettée, Abbé, writings of, ii, 119

Guibord, the burial of, ii, 196 *ff.*
Guicciardini, writings of, i, 200, ii, 84, 408
Guise, Duke of, and censorship, ii, 33
Guldenstubbe, L. V., writings of, ii, 189
Gunther, A., writings of, ii, 180
Gustavus Adolphus, ii, 358
Gutenberg, and printing, ii, 272 *ff.*
Gutzkow, C., writings of, ii, 430
Guyon, Mme., writings of, ii, 148

H

Haeckel, writings of, ii, 430
Hall, Bishop, on the Index, ii, 7
Hallam, writings of, ii, 162, 408
Hamburg, censorship in, ii, 252
Hannot, Index of, 1714, i, 298; Index of, 1719, i, 319
d'Harcourt, Maréchal, definition of "Jansenist," i, 365
Hardouin, writings of, ii, 42
Harlay, Index of, 1685, i, 317
Harnack, A., writings of, ii, 445
Havet, writings of, ii, 191
Heart of Jesus, the, festival of, ii, 167
Hebrew, the study of, in France, ii, 291, 335 *ff.*
Hebrew printers in Spain, ii, 313
Hebrew writings, destruction of, i, 25; prohibition of, i, 72 *ff.*
Hegel on censorship, ii, 276 *ff.*
Heidelberg, book-trade of, ii, 356; an early *imprimatur* in, ii, 348; University of, and Eckart, i, 69
Heine, writings of, ii, 130, 164
Heinrich, Duke of Mecklenburg, ii, 244
Heinze, the law of, ii, 252
Helvetius, writings of, ii, 80, 156
Henriquez, writings of, ii, 45; and the authority of the pope, ii, 99
Henry of Navarre, and Sixtus V, ii, 232; and Gregory XIV, ii, 232
Henry II, censorship edict of, i, 100

Henry III, and the Bull *Coenae Domini*, i, 113; and censorship, i, 103
Henry IV and literature, ii, 334
Henry VIII, censorship under, i, 41, 86 *ff.*, ii, 257
Herbert of Cherbury, writings of, ii, 128, 408
Hereford, Nicholas, i, 70
Heresbach and the study of Greek and Hebrew, ii, 336
Heresiarchs, list of, 1549, i, 151; in the Index of Quiroga, i, 240; in the Sistine Index, i, 247
Hermann of Ryswick, burned, i, 81
Hermes, George, writings of, ii, 180
Herrgott, J., execution of, ii, 351
Heymans on censorship, ii, 449
Hichins, William (Tyndale), i, 92
Hieronymites, ii, 36
Hieronymus, Bishop of Ascoli, and Luther, i, 109
Hilgers, on Benedict XIV, ii, 60; on censorship, i, 52, 78 *ff.*, ii, 207 *ff.*, 428 *ff.*; on the Jansenists, ii, 227; on Jesuit censorship, ii, 216 *ff.*; on Luther, ii, 245 *ff.*; on morality, ii, 462 *ff.*; on Protestant censorship, ii, 245 *ff.*, 268 *ff.*; on the reading of the Scriptures, ii, 33 *ff.*
Hincmar, i, 64
Hirscher, J. B., writings of, ii, 179
Hobbes, Thomas, writings of, ii, 85, 128, 253, 408
Hogan, W., and the Index, ii, 194
d'Holbach, writings of, ii, 175
Holland, censorship in, i, 40, ii, 253 *ff.*
Hollybushe, John, Bible of, ii, 31
Holstenius and Peiresc, ii, 75
Honorius and the University of Bologna, i, 120
Hoogstraaten, Jacob, and Reuchlin, i, 84 *ff.*, 337 *ff.*
Hopelcheen, censorship in, ii, 320
Houssaye, writings of, ii, 124
Houtin, Abbé, writings of, ii, 444

Hovius, H., ii. 362
Hübmayer, execution of, ii, 351
Hügel, Baron Friedrich von, on the Papal Commission, ii, 470 *ff.*
Hugo, Cardinal, the Bible of, ii, 12 *ff.*
Hugo, Victor, writings of, ii, 164, 408
Hulst, Franz van der, permit to, i, 93; appointed inquisitor, i. 94
Humanistic movement, the, ii, 278 *ff.*
Humanists, the, ii, 284, 294; and the authority of the Church, ii, 11 *ff.*
Hume, David, writings of, ii, 85, 155, 161, 435
Huss, John, i, 70
Hussites, condemned by Julius II, i, 111; writings of the, i, 71, ii, 355
Hutchinson, John, the *Principia of Moses*, i, 315
Hutten, Ulrich v.. in the Index, i, 155
Hutton, W H., i, 326

I

Immaculate Conception, the doctrine of, ii, 141 *ff.*, 437; writings on the, ii, 64
Index, the, as a guide for book-buyers, i, 42; as a serial, 1581, i, 220; Congregation of the, institution of the, i, 131
Index of books commended, Bavaria, 1569, i. 217
Index Revision and Reform, ii, 411 *ff.*
Index Librorum Haereticorum of the Frankfort Fair, ii, 362
Indexes, the, as guides for publishers, ii, 365 *ff.*, papal, the series of, i, 4; schedule of, ii, 480 *ff.*
Indulgences, the Congregation of, ii, 138; fraudulent, ii, 136
Infallibility of the pope, the, ii, 414 *ff.*
Inglis, Sir Robert, and the condemnation of Galileo, i. 311

Ingolstadt, University of, and censorship, ii, 215
Innocent I and Pelagius, i, 60
Innocent III, i, 65
Innocent IV, issues, 1252, Bull *Ad Extirpanda*, i, 121; and Louis IX, i, 73; and Talmudic writings, i, 73
Innocent VIII, Bull of *Contra Impressores*, i, 108; Bull of 1486, ii, 288; and the University of Cologne, i, 78
Innocent X and the (so called) propositions of Jansen, i, 346 *ff.*
Innocent XI, and Alexander, ii, 107; and Bossuet, ii, 104; and Louis XIV, ii, 104; and the doctrine of grace, ii, 3; and the Gallican controversy, ii, 106
Innocent XII, ii, 36; and Arnauld, ii, 451; and indulgences, ii, 138
Innocent XIII and the Bull *Unigenitus*. i, 364
Inquisition, the, in Central America, ii, 320; in the Middle Ages, i, 117 *ff.*; in France, i, 125; in Germany, i, 125; in Italy, i, 125; in Spain, i, 119, 125, ii, 26, 282, 316, 322 *ff.*: of Rome, i, 116, 123, 126, ii, 434; of Tarragona, i, 68; originated in Paradise, i, 127; burns Hebrew books, i, 74; and the Cabbala, i, 75; and Galileo and Copernicus, i, 128; and Hermann of Ryswick, i, 81; and Alexander IV, i. 121; and censorship in Venice, ii. 296: and the censorship of the stage, ii, 377 *ff.*; and the Copernican doctrine, i, 312 *ff.*; and the Freemasons, ii, 132 *ff.*; and Gregory IX, i, 120; and the art of printing, i, 121; and Philip the Fair, i, 121; and Settele, i, 314; and Urban IV, i, 121; and the writings of Jansen, i, 345 *ff.*
Italian, book-trade and the Inquisition, i, 123; *Giornale Ecclesiastico*, 1785–1798, i,

Italian (*Continued*) 326; patriotism and censorship, ii, 308; Protestant writings in the Index, ii, 126

Italy, censorship in, i, 29, 36 *ff.*, introduction of printing into, ii, 288; publishing in, ii, 273

J

Jacobins, the, and censorship, ii, 223

Jacolliot, writings of, ii, 191

James I (of England), and censorship, i, 266 *ff.*, ii, 259 *ff.*; writings of ii, 408; and Paul V, ii, 115; and the oath of allegiance, ii, 116 *ff.*; in the Index, i, 292

James, Thomas, *Index Generalis* of, i, 12, 270, ii, 369 *ff.*; and the Index of Quiroga, i, 239; on the editions of the Fathers, i, 278

Jansen, Cornelius, the writings of, i, 345 *ff.*, ii, 405; five propositions ascribed to, i, 346 *ff.*

Jansenist controversy, the, i, 345 *ff.*

Jansenist writings, i, 320 *ff.*, ii, 69 *ff.*

Jansenists, the, and censorship, ii, 451 *ff.*; and the French Revolution, ii, 227; and the Scriptures, ii, 32

Jena, censorship in, ii, 241; Index printed in, 1844, ii, 250

Jenson, the first nobleman among publishers, ii, 292

Jerome of Prague, i, 70

Jesuits, the, writings of, ii, 37 *ff.*, 237; in Germany, ii, 43; and censorship, ii, 428 *ff.*, 451 *ff.*; and censorship in Bavaria, i, 218; and censorship in the Empire, ii, 214, 357 *ff.*; and the Chinese and Malabar usages ii, 146; and the doctrine of probability, ii, 151; and the Index of Brasichelli, i, 276 *ff.*; and theological morality, i, 374 *ff.*

Jewish literature in the Index, ii, 123

Jobez, writings of, ii, 162

John XXI and the Schoolmen, i, 67

John XXII, condemnations by, i, 67 *ff.*

John of Jaudun, i, 68

Johnson, Samuel, on Francis Osborne, ii, 125

Jones, Spencer, *England and the Holy See*, ii, 432

Joris, David, condemnation of, ii, 238

Joseph I of Portugal, censorship under, ii, 236 *ff.*

Joseph II (of Austria) and the University of Pavia, ii, 174

Josephus, Michael, on the works of heretics, i, 296 *ff.*

Julius II, issues Bull *Coenae Domini*, 1511, i, 111; specifies sects classed as heretical, i, 111; and Louis XII, ii, 231

Julius III, brief of, 1551, permitting certain cardinals to read heretical books, i, 215; Bull of 1550, for control of book-trade, i, 124, 215; orders destruction of Hebrew, books i, 25, 74; and censorship, i, 105

Julius, Duke of Brunswick, and censorship, ii, 243

Jurists, writings of, in the Index, ii, 125

Justinian, Emperor, condemns books of Severus, i, 62

Justiniani, the history of Venice of, ii, 295 *ff.*

Juvencius on the Jesuits, ii, 147

K

Kant, writings of, ii, 158, 252, 408

Kapp, F., on book-production in Germany, ii, 270 *ff.*; on censorship in Germany, ii, 357

Kardec, Allan, writings of, ii, 189

Kempis, Thomas à, the "Imitation" of, ii, 411

Kepler, J., and censorship, ii, 248; and the Inquisition, i, 128 *ff.*

Kidder, Bishop, on French editions of the Testament, ii, 17

Kirchof and the German book-trade, i, 196

Koberger, A., and the Bible of Hugo, ii, 12 *ff.*; the publications of, ii, 354

Koniasch, Index of, 1760, i, 323

Königgrätz, Index of, 1729, i, 322

Koran, the, in the Index, i, 155

Köstlin on the writings of Luther, i, 343 *ff.*

Kotzebue and censorship, ii. 225

Kracow, Index of, 1603, i. 269; Index of, 1617, i, 269

Krantz, ii, 329

Kranz, Albert, *Historia Ecclesiastica*, i, 165

Krause (*Carus-Sterne*), writings of, ii, 430

Kulturkampf, the, ii, 2, 51

L

La Bigne, *Bibliotheca* of, expurgated by Brasichelli. i. 273: censored, i. 274

Laborde on usury, ii, 152

La Bruyère, writings of, ii, 344

La Châtre, writings of, ii, 163

Lacombe, writings of, ii, 150

Lacordaire, ii, 182 *ff.*

La Fontaine, writings of, ii, 170

La Guérronnière, writings of, ii, 201

Lajollais, de, Natalie, writings of, ii, 192

Lalande, writings of, ii, 163

Lamartine, writings of, ii, 164, 408

Lambardi, writings of. ii, 149

La Mennais, Abbé, writings of. ii, 181 *ff.*, 408

Lanfrey, writings of, ii, 408

Lang, Andrew, writings of, ii, 408

La Riva, writings of, ii, 198

Laroque, writings of, ii, 191

Lasalle and censorship, ii, 251

Lateran, Council of the, 1215, i, 66; 1516, i, 108

Latin the language of literature, ii, 275

Latin classics, editions of, in the Index, ii, 123

Latinus, i, 134; and the Index of Paul IV, i, 176

Launoy, de, writings of, ii, 107, 408

Laylande on the writings of Galileo, i, 314

Lazzeretti, writings of, ii, 193

Lea, Henry C., on censorship in Spain, ii, 324 *ff.;* on the Inquisition in the Middle Ages, i, 117 *ff.*; on the Papal Inquisition, i, 122: on the Scriptures in Spain, ii, 26

Lead tablets, chronicles of the, ii, 147 *ff.*

Le Bas, writings of, ii, 162

Lee, Edward, and Erasmus, i, 332

Lee, F. G., writings of, ii, 178

Lee, Roger, and Mary Ward, ii, 38

Legate, Bartholomew, burning of, ii, 257

Legrand, writings of, ii, 160

Leibnitz, writings of, ii, 435

Leighton, A., condemnation of, ii, 261

Leipsic, the book-trade of, ii, 350 *ff.*; censorship in, ii, 242 *ff.*, 351 *ff.*

Leo I condemns heretical writings. i, 61

Leo X, Bull of, 1519, i, 109; coronation of i, 81; issues (1521) Bull *Decet Romanum*, i, 110; issues, 1520, the Bull *Exurge*, i, 110; issues, 1515, Bull *Inter Solicitudines*, i, 82; and Cardinal Wolsey, i, 110; and censorship in Spain. i, 104; and Charles V, contract between, i, 85; and the *Epistolae obscurorum virorum*, i, 85; and Erasmus, i, 331 *ff.*; and literature, ii, 276; and Luther and von Hütten, i, 110; and the *Magister*, i, 133; and permits for heretical reading, i, 214; and the Testament of Erasmus, ii, 15

Leo XII, on the use of the Scriptures, ii, 28; on the Bible Societies, ii, 28; *mandatum* of, ii, 62 *ff.*; and censor-

Leo XII (*Continued*)
ship, ii, 443; and La Mennais,
ii, 181
Leo XIII, Indexes of, ii, 62, 379,
ff.; and Benedict XIV, ii,
60; and censorship, ii, 443;
and Father Tyrrell, ii, 467 *ff*.,
and "Romanus," ii, 417 *ff*.,
and Rosmini, ii, 186; and von
Hügel, ii, 472
Leopardi, writings of, ii, 161,
305
Lequeux, J. F. M., writings of,
ii, 119
Lessing, writings of, ii, 164, 408
Leti, Gregorio, writings of, ii,
122
Leyden, John of, ii, 352
Libellus, F., i, 309
"Liberal Catholics," the, ii, 118
ff., 417 *ff*.
License, application for, form of,
ii, 482; example of a, ii, 202
Liguori, writings of, ii, 151
Lilburne, condemnation of,
ii, 263
Limborch on the Inquisition,
ii, 122, 409
Lipsius, writings of, ii, 409, 447
Lisbon, Index of, 1581, i, 235
ff., Index of, 1624, i, 290 *ff*.
Literary policy of the modern
Church, the, ii, 379 *ff*.
Literary property, i, 7 *ff*.
Liturgy, use of the Roman,
ii, 120
Llorente, writings of, ii, 166
Locke, John, writings of, ii, 86,
409
Loisy, Abbé, writings of, ii, 444
Lollards, the, teachings of, ii,
256
London, first printing in, ii, 358;
Index of (1877), ii, 206 *ff*.
Louis IX, and Hebrew writ-
ings, i, 73; and Innocent IV,
i, 73
Louis XII, and Julius II, ii,
231; and the early printers,
ii, 329 *ff*.
Louis XIV, censorship decrees
of, i, 317 *ff*.; edict of (1685),
ii, 336; and the Bull *Unigenitus*, i, 361 *ff*.; and Cardinal

Noailles, i, 370 *ff*.; and Mme.
de Maintenon, ii, 340; and
Fénelon, ii, 149 *ff*.
Louis XV, and writings against
religion, ii, 156; and censorship, ii, 222
Louis XVIII, and the Concor-
dat, ii, 170
Louis, Duke of Würtemberg,
and censorship ii, 240, 243
Louvain, Index of, 1510, i, 140;
1546, i, 26, 141 *ff*., 145;
1550, i, 145; 1554, i, 160
Louvain, University of, and
censorship, i, 109; and the
doctrine of grace, ii, 3; and
Luther, i, 342; and publishing,
ii, 359
Luca, Cardinal de, ii, 411
Lucca, Index of, 1545, i, 147
Lully, Raymond, i, 69
Luther, i, 10; the Bible of, ii, 351;
characterised by Hilgers, ii,
245 *ff*., and the bishops of
Ascoli, i, 109; and Cardinal
Cajetanus, i, 109; and censorship, i, 140, 341 *ff*.; writings
of, burned in Rome, 1521, i,
111; writings of, i, 341 *ff*.,
ii, 217, 287 in the Index, i,
200, 294; and Erasmus, i, 332
ff.; and Leo X., i, 110; and
Protestant censorship, ii, 244
Lutherans, the, and the Copernican system, i, 315 *ff*.
Lutzenburg, Bernard, i, 23; the
catalogue of, i, 85
Lyons, censorship in, i, 100;
printing in, ii, 337; and heretical literature, ii, 335

M

Mabillon, writings of, ii, 108;
and censorship, ii, 344; and
the Congregation, ii, 76
Macaulay, T. B., on censorship,
ii, 264
Macchi, Cardinal, ii, 381 *ff*.
Macchiavelli, in the Index, i,
200; on the religion of Rome,
ii, 453
Maciciowski, Index of, 1603,
i, 269

Madrid, Index of, 1583. i. 236
ff.; Index of. 1640. i. 294 ff.

Maffei on usury, ii, 152

Magdalenus, *Elenchus* of, 1632,
i, 268; supplementary Index
of, 1619, i, 268

Magdeburg, book-trade of, ii,
352; a centre of heresy, i,
81; printing in, ii, 272

Magister Sacri Palatii, i, 133,
134, ii, 73; prohibitions by,
ii, 77

Magnetism, ii, 189

Maintenon, Mme. de. and censorship, ii. 340

Mainzer Katholik, the, on censorship, ii, 413, 450 ff., 459
ff.

Maittaire on censorship, ii, 333

Malabar usages, the, in the Index, ii, 146

Malebranche, writings of, ii, 127,
409

Malesherbes and censorship, ii,
222

Malou, bishop, ii, 447

Mandeville, writings of, ii, 264
ff., 409

Mangin, writings of, ii, 160

Manicheans, writings of, i, 61

Manning, Archbishop, ii, 178;
Cardinal, and Ffoulkes, ii, 174

Manrique, Archbishop of Seville,
and censorship, i, 104; and
Erasmus, i, 339

Mansion, Colard, ii, 11, 358

Manutius, Paul, printer in
Rome, ii, 306; prints writings
of Erasmus; i, 333

Marcello and censorship. i. 211

Maria of Agreda, ii, 146

Maria Theresa and censorship,
i, 323 ff., ii, 218

Mariana, Juan de, writings of,
ii, 37, 96; and the Index of
Quiroga, i, 239

Marillac and the Royal College,
i, ii, 335 ff.

Marin, V., Index of, 1707, i, 298

Mariology, ii, 141 ff.

Marloratus hanged, ii, 333

Marmontel, writings of, ii, 409

Marne, the writings of, ii, 190

Marriage, representation of, on
the stage, prohibited in Spain,
i. 304

Marsilius of Padua, i, 68

Martin I, decree of, i, 62

Martinez, Alfonso, i, 157

Martinez de Osma, Pedro, writings of, condemned, i, 72

Martinez, Seb., i, 163

Marvell, Andrew, on the Index,
ii, 8; writings of, ii, 409

Mary, Queen, of England, marriage of, ii, 368; and censorship, i, 91

Mascarenhan, Inquisitor-General, Index of, i, 290

Matter, J., on Swedenborg,
ii, 189

Maurice, F. D., writings of, ii,
171, 409

Maximilian and Reuchlin, i, 338
ff.

Mayence, capture of, ii, 275;
Inquisition of, i, 72; printing
in, ii, 276

Maynooth, College of, on the
papal authority, ii, 118

Mazazor (Machsor), the book,
condemned, i, 76

Melanchthon, in the Index, i,
164; writings of, ii, 237; and
Protestant censorship, ii,
244 ff.

Melchers, Archbishop, and the
Rheinische Merkur, ii, 200

Melchites, Synod of, ii, 173

Mendham, on censorship, ii, 456
ff., on expurgations, i, 21; on
the literary policy of Rome,
i, 17; reprint by, of the Sistine
Index, i, 246; and the Bull
Coenae Domini, i, 115; and
the Council of Trent, i, 203 ff.;
and the Index of Brasichelli,
i, 277 ff.

Mengus on exorcising, ii, 135 ff.

Mennonites, the, and Protestant
censorship, ii, 245

Mercassel, Joh., writings of,
ii, 187

Mercator, Atlas of, and the Index, i, 252 ff.

Mercedarians, ii, 36

Merle d'Aubigné, writings of,
ii, 409

Mesengui, the Catechism of, ii, 100 *ff*

Methods of Roman censorship, ii, 439 *ff*.

Mexico, writings of, in the Index, ii, 198

Meyer, C. F., writings of, ii, 430

Michael of Cesena, i, 68

Michelet, the writings of, ii, 190, 409

Mickiewicz, the writings of, ii, 190

Mignet, writings of, ii, 162

Milan, guild of printers, the, ii, 307 *ff*.; Index, lists of, 1624, i, 268; Index of, i, 152; publishing in, ii, 309

Mill, J. S., writings of, ii, 158, 409

Milman on censorship, ii, 257

Milner and the *Taxatio Papalis*, i, 226

Milton, John, the *Areopagitica* of, i, 54; and censorship, ii, 369; writings of, ii, 262, 365, 409, 435

Mirabeau, writings of, ii, 170

Mirandola, Pico della, theses of, i, 80, ii, 297 *ff*.

Mischna, the, condemned, i, 72

Missi Dominici of Charlemagne, i, 118

Mivart, St. George, writings of, ii, 409; and Father Tyrrell, ii, 465 *ff*.

Molière, writings of, ii, 131, 175, 344

Molina, writings of, ii, 39; and Clement VIII, ii, 69; and the Index, i, 241, 286

Molinists condemned by Sandoval, i, 285 *ff*.

Molinos, writings of, ii, 148, 409

Monastic orders and censorship, ii, 35 *ff*.

Mons, the Testament of, ii, 31

Montaigne, writings of, ii, 128, 344, 409

Montalembert, writings of, ii, 119

Montanus, A., edits the Polyglot Bible, ii, 19; expurgated by Brasichelli, i, 273; on the authors of expurgated works, i, 232 *ff*., Polyglot Bible of, ii, 361; writings of, ii, 375; and the Index of Paul IV, i, 178; and the Index of 1570, i, 227; and censorship, ii, 95

Montazet, writings of, ii, 304

Montesquieu, writings of, ii, 410

Montreal, the Literary Association of, and the censorship of Rome, ii, 194 *ff*.

More, Sir Thomas, and censorship, ii, 258; and the Scriptures, ii, 29; and the work of Caxton, ii, 367

Morgan, Lady, *Italy*, of, ii, 171, 410

Morin, Pierre, i, 134

Moscherosch, writings of, ii, 130

Mosheim, J. L., on the Index, ii, 9

Motto of the Index, i, 22

Moulins, the ordinance of (1566), ii, 339

Mourette, writings of, ii, 172

Moya, Matthaeus de, and the Jesuit causists, i, 374

Müller, Alexander, writings of, ii, 179

Municipal censorship, ii, 221

Munks, writings of, ii, 162

Münster, book-trade of, ii, 352; and the Anabaptists, ii, 352

Muratori, on usury, ii, 154; and Benedict, XIV, ii, 53

Murger, writings of, ii, 410, 435

Murner, the *Germania Nova* of, ii, 350

Murray, Archbishop, on the Index, ii, 457 *ff*.

Muzio, Girolamo, complaint of interference from the Index, i, 215

Musson, Abbé, *Les Histoires* of, ii, 36

Musurus and censorship, ii, 292

Mutianus, ii, 284

N

Nachtigall, the, ii, 213

Nantes, edict of, i, 318, ii, 17, 337, 339

Naples, Index of 1588, 241 *ff*.

Napoleon and the Concordat, ii,

170; and censorship, ii, 224 *ff*.; and Pigault, ii, 176; and Pius VII, ii, 233

Napoleon III, and Pius IX, ii, 233; and the Roman Question, ii, 201

Narbonne, Council of, 1227, i, 118

Navagero, A., censor in Venice, ii, 294

Necker, condemnation of, ii, 357

Nestorians, writings of, i, 60

Netherlands, book-trade of the, ii, 358 *ff*.; censorship in the, i, 93; manuscript trade in, ii, 280

Nicaea, second Council of, i, 63

Nicolai, Henry, ii, 259

Nicholas, Henry, writings of, ii, 259

Nicephorus, Patriarch, decree of, i, 63

Ninguarda, issues an Index for Bavaria, 1582, i, 218 *ff*.

Noailles, Archbishop, condemned, i, 370; Cardinal, writings of, ii, 62; Cardinal, and the Bull Unigenitus, i, 362 *ff*.

Nordlingen and the book-trade, ii, 279

Noris, Cardinal, the history of Pelagianism, by, i, 299, ii, 26; Cardinal, writings of, i, 353

Nuns, revelations by, in the Index, ii, 145 *ff*.

Nuremberg, the Bible of, ii, 13; book-trade of, ii, 355; censorship in, ii, 221; Diet of, i, 106; edict of, ii, 212; printing in, ii, 272

O

Ochinus, condemnation of, ii, 238

Odo, Cardinal, and Hebrew writings, i, 73

Oischinger, P. J. N., writings of, ii, 181

Olden-Barneveld, John of, ii, 253

Oliva, the Minorite, i, 68

Olivares and censorship, ii, 323

Ontology, ii, 186

Origen, the writings of, i, 60

Orleans, the Duchess of, and the Bull *Unigenitus*, i, 365, 371 *ff*.

Orsini, Cajetano, i, 122

Orvieto, Bishop of, and the Bull *Unigenitus*, i, 372

Osborne, Francis, writings of, ii, 124

Osnabrück, the Bishop of, ii, 463

Osservatore Romano, the, ii, 444

O'Sullivan, M., on the rights of kings, i, 292; on the Index, ii, 456 *ff*.

Oswald, H., on Mariology, ii, 145

Ottiere, writings of, ii, 111

Ottonelli and the censorship of the stage, ii, 377

Ovid in the Index, i, 192

Oxford, *Index Generalis* of, ii, 369 *ff*

P

Pacca, Cardinal, ii, 182 *ff*.

Padua, the University of, and censorship, ii, 295

Paine, Thomas, writings of, ii, 158

Palafox, Bishop, and the Jesuits, i, 355 *ff*.

Pallavicini, execution of, i, 130; writings of, ii, 92

Pallavicino, Cardinal, on censorship, i, 20, ii, 476 *ff*.; on the Inquisition, i, 127; writings of, ii, 301

Pannartz, printer, ii, 289

Panzer on the Index of Louvain, i, 140

Papal, authorisations, the authority of, ii, 311; Bulls repudiated in France, ii, 230 *ff*.; censorship and the Reformation, i, 108 *ff*.; Indexes, the series of, i, 4 *ff*.; infallibility, ii, 414 *ff*.; prohibitions in the 17th and 18th centuries, ii, 69 *ff*.

Papendrecht, Index of, 1735, i, 320 *ff*.

Paramo on the Inquisition, i, 127

Paravicino, V., writings of, ii, 126

Paris, François, and the Bull *Unigenitus*, i, 373

Paris, Index of, 1544, i, 140 *ff.*

Parliament, the, of England, and censorship, ii, 263 *ff.*; the Long, and censorship, ii, 369

Parliament of Paris, the, and censorship, i, 97 *ff.*, ii. 336

Parma, Index of. 1580, i, 234 *ff.*

Paruta, ambassador of Venice, ii, 298

Pascal, in the Index of 1664, i, 316 *ff.*, the *Lettres Provinciales* of, i, 280 *ff.*, ii, 341; writings of, ii, 410, 414; and Jansen, i, 346

Pastoral-Blatt, the, of Münster, on censorship, ii, 450

Pastoral theology, ii, 2 *ff.*

Patristic writings, editions of, on the Index, ii. 123

Patrizzi, ii, 178

Pattison, Mark, on the Humanists, ii, 285

Paul, the preaching of, i, 58

Paul, Bishop of Ascalon, and censorship, i, 82

Paul III, adds to Bull *Coenae Domini*, i, 113; and Erasmus, i, 331; and the Index of Casa, i, 148; and the Roman Inquisition, i, 122

Paul IV (Caraffa), Index of, i, 3, 14, 85. 168 *ff.*; prohibits Talmudic writings, i. 74; and Boccaccio, ii, 309 *ff.*: and Erasmus, i, 332 *ff.*; and Hebrew writings, i, 25; and the Inquisition, i, 123; and Lully, i, 69.

Paul V, and Beccanus, ii, 41; and the doctrine of grace, ii, 39; and Galileo, i, 310; and the Index of Lucca, i, 148; and Mariology, ii, 141; and Venice, ii, 91

Paulsen on the universities, ii, 284

Pavia, theologians of. ii, 174

Paw, Cornelius de. writings of. on the Americans, ii, 157

Peccatum Philosophicum, the, ii, 186

Pegna, F., edits Lutzenberg, i, 86

Peignot, on censorship, ii, 226; and the Bull *Coenae Domini*, i, 115

Peiresc and Holstenius, ii, 75

Pelagius, writings of, i, 60

Pelt, Johann, writings of, i, 95

Pentherbeus, or Putherbeus (Puy-Herbaut). Gabriel. writings of, ii, 374. 474

Perez, A., writings of, ii, 323

Periodicals, censorship of, ii, 198 *ff.*

Permits for heretical reading, i, 214 *ff.*, ii, 203

Peru, the Congress of, and the Index, ii, 197

Petra, Dom, on censorship, ii, 343

Petrarch. writings of, i, 238 *ff.*, ii, 281, 308

Péyrat. writings of, ii. 191

Peyrère, la, Isaac. ii, 2

Pfefferkorn and Reuchlin, ii, 44 *ff.*

Philip II, censorship under, i, 93, 164, ii, 323; ordinances of, ii, 359, 360; and the Bull *Coenae Domini*, i, 113; and the case of Carranza, i, 221 *ff.*; and the index of 1569, i, 226 *ff.*

Philip and Mary and censorship, i, 90 *ff.*

Philip IV, and censorship, ii, 323

Philip the Fair, edict of (1302), ii, 328; and the Inquisition, i, 121

Philip of Valois, edict of (1334), ii, 328

Philip Augustus, edict of (1200), ii, 328

Philosophical sin, Jesuit doctrine of, ii, 37

Pichler, writings of, ii, 173, 181

Pico della Mirandola, theses of, i, 80

Pigault, Le Brun, writings of, ii. 176

Pisa, the Council of, ii, 329; publishing in, ii, 309

Pistoja, Synod of, ii, 166 *ff.*
Pius II (Aeneas Sylvius), ii, 214;
condemnations by, i, 71 *ff.*;
writings of, in Index, i. 167,
336; and Bishop Pecock. i. 70
Pius IV, brief of, 1561, permitting legates to Trent to read
heretical books. i, 216; Index
of, i, 180 *ff.*; issues, 1563, Bull
re Inquisition, i, 126; and
censorship in France, ii, 334;
and the Index of Lucca, i. 148;
and the printing-press, ii, 306
Pius V (Ghislieri), i, 5; and
Cardinal Comendon, i, 216;
and the case of Carranza, i,
223 *ff.*; letters of. i, 223; and
censorship. i. 220 *ff.*; and the
Congregation of the Index, i,
131, ii, 96; and indulgences,
ii, 138; and the Inquisition, i,
123; and the printing-press,
ii, 306; and the book-dealers
of Como, ii, 307; and St.
Bartholomew, i, 224; and the
Corpus Juris Canonici, i, 225;
and the Scriptures, ii, 20; and
the writings of the Jansenists,
i, 351 *ff.*
Pius VI, general prohibition by.
ii, 155; and the French Revolution, ii, 168 *ff.*; and the
Jesuits, ii, 44; and the Synod
of Pistoja, ii, 166; and von
Eybel, ii, 414
Pius VII, recalls, 1822, condemnation of Copernican
theories, i, 129; and the Carbonari, ii, 132; and the Concordat, ii, 170; and Napoleon, ii,
169, 233; and Settele, i, 314
Pius IX, Indexes of, ii, 62;
modifies Bull *Coenae Domini*,
i, 112; on the use of the
classics. ii. 120; regulations
of. ii, 74 *ff*; and the Bull *Coenae
Domini*, i, 115; and censorship. ii. 65 *ff.*, 443; and
the Eastern Church, ii, 173;
and Gallicanism, ii, 118; and
the Immaculate Conception,
ii, 142; and the journals of
Rome, ii, 206; and the Montreal Association, ii, 195; and

Napoleon III, ii, 233; and
Victor Emmanuel, ii, 233;
and the Roman Question, ii,
201; and Rosmini. ii. 185 *ff.*
Pius X. ii, 379
Plantier, Bishop, and censor-
ship, ii, 460
Plantin, appointed proto-typo-
grapher, ii, 360; the Polyglot
Bible of, ii, 19; publishing
undertakings of ii, 359 *ff.*;
363 *ff.*
Pociej, Joh., writings of, ii, 173
Poggio in the Index, i, 160
Pole, Cardinal, and censorship.
i, 90, ii, 7
Political censorship. i, 50
Polliot, Estienne, condemnation
of. ii, 338
Porphyry, the books of, i, 59
Porrée, Gilbert de la, i, 65
Portalis and censorship, ii, 226
Port Royal and Jansen, i, 347 *ff.*
Possevinus and censorship,
ii, 335
Poynder, John, *History of the
Jesuits* by, ii, 41
Poza, J. B., and Benedict XIV,
ii, 53; and the Index, i, 292;
writings of, ii, 39, 410
Pozzo, Count F. dal, and the
Bull *Coenae Domini*, i, 115
Prado, Index of, 1747, i, 298
Prague, Index of, 1749, i, 322
Prayer, forms of, ii, 140 *ff.*
Precipiano, Archbishop, ii, 80;
Index of, 1695, i, 319; and
the Jansenists, i, 357 *ff.*
Pressensé, E. de, writings of, ii,
202, 410
Press-laws, in Spain, ii, 233 *ff.*;
of the French Empire, ii, 224
ff.
Preston, Thomas, writings of.
ii. 116. 300
Priestly, Joseph. writings of,
ii, 158
Primatt, Joseph, condemnation
of, ii, 263
Printer-publishers in Roman
Index, i, 173
Printing, influence of, i, 2;
early, in Italy, ii, 288 *ff.*; in
England, ii, 366; in France,

Printing (*Continued*)
ii, 328 *ff.*; introduced into
Venice, ii, 289

Probability, the doctrine of,
ii, 150 *ff.*

Prohibitions of books in Middle
Ages, i, 64 *ff.*

Propaganda, the Congregation
of, ii, 155

Protestant censorship, i, 49 *ff.*

Protestant Guardian, the, on
the expurgatory Indexes, i,
305

Proudhon, writings of, ii, 188,
251, 435

Prynne, condemnation of, ii,
261 *ff.*

Przichovsky, Index of, 1767,
i, 322 *ff*

Publishers in the Index, i, 157,
168

Publishing in Europe, conditions
of, ii, 271 *ff.*

Puffendorf, writings of, ii, 410

Puritans, the, and censorship, ii,
258 *ff.*

Putherbeus (or Pentherbeus),
Gabriel, ii, 374, 474

Pütter on printing and censorship, i, 2

Q

Querini, Cardinal, and the endowment of censorship, ii, 76
ff.

Quesnel, writings of, ii, 410;
and the Bull *Unigenitus*, i,
360 *ff.*; and censorship, i,
357 *ff.*

Quietism, writings on, ii, 148

Quinet, writings of, ii, 190, 410

Quiroga, and Erasmus, i, 333;
and the Index of 1571, i, 228;
Index of, 1583, i, 236 *ff.*;
Index of, 1584, i, 239 *ff.*

R

Rabardeau, ii, 102

Rabelais in Index, i, 101, ii, 343

Racine, writings of, ii, 225, 344

Ranke, writings of, ii, 161, 410

Rass, Bishop, ii, 447

Ratisbon, Diet of, 1541, i, 155

Rauchler, J., on printing, ii, 278

Raynaud, Théophile, on censorship, i, 138, ii, 39, 53; on
Reuchlin and Erasmus, ii, 343

Receuil des Actes du Clergé, ii, 82
ff.

Reeve, writings of, ii, 266

Reformation, the, i, 9; an intellectual revolution, i, 43; and
classical literature, i, 45 *ff.*,
ii, 271, and the universities
of Germany, i, 53

Reformation, the Catholic,
i, 206 *ff.*

Regalia Rights, the, ii, 104 *ff.*

Regalists, the, of Spain, ii, 98

"Regulars," the, contests of,
with the "Seculars," ii, 46 *ff.*

Renaissance, the, and literary
activities, ii, 281

Renan, E., the writings of,
ii, 190 *ff.*, 410

Renouf, writings of, ii, 202

Reserva-rechte, the, ii, 214

Reuchlin, Johannes, attacks
upon, i, 83 *ff.*; writings of, ii,
217, and Bertram, writings
of expurgated by the divines
of Douai, i, 233; and censorship, ii, 44 *ff.*; and Erasmus, i,
335 *ff.*; and Hoogstraaten,
i, 337 *ff.*

Revolution, the French, of 1789,
and censorship, ii, 222 *ff.*

Revue Ecclesiastique, la, on the
Index, ii, 448

Rheims, Synod of, i, 65

Rheinische Merkur, the, in the
Index, ii, 250

Ricci, Bishop, ii, 166

Riccioli on the infallibility of
the pope, ii, 122

Riccius, Index of, 1681, i, 324 *ff.*

Richard II and Wyclif, i, 69

Richardson, S., romances of,
ii, 131, 410

Richelieu, ii, 102; and censorship, ii, 344

Richet on Church and State,
ii, 114

Rifformatori, the, and censorship
in Venice, ii, 303

Rites, Congregation of, ii, 78 *ff.*,
434; and exorcising, ii, 135 *ff.*

and writings on the saints, ii, 140; and forms of prayer, ii, 140

Robertson, William, writings of, ii, 161

Rocaberti, Hippolyta, ii, 146

Rodrigues, writings of, ii, 191 *ff.*

Roman Indexes, 1670–1800, i, 324 *ff.*

Roman Question, the (1859–70), writings on, ii, 201

Roman Revolution of 1848. ii, 184 *ff.*

Roman World, the, on the Index, ii, 438 *ff.*

"Romanus" and *The Tablet*, ii, 417 *ff.*

Rome, Index of, 1632, i, 293 *ff.*; journals of, in the Index, ii, 200; the literary productions of, ii, 304 *ff.*; the artistic productions of, ii, 305; prohibitory edicts of, ii, 273 *ff.*

Roscoe, William, writings of, ii, 162, 410

Roselli, Antonio, the *Monarchia* of, i. 79, ii. 297

Rosmini, A., writings of, ii, 184 *ff.*, 410

Rossetti, D. G., writings of, ii, 166

Rousseau, writings of, ii, 81, 155 157, 170, 175, 229, 410

Ruchrath, Johann, of Overwesel (de Wesalia), i, 72

Rudolph II and the Bull *Coenae Domini*, i, 113

Rules, the ten, of the Index of Trent, i, 182 *ff.*

Rupella, Nicholas de, i, 73

S

Sa, Emmanuel, and the decree of 1688, i, 292; and the Index, i, 274, 286

Sabatier, writings of, ii, 410

Saccheri, H. P., ii, 62

Sacchino and Geneva, ii, 335

Sachs, Hans, and censorship, ii, 221, 335

Sachsenspiegel, the, and Gregory XI, i, 69

Sacramentists, the, writings of, ii, 242

Saint-Amour, William of, i, 24

St. Louis, edict of (1229), ii, 328

Saint-Simon, writings of, ii, 188, 410

Saints, writings on the, in the Index, ii, 138 *ff.*

Salamanca, University of, and censorship, ii, 328

Sales, St. Francis de, and Geneva, ii, 333

Salinas, Martin de, on censorship in Spain, ii, 315 *ff.*

Salisbury, Earl of, on Sarpi, ii, 93 *ff.*

Sall, Andrew, ii, 202 *ff.*

Salviati and the *Decameron*, ii, 310

Salzburg and the book-trade, ii, 279

"Sand, George" (Mme Dudevant), romances of, ii, 410, 435

Sandoval, Index of, 1612, i, 282 *ff.*

Sandys, Sir E., on the literary policy of the Church, ii. 453 *ff.*: writings of, ii, 126

Sannig, B., writings of, ii, 135

Santiago, Hernando de, and the Index, i, 289

Sarmiento, D., Index of, 1707, i, 297

Sarpi, Paolo, writings of, ii, 301 *ff.*, 410; and censorship, i, 37, 265, ii, 296 *ff.*; on Widdrington, ii, 117; and the Concordat, i, 280 *ff.*; and the contest with Rome, ii, 92 *ff.*

Savii sopra l'Eresia, the, ii, 295

Savile, Henry, and the oath of allegiance, ii, 117

Savonarola in the Index, i, 198 *ff.*

Sawtree, W., condemnation of, ii, 257

Saxony, censorship in, ii, 241

Scaliger, condemned under Gregory XIII, i, 225; writings of, ii, 275, 410

Schauenburg, A. von, Archbishop, i, 106

Scheeben on Mariology, ii, 145

Schell, Hermann, writings of, ii, 445

Scheurl on publishing, ii, 287
Schiller, writings of, ii. 212
Schmitt, Josef, writings of, ii, 174
Scholl, writings of, ii, 191
Schurius, Andrea, ii, 365
Schweinheim, ii, 289
Schwenckfeldians, the, and censorship, ii, 245
Science and the Church, ii, 461
Scioppius, writings of, ii, 37
Scotti, writings of, ii, 37
Scotus, Duns, ii, 428
Scotus, Erigena, i, 66
Scriptures, copies of, destroyed in England under Henry VIII, i, 86; in France, ii, 15 ff., 337; in the Index, i, 154, 156, 190, ii, 32; in the Netherlands, ii, 19 ff.; in Spain, ii, 22 ff.; in the vernacular, ii, 31, 63; reading of the, i, 24; treatment of, under censorship, ii, 11 ff., 475; and Clement VIII, i, 190
Scykowski, Index of, i, 286 ff.
Seabra on the Index, i, 290
Searle, Father, on censorship, ii, 461 ff.; on infallibility, ii, 415
Secchi and the Copernican system, i, 316
Secret societies in the Index, ii, 131 ff.
"Seculars," the, contests of, with the "Regulars," ii, 46 ff.
Segarelli of Parma, i, 67
Segesser on the reform of the Index, ii, 412
Segneri, writings of, ii, 148
Ségur, L. G. de, writings of, ii, 162, 189
Selvaggio and the Index of Trent, i, 181
Semenencho, P., writings of, ii, 173
Sens, Council of, i, 66, 97
Serarius and the Scriptures, i, 191
Serry and the Bull Unigenitus, i, 364
Servetus, M., in the Index, i, 155; trial of, ii, 237; the burning of, ii, 332

Settele and the Copernican system, i, 314
Settembrini, writings of, ii, 161
Sévigné, Mme. de, writings of, ii, 345
Seville, Index of, 1632, i, 293
Seymour, H., writings of, ii, 171
Shahan, Thomas J., on the Congregation of the Index, i, 134 ff.; on Erasmus, i, 340 ff.
Sheridan, R. B., and censorship, ii, 266
Sigoni, the history of Bologna of, ii, 311
Siguier, A., the writings of, ii, 190
Simler, Josias, and the Index of Trent, i, 196
Sirleto, correspondence of, with Montanus, Plantin, Valverde, et al, i, 209 ff.; and the Catholic Reformation, i, 207 ff., and censorship in Venice, ii, 296
Sismondi, writings of, ii, 162, 410
Sistine Index cancelled by Clement VIII, i, 253 ff.
Sixtus IV, and censorship, ii, 288; and the Immaculate Conception, ii, 142; and Pedro de Osma, i, 72; and printing, ii, 292; and Segarelli, i, 67
Sixtus V, ii, 306; Bull of, 1587, i, 216; Index of, 1590, i, 243 ff., issues, 1587, Bull Immensa, i, 133; and Baronius, ii, 311; and Boccaccio, ii, 310; and the Congregation of the Index, i, 131, 248 ff.; and Elizabeth, ii, 115; and Henry of Navarre, ii, 232
Sixtus of Siena destroys 12,000 Hebrew volumes, i, 74
Sleumer, A., the Index Romanus of, ii, 463
Slevin, Dr., on the Index, ii, 458; and the Bull Coenae Domini, i, 115
Smith, Adam, the Wealth of Nations of, on the Spanish Index, i, 303
Smith, Dr. Richard, and the Jesuits, ii, 46 ff.

Soanen and the Bull *Unigenitus*, i, 364

Socialism and the Index, ii, 188 *ff.*

Socinians, the. writings of, ii, 245. 253

Solier, writings of, ii, 37

Sorpon, Robert de, ii, 283

Sorbonne, College of the, ii, 283

Sorbonne, the, on the Bull *Unigenitus*, i, 370; and Bishop Monluc, i, 221; and censorship, i, 96 *ff.*; divines of the, on the oath of allegiance, ii, 118; Index of, in 1544, i, 100, 140 *ff.*; and the early printers, ii, 330 *ff.*; and the Gallican Church, ii, 103: and the Immaculate Conception, ii, 142: and Luther, i, 110

Sotomayor, Index of, i, 294 *ff.*

Soulié, writings of, ii, 435

Soury, Jules, writings of, ii, 191

South, Dr., and the Copernican doctrine, i, 315

South America, writings of, in the Index, ii, 197 *ff.*

Spain, censorship in, i, 16, 27 *ff.*, 104 *ff.*, ii, 282; press-laws in, ii, 233 *ff.*; printing in, ii, 313 *ff.*; and the Index of Trent, i, 194; and the Papacy, ii, 94 *ff.*; and the papal authority, ii, 84

Spalatro, Archbishop of, i, 130, ii, 301

Spanish Indexes, 1790–1844, i, 301 *ff.*

Speyer, the Bishop of, and Reuchlin, i, 84; the Diet of, i, 107

Spinoza, writings of, ii, 127, 253, 410

Spiritualism, ii, 189

Staël, Mme. de, and censorship, ii, 225

Star-Chamber, the, and censorship, ii, 259, 260 *ff.*

State. censorship of the. ii, 205 *ff.*

Stationers' Company. the. ii, 368: and censorship, i, 92

Stendhal, romances of, ii, 410

Stephanus, H. (Estienne), i, 296; and censorship, ii, 238

Stephanus, R. (Estienne), editions of Scriptures of, i, 102; and the Index. i, 228 *ff.*; writings of, ii, 411

Stephen III and Autpert, i, 63

Stephen, Leslie, on censorship, ii, 265

Sterne, L., romances of, ii, 411

Sternhold and Hopkins, version of the Psalms of, i, 306

Stowe, Harriet B., writings of, ii, 165

Strasburg, printing in, ii, 272; and censorship, ii, 350

Strauss, *Das Leben Jesu* of, ii, 171, 411

Stroud, writings of. ii, 171, 411

Stunica and the Inquisition, i. 128 *ff.*

Suarez, writings of, ii, 45 *ff.*

Subiaco, printing in, ii, 289

Sue, E., romances of, ii, 164, 411, 435

Sully and Casaubon, ii, 334

Sweden, censorship in, ii, 255 *ff.*

Swedenborg, writings of, ii, 189, 411

Swift, writings of, ii, 131

Switzerland, censorship in, ii, 237 *ff.*

Sylvius, Aeneas (Pius II). condemns his own writings, i. 71: writings of. in Index, i, 167, ii. 214

Synod, of Cologne, i, 106; of Naples (1619) and the Scriptures, ii, 33; of Paris, i, 66; of Sens, i, 66

Szyzkowski, Index of, 1617, i, 269

T

Tablet, the, and "Romanus," ii, 417 *ff.*

Tacitus, history of, condemned by Leo X, i, 111

Taine, H. A., writings of. ii. 160. 411

Talmud. the. editions of, ii, 291; ordered burned by Gregory IX, i, 72; prohibition of the, i, 25

Talmudic books and the Sistine Index, i, 262

Talon, Omer, and the authority of the pope, ii, 83
Tamburini, writings of, ii, 175
Targum, the, editions of, ii, 291
Tasso, writings of, ii, 212
Taxae, the, of the Church of Rome, i, 226
Taxatio Papalis, i, 226
Tempier, Bishop Stephen, i, 66
Ten, the Council of, and censorship, ii, 294
Tennemann, writings of, ii, 158
Testament, Greek, edition by Erasmus, i, 166; the New, in the Index, ii, 411
Thacher, execution of, ii, 258
Theatre, in France, censorship of the, ii, 378; in Italy, censorship of the, ii, 376 *ff.*; in Spain, censorship of the, ii, 377
Theodosius, Emperor, and the Nestorians, 1, 60
Theological controversies, in France, 1654–1700, ii, 1 *ff*; in the Netherlands, 1654–1690, ii, 2 *ff*
Theresa, Saint, i, 166, ii, 179
Thiers, A., on censorship, ii, 464
Thions, C., writings of, ii, 119
Thirty Years' War, influence of, on the book-trade, ii, 349, 364; and censorship, ii, 212; and the freedom of the press, ii, 358; and its influence on literature, i, 48
Thomai, historian of Ravenna, 1, 212 *ff.*
Thou, de, writings of, i, 286, ii, 124
Ticknor, George, on bookselling in Spain, ii, 316 *ff.*; on the Inquisition in Spain, ii, 327 *ff.*
Tillemont, writings of, ii, 107
Tillotson, J., sermons of, ii, 411
Tilly and Magdeburg, ii, 352
Toland, John, writings of, ii, 264
Toledo, Index of, 1584, i, 239 *ff.*
Tolstoy, Dimitri, writings of, ii, 173
Tonstal, Bishop of London, and censorship, i, 86, ii, 258 *ff.*
Torquemada, Cardinal, i, 70, 122; burns 7000 volumes, i, 242; and censorship, ii, 314

Torti, writings of, ii, 194
Toulouse, Council of, 1229, i, 119
Tournai, Synod of, ii, 362
Traditionalism, ii, 186
Trautmannsdorf, writings of, ii, 175
Trent, the Council of, i, 5, 180 *ff.*, ii, 78
Trent, the Index of, i, 5; printed in Liège, ii, 362; and Hebrew writings, i, 75
Triphenius, Abbé, writings of, ii, 129
Trutfetter, Canon, and censorship, i, 82
Tübingen, book-trade of, ii, 356; University of, ii, 243
Turrecremata, J., and the early printers, ii, 288
Tyler, Wat, insurrection of, ii, 256
Tyndale, Matthew, writings of, ii, 265
Tyndale, William, i, 92; the Bible of, ii, 29 *ff.*
Typesetters, censorship regulations for, ii, 66
Tyrrell, George, Father, on censorship, ii, 465 *ff.*

U

Ulm and the book-trade, ii, 279
Unigenitus, the Bull, i, 360 *ff.*
Universities, Continental, utterances of, on the English oath of allegiance, ii, 118; and the book-trade, ii, 282 *ff.*
University, of Berlin, the, censorship in, ii, 251; of Bologna, and jurisprudence, ii, 286; of Cologne, and censorship, ii, 288; of Erfurt, and censorship, ii, 349; of Louvain, and publishing, ii, 359; of Padua, and medicine, ii, 286; of Paris, and censorship, ii, 328 *ff.*, and printing, ii, 318, and theology, ii, 286; of Vienna, and literature, ii, 286
Upsala, Index of, ii, 255 *ff.*
Urban IV, appoints Inquisitor-General, i, 122; and the Inquisition, i, 121

Urban V issues Bull *Coenae Domini*, 1364, i, 111
Urban VIII, Index of, i, 293; and the astrologists, ii, 129; and censorship in Spain, ii, 98; and della Valle, ii, 125; and the doctrine of Grace, ii, 39; and forms of prayer, ii, 140 *ff.*; and Galileo, i, 311; and Jansenist writings, i, 346, ii, 69 *ff.*; and John Barnes, i, 130; and writings on the saints, ii, 139
Usher, Archbishop, on the Index, ii, 7
Usury, writings on, in the Index, ii, 152 *ff.*
Utrecht, the church of, i, 359 *ff.*; first printing in, ii, 358

V

Valdés, Index of, 1551, i, 146, 153; Index of, 1554, i, 156; Index of, 1559, i, 146, 161; and Erasmus, i, 339; and censorship, ii, 95; and the Index of Paul IV, i, 179; and the Scriptures, ii, 25
Valentia, Index of, 1551, i, 153
Valla, L., in the Index, i, 160; the New Testament of, ii, 14
Valladolid, Index of, 1554, i, 156; Index of, 1559, i, 161
Valle, della, Pietro, writings of, ii, 125
Valverde and Sirleto, i, 209 *ff*; on the ignorance of the censors, i, 210
Van Dyke, Paul, cited, i, 202
Van Espen on censorship, i, 138
Vanini, writings of, ii, 128
Varon, history of Sixena, ii, 322
Vatable, the Bible of, ii, 25
Vaughan, Archbishop, and Aquinas, i, 67
Vechietti, writings of, i, 130
Vega, Lope de, writings of, ii, 377
Venice, censorship in, ii, 281, 293 *ff.*; Index of, 1549, i, 148; Index of, 1543, i, 140; journals of, in the Index, ii, 200; publishing in, ii, 274 *ff.*, 289,
297; and the Papacy, ii, 90 *ff.*; Senate of, and Bull *Coenae Domini*, i, 113
Vercelli, Synod of, i, 65
Vergerio, Peter Paul, in the Index, i, 148, 149, 150, 199; works of, i, 170 *ff.*; and Paul IV, i, 169
Vergilius, Polydorus, on the Index, i, 274 *ff.*
Vermigli, the, writings of, ii, 242
Vernant, Jacques, writings of, ii, 47 *ff.*
Verona, inquisitors of, in 1228, i, 118
Verus, Gratianus, ii, 474
Viardot, writings of, ii, 163
Victor Emmanuel and Pius IX, ii, 233
Vidaurre, writings of, ii, 197
Vienna, book-trade of, ii, 356; censorship in, ii, 356; siege of, ii, 213; University of, and censorship, ii, 218 *ff.*
Vigil, writings of, ii, 197
Villanueva and the Scriptures in Spain, ii, 26
Villers on censorship, ii, 455 *ff.*
Viet on censorship, ii, 339 *ff.*
Volney, J. F., writings of, ii, 176, 411
Voltaire, writings of, ii, 81, 155, 170, 175, 411; and censorship, ii, 229; and Frederick the Great, ii, 251
Vondel, writings of, ii, 212, 253

W

Wagener, Hermann, on censorship, ii, 211
Waldenses, the, and the Scriptures, ii, 22
Waldie, writings of, ii, 171
Ward, Mary, and the *Jesuitissae*, ii, 38 *ff.*
Wareham, Archbishop of Canterbury, and censorship, i, 86
Weigelians, the, and censorship, ii, 245
Weimar, censorship in, ii, 241
Welschinger on censorship, ii, 224

Wessenberg, writings of, ii, 178
Westminister, printing in, ii, 366
Whately, Archbishop, the *Logic* of, ii, 158, 171, 411
White, Andrew D., and the condemnation of Galileo, i, 313 *ff.*
White, Thos., writings of, ii, 411
Whitgift, Archbishop of Canterbury, and censorship, i, 92
"Widdrington, Roger," writings of, ii, 116, 300
Wightman, Edward, burning of, ii, 257
Wilkes, John, writings of, ii, 266
Wilkins, J., the *New World* of, ii, 411
William V, Duke of Bavaria, and censorship, i, 218 *ff*
William of Occam, i, 68
Wittenberg, reformers of, i, 12; the book-trade of, ii, 350; University of, ii, 242
Wohlrab, Nicholas, ii, 242
Wolff, C., and censorship, ii, 249
Wolsey, Cardinal, and censorship, i, 86, ii, 257; and Luther, i, 110 *ff.*, 342 *ff.*
Woolston, Thomas, condemnation of, ii, 265
Worms, edict of, ii, 212
Wotton, Sir Henry, on Sarpi, ii, 93
Wyclif, the Bible of, ii, 29, 70, 256, 367

Wyclifites condemned by Julius II, i, 111

X

Ximenes, Inquisitor-General, i, 122; the Polyglot Old Testament of, ii, 19; and censorship, ii, 314; and printing, ii, 313; and the Scriptures, ii, 24

Y

Yucatan, censorship in, ii, 320

Z

Zamora, writings of, ii, 143
Zell, M., on the writings of Luther, ii, 287 *ff.*
Zola, romances of, ii, 169, 411, 435
Zürich, censorship in, ii, 237; the book-trade of, ii, 354; early printers of, ii, 12
Zwicher, G., writings of, ii, 411
Zwinger, Theodore, and the Index, i, 288
Zwingli, writings of, ii, 237; and censorship, ii, 354
Zwinglians, the, and censorship, ii, 244

Printed in the United Kingdom
 by Lightning Source UK Ltd.
120467UK00001B/3-4